PRENTICE HALL

WORLD STUDIES
ASIA and the PACIFIC

Geography • History • Culture

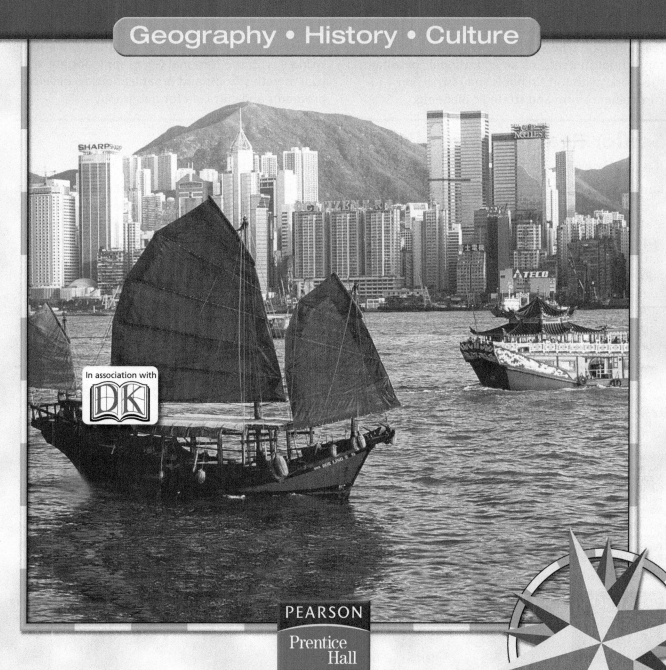

In association with
DK

PEARSON

Prentice
Hall

Boston, Massachusetts
Upper Saddle River, New Jersey

Program Consultants

Heidi Hayes Jacobs

Heidi Hayes Jacobs, Ed.D., has served as an education consultant to more than 1,000 schools across the nation and abroad. Dr. Jacobs serves as an adjunct professor in the Department of Curriculum on Teaching at Teachers College, Columbia University. She has written two best-selling books and numerous articles on curriculum reform. She received an M.A. from the University of Massachusetts, Amherst, and completed her doctoral work at Columbia University's Teachers College in 1981. The core of Dr. Jacobs' experience comes from her years teaching high school, middle school, and elementary school students. As an educational consultant, she works with K–12 schools and districts on curriculum reform and strategic planning.

Michal L. LeVasseur

Michal LeVasseur is the Executive Director of the National Council for Geographic Education. She is an instructor in the College of Education at Jacksonville State University and works with the Alabama Geographic Alliance. Her undergraduate and graduate work were in the fields of anthropology (B.A.), geography (M.A.), and science education (Ph.D.). Dr. LeVasseur's specialization has moved increasingly into the area of geography education. Since 1996 she has served as the Director of the National Geographic Society's Summer Geography Workshops. As an educational consultant, she has worked with the National Geographic Society as well as with schools and organizations to develop programs and curricula for geography.

Senior Reading Consultants

Kate Kinsella

Kate Kinsella, Ed.D., is a faculty member in the Department of Secondary Education at San Francisco State University. A specialist in second-language acquisition and content area literacy, she consults nationally on school-wide practices that support adolescent English learners and striving readers to make academic gains. Dr. Kinsella earned her M.A. in TESOL from San Francisco State University, and her Ed.D. in Second Language Acquisition from the University of San Francisco.

Kevin Feldman

Kevin Feldman, Ed.D., is the Director of Reading and Early Intervention with the Sonoma County Office of Education (SCOE) and an independent educational consultant. At the SCOE, he develops, organizes, and monitors programs related to K–12 literacy. Dr. Feldman has an M.A. from the University of California, Riverside, in Special Education, Learning Disabilities, and Instructional Design. He earned his Ed.D. in Curriculum and Instruction from the University of San Francisco.

Acknowledgments appear on page 282, which constitutes an extension of this copyright page.

Prentice Hall World Studies is published in collaboration with DK Designs, Dorling Kindersley Limited, 80 Strand, London WC2R 0RL. A Penguin Company.

ISBN 0-13-204145-6
11 V056 14

Cartography Consultant

📖 Andrew Heritage

Andrew Heritage has been publishing atlases and maps for more than 25 years. In 1991, he joined the leading illustrated nonfiction publisher Dorling Kindersley (DK) with the task of building an international atlas list from scratch. The DK atlas list now includes some 10 titles, which are constantly updated and appear in new editions either annually or every other year.

Academic Reviewers

Africa
Barbara B. Brown, Ph.D.
African Studies Center
Boston University
Boston, Massachusetts

Ancient World
Evelyn DeLong Mangie, Ph.D.
Department of History
University of South Florida
Tampa, Florida

Central Asia and the Middle East
Pamela G. Sayre
History Department,
    Social Sciences Division
Henry Ford Community College
Dearborn, Michigan

East Asia
Huping Ling, Ph.D.
History Department
Truman State University
Kirksville, Missouri

Eastern Europe
Robert M. Jenkins, Ph.D.
Center for Slavic, Eurasian and
    East European Studies
University of North Carolina
Chapel Hill, North Carolina

Latin America
Dan La Botz
Professor, History Department
Miami University
Oxford, Ohio

Medieval Times
James M. Murray
History Department
University of Cincinnati
Cincinnati, Ohio

North Africa
Barbara E. Petzen
Center for Middle Eastern Studies
Harvard University
Cambridge, Massachusetts

Religion
Charles H. Lippy, Ph.D.
Department of Philosophy
    and Religion
University of Tennessee
    at Chattanooga
Chattanooga, Tennessee

Russia
Janet Vaillant
Davis Center for Russian
    and Eurasian Studies
Harvard University
Cambridge, Massachusetts

United States and Canada
Victoria Randlett
Geography Department
University of Nevada, Reno
Reno, Nevada

Western Europe
Ruth Mitchell-Pitts
Center for European Studies
University of North Carolina
    at Chapel Hill
Chapel Hill, North Carolina

Reviewers

Sean Brennan
Brecksville-Broadview Heights
    City School District
Broadview Heights, Ohio

Stephen Bullick
Mt. Lebanon School District
Pittsburgh, Pennsylvania

Louis P. De Angelo, Ed.D.
Archdiocese of Philadelphia
Philadelphia, Pennsylvania

Paul Francis Durietz
Social Studies
    Curriculum Coordinator
Woodland District #50
Gurnee, Illinois

Gail Dwyer
Dickerson Middle School,
    Cobb County
Marietta, Georgia

Michal Howden
Social Studies Consultant
Zionsville, Indiana

Rosemary Kalloch
Springfield Public Schools
Springfield, Massachusetts

Deborah J. Miller
Office of Social Studies,
    Detroit Public Schools
Detroit, Michigan

Steven P. Missal
Plainfield Public Schools
Plainfield, New Jersey

Catherine Fish Petersen
Social Studies Consultant
Saint James, Long Island, New York

Joe Wieczorek
Social Studies Consultant
Baltimore, Maryland

ASIA and the PACIFIC

Develop Skills

Use these pages to develop your reading, writing, and geography skills.

Build a Regional Background

Learn about the geography, history, and culture of the region.

Focus on Countries

Create understanding of the region by focusing on specific countries.

- Learn map skills with the MapMaster Skills Handbook.
- Practice your skills with every map in this book.
- Interact with every map online and on CD-ROM.

Maps and illustrations created by DK help build your understanding of the world. The DK World Desk Reference Online keeps you up to date.

The *World Studies* Interactive Textbook online and on CD-ROM uses interactive maps and other activities to help you learn.

COUNTRY DATABANK

Read about the countries that make up Asia and the Pacific.

COUNTRY PROFILES

Theme-based maps and charts provide a closer look at countries.

Literature

A selection by an Asian author brings social studies to life.

Links

See the fascinating links between social studies and other disciplines.

Skills for Life

Learn skills that you will use throughout your life.

Target Reading Skills

Chapter-by-chapter reading skills help you read and understand social studies concepts.

Citizen Heroes

Meet people who have made a difference in their country.

DK Eyewitness Technology

Detailed drawings show how technology shapes places and societies.

Maps and Charts

MAP✶MASTER™

MAP✶MASTER™ Interactive

Go online to find an interactive version of every MapMaster map in this book. Use the Web Code provided to gain direct access to these maps.

How to Use Web Codes:

1. Go to **www.PHSchool.com**.
2. Enter the Web Code.
3. Click Go!

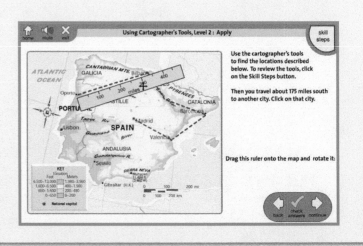

Building Geographic Literacy

Learning about a country often starts with finding it on a map. The MapMaster™ system in *World Studies* helps you develop map skills you will use throughout your life. These three steps can help you become a MapMaster!

The MAP★MASTER™ System

1 Learn

You need to learn geography tools and concepts before you explore the world. Get started by using the MapMaster Skills Handbook to learn the skills you need for success.

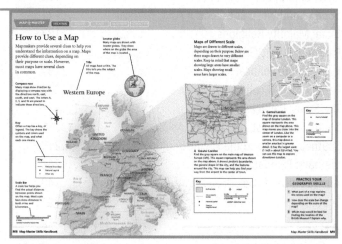

MAP★MASTER™ Skills Activity

Location The Equator runs through parts of Latin America, but it is far from other parts of the region.

Locate Find the Equator on the map. Which climates are most common in Latin America, and how far is each climate region from the Equator?

Draw Conclusions How do climates change as you move away from the Equator?

Go Online PHSchool.com Use Web Code lfp-1142 for step-by-step map skills practice.

2 Practice

You need to practice and apply your geography skills frequently to be a MapMaster. The maps in *World Studies* give you the practice you need to develop geographic literacy.

3 Interact

Using maps is more than just finding places. Maps can teach you many things about a region, such as its climate, its vegetation, and the languages that the people who live there speak. Every MapMaster map is online at **PHSchool.com,** with interactive activities to help you learn the most from every map.

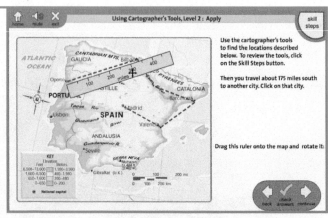

Learning With Technology

You will be making many exciting journeys across time and place in *World Studies*. Technology will help make what you learn come alive.

For: An activity on East Asia
Visit: PHSchool.com
Web Code: lcd-6101

For a complete list of features for this book, use Web Code lck-1000.

Go Online at PHSchool.com

Use the Web Codes listed below and in each Go Online box to access exciting information or activities.

How to Use the Web Code:
1. Go to **www.PHSchool.com**.
2. Enter the Web Code.
3. Click Go!

Asia and the Pacific Activities

Web Code	Activity
	History Interactive
lcp-7004	Explore Two Feudal Societies
lcp-7010	Learn About Military Technology in China
lcp-7011	Explore the Hagia Sofia
lcp-7012	Tour the Forbidden City
lcp-7013	Learn More About Technology in Han China
lcp-7014	Tour a Temple
lcp-7015	Discovering Indian Classic Dance
lcp-7017	Tour a Japanese Castle
lcp-7018	Learn More about Ancient Writing
lcp-7019	Tour the Temple of Confucius
lcp-7021	Experience Noh Drama
lcp-7025	Explore a Chinese Ship
lcp-7028	5 Pillars of Islam
lcp-7029	Inside a Mosque
lcp-7030	Investigating Ancient Trade
	MapMaster
lcp-7001	The Spread of Buddhism
lcp-7002	Geography of Japan
lcp-7003	China Under the Tang and Song Dynasties
lcp-7005	The Fertile Crescent
lcp-7006	The Maurya and Gupta Empires
lcp-7007	Early River Valley Civilizations
lcp-7008	Hinduism in the World Today
lcp-7016	The Indian Subcontinent
lcp-7020	Qin and Han Empires, 221 B.C.–A.D.220
lcp-7022	Mongolian Empire
lcp-7023	Geography of Ancient China
lcp-7024	Spread of Buddhism
lcp-7026	The Zhou Dynasty in China
lcp-7027	The Seasons

 **World Desk Reference Online**

There are more than 190 countries in the world. To learn about them, you need the most up-to-date information and statistics. The **DK World Desk Reference Online** gives you instant access to the information you need to explore each country.

Reading Informational Texts

Reading a magazine, an Internet page, or a textbook is not the same as reading a novel. The purpose of reading nonfiction texts is to acquire new information. On page M18 you'll read about some 🔄 **Target Reading Skills** that you'll have a chance to practice as you read this textbook. Here we'll focus on a few skills that will help you read nonfiction with a more critical eye.

Analyze the Author's Purpose

Different types of materials are written with different purposes in mind. For example, a textbook is written to teach students information about a subject. The purpose of a technical manual is to teach someone how to use something, such as a computer. A newspaper editorial might be written to persuade the reader to accept a particular point of view. A writer's purpose influences how the material is presented. Sometimes an author states his or her purpose directly. More often, the purpose is only suggested, and you must use clues to identify the author's purpose.

Distinguish Between Facts and Opinions

It's important when reading informational texts to read actively and to distinguish between fact and opinion. A fact can be proven or disproven. An opinion cannot—it is someone's personal viewpoint or evaluation.

For example, the editorial pages in a newspaper offer opinions on topics that are currently in the news. You need to read newspaper editorials with an eye for bias and faulty logic. For example, the newspaper editorial at the right shows factual statements in blue and opinion statements in red. The underlined words are examples of highly charged words. They reveal bias on the part of the writer.

> More than 5,000 people voted last week in favor of building a new shopping center, but the opposition won out. The margin of victory is irrelevant. Those radical voters who opposed the center are obviously self-serving elitists who do not care about anyone but themselves.
>
> This month's unemployment figure for our area is 10 percent, which represents an increase of about 5 percent over the figure for this time last year. These figures mean unemployment is getting worse. But the people who voted against the mall probably do not care about creating new jobs.

Identify Evidence

Before you accept an author's conclusion, you need to make sure that the author has based the conclusion on enough evidence and on the right kind of evidence. An author may present a series of facts to support a claim, but the facts may not tell the whole story. For example, what evidence does the author of the newspaper editorial on the previous page provide to support his claim that the new shopping center would create more jobs? Is it possible that the shopping center might have put many small local businesses out of business, thus increasing unemployment rather than decreasing it?

Evaluate Credibility

Whenever you read informational texts, you need to assess the credibility of the author. This is especially true of sites you may visit on the Internet. All Internet sources are not equally reliable. Here are some questions to ask yourself when evaluating the credibility of a Web site.

- ☐ Is the Web site created by a respected organization, a discussion group, or an individual?
- ☐ Does the Web site creator include his or her name as well as credentials and the sources he or she used to write the material?
- ☐ Is the information on the site balanced or biased?
- ☐ Can you verify the information using two other sources?
- ☐ Is there a date telling when the Web site was created or last updated?

Writing for Social Studies

Writing is one of the most powerful communication tools you will ever use. You will use it to share your thoughts and ideas with others. Research shows that writing about what you read actually helps you learn new information and ideas. A systematic approach to writing—including prewriting, drafting, revising, and proofing—can help you write better, whether you're writing an essay or a research report.

Narrative Essays

Writing that tells a story about a personal experience

1 Select and Narrow Your Topic

A narrative is a story. In social studies, it might be a narrative essay about how an event affected you or your family.

2 Gather Details

Brainstorm a list of details you'd like to include in your narrative.

3 Write a First Draft

Start by writing a simple opening sentence that conveys the main idea of your essay. Continue by writing a colorful story that has interesting details. Write a conclusion that sums up the significance of the event or situation described in your essay.

4 Revise and Proofread

Check to make sure you have not begun too many sentences with the word *I*. Replace general words with more colorful ones.

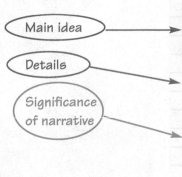

Main idea
Details
Significance of narrative

In my last year of college, I volunteered for an organization called Amigos De Las Americas (Friends of the Americas). I was sent to a remote village in Brazil and worked with villagers to improve the community's water supply and sanitation systems. The experience made me realize I wanted to work in the field of public health. When I went to Brazil, I never imagined what an incredible sense of purpose it would add to my life.

Persuasive Essays

Writing that supports an opinion or position

① Select and Narrow Your Topic

Choose a topic that provokes an argument and has at least two sides. Choose a side. Decide which argument will appeal most to your audience and persuade them to understand your point of view.

② Gather Evidence

Create a chart that states your position at the top and then lists the pros and cons for your position below, in two columns. Predict and address the strongest arguments against your stand.

③ Write a First Draft

Write a strong thesis statement that clearly states your position. Continue by presenting the strongest arguments in favor of your position and acknowledging and refuting opposing arguments.

④ Revise and Proofread

Check to make sure you have made a logical argument and that you have not oversimplified the argument.

Main Idea

Supporting (pro) argument

Opposing (con) argument

Transition words

It is vital to vote in elections. When people vote, they tell public officials how to run the government. Not every proposal is carried out; however, politicians do their best to listen to what the majority of people want. Therefore, every vote is important.

Expository Essays

Writing that explains a process, compares and contrasts, explains causes and effects, or explores solutions to a problem

1 Identify and Narrow Your Topic

Expository writing is writing that explains something in detail. It might explain the similarities and differences between two or more subjects (compare and contrast). It might explain how one event causes another (cause and effect). Or it might explain a problem and describe a solution.

2 Gather Evidence

Create a graphic organizer that identifies details to include in your essay.

Cause 1	Cause 2	Cause 3
Most people in the Mexican countryside work on farms.	The population in Mexico is growing at one of the highest rates in the world.	There is not enough farm work for so many people.

Effect
As a result, many rural families are moving from the countryside to live in Mexico City.

3 Write Your First Draft

Write a topic sentence and then organize the essay around your similarities and differences, causes and effects, or problem and solutions. Be sure to include convincing details, facts, and examples.

4 Revise and Proofread

Research Papers

Writing that presents research about a topic

1 Narrow Your Topic

Choose a topic you're interested in and make sure that it is not too broad. For example, instead of writing a report on Panama, write about the construction of the Panama Canal.

2 Acquire Information

Locate several sources of information about the topic from the library or the Internet. For each resource, create a source index card like the one at the right. Then take notes using an index card for each detail or subtopic. On the card, note which source the information was taken from. Use quotation marks when you copy the exact words from a source.

Source #1
McCullough, David. *The Path Between the Seas: The Creation of the Panama Canal, 1870-1914.* N.Y., Simon and Schuster, 1977.

3 Make an Outline

Use an outline to decide how to organize your report. Sort your index cards into the same order.

Outline
I. Introduction
II. Why the canal was built
III. How the canal was built
   A. Physical challenges
   B. Medical challenges
IV. Conclusion

Introduction

Building the Panama Canal

Ever since Christopher Columbus first explored the Isthmus of Panama, the Spanish had been looking for a water route through it. They wanted to be able to sail west from Spain to Asia without sailing around South America. However, it was not until 1914 that the dream became a reality.

Conclusion

It took eight years and more than 70,000 workers to build the Panama Canal. It remains one of the greatest engineering feats of modern times.

4 Write a First Draft

Write an introduction, a body, and a conclusion. Leave plenty of space between lines so you can go back and add details that you may have left out.

5 Revise and Proofread

Be sure to include transition words between sentences and paragraphs. Here are some examples:

To show a contrast—*however, although, despite.*

To point out a reason—*since, because, if.*

To signal a conclusion—*therefore, consequently, so, then.*

Evaluating Your Writing

Use this table to help you evaluate your writing.

	Excellent	Good	Acceptable	Unacceptable
Purpose	Achieves purpose—to inform, persuade, or provide historical interpretation—very well	Informs, persuades, or provides historical interpretation reasonably well	Reader cannot easily tell if the purpose is to inform, persuade, or provide historical interpretation	Purpose is not clear
Organization	Develops ideas in a very clear and logical way	Presents ideas in a reasonably well-organized way	Reader has difficulty following the organization	Lacks organization
Elaboration	Explains all ideas with facts and details	Explains most ideas with facts and details	Includes some supporting facts and details	Lacks supporting details
Use of Language	Uses excellent vocabulary and sentence structure with no errors in spelling, grammar, or punctuation	Uses good vocabulary and sentence structure with very few errors in spelling, grammar, or punctuation	Includes some errors in grammar, punctuation, and spelling	Includes many errors in grammar, punctuation, and spelling

CONTENTS

Go Online
PHSchool.com
Use Web Code **Icp-0000** for all of the maps
in this handbook.

Five Themes of Geography

Studying the geography of the entire world is a
huge task. You can make that task easier by using the
five themes of geography: location, regions, place,
movement, and human-environment interaction. The
themes are tools you can use to organize information
and to answer the where, why, and how of geography.

▲ **Location**
This museum in England has a
line running through it. The line
marks its location at 0° longitude.

LOCATION

1   Location answers the question, "Where is it?"
You can think of the location of a continent
or a country as its address. You might give an
absolute location such as 40° N and 80° W. You
might also use a relative address, telling where
one place is by referring to another place.
Between school and the mall and
*eight miles east of Pleasant
City* are examples of
relative locations.

REGIONS

Regions are areas that share at least one common feature. Geographers divide the world into many types of regions. For example, countries, states, and cities are political regions. The people in any one of these places live under the same government. Other features, such as climate and culture, can be used to define regions. Therefore the same place can be found in more than one region. For example, the state of Hawaii is in the political region of the United States. Because it has a tropical climate, Hawaii is also part of a tropical climate region.

MOVEMENT

Movement answers the question, "How do people, goods, and ideas move from place to place?" Remember that what happens in one place often affects what happens in another. Use the theme of movement to help you trace the spread of goods, people, and ideas from one location to another.

PLACE

Place identifies the natural and human features that make one place different from every other place. You can identify a specific place by its landforms, climate, plants, animals, people, language, or culture. You might even think of place as a geographic signature. Use the signature to help you understand the natural and human features that make one place different from every other place.

INTERACTION

Human-environment interaction focuses on the relationship between people and the environment. As people live in an area, they often begin to make changes to it, usually to make their lives easier. For example, they might build a dam to control flooding during rainy seasons. Also, the environment can affect how people live, work, dress, travel, and communicate.

◄ **Interaction**
These Congolese women interact with their environment by gathering wood for cooking.

PRACTICE YOUR GEOGRAPHY SKILLS

1 Describe your town or city, using each of the five themes of geography.

2 Name at least one thing that comes into your town or city and one that goes out. How is each moved? Where does it come from? Where does it go?

Understanding Movements of Earth

The planet Earth is part of our solar system. Earth revolves around the sun in a nearly circular path called an orbit. A revolution, or one complete orbit around the sun, takes 365¼ days, or one year. As Earth orbits the sun, it also spins on its axis, an invisible line through the center of Earth from the North Pole to the South Pole. This movement is called a rotation.

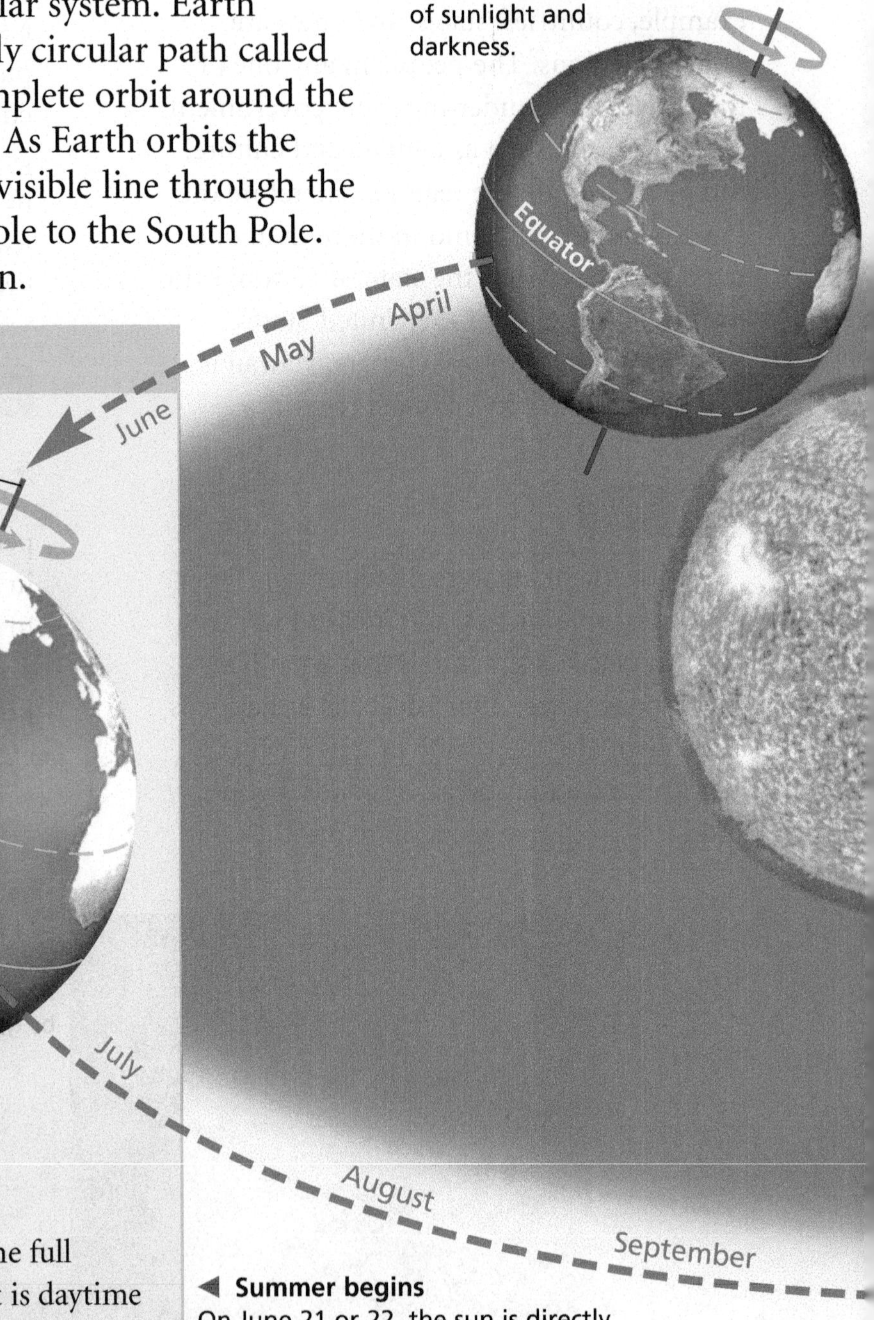

How Night Changes Into Day

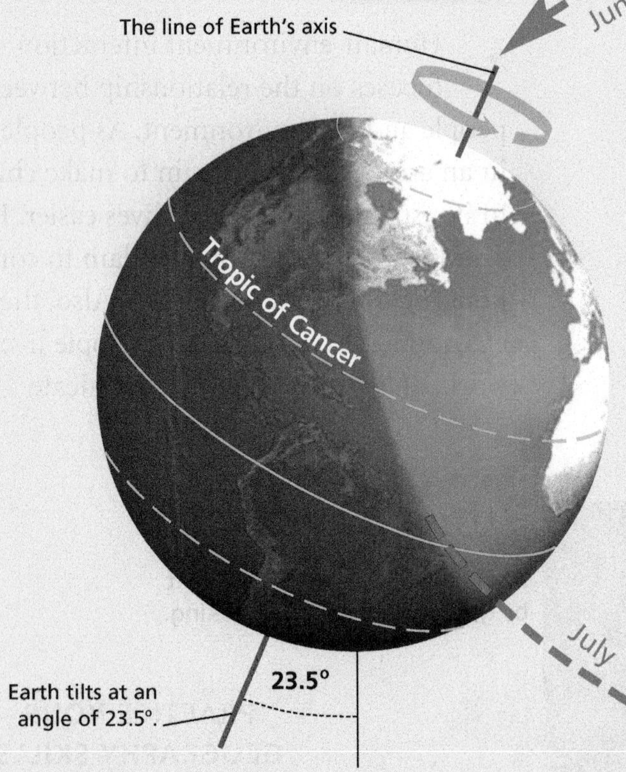

The line of Earth's axis

Tropic of Cancer

23.5°

Earth tilts at an angle of 23.5°.

Earth takes about 24 hours to make one full rotation on its axis. As Earth rotates, it is daytime on the side facing the sun. It is night on the side away from the sun.

▼ Spring begins
On March 20 or 21, the sun is directly overhead at the Equator. The Northern and Southern Hemispheres receive almost equal hours of sunlight and darkness.

Equator

April
May
June
July
August
September

◀ Summer begins
On June 21 or 22, the sun is directly overhead at the Tropic of Cancer. The Northern Hemisphere receives the greatest number of sunlight hours.

The Seasons

Earth's axis is tilted at an angle. Because of this tilt, sunlight strikes different parts of Earth at different times in the year, creating seasons. The illustration below shows how the seasons are created in the Northern Hemisphere. In the Southern Hemisphere, the seasons are reversed.

PRACTICE YOUR GEOGRAPHY SKILLS

1 What causes the seasons in the Northern Hemisphere to be the opposite of those in the Southern Hemisphere?

2 During which two days of the year do the Northern Hemisphere and Southern Hemisphere have equal hours of daylight and darkness?

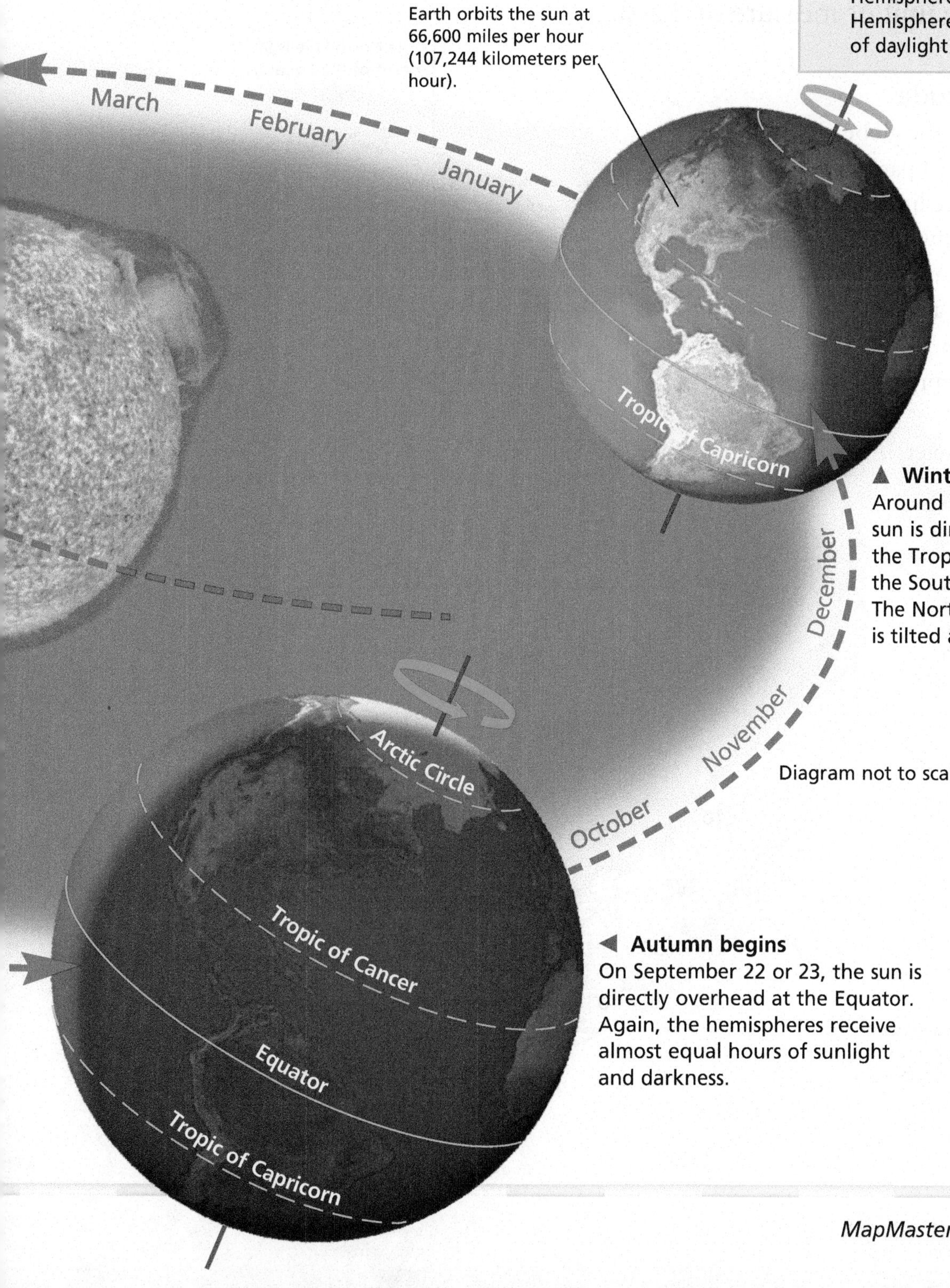

Earth orbits the sun at 66,600 miles per hour (107,244 kilometers per hour).
March
February
January
Tropic of Capricorn
December
November
October
Arctic Circle
Tropic of Cancer
Equator
Tropic of Capricorn
Diagram not to scale

▲ **Winter begins**
Around December 21, the sun is directly overhead at the Tropic of Capricorn in the Southern Hemisphere. The Northern Hemisphere is tilted away from the sun.

◀ **Autumn begins**
On September 22 or 23, the sun is directly overhead at the Equator. Again, the hemispheres receive almost equal hours of sunlight and darkness.

Understanding Globes

A globe is a scale model of Earth. It shows the actual shapes, sizes, and locations of all Earth's landmasses and bodies of water. Features on the surface of Earth are drawn to scale on a globe. This means that a small unit of measure on the globe stands for a large unit of measure on Earth.

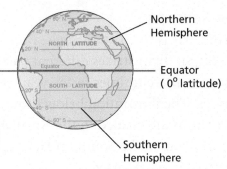

Northern Hemisphere

Equator (0° latitude)

Southern Hemisphere

Parallels of Latitude

Geographers divide the globe along imaginary horizontal lines called parallels of latitude. One of these latitude lines is the Equator, located halfway between the North and South Poles. Parallels of latitude are measured in degrees (°). One degree of latitude represents a distance of about 69 miles (111 kilometers).

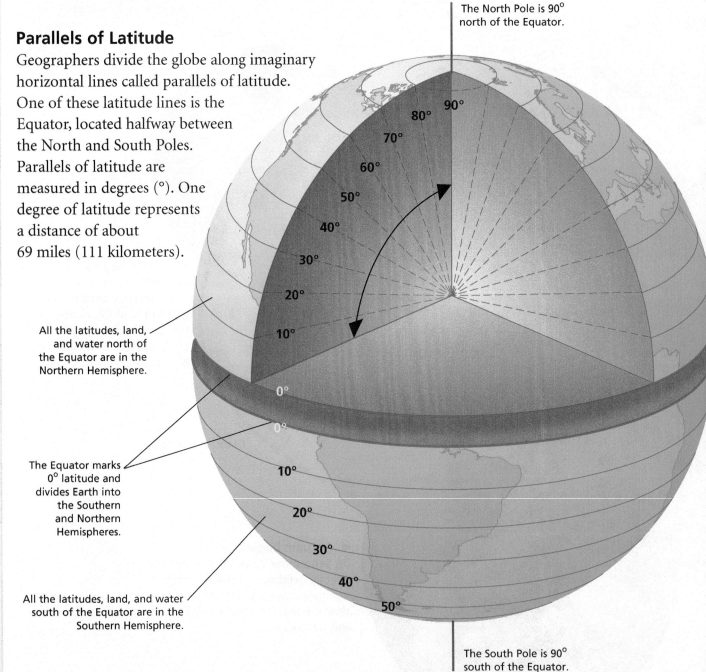

The North Pole is 90° north of the Equator.

90°
80°
70°
60°
50°
40°
30°
20°
10°
0°
0°
10°
20°
30°
40°
50°

All the latitudes, land, and water north of the Equator are in the Northern Hemisphere.

The Equator marks 0° latitude and divides Earth into the Southern and Northern Hemispheres.

All the latitudes, land, and water south of the Equator are in the Southern Hemisphere.

The South Pole is 90° south of the Equator.

Meridians of Longitude

Geographers also divide the globe along imaginary vertical lines called meridians of longitude, which are measured in degrees (°). The longitude line called the Prime Meridian runs from pole to pole through Greenwich, England. All meridians of longitude come together at the North and South Poles.

PRACTICE YOUR GEOGRAPHY SKILLS

1 Which continents lie completely in the Northern Hemisphere? In the Western Hemisphere?

2 Is there land or water at 20° S latitude and the Prime Meridian? At the Equator and 60° W longitude?

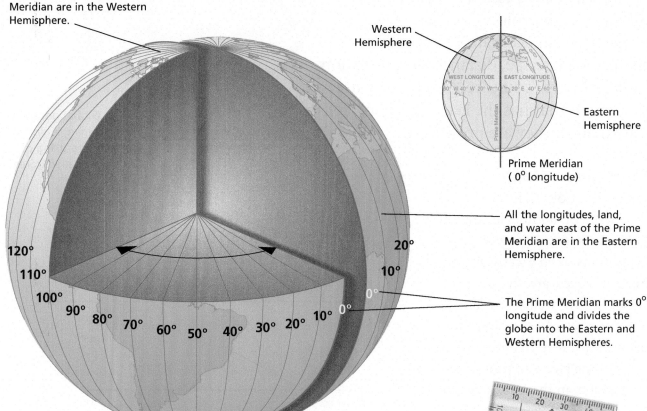

All the longitudes, land, and water west of the Prime Meridian are in the Western Hemisphere.

Western Hemisphere

Eastern Hemisphere

Prime Meridian (0° longitude)

All the longitudes, land, and water east of the Prime Meridian are in the Eastern Hemisphere.

The Prime Meridian marks 0° longitude and divides the globe into the Eastern and Western Hemispheres.

The Global Grid

Together, the pattern of parallels of latitude and meridians of longitude is called the global grid. Using the lines of latitude and longitude, you can locate any place on Earth. For example, the location of 30° north latitude and 90° west longitude is usually written as 30° N, 90° W. Only one place on Earth has these coordinates—the city of New Orleans, in the state of Louisiana.

▲ **Compass**
Wherever you are on Earth, a compass can be used to show direction.

Map Projections

Maps are drawings that show regions on flat surfaces. Maps are easier to use and carry than globes, but they cannot show the correct size and shape of every feature on Earth's curved surface. They must shrink some places and stretch others. To make up for this distortion, mapmakers use different map projections. No one projection can accurately show the correct area, shape, distance, and direction for all of Earth's surface. Mapmakers use the projection that has the least distortion for the information they are presenting.

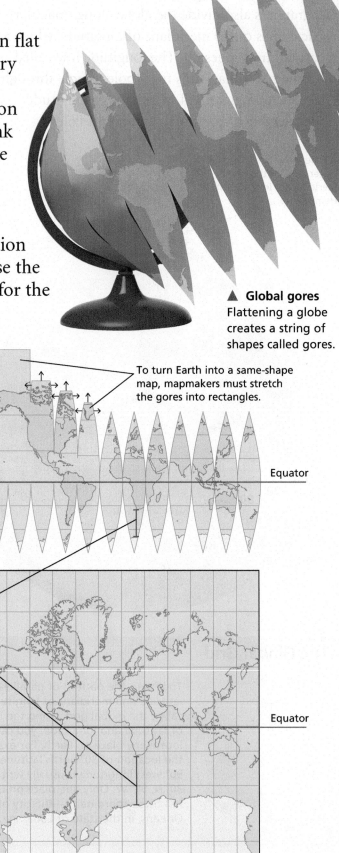

▲ **Global gores**
Flattening a globe creates a string of shapes called gores.

Same-Shape Maps

Map projections that accurately show the shapes of landmasses are called same-shape maps. However, these projections often greatly distort, or make less accurate, the size of landmasses as well as the distance between them. In the projection below, the northern and southern areas of the globe appear more stretched than the areas near the Equator.

To turn Earth into a same-shape map, mapmakers must stretch the gores into rectangles.

Equator

Stretching the gores makes parts of Earth larger. This enlargement becomes greater toward the North and South Poles.

Mercator projection ▶
One of the most common same-shape maps is the Mercator projection, named for the mapmaker who invented it. The Mercator projection accurately shows shape and direction, but it distorts distance and size. Because the projection shows true directions, ships' navigators use it to chart a straight-line course between two ports.

Equator

Equal-Area Maps

Map projections that show the correct size of landmasses are called equal-area maps. In order to show the correct size of landmasses, these maps usually distort shapes. The distortion is usually greater at the edges of the map and less at the center.

PRACTICE YOUR GEOGRAPHY SKILLS

1. What feature is distorted on an equal-area map?

2. Would you use a Mercator projection to find the exact distance between two locations? Tell why or why not.

To turn Earth's surface into an equal-area map, mapmakers have to squeeze each gore into an oval.

Equator

The tips of all the gores are then joined together. The points at which they join form the North and South Poles. The line of the Equator stays the same.

North Pole

Equator

South Pole

Robinson Maps

Many of the maps in this book use the Robinson projection, which is a compromise between the Mercator and equal-area projections. The Robinson projection gives a useful overall picture of the world. It keeps the size and shape relationships of most continents and oceans, but distorts the size of the polar regions.

The entire top edge of the map is the North Pole.

The map is least distorted at the Equator.

Equator

The entire bottom edge of the map is the South Pole.

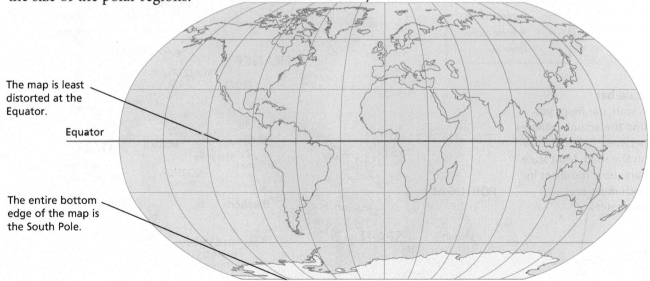

How to Use a Map

Mapmakers provide several clues to help you understand the information on a map. Maps provide different clues, depending on their purpose or scale. However, most maps have several clues in common.

Locator globe
Many maps are shown with locator globes. They show where on the globe the area of the map is located.

Title
All maps have a title. The title tells you the subject of the map.

Compass rose
Many maps show direction by displaying a compass rose with the directions north, east, south, and west. The letters N, E, S, and W are placed to indicate these directions.

Western Europe

Key
Often a map has a key, or legend. The key shows the symbols and colors used on the map, and what each one means.

Key

——	National border
⊛	National capital
•	Other city

Scale bar
A scale bar helps you find the actual distances between points shown on the map. Most scale bars show distances in both miles and kilometers.

0 miles 300

0 kilometers 300

Lambert Azimuthal Equal Area

SHETLAND ISLANDS (U.K.)

North Sea

Glasgow

Dublin

IRELAND

UNITED KINGDOM

London

English Channel

Copenhagen

DENMARK

Hamburg
Berlin

NETHERLANDS
Amsterdam

The Hague
Brussels
BELGIUM
LUXEMBOURG

GERMANY

Frankfurt

Prague
CZECH REPUBLIC

Paris

Luxembourg

Munich

Vienna

AUSTRIA

Bay of Biscay

FRANCE

Lyon

Bern LIECHTENSTEIN
SWITZERLAND

Milan

SAN MARINO

Toulouse

Marseille
MONACO

ANDORRA

ITALY

Adriatic Sea

CORSICA (France)

VATICAN CITY
Rome

PORTUGAL

Madrid

Barcelona

SARDINIA (Italy)

Tyrrhenian Sea

Lisbon

SPAIN

BALEARIC ISLANDS (Spain)

Seville

Mediterranean Sea

SICILY (Italy)

Maps of Different Scales

Maps are drawn to different scales, depending on their purpose. Here are three maps drawn to very different scales. Keep in mind that maps showing large areas have smaller scales. Maps showing small areas have larger scales.

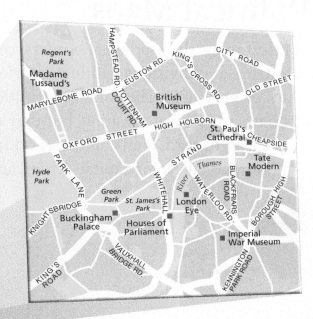

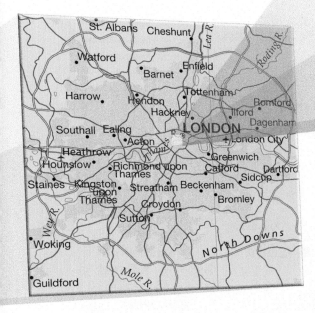

▲ Central London
Find the gray square on the map of Greater London. This square represents the area shown on the map above. This map moves you closer into the center of London. Like the zoom on a computer or a camera, this map shows a smaller area but in greater detail. It has the largest scale (1 inch represents about 0.9 mile). You can use this map to explore downtown London.

Key

■ Point of interest

Park

0 miles 0.5 1
0 kilometers 1

▲ Greater London
Find the gray square on the main map of Western Europe (left). This square represents the area shown on the map above. It shows London's boundaries, the general shape of the city, and the features around the city. This map can help you find your way from the airport to the center of town.

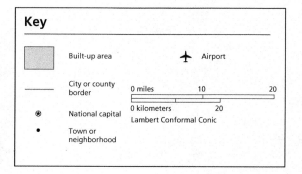

Key

▢ Built-up area   ✈ Airport

―― City or county border

⊛ National capital

• Town or neighborhood

0 miles 10 20
0 kilometers 20
Lambert Conformal Conic

PRACTICE YOUR GEOGRAPHY SKILLS

1 What part of a map explains the colors used on the map?

2 How does the scale bar change depending on the scale of the map?

3 Which map would be best for finding the location of the British Museum? Explain why.

Political Maps

Political maps show political borders: continents, countries, and divisions within countries, such as states or provinces. The colors on political maps do not have any special meaning, but they make the map easier to read. Political maps also include symbols and labels for capitals, cities, and towns.

PRACTICE YOUR GEOGRAPHY SKILLS

1 What symbols show a national border, a national capital, and a city?

2 What is Angola's capital city?

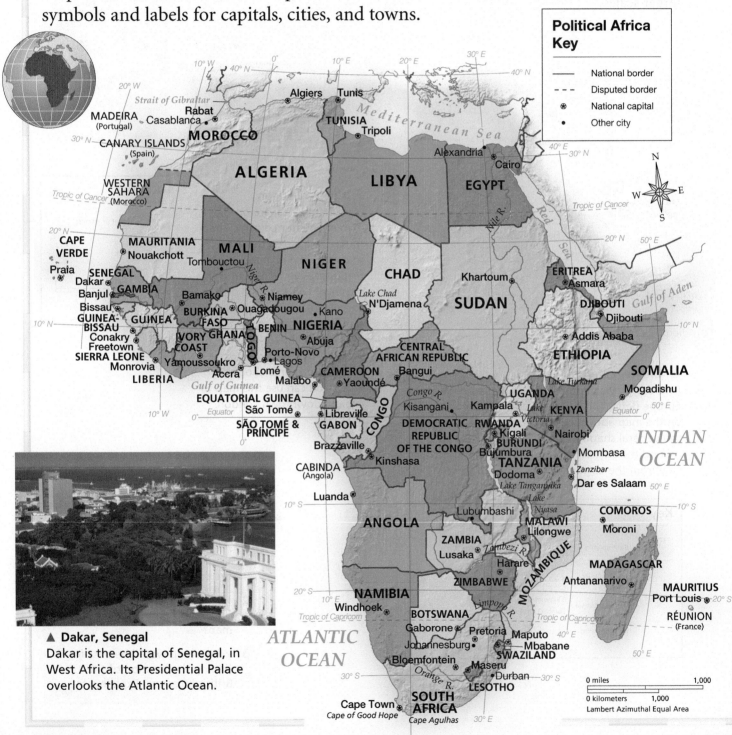

Political Africa Key

——— National border

- - - - Disputed border

⊛ National capital

• Other city

▲ **Dakar, Senegal**
Dakar is the capital of Senegal, in West Africa. Its Presidential Palace overlooks the Atlantic Ocean.

0 miles 1,000
0 kilometers 1,000
Lambert Azimuthal Equal Area

Physical Maps

Physical maps represent what a region looks like by showing its major physical features, such as hills and plains. Physical maps also often show elevation and relief. Elevation, indicated by colors, is the height of the land above sea level. Relief, indicated by shading, shows how sharply the land rises or falls.

PRACTICE YOUR GEOGRAPHY SKILLS

1 Which areas of Africa have the highest elevation?

2 How can you use relief to plan a hiking trip?

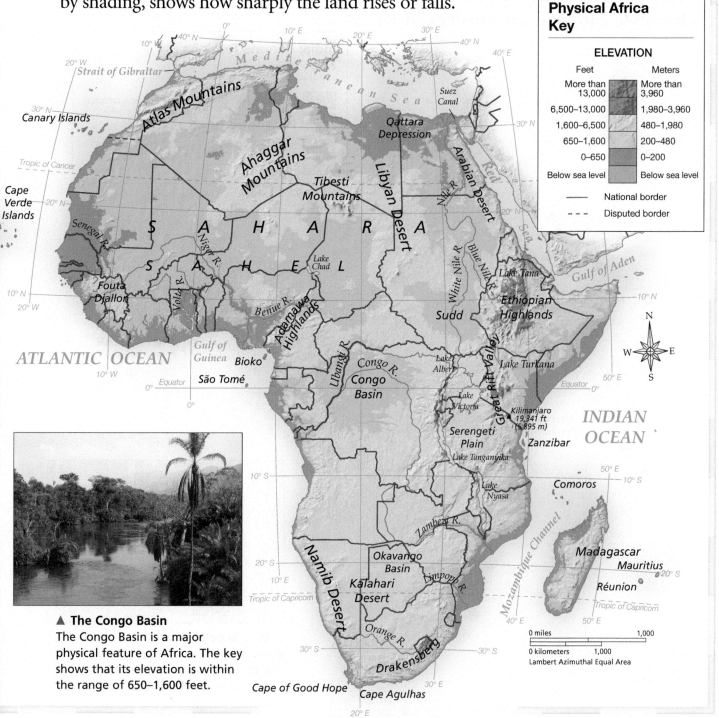

Physical Africa Key

ELEVATION

Feet	Meters
More than 13,000	More than 3,960
6,500–13,000	1,980–3,960
1,600–6,500	480–1,980
650–1,600	200–480
0–650	0–200
Below sea level	Below sea level

—— National border
- - - Disputed border

▲ **The Congo Basin**
The Congo Basin is a major physical feature of Africa. The key shows that its elevation is within the range of 650–1,600 feet.

Special-Purpose Maps: Climate

Unlike the boundary lines on a political map, the boundary lines on climate maps do not separate the land into exact divisions. For example, in this climate map of India, a tropical wet climate gradually changes to a tropical wet and dry climate.

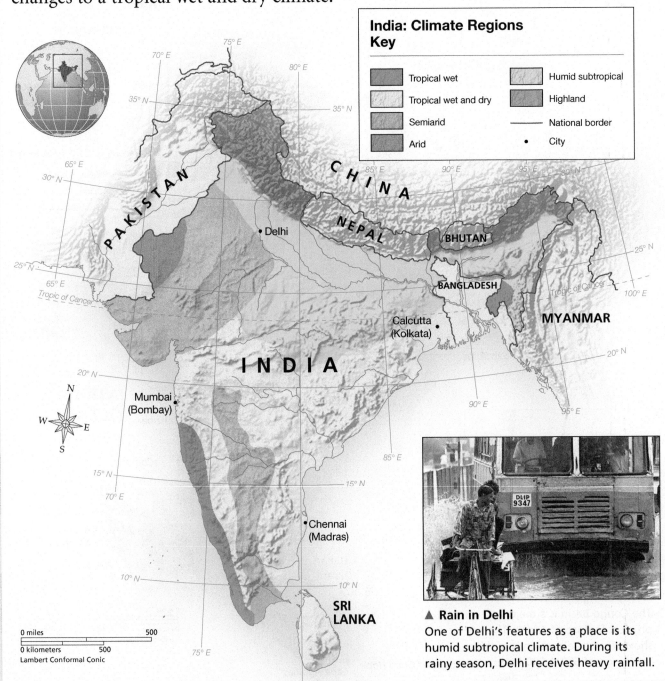

India: Climate Regions Key

- Tropical wet
- Tropical wet and dry
- Semiarid
- Arid
- Humid subtropical
- Highland
- National border
- • City

▲ **Rain in Delhi**
One of Delhi's features as a place is its humid subtropical climate. During its rainy season, Delhi receives heavy rainfall.

Special-Purpose Maps: Language

This map shows the official languages of India. An official language is the language used by the government. Even though a region has an official language, the people there may speak other languages as well. As in other special-purpose maps, the key explains how the different languages appear on the map.

PRACTICE YOUR GEOGRAPHY SKILLS

1 What color represents the Malayalam language on this map?

2 Where in India is Tamil the official language?

The Hindi language ▶
Hindi is the most widely spoken language in India. It is also the most popular language in Delhi.

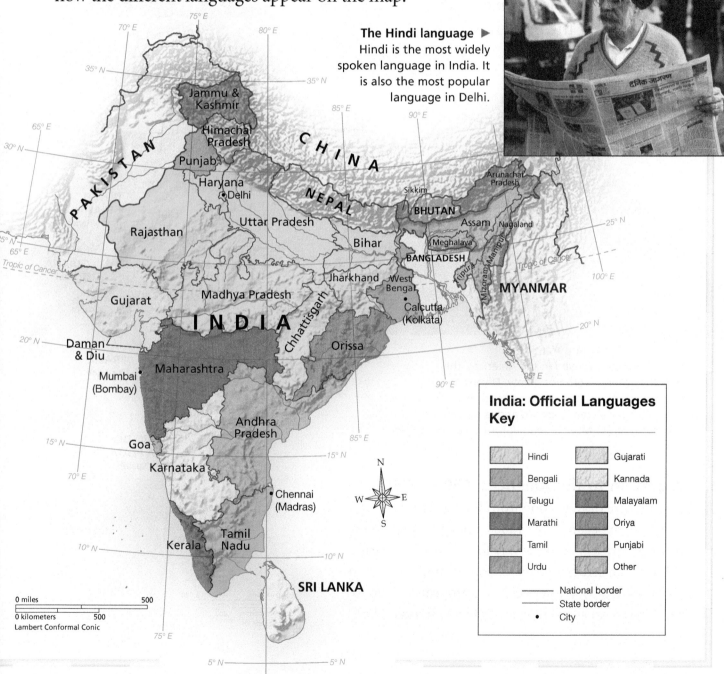

India: Official Languages Key

Hindi	Gujarati
Bengali	Kannada
Telugu	Malayalam
Marathi	Oriya
Tamil	Punjabi
Urdu	Other

— National border
— State border
• City

Human Migration

Migration is an important part of the study of geography. Since the beginning of history, people have been on the move. As people move, they both shape and are shaped by their environments. Wherever people go, the culture they bring with them mixes with the cultures of the place in which they have settled.

Explorers arrive ▼
In 1492, Christopher Columbus set sail from Spain for the Americas with three ships. The ships shown here are replicas of those ships.

▲ **Native American pyramid**
When Europeans arrived in the Americas, the lands they found were not empty. Diverse groups of people with distinct cultures already lived there. The temple-topped pyramid shown above was built by Mayan Indians in Mexico, long before Columbus sailed.

Migration to the Americas, 1500–1800

A huge wave of migration from the Eastern Hemisphere began in the 1500s. European explorers in the Americas paved the way for hundreds of years of European settlement there. Forced migration from Africa started soon afterward, as Europeans began to import African slaves to work in the Americas. The map to the right shows these migrations.

ATLANTIC OCEAN

NEW SPAIN
(Spain)
Mexico City

Caribbean Sea

Panama City

DUTCH GUIANA
(Netherlands)

NEW GRENADA
(Spain)

FRENCH GUIANA
(France)

Amazon R.

PERU
(Spain)
Lima
Cuzco

BRAZIL
(Portugal)

Potosí

RIO DE LA PLATA
(Spain)

Concepción

Buenos Aires

0 miles 1,000
0 kilometers 1,000
Wagner VII

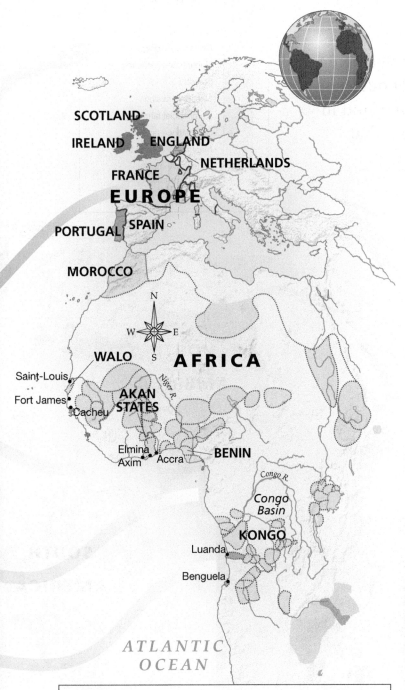

SCOTLAND
IRELAND ENGLAND
NETHERLANDS
FRANCE
EUROPE
PORTUGAL SPAIN
MOROCCO

AFRICA

WALO
Saint-Louis
Fort James
Cacheu
AKAN STATES
Elmina
Axim Accra **BENIN**
Niger R.

Congo R.
Congo Basin

KONGO
Luanda
Benguela

ATLANTIC OCEAN

Migration to Latin America, 1500–1800 Key

← European migration	Spain and possessions
← African migration	Portugal and possessions
— National or colonial border	Netherlands and possessions
···· Traditional African border	France and possessions
African State	England and possessions

PRACTICE YOUR GEOGRAPHY SKILLS

1 Where did the Portuguese settle in the Americas?

2 Would you describe African migration at this time as a result of both push factors and pull factors? Explain why or why not.

"Push" and "Pull" Factors

Geographers describe a people's choice to migrate in terms of "push" factors and "pull" factors. Push factors are things in people's lives that push them to leave, such as poverty and political unrest. Pull factors are things in another country that pull people to move there, including better living conditions and hopes of better jobs.

▲ **Elmina, Ghana**
Elmina, in Ghana, is one of the many ports from which slaves were transported from Africa. Because slaves and gold were traded here, stretches of the western African coast were known as the Slave Coast and the Gold Coast.

World Land Use

People around the world have many different economic structures, or ways of making a living. Land-use maps are one way to learn about these structures. The ways that people use the land in each region tell us about the main ways that people in that region make a living.

World Land Use Key

	Nomadic herding
	Hunting and gathering
	Forestry
	Livestock raising
	Commercial farming
	Subsistence farming
	Manufacturing and trade
	Little or no activity
———	National border
- - - -	Disputed border

▲ **Wheat farming in the United States**
Developed countries practice commercial farming rather than subsistence farming. Commercial farming is the production of food mainly for sale, either within the country or for export to other countries. Commercial farmers like these in Oregon often use heavy equipment to farm.

Levels of Development

Notice on the map key the term *subsistence farming*. This term means the production of food mainly for use by the farmer's own family. In less-developed countries, subsistence farming is often one of the main economic activities. In contrast, in developed countries there is little subsistence farming.

▲ **Growing barley in Ecuador**
These farmers in Ecuador use hand tools to harvest barley. They will use most of the crop they grow to feed themselves or their farm animals.

NORTH AMERICA

SOUTH AMERICA

0 miles		2,00
0 kilometers		2,000

Robinson

▲ **Growing rice in Vietnam**
Women in Vietnam plant rice in wet rice paddies, using the same planting methods their ancestors did.

PRACTICE YOUR GEOGRAPHY SKILLS

1 In what parts of the world is subsistence farming the main land use?

2 Locate where manufacturing and trade are the main land use. Are they found more often near areas of subsistence farming or areas of commercial farming? Why might this be so?

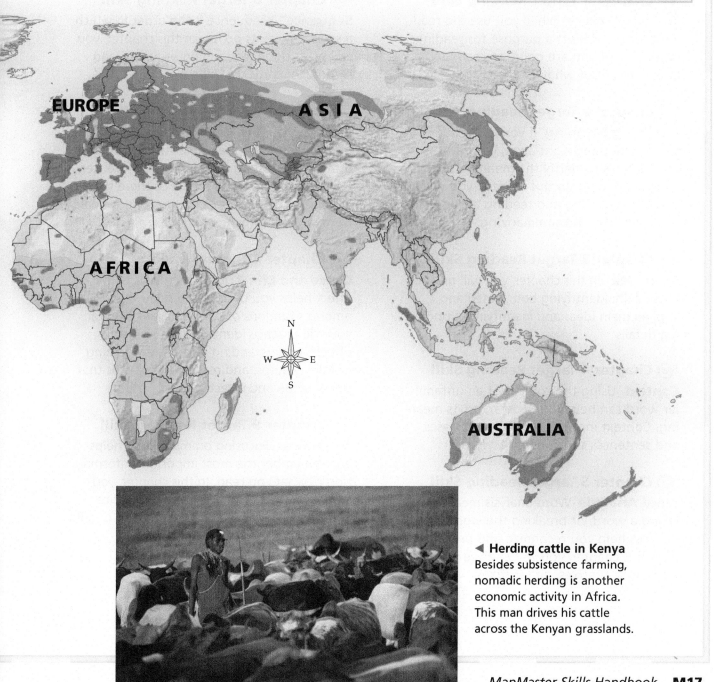

EUROPE

ASIA

AFRICA

AUSTRALIA

◄ **Herding cattle in Kenya**
Besides subsistence farming, nomadic herding is another economic activity in Africa. This man drives his cattle across the Kenyan grasslands.

How to Read Social Studies

 ## Target Reading Skills

The Target Reading Skills introduced on this page will help you understand the words and ideas in this book and in other social studies reading you do. Each chapter focuses on one of these reading skills. Good readers develop a bank of reading strategies, or skills. Then they draw on the particular strategies that will help them understand the text they are reading.

Chapter 1 Target Reading Skill

Reading Process When you use the reading process, you set a purpose for reading, predict what you are going to read, and ask questions about what you read.

Chapter 2 Target Reading Skill

Clarifying Meaning If you do not understand something right away, you can use several skills to clarify the meaning of words and ideas. In this chapter, you will practice rereading and reading ahead, paraphrasing, and summarizing.

Chapter 3 Target Reading Skill

Main Idea In this chapter, you will practice these skills: identifying both stated and implied main ideas and identifying supporting details.

Chapter 4 Target Reading Skill

Context Using the context of an unfamiliar word can help you understand its meaning. Context includes the words, phrases, and sentences surrounding a word.

Chapter 5 Target Reading Skill

Word Analysis Word analysis means analyzing a word, or breaking the word into parts to help you recognize and pronounce it. In this chapter, you will analyze words to find roots, prefixes, and suffixes.

Chapter 6 Target Reading Skill

Sequence A sequence is the order in which a series of events occurs. In this chapter, you will practice understanding sequence and recognize words that signal sequence.

Chapter 7 Target Reading Skill

Comparison and Contrast Comparing means examining the similarities between things. Contrasting is looking at differences. In this chapter, you will practice these skills: comparing and contrasting, making comparisons, and identifying contrasts.

Chapter 8 Target Reading Skill

Cause and Effect Identifying cause and effect helps you understand relationships among situations or events. In this chapter, you will practice identifying causes and effects, understanding effects, recognizing multiple causes, and recognizing words that signal cause and effect.

Chapter 9 Target Reading Skill

Main Ideas Focusing on main ideas helps you remember the most important information in what you read. In this chapter, you will have another opportunity to practice identifying main ideas and supporting details.

ASIA and the PACIFIC

Asia and the Pacific is a huge region that covers more than one third of Earth's surface. Asia is the largest continent. It includes some of the world's largest and smallest countries. This region also includes the only continent that is also a country—Australia.

Guiding Questions

The text, photographs, maps, and charts in this book will help you discover answers to these Guiding Questions.

1. **Geography** What are the main physical features of Asia and the Pacific?

2. **History** How have ancient civilizations of Asia and the Pacific influenced the world today?

3. **Culture** What are the main characteristics of the cultures of Asia and the Pacific?

4. **Government** What types of government exist in Asia and the Pacific today?

5. **Economics** How do the people of this region make a living?

Project Preview

You can also discover answers to the Guiding Questions by working on projects. Two projects are listed on page 246 of this book.

Investigate Asia and the Pacific Islands

Asia is the largest continent in the world. The vast Pacific Ocean contains thousands of scattered islands and another continent—the country of Australia. The continent of Asia includes part of Russia. However, Russian Asia is not covered in these pages. Because most of Russia's people live in Europe, Russia is discussed with Europe.

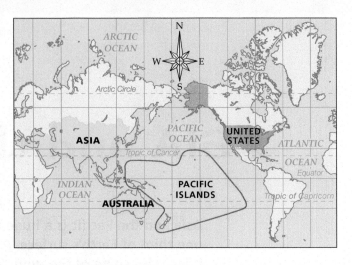

▲ **Myanmar, Asia**
Shwedagon Buddhist Temple dates from about A.D. 1000.

LOCATION

1 Locate Asia and the Pacific Islands
In this book you will read about Asia, Australia, and the islands of the Pacific Ocean. This region is shaded green on the map above. What ocean lies between Asia and the United States? If you lived on the west coast of the United States, in which direction would you travel to reach Asia? If you lived on the most eastern tip of the Pacific islands, in which direction would you travel to reach the west coast of the United States?

REGIONS

2 Estimate Asia's Size
Compare Asia's mainland to the continental United States (all states except Alaska and Hawaii). With a ruler, measure mainland Asia from north to south. Measure the distance from east to west. Now make the same measurements for the continental United States. About how many times longer and wider is mainland Asia (not including Russia) than the continental United States?

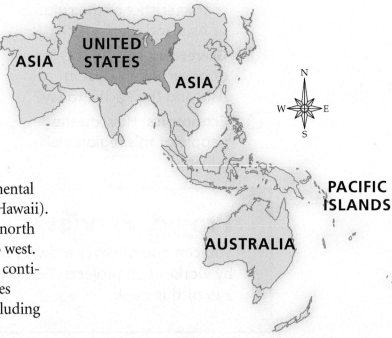

Political Asia

LOCATION

3 Investigate the Countries of Asia and the Pacific

Which Asian country on the map below is the largest? Which country is the second largest? Asia has many countries that are located on islands. Name three of them. Iran is a large country in the western part of Asia. Name three countries that border Iran.

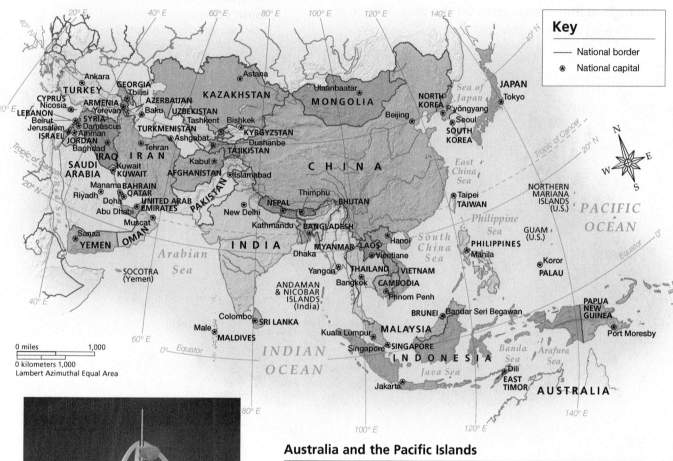

Key

— National border

⊛ National capital

▲ **Dubai, United Arab Emirates**
Wealth from the region's oil resources paid for elaborate buildings like this hotel.

Australia and the Pacific Islands

Physical Asia

LOCATION

4 Examine the Physical Features of Asia

Asia is a continent of great physical contrasts, including towering mountains, high plateaus, and low-lying plains. Use the elevation key to identify the highest and lowest areas on the map. Where are they? Describe their physical features.

▲ **Mount Fuji, Japan**
Japan's tallest mountain is actually a volcano, which last erupted in 1707.

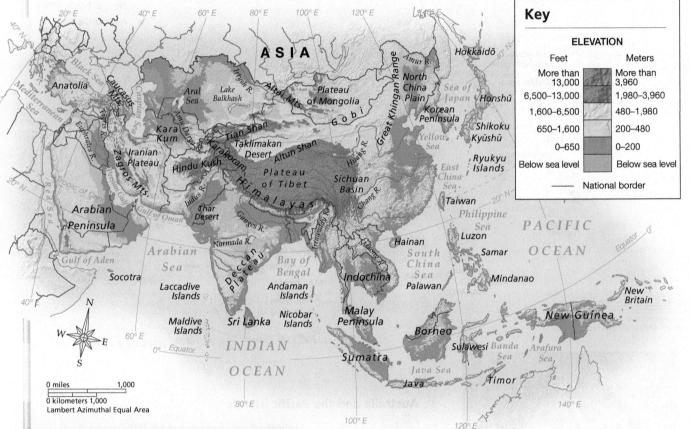

Key

ELEVATION

Feet	Meters
More than 13,000	More than 3,960
6,500–13,000	1,980–3,960
1,600–6,500	480–1,980
650–1,600	200–480
0–650	0–200
Below sea level	Below sea level

—— National border

▲ **Australian Outback**
The Outback, in the dry, hot center of the country, is grassland and desert where few people live. Here ranchers raise sheep and cattle.

Australia and the Pacific Islands

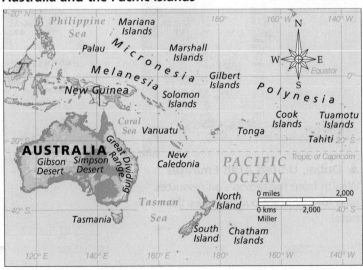

The Ring of Fire

Earth's crust is made up of plates that ride on top of molten rock called magma. The magma escapes in the form of lava when volcanoes erupt. Ninety percent of the world's active volcanoes circle the Pacific Ocean. Look at the map below. Why is this region described as a "Ring of Fire"?

▲ **Puu Oo Volcano, Hawaii**
The Puu Oo volcano spews molten lava as it erupts. The islands that we call Hawaii are the tops of volcanoes that rest on the ocean floor.

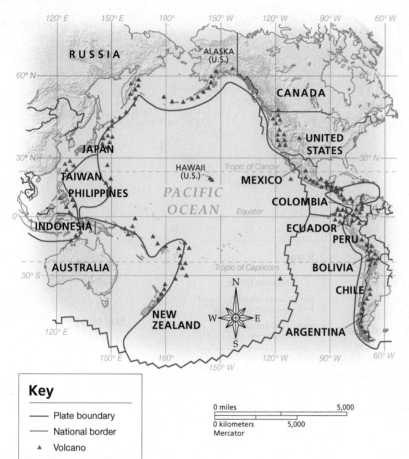

Key

—— Plate boundary
—— National border
▲ Volcano

0 miles 5,000
0 kilometers 5,000
Mercator

INTERACTION

5 Investigate the Ring of Fire

Where Earth's plates meet, plate boundaries are formed. With your finger, trace the plate boundaries on the map at left. Notice where the volcanoes are located in relation to the plate boundaries. Compare the location of volcanoes to the location of cities on the political maps on page 3. Where might volcano eruptions cause the most harm to people?

PRACTICE YOUR GEOGRAPHY SKILLS

1. You begin your boat trip from Australia's north coast and travel west through Indonesia. After you pass Borneo and Java, you cross the Equator and enter a large body of water. What is its name?

2. Today you fly from the Himalayas along the 30° N parallel across the Indus River to the Zagros Mountains. What body of water are you near?

3. There are many volcanoes to the east of this island nation north of the East China Sea. What is the name of this country?

▲ **Boats moored in Indonesia**

Focus on Countries in Asia

Now that you've investigated the geography of Asia and the Pacific, take a closer look at some of the countries that make up this vast region. The map shows the countries of Asia and the Pacific. The countries that you will study in depth in the second half of this book appear in yellow on the map.

Go Online
PHSchool.com
Use Web Code **lcp-6000** for the **interactive maps** on these pages.

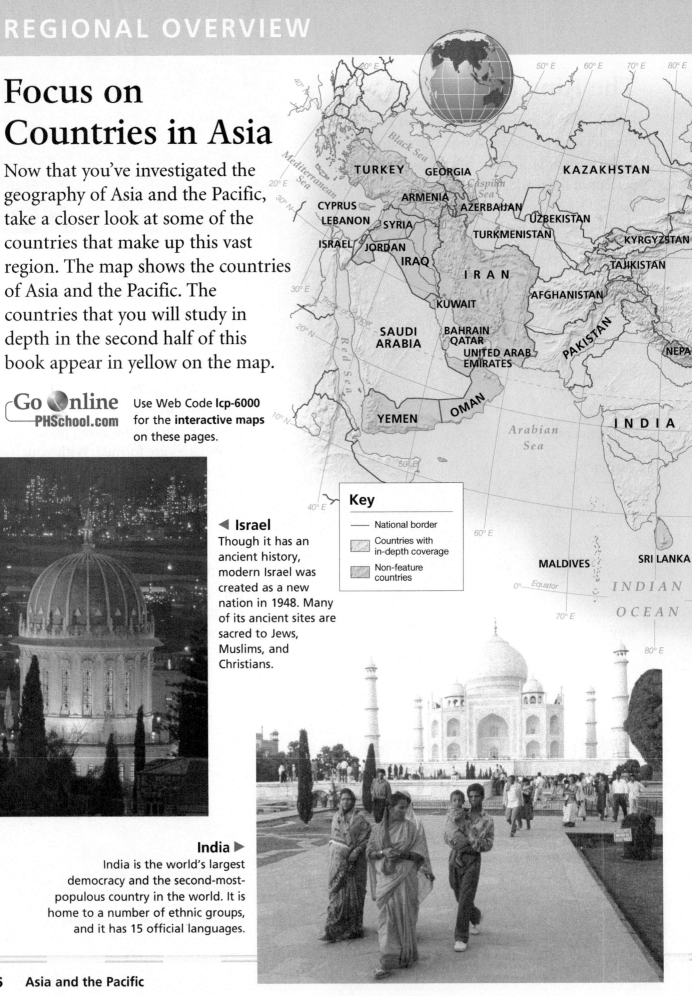

Key
- —— National border
- Countries with in-depth coverage
- Non-feature countries

Map labels: TURKEY, GEORGIA, KAZAKHSTAN, CYPRUS, ARMENIA, AZERBAIJAN, UZBEKISTAN, LEBANON, SYRIA, TURKMENISTAN, KYRGYZSTAN, ISRAEL, JORDAN, IRAQ, I R A N, TAJIKISTAN, AFGHANISTAN, KUWAIT, SAUDI ARABIA, BAHRAIN, QATAR, UNITED ARAB EMIRATES, PAKISTAN, NEPAL, YEMEN, OMAN, I N D I A, MALDIVES, SRI LANKA, INDIAN OCEAN

Seas: Black Sea, Mediterranean Sea, Caspian Sea, Red Sea, Arabian Sea

◀ **Israel**
Though it has an ancient history, modern Israel was created as a new nation in 1948. Many of its ancient sites are sacred to Jews, Muslims, and Christians.

India ▶
India is the world's largest democracy and the second-most-populous country in the world. It is home to a number of ethnic groups, and it has 15 official languages.

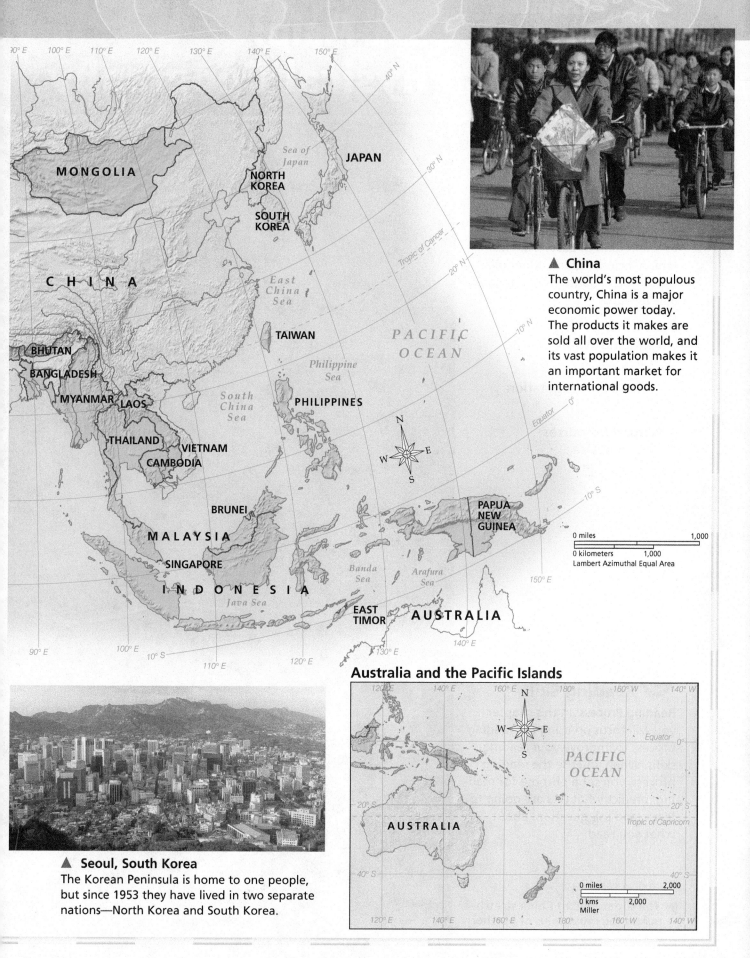

MONGOLIA

NORTH KOREA

JAPAN

SOUTH KOREA

CHINA

BHUTAN

BANGLADESH

MYANMAR LAOS

THAILAND

VIETNAM

CAMBODIA

BRUNEI

MALAYSIA

SINGAPORE

INDONESIA

TAIWAN

PHILIPPINES

PAPUA NEW GUINEA

EAST TIMOR

AUSTRALIA

Sea of Japan

East China Sea

Philippine Sea

South China Sea

PACIFIC OCEAN

Banda Sea

Arafura Sea

Java Sea

Tropic of Cancer

Equator

N
W E
S

90° E 100° E 110° E 120° E 130° E 140° E 150° E
40° N
30° N
20° N
10° N
0°
10° S

0 miles   1,000
0 kilometers   1,000
Lambert Azimuthal Equal Area

▲ **China**
The world's most populous
country, China is a major
economic power today.
The products it makes are
sold all over the world, and
its vast population makes it
an important market for
international goods.

Australia and the Pacific Islands

AUSTRALIA

PACIFIC OCEAN

N
W E
S

Equator
Tropic of Capricorn

120° E 140° E 160° E 180° 160° W 140° W
20° S
40° S

0 miles   2,000
0 kms   2,000
Miller

▲ **Seoul, South Korea**
The Korean Peninsula is home to one people,
but since 1953 they have lived in two separate
nations—North Korea and South Korea.

Chapter 1

East Asia: Physical Geography

Chapter Preview

This chapter will introduce you to the region of East Asia. This region includes China, Mongolia, North Korea, South Korea, Japan, and Taiwan.

Section 1
Land and Water

Section 2
Climate and Vegetation

Section 3
Natural Resources and Land Use

Target Reading Skill

Reading Process In this chapter you will focus on using the reading process to improve your reading skills. When you use the reading process, you set a purpose for reading, predict what you are going to learn, and ask questions about what you read.

▶ The Great Wall of China stretches across the mountains of northern China.

East Asia: Physical

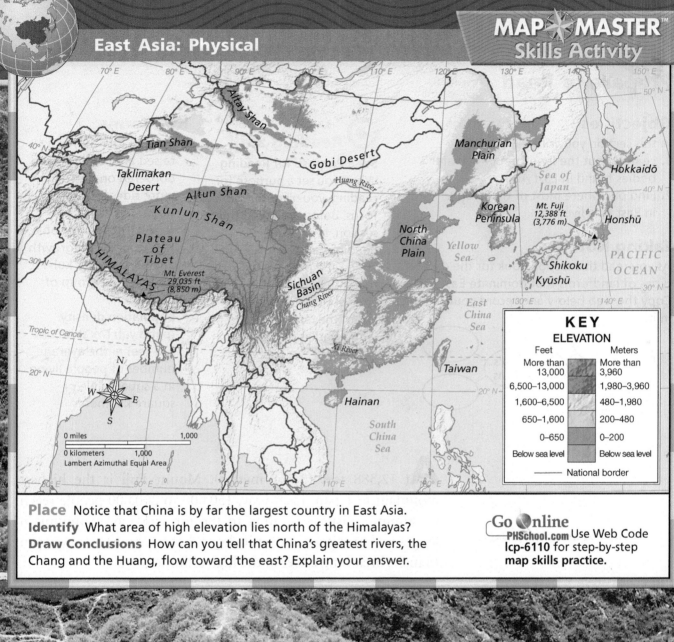

KEY
ELEVATION

Feet		Meters
More than 13,000		More than 3,960
6,500–13,000		1,980–3,960
1,600–6,500		480–1,980
650–1,600		200–480
0–650		0–200
Below sea level		Below sea level
	—— National border	

Place Notice that China is by far the largest country in East Asia.
Identify What area of high elevation lies north of the Himalayas?
Draw Conclusions How can you tell that China's greatest rivers, the Chang and the Huang, flow toward the east? Explain your answer.

Go Online
PHSchool.com Use Web Code
lcp-6110 for step-by-step
map skills practice.

Prepare to Read

Objectives

In this section you will
1. Learn about the landforms and water bodies found in East Asia.
2. Find out where most of the people in East Asia live.

Taking Notes

As you read this section, look for the different types of landforms that dominate East Asia. Copy the web below and record your findings in it.

East Asia's Landforms

Target Reading Skill

Set a Purpose for Reading
When you set a purpose for reading, you give yourself a focus. Before you read this section, look at the headings and pictures. Then set a purpose for reading. In this section, your purpose is to learn about the landforms and water bodies of East Asia.

Key Terms

- **plateau** (pla TOH) *n.* a raised area of level land bordered on one or more sides by steep slopes or cliffs
- **fertile** (FUR tul) *adj.* able to support plant growth
- **archipelago** (ahr kuh PEL uh goh) *n.* a group of islands
- **population density** (pahp yuh LAY shun DEN suh tee) *n.* the average number of people living in a square mile or square kilometer

A view of Mount Fuji, Japan

At 12,388 feet (3,776 meters), Mount Fuji is the highest mountain in Japan. Each year, 150,000 to 200,000 people reach its summit. Visitors heading to the top can stay in mountain lodges and browse in souvenir shops that sell canisters of oxygen to make breathing easier at the high altitude.

Landforms and Water Bodies

Mount Fuji is one of the many spectacular landforms that make up East Asia. A single nation, China, takes up most of East Asia's land. Mountains, highlands, and **plateaus,** or raised areas of level land bordered on one or more sides by steep slopes or cliffs, make up much of China's land-scape. The other countries of this region are mountainous, like China. But only China and Mongolia also have wide plains and plateaus. Japan, Taiwan, North Korea, and South Korea have narrow plains that lie mainly along coasts and rivers.

The Himalayas Powerful natural forces created the rugged landscape of East Asia. About 50 million years ago, a huge piece of a continent collided with Asia. The collision caused Earth's surface to fold and buckle, forming the Himalayas and the Plateau of Tibet. The Himalayas are the highest mountains in the world. They include Mount Everest, the highest peak in the world. The Himalayas extend along the border of China and Nepal. The Plateau of Tibet is a huge highland area that lies north of the Himalaya mountains.

Island Landscapes Natural forces also shaped the islands that make up Japan. Earthquakes forced some parts of the country to rise and others to sink. Erupting volcanoes piled up masses of lava and ash, forming new mountains. Japan's Mount Fuji is actually a volcano that has not erupted since 1707. Today, earthquakes and volcanoes are still changing the landscape in many parts of East Asia.

China: More Than One Billion People China is home to one of the oldest civilizations on Earth. With a population of more than one billion people, it also has more people than any other nation in the world.

Mountains and deserts make up more than two thirds of China's land. A desert is a dry region with little vegetation. The area of western and southwestern China has some of the highest mountains in the world. China's Gobi is the northernmost desert on Earth.

China's most important rivers, the Chang and the Huang, begin in Tibet and flow east. The Chang River is deep enough for cargo ships to sail on. More than 100 million people live along the banks of the Huang River. It runs through one of the most fertile regions of China, the North China Plain. **Fertile** soil is capable of supporting abundant plant growth. The North China Plain is covered with deposits of loess (LOH es), a brownish-yellow soil that is very fertile.

The Plateau of Tibet
The Plateau of Tibet is a vast, high area in China that includes the region of Tibet. These Tibetan women make their living by herding livestock. **Infer** *The Plateau of Tibet is called "the roof of the world." Why do you think this is so?*

Set a Purpose for Reading
If your purpose is to learn about East Asia's landforms and water bodies, how does this paragraph help you meet your goal?

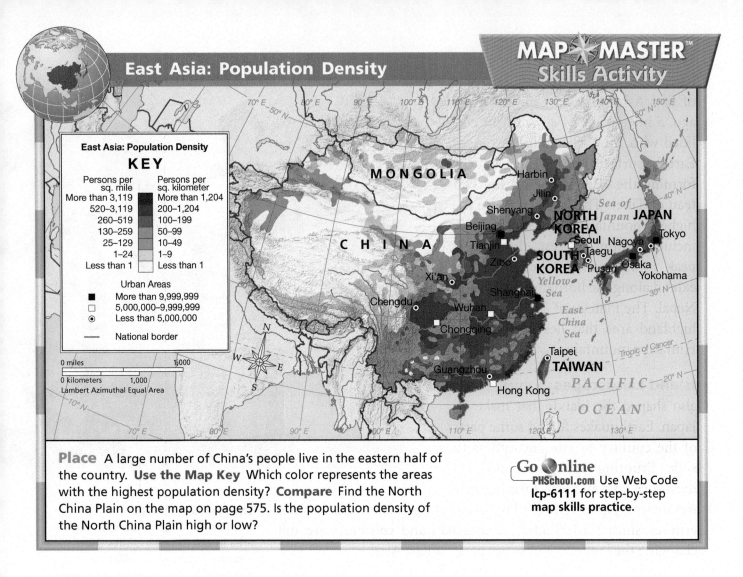

East Asia: Population Density

East Asia: Population Density

KEY

Persons per sq. mile	Persons per sq. kilometer
More than 3,119	More than 1,204
520–3,119	200–1,204
260–519	100–199
130–259	50–99
25–129	10–49
1–24	1–9
Less than 1	Less than 1

Urban Areas
- ■ More than 9,999,999
- □ 5,000,000–9,999,999
- ◉ Less than 5,000,000
- — National border

0 miles 1,000
0 kilometers 1,000
Lambert Azimuthal Equal Area

Place A large number of China's people live in the eastern half of the country. **Use the Map Key** Which color represents the areas with the highest population density? **Compare** Find the North China Plain on the map on page 575. Is the population density of the North China Plain high or low?

Go Online
PHSchool.com Use Web Code
lcp-6111 for step-by-step
map skills practice.

Japan: An Island Country Japan is an **archipelago** (ahr kuh PEL uh goh), or group of islands, in the western Pacific Ocean. Japan has four main islands and more than 3,000 smaller ones. Every major Japanese city is located on the coast. As the map above shows, most of Japan's people live in coastal areas. Nearly 80 percent of the country is mountainous.

Japan's four main islands are Hokkaidō (hoh ky doh), Honshū (hahn shoo), Shikoku (shee koh koo), and Kyūshū (kyoo shoo). The largest and most populated of these is Honshū. Most of Japan's major cities, including its capital city of Tokyo, are located on Honshū.

The Koreas: Two Countries, One Peninsula The Korean Peninsula extends south into the Yellow Sea between China and Japan. A peninsula is a piece of land nearly surrounded by water. Since 1953, Korea has been divided into two separate countries, North Korea and South Korea.

✓ **Reading Check** Which type of landform dominates Japan— mountains or plains?

Population in East Asia

As you can see on the map on the previous page, the population of East Asia is spread unevenly across the land. Few people live in the deserts, plateaus, and mountains. Yet almost 1.5 billion people make their homes in East Asia. Most of the people live in the plains and coastal areas, where living and growing food are easier. These parts of East Asia have a very high **population density,** or average number of people living in a square mile (or square kilometer).

Look at the physical map of East Asia on page 9 and find the North China Plain. Now look at the population density map of East Asia on page 12. You can see that this area of China has a very high population density. That is because the land in the North China Plain is better suited for human settlement than the mountains and deserts of China. For example, the North China Plain is level and has fertile soil.

In East Asia, level ground must be shared by cities, farms, and industries. Almost half the population of Japan is crowded onto less than 3 percent of the country's land. In China, most of the population is located in the eastern half of the country, where the plains and coastal areas are located.

A crowded street in Seoul, the capital of South Korea

 Reading Check Why does the North China Plain have such a high population density?

 ## Section 1 Assessment

Key Terms
Review the key terms at the beginning of this section. Use each term in a sentence that explains its meaning.

Target Reading Skill
How did having a purpose help you understand important ideas in this section?

Comprehension and Critical Thinking
1. (a) **Recall** What are the major landforms in East Asia?

(b) **Locate** In what part of China is the Plateau of Tibet?
(c) **Contrast** How are the landforms in eastern China different from the landforms in western China?
2. (a) **Identify** Name one type of landform in China where there is a high population density. You may refer to the maps in the section to answer.
(b) **Draw Conclusions** How does the physical geography of East Asia help explain why the eastern part of China is the most densely populated part of the country?

Writing Activity
Suppose that you are a travel agent helping a customer who wants to visit East Asia. Which landforms would you suggest that your customer visit? In which countries are these landforms located? Record your suggestions.

For: An activity on East Asia
Visit: PHSchool.com
Web Code: lcd-6101

Climate and Vegetation

Prepare to Read

Objectives

In this section you will
1. Examine the major climate regions in East Asia.
2. Discover how climate affects people and vegetation in East Asia.

Taking Notes

As you read this section, look for details about how climate affects the people and vegetation in East Asia. Copy the table below and record your findings in it.

East Asia's Climates	
Effect on Vegetation	Effect on People
•	• Rice is the main food in southern China.

Target Reading Skill

Predict Making predictions about your text helps you set a purpose for reading and helps you remember what you read. Preview the section by looking at the headings, pictures, and maps. Then predict what the text might discuss about climate and vegetation in East Asia.

Key Terms

• **monsoon** (mahn SOON) *n.* a wind that changes direction with the change of season
• **typhoon** (ty FOON) *n.* a tropical storm that develops over the Pacific Ocean, with winds that reach speeds greater than 74 miles per hour
• **deciduous** (dee SIJ oo us) *adj.* falling off or shedding, as in leaves, seasonally or at a certain stage of development

You and your family are visiting Japan in the middle of February. All of you are trying to decide where to go for a long weekend. Your brother wants to go north to the island of Hokkaidō, where the skiing is perfect. Your parents, though, have had enough of winter. They would like to go to the island of Okinawa (oh kee nah wuh). The water there is warm enough for swimming. Which would you prefer—sun or snow?

East Asia's Climate Regions

Look at the climate map on the next page. It shows that East Asia has seven climate regions. Two of them—the tropical wet region and the subarctic region—cover a comparatively small part of the land. The five major climate regions are semiarid, arid, humid subtropical, humid continental, and highland.

Downhill skiing in Japan

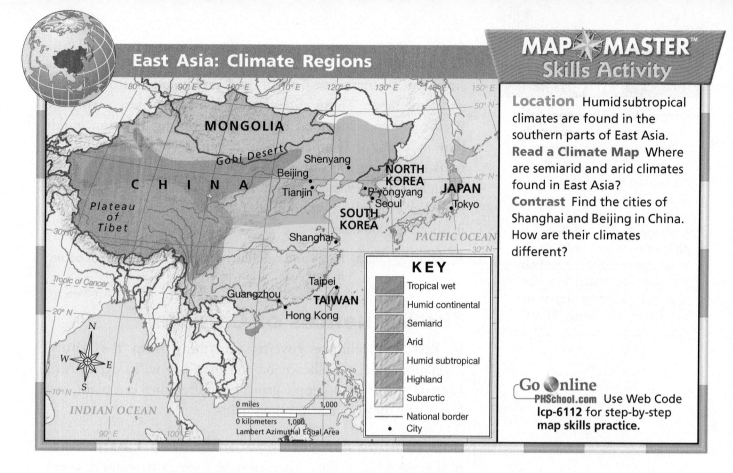

East Asia: Climate Regions

MONGOLIA

Gobi Desert
Shenyang
Beijing
Tianjin

C H I N A

Plateau of Tibet

NORTH KOREA
P'yŏngyang
Seoul
SOUTH KOREA

JAPAN
Tokyo

Shanghai

PACIFIC OCEAN

Tropic of Cancer

Guangzhou
Taipei
TAIWAN
Hong Kong

INDIAN OCEAN

N
W   E
S

0 miles   1,000
0 kilometers   1,000
Lambert Azimuthal Equal Area

KEY
- Tropical wet
- Humid continental
- Semiarid
- Arid
- Humid subtropical
- Highland
- Subarctic
- National border
- • City

A Variety of Climates A large part of eastern China has a humid subtropical climate—cool winters and hot summers with plenty of rain. To the north is a humid continental area of warm summers and cold winters. Because South Korea and Japan are almost completely surrounded by water, summers are a bit cooler and winters are a bit warmer than in other places at the same latitude.

In contrast, the northern interior of China is very dry, with arid and semiarid climate regions. There, temperatures can range from very hot to very cold. To the south, the Plateau of Tibet has a cool, dry, highland climate.

Monsoons Monsoons strongly affect the climates of East Asia. Monsoons are winds that change direction with the change of season. In summer, Pacific Ocean winds blow northwest toward the Asian continent. They bring rainfall that starts in June as a drizzle. The Japanese call this the "plum rain" because it begins just as the plums begin to ripen on the trees. The winds cause hot, humid weather and heavier rain in July.

In winter, the winds blow toward the east. The winds that begin in the interior of northern Asia are icy cold and very dry. In parts of China, the winds produce dust storms that can last for days. Where they cross warm ocean waters, these monsoons pick up moisture. Farther inland, they drop it as rain or snow.

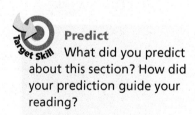

Predict
What did you predict about this section? How did your prediction guide your reading?

Typhoons East Asia has hurricanes like those that sometimes strike the southern coastline of the United States during August and September. These violent storms, which develop over the Pacific Ocean, are called **typhoons.** Whirling typhoon winds blow at speeds of 74 miles an hour or more. The winds and heavy rains they bring can cause major damage. Killer typhoons have brought great devastation and death to some countries in East Asia. For example, a typhoon that struck China in 1922 resulted in about 60,000 deaths.

✓ **Reading Check** **Name and describe two types of storms that occur in East Asia.**

The Influences of Climate

In East Asia, climate governs everything from the natural vegetation, which is shown on the map below, to agriculture. Climate affects what people grow, how often they can plant, and how easily they can harvest their fields.

How Climate Affects Vegetation in East Asia Much of the plant life in East Asia is strong enough to stand seasonal differences in temperature and rainfall. Bamboo, for example, grows remarkably quickly during the wet season in southern China and Japan. Yet it can also survive dry spells by storing food

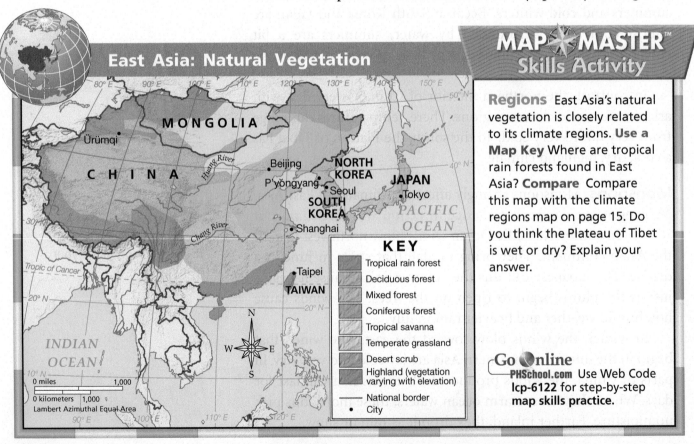

East Asia: Natural Vegetation

KEY
- Tropical rain forest
- Deciduous forest
- Mixed forest
- Coniferous forest
- Tropical savanna
- Temperate grassland
- Desert scrub
- Highland (vegetation varying with elevation)
- National border
- City

Lambert Azimuthal Equal Area

MAP MASTER™ Skills Activity

Regions East Asia's natural vegetation is closely related to its climate regions. **Use a Map Key** Where are tropical rain forests found in East Asia? **Compare** Compare this map with the climate regions map on page 15. Do you think the Plateau of Tibet is wet or dry? Explain your answer.

Go Online
PHSchool.com Use Web Code lcp-6122 for step-by-step map skills practice.

in its huge root system. Shrubs and many small flowering plants in the deserts of China spring up rapidly after summer rains. **Deciduous** (dih SIJ oo us), or leaf-shedding, trees change with the seasons. Maples, birches, and other trees turn the hillsides of Japan and the Koreas gold, orange, and red, once summer gives way to fall.

How Climate Affects People in East Asia

Climate greatly affects life in East Asia. The region around the Huang River in China is a good example. The Chinese word *Huang* means "yellow." The river gets its name from the brownish-yellow loess that is blown by the desert winds. The river picks up the loess and deposits it to the east on the North China Plain. The loess covers a huge 125,000-square-mile (324,000-square-kilometer) area around the river. This plain is one of the best farming areas in China.

The Huang River also floods. A system of dams helps control the waters. But the river can still overflow during the monsoons. Floods gave the Huang River its nickname, "China's Sorrow."

The diet of East Asians is also affected by climate. Because rice grows best in warm weather, it is the main crop—and food—of people in southern China. In the cooler north, wheat and other grains grow better than rice. This means that people in the north eat more flour products, such as noodles.

Brilliant Fall Colors in Japan
Most parts of Japan have spring, summer, fall, and winter. At this teahouse in the city of Nara, it is still warm enough to sit outdoors in October and November. **Analyze Images** *How can you tell the trees in the photo are deciduous trees?*

✓ **Reading Check** **How does bamboo survive during dry spells in southern China and Japan?**

Section 2 Assessment

Key Terms
Review the key terms at the beginning of this section. Use each term in a sentence that explains its meaning.

Target Reading Skill
What did you predict about this section? How did your prediction guide your reading?

Comprehension and Critical Thinking
1. (a) Recall What are the five major climate regions in East Asia?

(b) Summarize What kind of winters and summers are found in a humid subtropical climate?
2. (a) Identify Name three ways climate affects agriculture in East Asia.
(b) Generalize How does the climate affect what people eat in China?

Writing Activity
Write a letter to a friend who is planning a long trip to East Asia. Explain what climate conditions can occur in different areas. Include suggestions for clothing.

For: An activity on East Asia's climate
Visit: PHSchool.com
Web Code: lcd-6102

Skills for Life

Using Reliable Information on the Internet

Your teacher has given you an assignment to write a report about the Gobi Desert in Mongolia and China. To research your report, you are asked to find articles, photos, and statistics about the Gobi Desert.

"Use a variety of good sources on the Internet," your teacher urges. "An encyclopedia article is a good start for basic facts. But if you search further, you might find stories from people who live there. You might also find photographs that will help you to describe the land in your own words."

You enter the word *Gobi* on an Internet search engine, and receive 123,000 "hits"—that is, Web sites that contain the word *Gobi*. How can you find reliable, useful information among all these sites?

Learn the Skill

To find information from Web sites you can trust, follow the steps below.

1. **Decide on your search terms.** Make a list of what you are looking for. For example, try *Gobi Desert* or *Gobi climate.*

2. **Notice the Web site's Internet address.** The address, or URL, will include a period followed by a three-letter abbreviation. Among the most common are ".com," ".edu," ".gov," and ".org." Just about anyone can set up a Web site with a .com (commercial) address. Schools and universities use a .edu (education) address. Nonprofit organizations such as museums use .org. Official government sites carry a .gov address.

3. **Try to identify the author and date of information on a Web site.** The author and date often appear on the Web page. But many sites are anonymous—they do not identify the author. Do not use information from anonymous sites. It may be out of date or it may be written by an author who has no particular expertise about the topic.

4. **Choose a reliable source, or use more than one source, if needed.** Encyclopedias are reliable. They are written by people who have knowledge about a wide range of subject areas and they present facts. Sources with .gov and .edu are generally reliable, as are newspapers, magazines, and television network news sites.

Practice the Skill

Use the steps in the skill to do some research on a computer.

1. If a search for *Gobi* gives you thousands of results, what additional search terms could you use to narrow the search?

2. Look for a site with a .gov address from the government of China or Mongolia. Or try a United States government Web site for statistics about the location and size of the Gobi. Why is it a good idea to go to an .edu address to research the Gobi?

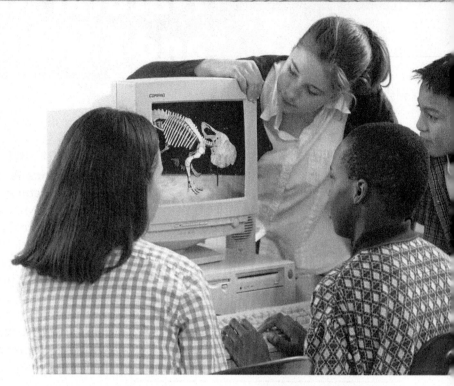

Reliable Web sites can help you research Gobi dinosaurs—or any school assignment.

3. Would it matter if an online map of the Gobi was created this year or 50 years ago? Would it matter if a graph of average rainfall in the Gobi was from this year or 50 years ago? Explain.

4. Say you read about a recent discovery of dinosaur bones in the Gobi. The news appears on an archaeology Web site, but the author and date are unidentified. Where would you find a reliable source of this news?

Apply the Skill

Suppose your neighbor writes a letter to the editor of the Internet edition of your local newspaper. In the letter, she writes, "The population in our community has doubled in the last year." Is this reliable information? Then you go to your local government's Web site and read this: "Town population doubles in just one year, according to government statistics." Is this information reliable? Name two Web sites you could go to in order to find the actual statistics. Explain why each is reliable.

Natural Resources and Land Use

Prepare to Read

Objectives
In this section you will
1. Learn about East Asia's major natural resources.
2. Find out how the people of East Asia use land to produce food.

Taking Notes
Copy the table below. As you read, look for the headings that appear in large red type. Turn these headings into questions. Use the table to record your answers to these questions.

Natural Resources and Land Use in East Asia	
Questions	Answers

Target Reading Skill

Ask Questions Preview the headings, pictures, and maps to see what this section is about. Find the main headings in this section. (They appear in large red type.) Turn these headings into questions. Then read to answer your questions. Write your questions and answers in the Taking Notes table.

Key Terms
- **developing country** (dih VEL up ing KUN tree) *n.* a country that has low industrial production and little modern technology
- **developed country** (dih VEL upt KUN tree) *n.* a country with many industries and a well-developed economy
- **terrace** (TEHR us) *n.* a level area in a hillside
- **double-cropping** (DUB ul KRAHP ing) *v.* to grow two or more crops on the same land

Coal miners in China

When planning their economies, all countries ask these three basic questions: What will be produced? How will it be produced? For whom will it be produced? For the countries of East Asia, the answers to these questions depend largely on factors surrounding these two things: natural resources and land use.

Natural resources are materials found in nature. They include fertile land, minerals, water, and forests. Natural resources can be used to produce all sorts of goods, from cars to sweatshirts. Land use is linked to natural resources. To improve their economies, governments have to decide how to use the land and the natural resources they contain.

East Asia's Natural Resources

East Asia's lands and waters are filled with abundant natural resources. As the map on the next page shows, East Asia has natural resources that can be used to produce energy, such as coal, oil, and water for hydroelectric power. Other resources in East Asia are the raw materials for manufactured goods, such as electronic equipment. The water bodies and fertile land of East Asia are also important resources.

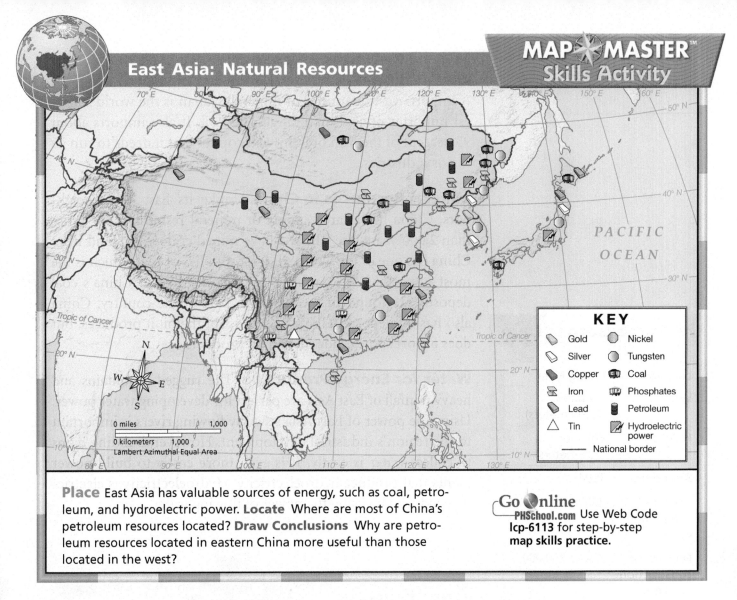

KEY

◇	Gold	◉	Nickel
▱	Silver	○	Tungsten
◈	Copper	▦	Coal
⌇	Iron	▦	Phosphates
◇	Lead	▮	Petroleum
△	Tin	▨	Hydroelectric power
		——	National border

Place East Asia has valuable sources of energy, such as coal, petroleum, and hydroelectric power. **Locate** Where are most of China's petroleum resources located? **Draw Conclusions** Why are petroleum resources located in eastern China more useful than those located in the west?

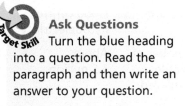

Go Online
PHSchool.com Use Web Code lcp-6113 for step-by-step map skills practice.

Mineral Resources in the Two Koreas

East Asia has plenty of mineral resources, but they are unevenly distributed. Some countries have more and other countries have less. The two Koreas, for example, have limited mineral resources. Coal and iron, which are used in manufacturing, are plentiful in North Korea. But there is little coal or iron in South Korea, where much more manufacturing takes place. The only minerals that are in large supply in the South are tungsten and graphite.

If South Korea could share North Korea's coal and iron, both countries would benefit. But the two do not share resources, since they are hostile toward each other. North Korea is a **developing country**—one that has low industrial production and little modern technology. South Korea is a **developed country**—one with many industries and a well-developed economy. Because of its limited resources, South Korea must import the iron, crude oil, and chemicals it needs for its industries. Nevertheless, it has become one of East Asia's richest economies. It exports, or sells, many manufactured goods to other nations.

Ask Questions Turn the blue heading into a question. Read the paragraph and then write an answer to your question.

Mineral Resources in Japan Japan is a modern industrial society. Yet Japan—like South Korea—has few mineral resources. It imports vast quantities of minerals. Japan is the world's largest importer of coal, natural gas, and oil. It also imports about 95 percent of the iron ore, tin, and copper that it needs to run its major industries.

Mineral Resources in China Unlike its East Asian neighbors, China has a large supply of mineral resources. For more than 2,000 years, the Chinese have mined copper, tin, and iron. China has one of the world's largest supplies of coal, which is the most important of its mineral resources. Most of China's coal deposits are found in the northern part of the country. China also has oil deposits. China uses most of the oil it produces, but does export some crude oil and oil products.

Water for Energy Production The rugged mountains and heavy rainfall of East Asia are perfect for developing water power. Using the power of East Asia's swiftly flowing rivers is important to the region's industrial development. However, building dams to collect water is costly. It is even more costly to build power plants that produce hydroelectricity. Hydroelectricity is electricity produced by using the power of flowing water.

The Three Gorges Dam

Location	Chang River
Width	1.4 miles (2,309 meters)
Height	607 feet (185 meters)
Start date	1994
Expected completion date	2009
Number of construction workers	About 250,000
Purpose	Flood control, hydroelectricity
Number of people displaced	About 1.5 million

In 2004, China produced about 20 percent of its electricity from hydroelectric power. The Chinese government expects this figure to increase when China finishes building the Three Gorges Dam across the Chang River. The Three Gorges Dam will be one and a half miles wide and more than 600 feet high. China is building the dam not only to produce electricity but also to control the frequent floods on the Chang River.

Water for Aquaculture East Asia's ocean and inland waters have been an important source of food for the region's people. Aquaculture, or fish farming, has been practiced in Asia for centuries. During the 1980s and 1990s, however, aquaculture production in Asia greatly expanded. This was due, in part, to the fact that overfishing and pollution had decreased the supply of saltwater and freshwater fish. The increase was also due to advances in the practice of aquaculture. In East Asia, China is the leading aquaculture producer. Japan, South Korea, and Taiwan are also among the top aquaculture producers in the world. Aquaculture includes farm-raised fish, shrimp, oysters, mussels, clams, and seaweed.

✓ **Reading Check** **Based on what you have read, is Japan a developed country or a developing country?**

The World's Largest Dam
The bottom photo shows the Three Gorges Dam in China under construction. The top photo shows what the Three Gorges area looked like before construction began. The middle photo shows a model of the completed dam. China is building the dam to produce hydroelectricity. **Contrast** *Study the two small photos. How will the dam change the landscape of the Three Gorges area?*

A Japanese farmer displays his harvest of rice.

Using the Land to Produce Food

In order to feed its large population, East Asians need to farm every bit of available land. With so many mountains and plateaus, only a small percentage of the land can be cultivated. Only about 14 percent of China, 12 percent of Japan, and 14 percent of North Korea can be farmed. South Korea's 19 percent is about equal to the percentage of land farmed in the United States.

Terrace Farming In China, Japan, and parts of Korea, farmers cut horizontal steps called **terraces** into steep hillsides to gain a few precious yards of soil for crops. Farmers even use the land at the sides of roads and railway lines for planting.

Double-Cropping Where climate and soil allow, farmers practice **double-cropping,** growing two or more crops on the same land in the same season or at the same time. In China, farmers often plant one type of crop between the rows of another crop in order to grow more food. In some parts of southern China, farmers are even able to grow three crops in a year. In southern Japan, rice seeds are sowed in small fields. When the seedlings are about a foot high, they are replanted in a larger field after wheat has been harvested from it.

✓ **Reading Check** What is the difference between terrace farming and double-cropping?

Section 3 Assessment

Key Terms
Review the key terms at the beginning of this section. Use each term in a sentence that explains its meaning.

Target Reading Skill
What questions did you ask about this section?

Comprehension and Critical Thinking
1. **(a) Recall** Name three natural resources in East Asia that can be used to produce energy.

(b) Contrast Which country has a larger supply of mineral resources, China or Japan?
(c) Infer How could a country develop its economy without a large supply of mineral resources?
2. **(a) Recall** What two farming techniques do East Asian farmers use to make up for a shortage of farmland?
(b) Infer Why might East Asian farmers be interested in learning about faster-growing crops?

Writing Activity
Suppose you are a reporter for a television news program. Write a report that tells how the waters of East Asia are an important resource for its people. Include at least two ways water is used in East Asia.

Go Online
PHSchool.com

For: An activity on East Asia
Visit: PHSchool.com
Web Code: lcd-6103

Review and Assessment

◆ Chapter Summary

Section 1: Land and Water

- Mountains, plains, and plateaus are the main landforms in East Asia. The Chang and Huang rivers are major bodies of water.
- Most people in East Asia live in the plains and coastal areas.

China

Section 2: Climate and Vegetation

- East Asia's five major climate regions are semi-arid, arid, humid subtropical, humid continental, and highlands. Monsoons have a strong effect on the climate of East Asia.
- The climate of East Asia supports vegetation, such as bamboo, that is strong enough to stand seasonal differences in temperature and rainfall. Winds blow fertile soil, which is then carried by the Huang River to the North China Plain.

Japan

Section 3: Natural Resources and Land Use

- China has more mineral resources than its neighbors. Water in East Asia is used to produce hydroelectricity and to support aquaculture.
- East Asia's physical landscape leaves a small amount of land available for farming. Terraces and double-cropping are two ways East Asian farmers get the most food out of the land that is used for farming.

◆ Key Terms

Each of the statements below contains a key term from the chapter. If the statement is true, write *true*. If the statement is false, rewrite the statement to make it true.

1. A plateau is a dry region with little vegetation.

2. When soil is fertile, it is capable of supporting abundant plant growth.

3. Population density measures the average number of people living in a square mile or square kilometer.

4. A monsoon is a tropical storm that occurs over the Pacific Ocean.

5. Deciduous trees shed their leaves in the fall.

6. A developed country has a low level of industrial production.

7. A developing country has many industries and a well-developed economy.

8. When farmers use double-cropping, they build steps into hillsides to increase farmland.

Review and Assessment (continued)

◆ Comprehension and Critical Thinking

9. (a) Recall Which East Asian countries have mountains, wide plains, and plateaus?
(b) Locate Where are the Himalayas located?

10. (a) Name Name two major rivers in China.
(b) Recall Which of these rivers flows through the North China Plain?
(c) Identify Effect How does this river make the North China Plain a fertile region?

11. (a) List What are Japan's four main islands?
(b) Compare and Contrast How is the physical geography of Japan different from the physical geography of the Koreas?

12. (a) Identify Which parts of East Asia have a very high population density?
(b) Summarize Why does most of the population in China live in the eastern half of the country?

13. (a) Explain How does water affect the climates of the Koreas and Japan?
(b) Summarize What does the summer monsoon do in East Asia and in what direction does it blow?

14. (a) Define What three basic questions do countries ask when planning their economies?

(b) Summarize How do Japan and South Korea make up for their lack of mineral resources?

15. (a) Locate Where is the Three Gorges Dam?
(b) Predict How might the Three Gorges Dam affect energy production in China?

16. (a) Explain How have the farmers of East Asia made the best use of the land for farming?
(b) Apply Information Which farming method is linked to the physical landscape of East Asia?

◆ Skills Practice

Using Reliable Information on the Internet
Review the steps you followed to learn this skill. Then explain why an Internet encyclopedia is a reliable source.

◆ Writing Activity: Geography

Create a geographic dictionary of these items: plateau, plain, volcano, monsoon, mountain, peninsula. Arrange the list in alphabetical order. Write a definition, using your textbook to find a real-life example of each term. The example must be located in East Asia. Include the country where your example is located.

MAP MASTER™
Skills Activity

East Asia

Place Location For each place listed below, write the letter from the map that shows its location.

1. Himalayas
2. North China Plain
3. Huang River
4. Plateau of Tibet
5. Chang River
6. Mount Fuji

Go Online
PHSchool.com Use Web Code ldp-6120 for an interactive map.

Standardized Test Prep

Test-Taking Tips

Some questions on standardized tests ask you to identify the main topic of a reading passage. Study the passage below. Then follow the tips to answer the sample question.

> Desert winds blow silt into the Huang River. The Huang, or Yellow, River gets its name from this brownish-yellow loess. The river carries and deposits loess to the east. The loess covers 125,000 square miles (324,000 square kilometers) on the North China Plain. This great plain is one of China's best farming regions.

> **TIP** Some paragraphs contain a topic sentence that states its main idea. All other sentences in the paragraph support this point.

Pick the letter of the statement that best answers the question.

Which is the best topic sentence for this paragraph?

A ~~Climate influences everything from natural vegetation to agriculture.~~

B ~~Loess is rich yellow-brown silt or clay.~~

C Climate affects life in the region around the Huang River.

D The Huang River is known as China's Sorrow because of its damaging floods.

> **TIP** Rule out answer choices that don't make sense. Then pick the best answer from the remaining choices.

Think It Through You can rule out A because the statement is too general. It could be the topic for a paragraph on any region of the world. However, B is too specific; it could be another detail in the paragraph. Similarly, D is another detail, one that might be included in a different paragraph about flooding on the Huang. The correct answer is C.

Practice Questions

Use the passage below to answer Question 1. Use the tips above to help you.

> In summer, the monsoon blows northwest from the Pacific Ocean toward the Asian continent. The summer monsoon brings hot, humid weather and rainfall to East Asia. In winter, the monsoon blows toward the east. Where they cross warm ocean waters, such as the South China Sea, these monsoons pick up moisture. Later, they drop it as rain or snow.

1. Which is the best topic sentence for the above paragraph?

   A People need rain to grow crops.

   B Monsoons have a strong effect on climate in East Asia.

   C The South China Sea is located off China's southern coast.

   D The Pacific Ocean is the deepest ocean in the world.

Use the tips above and other tips in this book to help you answer the following questions.

2. Which country takes up most of East Asia's land?

   A Japan   C Mongolia

   B China   D South Korea

3. Most of the people in Japan live

   A in coastal areas.

   B in mountainous areas.

   C on Japan's wide plains.

   D on plateaus.

4. The Huang River runs through a fertile region of East Asia called

   A Mongolia.

   B Taiwan.

   C the North China Plain.

   D Tibet.

Use Web Code lca-6100 for a **Chapter 1 self-test**.

Chapter Preview

In this chapter, you will examine the physical geography of South, Southwest, and Central Asia. This huge region includes many countries and a range of landforms.

Section 1
South Asia
Physical Geography

Section 2
Southwest Asia
Physical Geography

Section 3
Central Asia
Physical Geography

 **Target Reading Skill**

Clarifying Meaning In this chapter, you will focus on understanding what you read by rereading and reading ahead, paraphrasing, and summarizing.

▶ An American climbing team below the summit of Mount Everest, the world's tallest peak

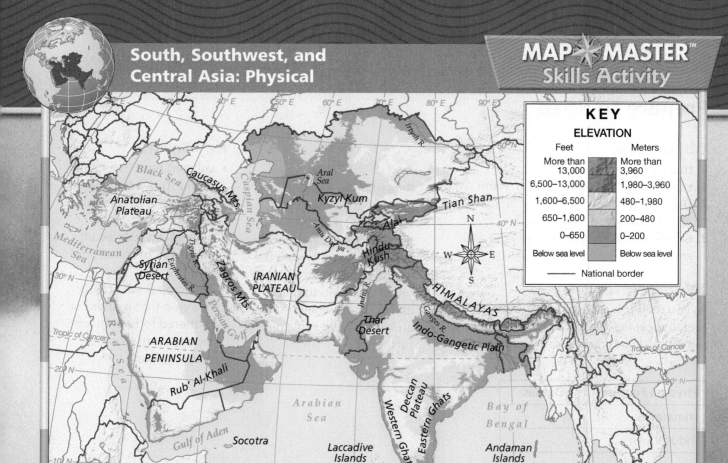

KEY

ELEVATION

Feet		Meters
More than 13,000		More than 3,960
6,500–13,000		1,980–3,960
1,600–6,500		480–1,980
650–1,600		200–480
0–650		0–200
Below sea level		Below sea level

—— National border

Regions South, Southwest, and Central Asia extend from Turkey in the west to India in the east. **Identify** Find and name the bodies of water that surround this region. **Contrast** This region includes both large and small countries. How are the sizes of Saudi Arabia, Iran, and India different from the sizes of Israel and Nepal?

Go Online
PHSchool.com Use Web Code
lcp-6210 for step-by-step
map skills practice.

Prepare to Read

Objectives

In this section, you will

1. Learn about the landforms of South Asia.
2. Discover the most important factor that affects climate in South Asia.
3. Examine how people use the land and resources of South Asia.

Taking Notes

As you read this section, look for details about the physical features of South Asia. Copy the table below and record your findings in it.

Physical Features	Details
Himalayas	
Indus River	

Target Reading Skill

Rereading or Reading Ahead If you do not understand a certain passage, reread it to look for connections among the words and sentences. It might also help to read ahead, because a word or an idea may be explained further on.

Key Terms

- **subcontinent** (SUB kahn tih nunt) *n.* a large landmass that is a major part of a continent
- **alluvial** (uh LOO vee ul) *adj.* made of soil deposited by rivers
- **cash crop** (kash krahp) *n.* a crop that is raised or gathered to be sold for money on the local or world market

Mountain climbing in the Himalayas

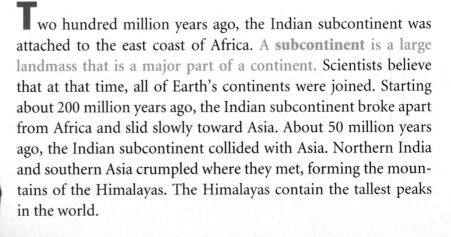

Two hundred million years ago, the Indian subcontinent was attached to the east coast of Africa. A **subcontinent** is a large landmass that is a major part of a continent. Scientists believe that at that time, all of Earth's continents were joined. Starting about 200 million years ago, the Indian subcontinent broke apart from Africa and slid slowly toward Asia. About 50 million years ago, the Indian subcontinent collided with Asia. Northern India and southern Asia crumpled where they met, forming the mountains of the Himalayas. The Himalayas contain the tallest peaks in the world.

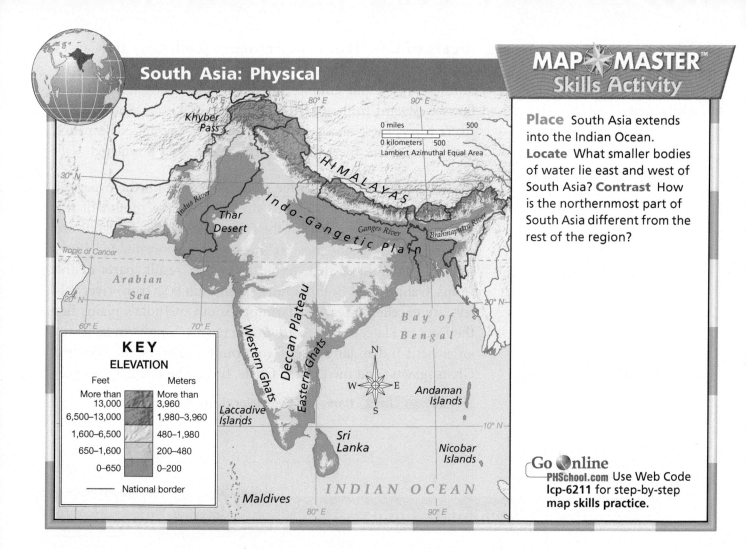

South Asia: Physical

MAP MASTER™
Skills Activity

Khyber Pass

HIMALAYAS

Indus River

Thar Desert

Indo-Gangetic Plain

Ganges River

Brahmaputra River

Tropic of Cancer

Arabian Sea

Deccan Plateau

Western Ghats

Eastern Ghats

Bay of Bengal

Laccadive Islands

Andaman Islands

Sri Lanka

Nicobar Islands

INDIAN OCEAN

Maldives

0 miles 500
0 kilometers 500
Lambert Azimuthal Equal Area

KEY
ELEVATION

Feet		Meters
More than 13,000		More than 3,960
6,500–13,000		1,980–3,960
1,600–6,500		480–1,980
650–1,600		200–480
0–650		0–200

——— National border

Place South Asia extends into the Indian Ocean.
Locate What smaller bodies of water lie east and west of South Asia? **Contrast** How is the northernmost part of South Asia different from the rest of the region?

Go Online
PHSchool.com Use Web Code lcp-6211 for step-by-step map skills practice.

Major Landforms of South Asia

The largest nation in South Asia is India. It extends from the Himalayas down to the narrow tip of the Indian subcontinent in the south. Pakistan (PAK ih stan) and Afghanistan (af GAN ih stan) lie to the west of India. Along India's northern border, the kingdoms of Nepal (nuh PAWL) and Bhutan (BOO tahn) lie along the slopes of the Himalayas. To the east is Bangladesh (BAHNG luh DESH). The island nations of Sri Lanka (sree LAHNG kuh) and the Maldives (MAL dyvz) lie off the southern tip of India.

A Natural Barrier Find the Himalayas on the map above. Notice that they form a barrier between South Asia and the rest of Asia. This huge mountain range stretches some 1,550 miles (2,500 kilometers) from east to west. Mount Everest, the world's tallest mountain, is located in the Himalayas. Mount Everest rises to 29,035 feet (8,850 meters). That's about five and a half miles high! More than 100 mountains in the Himalayas soar above 24,000 feet (7,300 meters). The Himalayas present the greatest challenge in the world to mountain climbers.

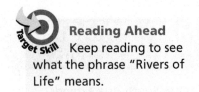

Reading Ahead
Keep reading to see what the phrase "Rivers of Life" means.

Rivers of Life The two major rivers in South Asia—the Ganges and the Indus—begin in the Himalayas. The Ganges flows across northern India and empties into the Bay of Bengal. The Indus flows westward from the Himalayas into Pakistan. South Asia's rivers carry water and minerals to support farming. The plains around the rivers, therefore, are fertile and heavily populated.

Plains and Plateaus Huge plains cover the northern part of the Indian subcontinent. They stretch from the mouth of the Indus River to the mouth of the Ganges River. These plains are **alluvial,** which means they are made of soil deposited by rivers. Alluvial plains have rich, fertile soil. As a result, parts of the Indus, Ganges, and Brahmaputra (brah muh POO truh) river valleys are excellent areas for farming. South of India's plains lies the Deccan Plateau. The word *deccan* means "south" in Sanskrit, an ancient Indian language. Two mountain ranges, the Western Ghats (gawts) and the Eastern Ghats, frame the Deccan Plateau.

✓ **Reading Check** **Name the two major rivers in South Asia.**

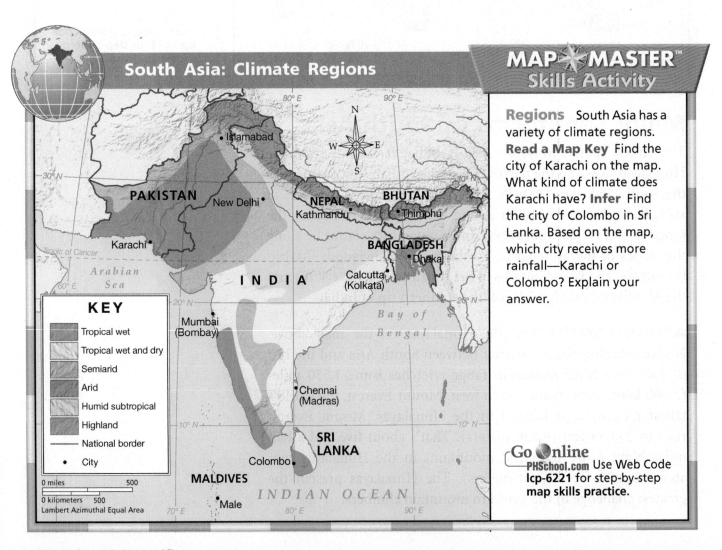

South Asia: Climate Regions

MAP MASTER™
Skills Activity

KEY

- Tropical wet
- Tropical wet and dry
- Semiarid
- Arid
- Humid subtropical
- Highland
- National border
- • City

0 miles 500
0 kilometers 500
Lambert Azimuthal Equal Area

Regions South Asia has a variety of climate regions. **Read a Map Key** Find the city of Karachi on the map. What kind of climate does Karachi have? **Infer** Find the city of Colombo in Sri Lanka. Based on the map, which city receives more rainfall—Karachi or Colombo? Explain your answer.

Go Online
PHSchool.com Use Web Code lcp-6221 for step-by-step map skills practice.

The Climates of South Asia

Monsoons are the single most important factor that affects the climate of South Asia. Monsoons are winds that change direction with the change of seasons. The summer monsoons blow across South Asia from the southwest. During the winter, the winds change direction and blow from the northeast.

The Summer Monsoons From June to early October, steady winds blow over the surface of the Arabian Sea and the Indian Ocean. The air picks up a great deal of moisture. Then, the air passes over the hot land along the western tip of India. As the moist air passes over the hot land, it rises and loses its moisture in the form of rain. The rains that fall along the coastline cool the land somewhat. When the next air mass blows in, it travels farther inland before losing its supply of moisture. In this way, the monsoon rains work their way inland until they finally reach the Himalayas.

The Winter Monsoons During the winter months, the monsoons change direction, and the winds blow from the frigid northeast. These winds move dry, cold air toward South Asia. The Himalayas block the cold air. The countries of South Asia enjoy dry winter weather, with temperatures averaging 70°F (21°C).

✓ **Reading Check** What are monsoons?

Land Use in South Asia

About 70 percent of the population in South Asia live in rural areas. Most of these people are crowded into fertile river valleys. Here, they grow whatever crops the soil and climate of their particular region will allow.

Links to Science

India's Salt Lake During the hot months, the 90-square-mile (230-square-kilometer) Sambhar (SAM bar) Lake in northwestern India is dry. Oddly, during this time the lake bed looks as though it is covered in snow. The white blanket is not snow but a sheet of salt. This salt supply has been harvested as far back as the 1500s. It is still an important resource for the region today.

Tea Harvest in India
Tea is a major crop in India. Workers harvest fresh tea leaves by hand. The leaves are then processed and dried. Dried tea is sometimes packed in tea bags. *Infer How can you tell harvesting leaves is labor intensive?*

Cash Crops Some countries of South Asia produce cash crops such as tea, cotton, coffee, and sugar cane. A **cash crop** is one that is raised or gathered to be sold for money on the local or world market. Growing cash crops often brings in a great deal of money, but it can also cause problems. The economy of a region can become dependent on world prices for the crops. When prices fall, the cash crops do not bring in enough money. When cash crops fail, farmers may not earn enough money.

Mineral Resources The earth beneath India holds a vast supply of mineral wealth. Iron ore and coal are plentiful. Other important minerals include copper, limestone, and bauxite—an ore that contains aluminum. India has only a small amount of oil. Because of this, India relies heavily on hydroelectricity and nuclear power plants.

Population and Land Use South Asia is one of the most densely populated regions in the world. Most of the people live in areas that have plenty of rainfall. These include coastal areas, as well as northeastern India and the country of Bangladesh. The population is lower in areas where it is more difficult for people to live.

√ **Reading Check** Where do most of the people in South Asia live?

The densely populated city of Dhaka is Bangladesh's capital.

Section 1 Assessment

Key Terms
Review the key terms at the beginning of this section. Use each term in a sentence that explains its meaning.

 Target Reading Skill
What words were you able to clarify by rereading?

Comprehension and Critical Thinking
1. (a) Recall Which landform forms a natural barrier between South Asia and the rest of Asia?

(b) Connect How do the Ganges and the Indus rivers relate to this landform?
2. (a) Identify From which direction does the summer monsoon blow across South Asia?
(b) Contrast How is the winter monsoon different from the summer monsoon in South Asia?
3. (a) List Give some examples of the cash crops raised in South Asia.
(b) Summarize Why may cash crops cause problems for the economies of South Asian countries?

Writing Activity
Write a two-paragraph description of a television show about the geography and resources of South Asia. In your description, include at least three locations in South Asia. Tell what your camera crew will film in each location.

For: An activity on South Asia
Visit: PHSchool.com
Web Code: lcd-6201

Southwest Asia
Physical Geography

Prepare to Read

Objectives

In this section, you will

1. Learn about the major landforms of Southwest Asia.
2. Find out what the two most important resources in Southwest Asia are.
3. Examine how people use the land in Southwest Asia.

Taking Notes

As you read this section, look for details about Southwest Asia's major physical features, including climate. Copy the table below and record your findings in it.

Physical Features of Southwest Asia	Details
Desert	
Persian Gulf	
Arabian Peninsula	
Dry climate	

Target Reading Skill

Paraphrasing When you paraphrase, you state what you have read in your own words. Here is a paraphrase of the first paragraph under the red heading on page 41: "Land in Southwest Asia is used mainly for agriculture, nomadic herding, and producing oil. The region has a small percentage of arable land. Most farming takes place in the northern part of the region."

As you read this section, paraphrase the first paragraph after each red heading.

Key Terms

- **oasis** (oh AY sis) *n.* an area in a desert region where fresh water is usually available from an underground spring or well
- **petroleum** (puh TROH lee um) *n.* an oily liquid formed from the remains of ancient plants and animals; a fuel
- **nonrenewable resource** (nahn rih NOO uh bul REE sawrs) *n.* a natural resource that cannot be quickly replaced once it is used
- **standard of living** (STAN durd uv LIV ing) *n.* a measurement of a person's or a group's education, housing, health, and nutrition

A parachutist lands in the Rub' al-Khali desert in Saudi Arabia.

The Rub' al-Khali (roob ahl KHAH lee), or "Empty Quarter," of the Arabian Peninsula is the largest all-sand desert in the world. Almost nothing lives in this flat, hot territory. Ten years may pass between rainfalls. The sand dunes do not stay in one place—they gradually move as they are blown by the wind.

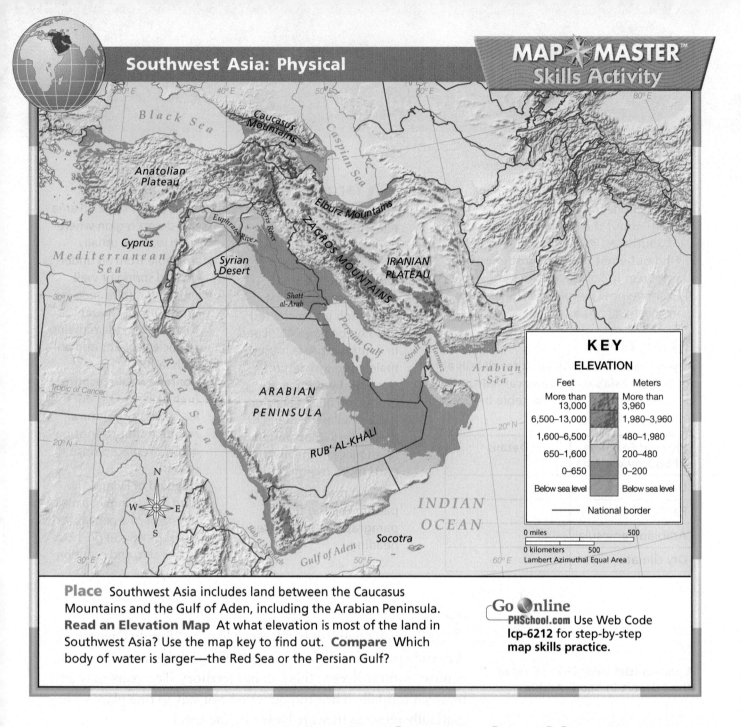

Black Sea

Caucasus Mountains

Anatolian Plateau

Caspian Sea

Elburz Mountains

Euphrates River

Tigris River

ZAGROS MOUNTAINS

Cyprus

Mediterranean Sea

Syrian Desert

IRANIAN PLATEAU

30° N

Shatt al-Arab

Persian Gulf

Strait of Hormuz

Arabian Sea

Red Sea

Tropic of Cancer

ARABIAN PENINSULA

20° N

20° N

RUB' AL-KHALI

INDIAN OCEAN

Bab el Mandeb

Socotra

Gulf of Aden

KEY
ELEVATION

Feet		Meters
More than 13,000		More than 3,960
6,500–13,000		1,980–3,960
1,600–6,500		480–1,980
650–1,600		200–480
0–650		0–200
Below sea level		Below sea level

——— National border

0 miles 500
0 kilometers 500
Lambert Azimuthal Equal Area

Place Southwest Asia includes land between the Caucasus Mountains and the Gulf of Aden, including the Arabian Peninsula. **Read an Elevation Map** At what elevation is most of the land in Southwest Asia? Use the map key to find out. **Compare** Which body of water is larger—the Red Sea or the Persian Gulf?

Go Online
PHSchool.com Use Web Code
lcp-6212 for step-by-step
map skills practice.

A Dry Region Bordered by Water

Southwest Asia contains some of Earth's largest deserts. The Rub'al-Khali is almost as big as the state of Texas. Deserts also cover much of the country of Iran, Syria, and Iraq. Many parts of Southwest Asia receive little rain. Water is very valuable here.

Some of the region's deserts are covered with sand. In others, the land is strewn with pebbles, gravel, and boulders. Travelers passing through these dry areas are relieved when they find an oasis (oh AY sis). **An oasis is a small area in a desert region where fresh water is usually available from an underground spring or well.** Sometimes, an oasis can support a community of people. Farmers can grow crops. Nomadic shepherds can raise livestock.

Paraphrasing
Use your own words to paraphrase the paragraph at the right. Use a synonym for the word *relieved*.

Target Skill

Two Historic Rivers Few plants grow in most Southwest Asian deserts. Some of the most fertile soil in the world, however, lies along the Tigris (TY gris) and Euphrates (yoo FRAY teez) rivers. When these rivers flood, they deposit rich soil along their banks. The Tigris and the Euphrates rivers begin in Turkey and flow south through Iraq. They join to form the Shatt-al-Arab, which flows into the Persian Gulf. In ancient times, the land between these two rivers supported one of the world's first civilizations. The region was known as Mesopotamia. Here, people learned to raise plants and animals for food, relying on the rich soil provided by the rivers.

Iraq's capital, Baghdad, lies on both banks of the Tigris River. The small photo shows a mosque, or Islamic place of worship, in Istanbul, Turkey.

Mountains and Plateaus As you can see on the physical map of Southwest Asia, the Tigris and Euphrates rivers begin in the mountains of Turkey. Iran also has mountains. The Zagros Mountains extend along the western part of Iran. The Elburz Mountains extend along the northern coast of Iran. The mountains give way to large plateaus in both Turkey and Iran.

Seas and Gulfs Much of the land of Southwest Asia borders bodies of water that separate countries within the region. These bodies of water also separate Southwest Asia from other regions. The Red Sea separates Southwest Asia and Africa. The Mediterranean Sea forms Southwest Asia's western border. The Black Sea forms Turkey's northern border. The Caspian Sea forms part of the boundary between Southwest Asia and Central Asia. The Persian Gulf separates Iran from the Arabian Peninsula.

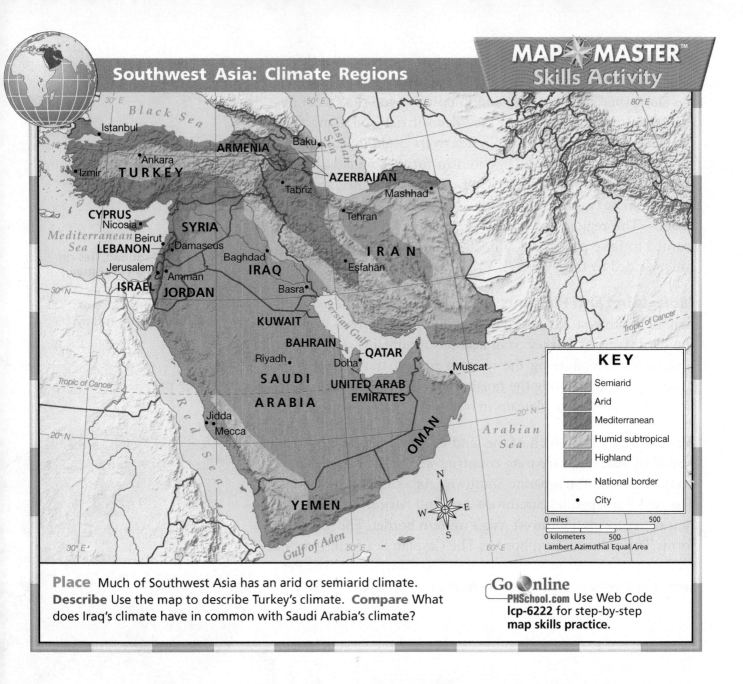

KEY

	Semiarid
	Arid
	Mediterranean
	Humid subtropical
	Highland
——	National border
•	City

0 miles 500
0 kilometers 500
Lambert Azimuthal Equal Area

Place Much of Southwest Asia has an arid or semiarid climate.
Describe Use the map to describe Turkey's climate. **Compare** What does Iraq's climate have in common with Saudi Arabia's climate?

Go Online
PHSchool.com Use Web Code
lcp-6222 for step-by-step
map skills practice.

A Hot, Dry Climate Most of Southwest Asia has an arid or a semiarid climate. Much of the region receives less than 10 inches (25 centimeters) of rain each year. It is no wonder, then, that nearly two thirds of Southwest Asia is desert!

Because the desert air contains little moisture, few clouds form over the dry land. As a result, temperatures may reach as high as 125°F (52°C) during the day. At night, they may drop to as low as 40°F (4°C).

Some parts of Southwest Asia have a Mediterranean climate, with hot, dry summers and mild, rainy winters. The coasts of the Mediterranean, Black, and Caspian seas as well as the mountainous areas of the region have a Mediterranean climate.

✓ **Reading Check** Which two countries in Southwest Asia have mountains?

Southwest Asia's Major Natural Resources

The two most important natural resources in Southwest Asia are petroleum and water. **Petroleum** (puh TROH lee um) is an oily, flammable liquid formed from the remains of ancient plants and animals. It is found under Earth's surface. Petroleum deposits take millions of years to form. Petroleum is a **nonrenewable resource**—a natural resource that cannot be quickly replaced once it is used.

Petroleum is the source of gasoline and other fuels. People all over the world depend on petroleum to fuel cars and trucks, provide energy for industry, and heat homes. Petroleum is the natural resource that brings the most money into Southwest Asia. Water, however, is the resource that people there need most. Since much of Southwest Asia has a dry climate, the water in the region must be used carefully.

Petroleum Large deposits of petroleum, also called oil, can be found in only a few places on Earth. As a result, petroleum-rich countries play a key role in the world's economy. Southwest Asia is the largest oil-producing region in the world. Petroleum is Southwest Asia's greatest export.

Oil wealth allows many Southwest Asian countries to increase the standard of living of their people. **Standard of living** is a measurement of a person's or a group's education, housing, health, and nutrition. These countries have enough money to build schools and hospitals and to import goods from other countries. They can also import workers. Most of the people living in oil-rich Kuwait are citizens of other countries, including Pakistan, India, and Bangladesh.

Southwest Asia has more than half of the world's oil reserves. But some countries in the region have little or no oil. These countries tend to have a lower standard of living than their oil-rich neighbors. They do not have the income that petroleum brings.

Oil pipelines in Saudi Arabia

Water from the Sea of Galilee is carried to southern Israel by the National Water Carrier.

Water To grow crops in this dry region, people usually must irrigate their land. Saudi Arabia, for example, has no permanent rivers. It has wadis (WAH deez), or stream beds that may hold water when seasonal rains fall but are dry much of the year. People there irrigate their crops by pumping water from deep underground wells. In other parts of Southwest Asia, wells are not as necessary. People use water from rivers and streams to irrigate the dry areas of the country.

The nations of Southwest Asia have continued to build irrigation systems. But irrigation cannot solve the problem of water scarcity. Too much irrigation can use up the water that is available. In an area with little rainfall, water that is taken from a river is not soon replaced. When a river runs through more than one nation, each nation is affected by the others' irrigation systems.

✓ **Reading Check** What benefits has petroleum brought to the countries of Southwest Asia?

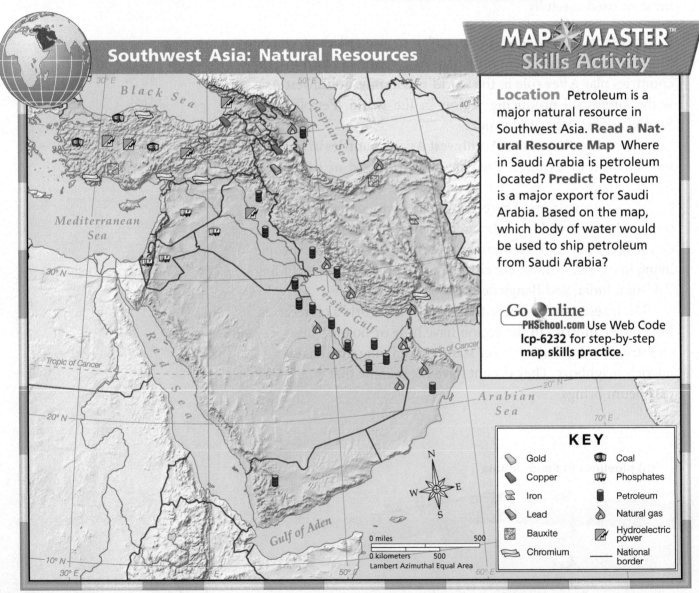

Southwest Asia: Natural Resources

MAP ✦ MASTER™
Skills Activity

Location Petroleum is a major natural resource in Southwest Asia. **Read a Natural Resource Map** Where in Saudi Arabia is petroleum located? **Predict** Petroleum is a major export for Saudi Arabia. Based on the map, which body of water would be used to ship petroleum from Saudi Arabia?

Go Online
PHSchool.com Use Web Code lcp-6232 for step-by-step map skills practice.

KEY

Gold		Coal	
Copper		Phosphates	
Iron		Petroleum	
Lead		Natural gas	
Bauxite		Hydroelectric power	
Chromium		National border	

0 miles 500
0 kilometers 500
Lambert Azimuthal Equal Area

Using the Land in Southwest Asia

People use the land in Southwest Asia in three major ways: for agriculture, for nomadic herding, and for producing oil. Because of the region's climate, only a small percentage of the region is made up of arable land. Most of this farmland is located in the northern part of the region, with commercial farming taking place along the coasts. There, the Mediterranean climate makes it possible for people to grow a wide variety of crops.

Various commercial farm products are raised in Israel and Turkey. In Israel, these include citrus fruits, cotton, peanuts, and sugar cane. Turkey's commercial farms produce such crops as wheat, barley, cotton, sugar beets, fruits, olives, and corn.

For centuries, Arabic-speaking nomadic herders known as Bedouins (BED oo inz) have lived in Southwest Asia's deserts herding camels, goats, and sheep. Instead of settling in one place, Bedouins moved over a large area of land, seeking grass and water for their animals. Today the Bedouin make up about 10 percent of the population of Southwest Asia. In recent times, settlement policies of countries in Southwest Asia have forced many Bedouins to settle in one place.

✓ **Reading Check** **What are some of Turkey's commercial farming crops?**

Links to Science

Dead Sea Alive With Minerals The Dead Sea, a lake between Israel and Jordan, is too salty to support fish or plant life. But it does help support Israel's economy. The sea is full of minerals. The Israelis take out potash—a mineral used for explosives and fertilizer—as well as table salt and a variety of other minerals for export.

Section 2 Assessment

Key Terms
Review the key terms at the beginning of this section. Use each term in a sentence that explains its meaning.

Target Reading Skill
Reread the first paragraph after the heading Two Historic Rivers on page 37. Then, using your own words, paraphrase the paragraph. Begin your paraphrase with the sentence, "Rich soil lies along the banks of the Tigris and Euphrates rivers."

Comprehension and Critical Thinking
1. (a) Recall What kind of land covers much of Southwest Asia?

(b) Identify Name one major desert, two seas, and one mountain range in Southwest Asia.
(c) Explain Give a location for the desert, the seas, and the mountain range in the previous question.
2. (a) Identify What are the two most important natural resources in Southwest Asia?
(b) Explain Why are irrigation systems important in Southwest Asia?
3. (a) Recall What are three major ways that people use the land in Southwest Asia?
(b) Summarize What are some commercial farm products of Southwest Asia?

Writing Activity
Write a paragraph that describes water from the point of view of a person living in the United States on the coast of the Atlantic Ocean. Then write another paragraph from the point of view of a person living in a desert region in Southwest Asia. Exchange your paragraphs with a partner. How are your paragraphs similar to or different from those of your partner?

Go Online
PHSchool.com

For: An activity on Southwest Asia
Visit: PHSchool.com
Web Code: lcd-6202

Identifying Main Ideas

Keith was just starting his homework when his mother popped her head into the room.

"What assignment are you working on?" she asked.

"I'm reading an article on petroleum mining in Southwest Asia," Keith replied. "Did you know that more than half of Saudi Arabia's oil reserves are found in just eight oil fields, including the largest onshore oil field in the world?"

"That's a fascinating detail," Keith's mother said. "What's the main idea of the article?"

"That's the assignment," Keith answered. "We have to read the article and identify the main idea."

Identifying main ideas is an essential study skill.

A main idea is the most important information in a paragraph or reading passage. A main idea is not the same as a topic. Knowing how to identify main ideas will make you a better reader and a better student.

Learn the Skill

To identify the main idea in a paragraph, follow these steps:

1 **Identify the topic of the paragraph.** The topic of a paragraph tells what the paragraph is about. Look for a sentence that identifies the topic. It is called a "topic sentence," and it is often the first sentence of a paragraph. Also, it sometimes—but not always—states the main idea.

2 **Look for an idea that all the sentences in the paragraph have in common.** In a well-written paragraph, most of the sentences provide details that support or explain the main idea.

3 **State the main idea in your own words.** Write what you think is the main idea in your own words. Write a complete sentence. Avoid writing a sentence that is too broad or too specific. Remember that a main idea focuses on the most important information about the topic. Even if a detail is interesting, it may not be the most important information. A main idea should always be a complete sentence.

Practice the Skill

Now turn to page 39 and study the first paragraph under the heading Southwest Asia's Major Natural Resources. Use the steps on the previous page to find the main idea of the paragraph.

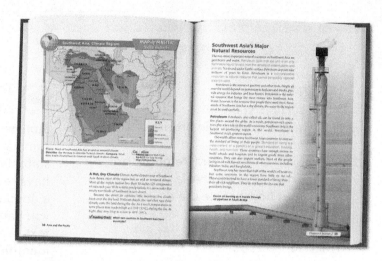

1 What is the topic of the paragraph? Remember that the topic of a paragraph is not necessarily the same as a main idea. For example, the topic of a paragraph is usually a subject, such as petroleum mining in Southwest Asia.

2 In a word or phrase, write down what you think each sentence is about. Then look at the words you've listed and find a common idea among them.

3 Look for the most important information about the topic. Write a complete sentence that states the most important information. Be sure your sentence focuses on the most important information. Why is the following statement too broad? *Southwest Asia has many natural resources.* Why is the following statement too specific? *Petroleum is found under Earth's surface.*

Apply the Skill

Read the following paragraph. Use the steps you learned to write a statement giving the main idea of this paragraph.

   With about one fourth of the world's oil, Saudi Arabia is the leading country in the Organization of Petroleum Exporting Countries (OPEC). OPEC is an organization of countries with economies that rely on money from oil exports. As a group, OPEC decides how much oil its members will produce and at what price to sell it. Besides Saudi Arabia, members consist of Algeria, Indonesia, Iran, Iraq, Kuwait, Libya, Nigeria, Qatar, the United Arab Emirates, and Venezuela. OPEC produces about 40 percent of the world's crude oil.

Prepare to Read

Objectives

In this section, you will
1. Learn about the main physical features of Central Asia.
2. Discover which natural resources are important in Central Asia.
3. Find out how people use the land in Central Asia.

Taking Notes

As you read this section, look for details about the physical geography of Central Asia. Copy the diagram below and record your findings in it.

Land	Climate	Natural Resources
• •	• •	• •

Target Reading Skill

Summarizing When you summarize, you review and state the main points you have read. Summarizing is a good technique to help you better understand a text. A good summary identifies the main ideas, states them in the order in which they appear, and notes when one event causes another to happen. As you read, pause occasionally to summarize what you have read.

Key Term

- **steppe** (step) *n.* vast, mostly level, treeless plains that are covered in grasses

On the treeless plains of Central Asia sprawls the Baikonur (by kuh NOOR) Cosmodrome, the largest space-launch center in the world. Baikonur is the site of several historic spaceflights. In 1957, the first artificial satellite was launched from Baikonur. The first mission to put a human in space blasted off from Baikonur in 1961. In 2003, the *Mars Express*, a European mission to send a spacecraft to Mars, was launched from Baikonur.

Baikonur is located in Kazakhstan (kah zahk STAHN), the largest and northernmost country in Central Asia. To its south are Uzbekistan (ooz BEK ih stan), Kyrgyzstan (kihr gih STAN), Turkmenistan (turk MEN ih stan), and Tajikistan (tah jik ih STAN). Afghanistan forms the southern border of Central Asia. Except for Afghanistan, the countries of Central Asia were once part of the Soviet Union.

This rocket, carrying the *Mars Express*, was launched from Baikonur in 2003.

Central Asia's Main Physical Features

Central Asia's main physical features are highlands, deserts, and steppes. **Steppes** are vast, mostly level, treeless plains covered with grassland vegetation. Central Asia's mountains are in the southeastern part of the region. The Tian Shan and Pamir mountain ranges cover much of Kyrgyzstan and Tajikistan. The Tian Shan range also extends into China. The Pamir extend into Afghanistan, where they meet the Hindu Kush mountains.

To the west of these mountain ranges, the elevation drops and the land flattens. The Kara Kum desert covers much of the land in Turkmenistan. The Kyzyl Kum desert covers much of neighboring Uzbekistan. The Kirghiz Steppe is located in Kazakhstan.

Steppes in Central Asia

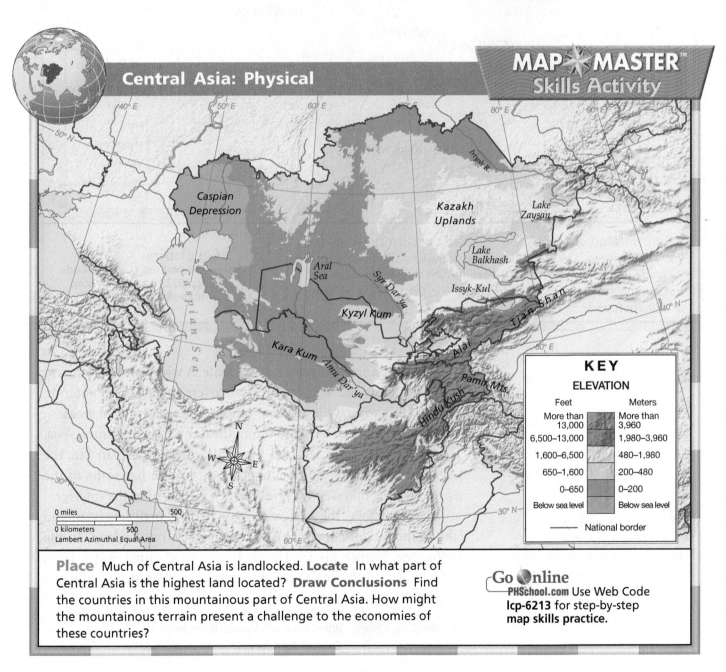

Central Asia: Physical

MAP★MASTER™
Skills Activity

KEY
ELEVATION

Feet		Meters
More than 13,000		More than 3,960
6,500–13,000		1,980–3,960
1,600–6,500		480–1,980
650–1,600		200–480
0–650		0–200
Below sea level		Below sea level
——— National border		

Place Much of Central Asia is landlocked. **Locate** In what part of Central Asia is the highest land located? **Draw Conclusions** Find the countries in this mountainous part of Central Asia. How might the mountainous terrain present a challenge to the economies of these countries?

Go Online
PHSchool.com Use Web Code **lcp-6213** for step-by-step map skills practice.

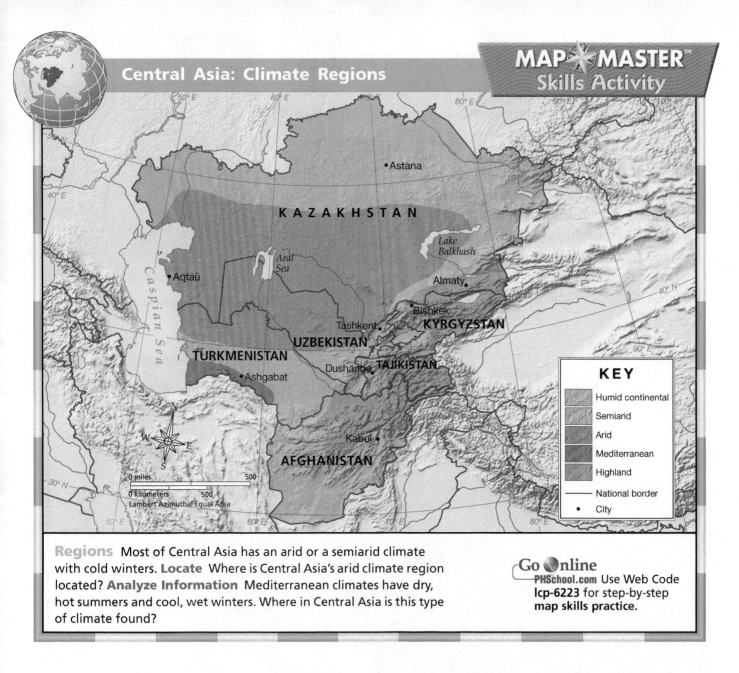

MAP MASTER™
Skills Activity

KEY

- Humid continental
- Semiarid
- Arid
- Mediterranean
- Highland
- National border
- • City

0 miles 500
0 kilometers 500
Lambert Azimuthal Equal Area

Regions Most of Central Asia has an arid or a semiarid climate with cold winters. **Locate** Where is Central Asia's arid climate region located? **Analyze Information** Mediterranean climates have dry, hot summers and cool, wet winters. Where in Central Asia is this type of climate found?

Go Online
PHSchool.com Use Web Code **lcp-6223** for step-by-step map skills practice.

Summarizing
Summarize the paragraph at the right. Be sure to include the reason why the Aral Sea is drying up.

Most of Central Asia has a dry climate. A wide band of semiarid land surrounds the arid region that covers much of the interior. The arid areas receive less precipitation than the semiarid areas.

Two bodies of water stand out in the dry region of Central Asia. They are the Caspian Sea and the Aral Sea. The Caspian Sea, the largest lake in the world, is actually a salt lake. It has some of the world's largest oil reserves. The Aral Sea is located in the interior.

Also a salt lake, the Aral Sea was once the fourth-largest inland lake in the world. Now many boats there rest on dry land. In the 1960s, the former Soviet Union began to channel water from rivers that feed the sea to irrigate crops. As a result, the Aral Sea began to dry up.

✓ **Reading Check** What type of climate does most of Central Asia have?

Natural Resources in Central Asia

As in Southwest Asia, petroleum is a major natural resource in Central Asia. Another major natural resource in the region is natural gas. Kazakhstan is one of three Central Asian countries that have large oil and gas reserves. The other two are Uzbekistan and Turkmenistan. Turkmenistan has the fifth-largest reserve of natural gas in the world. These countries are working to develop the oil and gas industry.

Central Asia has other valuable minerals in addition to petroleum and natural gas. Kazakhstan has rich deposits of coal, much of which it exports to Russia, Ukraine, and Kyrgyzstan. Kazakhstan is the largest exporter of coal to other former Soviet republics as well. Kyrgyzstan, Tajikistan, and Uzbekistan are important gold producers. Other major mineral resources in the region are copper, iron ore, lead, and uranium.

✓ **Reading Check** What are two major natural resources in Central Asia?

Drilling for oil in Kazakhstan

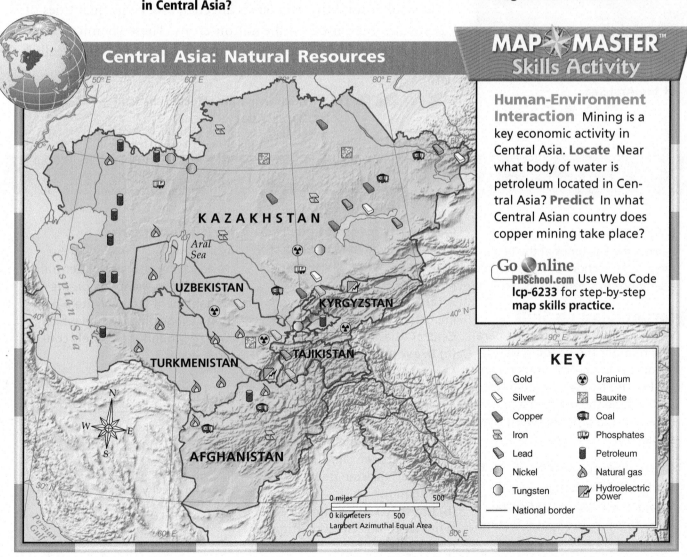

Central Asia: Natural Resources

MAP★MASTER™ Skills Activity

Human-Environment Interaction Mining is a key economic activity in Central Asia. **Locate** Near what body of water is petroleum located in Central Asia? **Predict** In what Central Asian country does copper mining take place?

Go Online
PHSchool.com Use Web Code **lcp-6233** for step-by-step map skills practice.

KEY

◇ Gold	☢ Uranium
◇ Silver	▨ Bauxite
◆ Copper	⬛ Coal
⊠ Iron	⬛ Phosphates
◇ Lead	⬛ Petroleum
◯ Nickel	◊ Natural gas
◯ Tungsten	▨ Hydroelectric power
— National border	

0 miles 500
0 kilometers 500
Lambert Azimuthal Equal Area

Abandoned boats lie rusting on land that was once the bottom of the Aral Sea.

Land Use in Central Asia

Most of the land in Central Asia is used for agriculture, especially livestock raising and commercial farming. People in Central Asia have raised sheep, horses, goats, and camels for thousands of years. Cotton is a major crop in Uzbekistan, Turkmenistan, and Tajikistan.

Agriculture in Central Asia depends on irrigation. In the 1960s, the Soviet Union started a huge irrigation project to bring water to Central Asia. The Soviet Union wanted to increase cotton production. Canals were built to carry fresh water from two rivers to irrigate the cotton fields. Between 1960 and 1980, cotton production in the Soviet Union more than tripled.

The irrigation projects turned Central Asia into a leading cotton producer. But they also caused major damage to the Aral Sea. The Amu Darya and Sry Darya rivers flow into the Aral Sea. Over the decades, heavy irrigation has taken great amounts of water from these two rivers. As a result, the Aral Sea is drying up. The land around the Aral Sea is affected, too. Huge quantities of pesticides were used on the cotton crops. These chemicals have polluted the soil. The destruction of the Aral Sea has been called one of the world's worst environmental disasters.

√ **Reading Check** How has irrigation affected the land in Central Asia?

 Section 3 Assessment

Key Terms

Review the key terms at the beginning of the section. Use each term in a sentence that explains its meaning.

Target Reading Skill

Write a summary of the first paragraph under the heading Natural Resources in Central Asia on page 47. Be sure to use your own words and include the main idea and details in the order in which they appeared.

Comprehension and Critical Thinking

1. (a) Recall What are Central Asia's three main physical features?

(b) Transfer Information If you were to draw a map of Central Asia, where would these main physical features be located?

2. (a) Identify What are two important natural resources in Central Asia?

(b) Draw Inferences With which Central Asian country might an American energy company want to work to develop natural gas resources? Explain why.

3. (a) Explain What major crop raised in Uzbekistan, Turkmenistan, and Tajikistan depends on irrigation?

(b) Identify Cause and Effect What were the effects of irrigation on the Aral Sea?

Writing Activity

As in many regions around the world, the economies of Central Asian countries depend on the availability of water. Write a paragraph suggesting ways in which your community can wisely conserve water.

Go Online
PHSchool.com

For: An activity on Central Asia
Visit: PHSchool.com
Web Code: lcd-6203

Chapter **2** Review and Assessment

◆ Chapter Summary

Section 1: South Asia: Physical Geography
- The Himalayas are a major landform in South Asia. The region also includes the Ganges and Indus rivers, fertile plains, and a plateau framed by the Western Ghats and the Eastern Ghats.
- The climate of South Asia is greatly affected by the monsoons.
- South Asia is a densely populated and generally rural region. Most of the people work in agriculture, and most of the land is used for farming.

Section 2: Southwest Asia: Physical Geography

Israel

- Much of Southwest Asia is a peninsula. The region has a dry climate and contains some of Earth's largest deserts.
- Petroleum and water are Southwest Asia's most important and valuable natural resources.
- Land in Southwest Asia is used mainly for agriculture, for nomadic herding, and for producing oil.

Section 3: Central Asia: Physical Geography
- Highlands, deserts, steppes, and a generally dry climate are Central Asia's main physical features. Much of the region is located inland.
- Central Asia's most valuable natural resources are oil and natural gas.
- Most of the land in Central Asia is used for agriculture, especially livestock raising and commercial farming. Because the region is dry, agriculture in Central Asia depends on irrigation.

India

◆ Key Terms

Match the definitions in Column I with the key terms in Column II.

Column I
1. a large landmass that is a major part of a continent
2. a crop that is raised to be sold for money on the local or world market
3. an oily liquid used as a fuel
4. an area in a desert region where fresh water is usually found
5. a natural resource that cannot be quickly replaced once it is used up
6. a measurement of a person's or group's education, housing, health, and nutrition
7. a vast, mostly level, treeless plain

Column II
A standard of living
B oasis
C steppe
D petroleum
E subcontinent
F nonrenewable resource
G cash crop

Review and Assessment (continued)

◆ Comprehension and Critical Thinking

8. (a) Define What are the two most important rivers in South Asia?
(b) Identify Effects How do the rivers of South Asia affect farmland?

9. (a) Recall What percentage of the population in South Asia lives in rural areas?
(b) Apply Information How does rainfall relate to population patterns in South Asia?

10. (a) Locate Where are the Tigris and Euphrates rivers located?
(b) Analyze Information What are some of the factors that explain why one of the world's first civilizations grew in Mesopotamia rather than on the Arabian Peninsula?

11. (a) Identify What is Southwest Asia's greatest export?
(b) Infer Southwest Asia has more than half of the world's oil reserves. Why might the United States have an interest in this region?

12. (a) Name Name one way that people use the land in Southwest Asia.

(b) Predict Where would you expect to find a commercial farm in Southwest Asia—in Saudi Arabia or in Turkey? Give at least two reasons to support your answer.

13. (a) List What are three facts about the geography of Central Asia?
(b) Summarize Why is the Aral Sea shrinking?

◆ Skills Practice

Identifying Main Ideas Review the steps you followed on page 42 to learn how to identify main ideas. Then re-read the first paragraph on page 47. Write a sentence that states the main idea.

◆ Writing Activity: Science

Suppose that you are a science reporter assigned to write about the Aral Sea. Do research to learn more about how the area around the Aral Sea has been affected by heavy irrigation. Write a brief article about the current situation.

MAP★MASTER™ Skills Activity

Place Location For each place listed below, write the letter from the map that shows its location.

1. Rub' al-Khali
2. Mediterranean Sea
3. Euphrates River
4. Himalayas
5. Indian Ocean
6. Aral Sea

Go Online
PHSchool.com Use Web Code **lcp-6220** for step-by-step **map skills practice.**

South, Southwest, and Central Asia

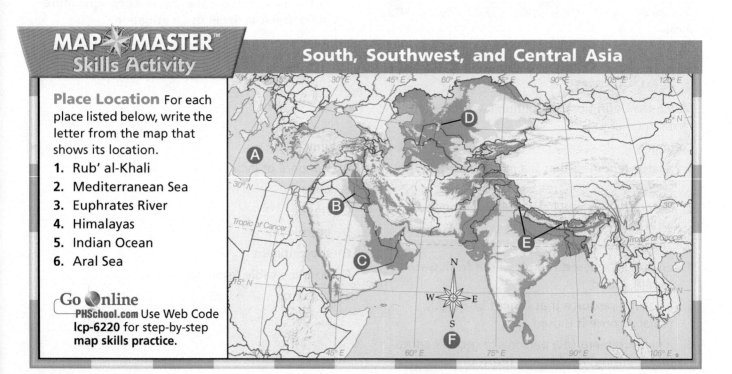

Standardized Test Prep

Test-Taking Tips

Some questions on standardized tests ask you to analyze parts of a map. Study the map key below. Then follow the tips to answer the sample question.

KEY

Feet	Elevation	Meters
Over 13,000	▬	Over 3,960
6,500–13,000	▬	1,980–3,960
1,600–6,500	▬	480–1,980
650–1,600	▬	200–480
0–650	▬	0–200
Below sea level	▬	Below sea level

TIP On a map key, the color column lines up with the data on the information column or columns. To find the required information, move from a given color to the data on the left or right.

Pick the letter that best answers the question.

On an elevation map, most of the area around the Ganges River is colored green. According to the key at the left, how many meters is the elevation in that area?

A below sea level

B 0–200

C 0–650

D 650–1,600

TIP Preview the question. Keep it in mind as you study the information on the map key.

Practice Questions

Use the tips above and other tips in this book to help you answer the following questions.

1. Scientists think that about 40 million years ago, the Indian subcontinent slowly collided with Asia to form

   A the island nation of Sri Lanka.

   B the Western Ghats.

   C the Himalayas.

   D Mesopotamia.

2. The alluvial plains in northern India make the area ideal for

   A mining.

   B farming.

   C aquaculture.

   D hydroelectricity.

3. South Asian countries have climates with warm, dry winters because

   A they are located along the Equator.

   B they are located in a desert region.

   C the Himalayas block cold air blown by the winter monsoon.

   D the Eastern Ghats block cold air blown by the winter monsoon.

Use the passage below to answer Question 4.

In the winter, the people of eastern Kazakhstan wrap themselves in fur to brave the freezing temperatures. Snow covers the ground as far as the eye can see. Livestock must dig through the ice to feed on the tough grass underneath. But the straight roads of the countryside never need to be plowed. Engineers built the roads slightly higher than the surrounding land. The strong winds keep the roads free of snow.

4. This paragraph is missing a topic sentence. What is the best topic sentence for this paragraph?

   A Winters in eastern Kazakhstan are extremely cold and snowy.

   B Engineers in Kazakhstan are among the best in the world.

   C Some people in eastern Kazakhstan raise livestock for a living.

   D Summers in Kazakhstan are extremely hot.

Use Web Code **lca-6200** for **Chapter 2 self-test**.

Chapter 3

Southeast Asia and the Pacific Region: Physical Geography

Chapter Preview

In this chapter, you will learn about Southeast Asia and the Pacific Region—a region of the world that includes islands, peninsulas, and the world's smallest continent.

Section 1
Southeast Asia
Physical Geography

Section 2
Australia and New Zealand
Physical Geography

Section 3
The Pacific Islands
Physical Geography

🎯 Target Reading Skill

Main Idea In this chapter, you will focus on identifying the main ideas in the sections and paragraphs you read. You will also focus on identifying the details that support each main idea.

▶ A lush rain forest in the Philippines

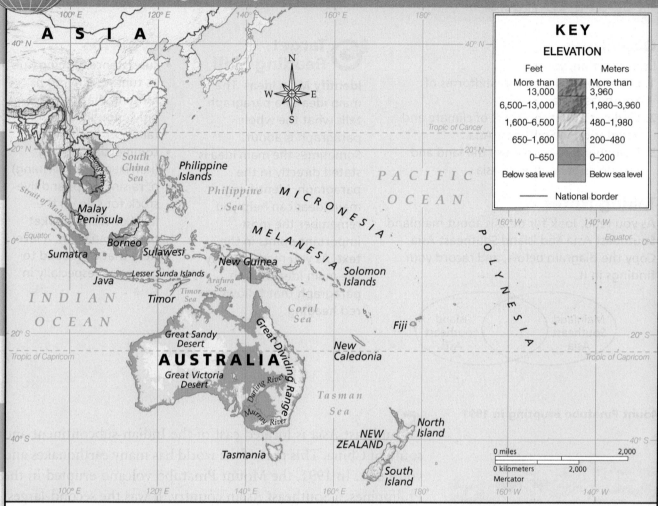

KEY

ELEVATION

Feet	Meters
More than 13,000	More than 3,960
6,500–13,000	1,980–3,960
1,600–6,500	480–1,980
650–1,600	200–480
0–650	0–200
Below sea level	Below sea level

—— National border

ASIA

South China Sea

Philippine Islands

Philippine Sea

MICRONESIA

PACIFIC OCEAN

Strait of Malacca

Malay Peninsula

MELANESIA

POLYNESIA

Borneo

Sumatra

Sulawesi

New Guinea

Solomon Islands

Java

Lesser Sunda Islands

Arafura Sea

Timor

Timor Sea

Coral Sea

Fiji

INDIAN OCEAN

Great Sandy Desert

AUSTRALIA

Great Dividing Range

New Caledonia

Great Victoria Desert

Darling River

Murray River

Tasman Sea

Murray River

NEW ZEALAND

North Island

Tasmania

South Island

Equator

Tropic of Cancer

Tropic of Capricorn

0 miles 2,000
0 kilometers 2,000
Mercator

Place Much of Southeast Asia and the Pacific Region is located
between the Tropic of Cancer and the Tropic of Capricorn.
Identify Name the continents in Southeast Asia and the Pacific
Region. **Draw Conclusions** What kind of climate would you
expect most of these countries to have? Explain your answer.

Go Online
PHSchool.com Use Web Code
lcp-6310 for step-by-step
map skills practice.

Southeast Asia
Physical Geography

Prepare to Read

Objectives
In this section, you will
1. Learn about the major landforms of Southeast Asia.
2. Find out about the kinds of climate and vegetation in Southeast Asia.
3. Examine how people use the land and resources of Southeast Asia.

Taking Notes
As you read, look for details about mainland Southeast Asia and island Southeast Asia. Copy the diagram below, and record your findings in it.

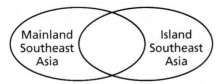

Mainland Southeast Asia   Island Southeast Asia

Target Reading Skill

Identify Main Ideas The main idea of a paragraph tells what the whole paragraph is about. Sometimes the main idea is stated directly in the paragraph. Identifying main ideas can help you remember the most important points in the text. As you read, identify the main idea of each paragraph that follows a red heading.

Key Terms
- **subsistence farming** (sub SIS tuns FAHR ming) *n.* farming that provides only enough food for a family or for a village
- **commercial farming** (kuh MUR shul FAHR ming) *n.* raising crops and live-stock for sale on the local or world market
- **paddy** (PAD ee) *n.* a level field that is flooded to grow rice, especially in Asia

Mount Pinatubo erupting in 1991

Southeast Asia is located east of the Indian subcontinent and south of China. This part of the world has many earthquakes and volcanoes. In 1991, the Mount Pinatubo volcano erupted in the Philippines, a Southeast Asian country. It was the second-largest volcanic eruption of the twentieth century. About 58,000 people moved to safety, but about 800 people died. The eruption threw nearly 20 millions tons of gas and ash 21 miles (34 kilometers) into the atmosphere. The gas cloud spread around Earth. For two years, this gas cloud caused global temperatures to drop by about 1°F (0.5°C). Volcanoes are one physical feature of Southeast Asia. What are other major physical features of Southeast Asia? How do they affect land use in the region?

The Land of Southeast Asia

Southeast Asia is divided into mainland and island areas. The mainland is a peninsula that juts south from the main area of Asia. The islands extend east and west between the Indian and the Pacific oceans. Locate the mainland and the islands on the map on the next page.

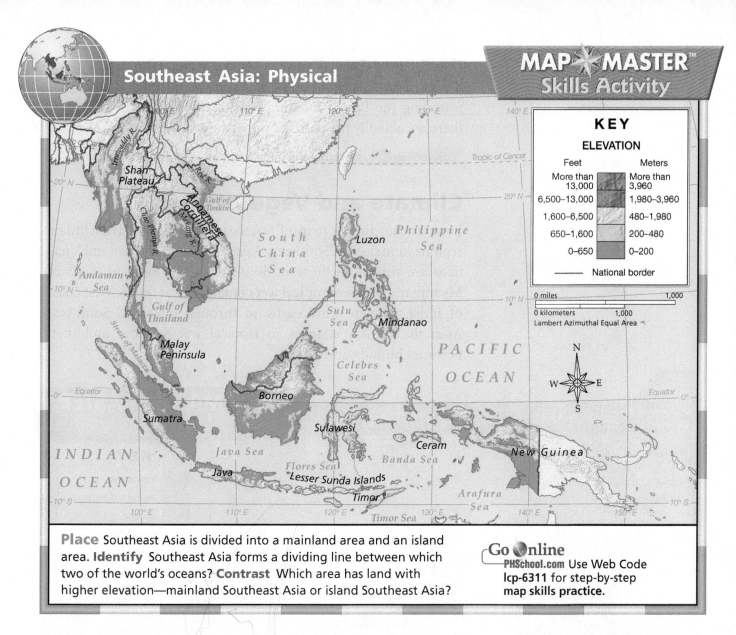

MAP★MASTER™
Skills Activity

KEY

ELEVATION

Feet		Meters
More than 13,000		More than 3,960
6,500–13,000		1,980–3,960
1,600–6,500		480–1,980
650–1,600		200–480
0–650		0–200

—— National border

0 miles   1,000
0 kilometers   1,000
Lambert Azimuthal Equal Area

Place Southeast Asia is divided into a mainland area and an island area. **Identify** Southeast Asia forms a dividing line between which two of the world's oceans? **Contrast** Which area has land with higher elevation—mainland Southeast Asia or island Southeast Asia?

Go Online
PHSchool.com Use Web Code
lcp-6311 for step-by-step
map skills practice.

Mainland Southeast Asia The nations of mainland Southeast Asia are Cambodia, Laos (LAH ohs), Malaysia (muh LAY zhuh), Myanmar (MYUN mahr), Thailand (TY land), and Vietnam. Note that Malaysia is part of mainland Southeast Asia as well as of island Southeast Asia. Much of this area is covered by forested mountains. Most people live in the narrow river valleys between mountain ranges.

Island Southeast Asia Five major nations make up island Southeast Asia: Singapore, Malaysia, Brunei (broo NY), Indonesia, and the Philippines. The largest of the island nations is Indonesia. Indonesia's biggest island is Sumatra. Singapore is a tiny nation, located at the tip of the Malay Peninsula. The country of Malaysia lies partly on the mainland and partly on the island of Borneo. The Philippines is a country made up of some 7,000 islands.

Tourists riding elephants through the forests of Thailand

The Ring of Fire The islands of Southeast Asia are part of the Ring of Fire. That is a region of volcanoes and earthquakes surrounding the Pacific Ocean. Most of the mountainous islands there are actually the peaks of underwater volcanoes.

✓ **Reading Check** **Name the largest nation in island Southeast Asia.**

Climate and Vegetation

Look at the climate map of Southeast Asia below. The climate regions in mainland Southeast Asia between Myanmar and Vietnam are similar to those in South Asia. On the west coast of Myanmar, there is a tropical wet climate, just as on the west coast of India. As you move eastward through mainland Southeast Asia, the climate changes to tropical wet and dry and then becomes humid subtropical.

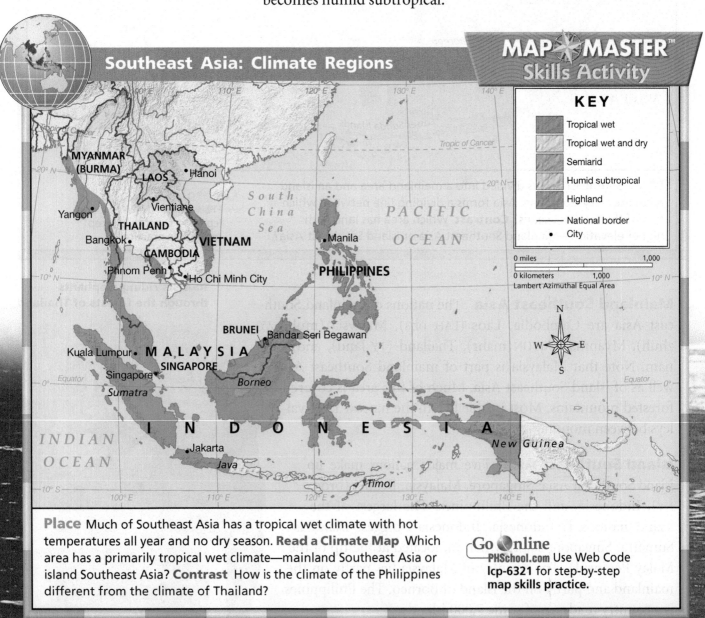

Southeast Asia: Climate Regions

MAP MASTER™
Skills Activity

KEY
- Tropical wet
- Tropical wet and dry
- Semiarid
- Humid subtropical
- Highland
- ⎯ National border
- • City

0 miles 1,000
0 kilometers 1,000
Lambert Azimuthal Equal Area

Place Much of Southeast Asia has a tropical wet climate with hot temperatures all year and no dry season. **Read a Climate Map** Which area has a primarily tropical wet climate—mainland Southeast Asia or island Southeast Asia? **Contrast** How is the climate of the Philippines different from the climate of Thailand?

Go Online
PHSchool.com Use Web Code
lcp-6321 for step-by-step
map skills practice.

Multiple Monsoons However, when you get to the southeastern coast of Vietnam, the pattern changes. The climate is again tropical wet. It supports tropical rain forests—thick forests that receive at least 60 inches (152 centimeters) of rain a year. Why is this area so wet? The answer is that summer monsoons bring rains to this coast just as they do to the western coast.

In fact, there are two separate summer monsoons. An Indian Ocean monsoon blows from the southwest, and a Pacific Ocean monsoon blows from the southeast. Each brings heavy summer rain to the Southeast Asian coast that it hits. Also, during the Northern Hemisphere's winter, winds off the central Pacific Ocean blow from the northeast. This winter monsoon brings heavy rains to the southern Philippines and Indonesia. Because most of Indonesia is in the Southern Hemisphere, the heavy rain from December to March is a summer monsoon there.

Effects of a Tropical Wet Climate Most of island Southeast Asia has a tropical wet climate that supports tropical rain forests. Southeast Asia contains the second-largest tropical rain forest region in the world.

The rain forests of Southeast Asia are lush and thick with vegetation. However, there are disadvantages to living in the tropical climate of Southeast Asia—typhoons. When typhoons hit land, the high winds and heavy rain often lead to widespread property damage and loss of life.

✓ **Reading Check** How does the northeast monsoon affect the southern Philippines and Indonesia?

Monsoons in Southeast Asia
The photos below show the effect of monsoons in Cambodia. Monsoons bring rains that can sometimes flood streets. **Analyze Images** *How do people get around when monsoon flooding is severe?*

Using the Land and Resources of Southeast Asia

Many of the people in Southeast Asia make their living from the land. Some live in villages, where they build their own houses and grow their own food. Farming that provides only enough for a family or for a village is called **subsistence farming.** Many use the same building and farming methods that their ancestors relied upon thousands of years ago. Other people in Southeast Asia work on plantations—large farming operations designed to raise crops for profit, or cash crops. Plantation agriculture is a type of commercial farming. **Commercial farming** is the raising of crops and livestock for sale on the local or world market.

Farming   Farming is a major economic activity in Southeast Asia, even though the region's cities and industries have been growing rapidly. In most Southeast Asian countries, more than 40 percent of the population work in agriculture. People farm—and live—in the river valleys of mountainous mainland Southeast Asia and on the lowland plains of island Southeast Asia. Crops include cash crops such as coffee, tea, and rubber. In Indonesia and Malaysia, rubber is grown on plantations and is a major export crop. Other major crops are soybeans, sugar cane, fruit, and, most important, rice.

The Importance of Rice   Rice has been the chief crop in Southeast Asia for centuries. Rice needs a hot climate and plenty of water to grow. In fact, rice grows best when it is planted in the water. In Southeast Asia, farmers use the paddy system to grow rice. A **paddy** is a level field that is flooded to grow rice. Indonesia and Thailand are among the top rice-producing countries in the world. In Southeast Asia, rice is also an important part of the people's diet. It is a food crop as well as a cash crop.

Growing Rice in Indonesia
In most of Southeast Asia, people grow rice by hand. Farmers use water buffalo to plow the fields. Rice seedlings are transplanted by hand to the fields, which have been flooded with water. **Analyze Images** *Which photo shows people transplanting rice seedlings to the fields?*

MAP MASTER™
Skills Activity

KEY

	Extent of rain forest, 3000 B.C.
	Present-day extent of rain forest
——	National border
•	City

0 miles 600
0 kilometers 600
Lambert Azimuthal Equal Area

Human-Environment Interaction Rain forests have a thin layer of topsoil. When people clear rain forests for farms, heavy rains often wash the topsoil away. Then people must clear more land for crops. **Locate** Where are rain forests located in Southeast Asia today? **Compare** On which island has rain forest destruction been greater—Sumatra or Java?

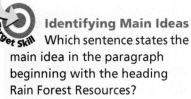
Go Online
PHSchool.com Use Web Code **lcp-6331** for step-by-step **map skills practice.**

Rain Forest Resources Southeast Asia's tropical rain forests cover large areas in the region. Rain forests contain a great variety of plant and animal life. In Southeast Asia, rain forests are a source of lumber, medicines, and chemicals used in industry. Tropical rain forests once covered nearly all of Southeast Asia. Over the years, huge sections have been cut down to provide lumber and to create farmland. On the island of Java in Indonesia, more than 90 percent of the rain forest has been cleared.

One challenge for the nations of Southeast Asia is balancing the need for economic growth with the need for rain forests. Thailand has made some progress toward conserving its rain forests. In 1988, hundreds of people in Thailand were killed by huge mudslides. The mudslides occurred because trees that had held the soil on the hillsides had been cut down. In 1989, Thailand banned logging in natural forests.

Identifying Main Ideas
Target Skill Which sentence states the main idea in the paragraph beginning with the heading Rain Forest Resources?

Chapter 3 Section 1 **59**

Bamboo as a Resource One forest resource that Southeast Asian people have long used for shelter is bamboo. Bamboo is a type of fast-growing grass that produces a woody stem. Giant bamboo can grow to about 100 feet (30 meters) tall. Millions of people in Southeast Asia live in houses made of bamboo. It is also used to make irrigation pipes, ropes, and bridges. Bamboo is important to the economies of several Southeast Asian countries. The Philippines is one of the world's largest suppliers of bamboo to the world market.

Mineral Resources The countries of Southeast Asia are rich in minerals. Indonesia, Myanmar, and Brunei have large deposits of oil. Even more plentiful, however, are the region's reserves of natural gas. Among the Southeast Asian countries, Indonesia and Malaysia have the largest reserves of natural gas. Thailand has large natural gas reserves in the Gulf of Thailand. These countries are using their own supplies of natural gas to generate electricity instead of importing oil.

✓ **Reading Check** Why does Southeast Asia now have fewer areas of tropical rain forests than in the past?

Bamboo stems being used as scaffolding in Laos

Section 1 Assessment

Key Terms
Review the key terms at the beginning of this section. Use each term in a sentence that explains its meaning.

Target Reading Skill
Write the main idea of each paragraph that follows a red heading in this section.

Comprehension and Critical Thinking
1. (a) Recall What kind of landform makes up mainland Southeast Asia?

(b) Compare and Contrast How is mainland Southeast Asia similar to and different from island Southeast Asia?

2. (a) Recall What kind of climate does most of island Southeast Asia have?

(b) Synthesize Information Why does the southeastern coast of Vietnam have the same climate as most of island Southeast Asia?

3. (a) List Give some examples of cash crops raised in Southeast Asia.

(b) Contrast What is the difference between subsistence farming and commercial farming?

(c) Draw Conclusions How can rice be a product of both commercial and subsistence farming?

Writing Activity
Write a paragraph that explains why commercial logging and commercial farming have a destructive effect on tropical rain forests.

For: An activity about Southeast Asia's geography
Visit: PHSchool.com
Web Code: lcd-6301

Prepare to Read

Objectives

In this section, you will

1. Find out why Australia and New Zealand have unique physical environments.
2. Learn about Australia's physical geography.
3. Explore New Zealand's physical geography.

Taking Notes

As you read, look for details about the physical geography of Australia and New Zealand. Copy the table below, and record your findings in it.

Physical Geography	
Australia	New Zealand

Target Reading Skill

Identify Supporting Details The main idea of a paragraph is supported by details that give further information about it. These details may explain the main idea or give examples or reasons. Look at the first paragraph on page 62. The first sentence is the main idea. The rest of the sentences support this main idea. How do the details about marsupials support the main idea?

Key Terms

- **marsupial** (mahr SOO pea ul) *n.* an animal, such as a kangaroo, that carries its young in a body pouch
- **tectonic plate** (tek TAHN ik playt) *n.* a huge slab of rock that moves very slowly over a softer layer beneath the surface of Earth's crust
- **geyser** (GY zur) *n.* a hot spring that shoots a jet of water and steam into the air
- **fiord** (fyawrd) *n.* a long, narrow inlet or arm of the sea bordered by steep slopes created by glaciers

What bird is strange looking, has a long bill, does not fly, and only comes out at night to hunt? If you said a kiwi, you are right. The people of New Zealand are so proud of this unusual bird that they have made it their national symbol. The people even call themselves "Kiwis." The bird is one of many unique animals found in New Zealand and its neighbor to the west, Australia.

Unique Physical Environments

Australia lies between the Pacific Ocean and the Indian Ocean. New Zealand lies in the Pacific Ocean to the east of Australia. Both countries are in the Southern Hemisphere, south of the Equator. This means that their seasons are the opposite of those in the United States. They are far from other continents, which has made them unique.

The kiwi has appeared on New Zealand stamps since 1898.

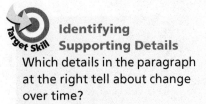

Ayers Rock, known in the Aboriginal language as Uluru, is located in central Australia. Kangaroos are common in Australia.

Target Skill

Identifying Supporting Details
Which details in the paragraph at the right tell about change over time?

Unique Plants and Animals New Zealand and Australia are so far from other continents that many of their animals and plants are found nowhere else on Earth. Only in New Zealand can you find kiwis and yellow-eyed penguins. Eighty-four percent of the plants in New Zealand's forests grow nowhere else. Australia has many unique creatures, such as the kangaroo and the koala. They are **marsupials** (mahr SOO pea ulz), or animals that carry their young in a body pouch. Marsupials *are* found elsewhere in the world. The opossum of North America, for instance, is a marsupial. But in Australia, almost all mammals are marsupials. This is not true anywhere else on Earth.

Moving Plates of Rock The uniqueness of New Zealand and Australia is the result of forces beneath Earth's surface. According to the theory of plate tectonics, the outer "skin," or crust of Earth, is broken into huge, moving slabs of rock called **tectonic plates.** These plates move independently, sometimes colliding and sometimes sliding against one another. Australia, New Zealand, and the Pacific islands are all part of the Indo-Australian plate. Once, it was part of a landmass that included Africa. Then, several hundred million years ago, the Indo-Australian plate broke away. Slowly—at a rate of an inch or two each year—it moved northeast toward Asia.

Movement and Change Over Time As the plates moved, Australia and the Pacific islands moved farther from Africa. Over the centuries, small changes have occurred naturally in the animals and plants of Australia and the islands. For instance, many birds have lost the ability to fly, even though they still have small wings. Because Australia and the islands are so isolated, these animals have not spread to other regions.

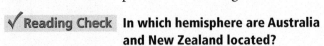 **Reading Check** **In which hemisphere are Australia and New Zealand located?**

Australia's Physical Geography

Australia is Earth's smallest continent. It is about as large as the continental United States (the part of the United States located between Canada and Mexico, not including Alaska and Hawaii). Most Australians live along Australia's eastern and southeastern coasts. Australia's physical geography explains why.

Find the region along Australia's east coast on the map below. This region receives ample rain. Winds blowing westward across the Pacific Ocean pick up moisture. As the winds rise to cross the Great Dividing Range, the moisture falls as rain. These winds also help make the climate mild and pleasant. Most Australians live here, in cities. Australia's most important rivers, the Murray and the Darling, flow through the region. They flow across a vast plain that contains Australia's most fertile farmland.

✔ **Reading Check** **How does the physical geography of Australia explain where the people live?**

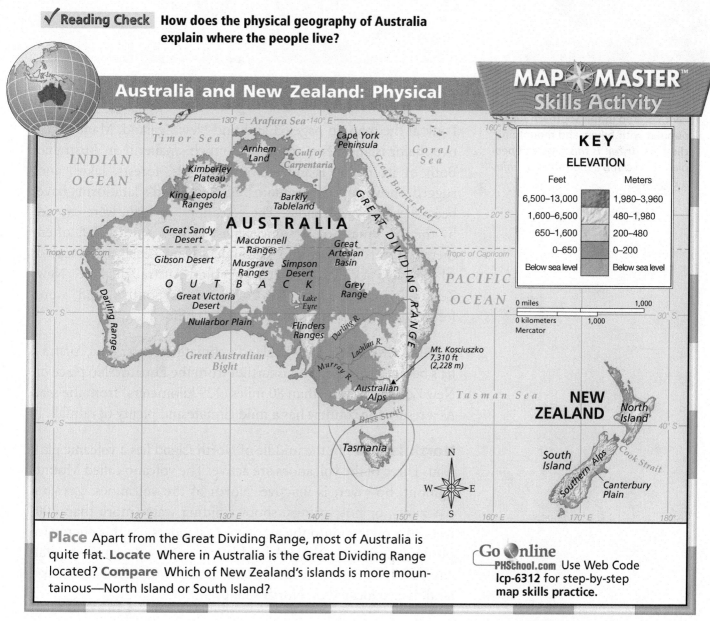

Australia and New Zealand: Physical

MAP MASTER™ Skills Activity

KEY
ELEVATION

Feet		Meters
6,500–13,000		1,980–3,960
1,600–6,500		480–1,980
650–1,600		200–480
0–650		0–200
Below sea level		Below sea level

0 miles 1,000
0 kilometers 1,000
Mercator

Place Apart from the Great Dividing Range, most of Australia is quite flat. **Locate** Where in Australia is the Great Dividing Range located? **Compare** Which of New Zealand's islands is more mountainous—North Island or South Island?

Go Online
PHSchool.com Use Web Code
lcp-6312 for step-by-step
map skills practice.

Mount Cook National Park
New Zealand's Mount Cook National Park, located in the Southern Alps, is popular with hikers and mountain climbers. **Infer** *Is this group of people out to climb a mountain or enjoy a day hike?*

New Zealand's Physical Geography

Look at the map on page 63 and find New Zealand. Made up of two major islands, New Zealand is much smaller than Australia. Both of its major islands have highlands, forests, lakes, and rugged, snowcapped mountains. New Zealand's landforms have been shaped by volcanoes. The volcanoes, in turn, were caused by the movement of tectonic plates. Where plates meet, often there are earthquakes and volcanoes. New Zealand is located where the Pacific plate meets the Indo-Australian plate. New Zealand's major islands, North Island and South Island, were formed by volcanoes when these plates collided.

A Mild Climate New Zealand's climate is cooler than Australia's because New Zealand is farther from the Equator. No place in New Zealand is more than 80 miles (129 kilometers) from the sea. As a result, the country has a mild climate and plenty of rainfall.

North Island In the middle of North Island lies a volcanic plateau. Three of the volcanoes are active. The volcano called Mount Egmont, however, is inactive. North of the volcanoes, **geysers** (GY zurz), or hot springs, shoot scalding water more than 100 feet (30.5 meters) into the air. New Zealanders use this energy to produce electricity. North Island is where New Zealand's capital city of Wellington is located. The country's largest city, Auckland, is also located on North Island.

South Island South Island has a high mountain range called the Southern Alps. Mount Cook, the highest peak in the range, rises to 12,349 feet (3,764 meters). Glaciers cover the mountainsides. Below, crystal-clear lakes dot the landscape. Fiords (fyawrds), or narrow inlets bordered by steep slopes, slice the southwest coastline. Here, the mountains reach the sea. To the southeast lies a flat, fertile land called the Canterbury Plain. This is where farmers produce most of New Zealand's crops. Ranchers also raise sheep and cattle here.

Comparing Australia and New Zealand New Zealand is like Australia in several ways. In both countries, most of the population lives in cities along the coast. More than four out of five New Zealanders live in towns and cities. Both Australia and New Zealand have important natural resources such as coal, iron ore, and natural gas. The two countries also raise sheep and cattle and grow similar crops.

New Zealand is different from Australia in a number of ways, too. New Zealand is much smaller but has higher mountains than those in Australia. New Zealand has glaciers, while Australia does not. The two countries also have different climates.

 **Reading Check** Where do most people in New Zealand live—in urban areas or in rural areas?

Section 2 Assessment

Key Terms
Review the key terms at the beginning of this section. Use each term in a sentence that explains its meaning.

Target Reading Skill
The main idea of the last paragraph in this section is that Australia and New Zealand are different in many ways. State the details that support this main idea.

Comprehension and Critical Thinking
1. (a) Recall Where do most of the people in Australia live?

(b) Identify Cause and Effect How have Australia's geography and climate affected where Australians live?

2. (a) Recall How were New Zealand's North Island and South Island formed?

(b) Compare and Contrast How is the physical geography of New Zealand different from that of Australia? How is it similar?

3. (a) Explain How are the population patterns similar in Australia and New Zealand?

(b) Draw Conclusions Why do most of the people in New Zealand live near the coasts?

Writing Activity
Write a list of adjectives that describe Australia. Then write a list of adjectives that describe New Zealand. Include at least three adjectives for each country. Using the information in this section, write a fact related to each adjective on your list.

For: An activity about Australia
Visit: PHSchool.com
Web Code: lcd-6302

Identifying Cause and Effect

Have you ever tossed a stone into a pond and watched what happens? As soon as that stone hits the surface and sinks, circles of ripples, or waves, begin to move away from that spot in ever-widening circles. This is one case of cause and effect. Tossing the stone started the waves moving away from the spot where the stone landed. Understanding this relationship between cause and effect is useful in school and in daily life.

Learn the Skill

Being able to identify causes and effects helps you to understand what you read. To learn this skill, follow the steps below.

1 **Look for a cause-and-effect relationship.** Remember the pebble in the pond. As you read, ask yourself, "Why did this happen?" or "How did this happen?" Look for words such as *because, so,* and *as a result.* These words sometimes signal a cause-and-effect relationship.

2 **Identify the effect or effects.** Like the ripples that appear in a pond, an effect is what happens. A cause may have more than one effect. List the effect(s) you have identified.

3 **Identify the cause or causes.** A cause makes something happen. An effect may have more than one cause. List the cause(s) of the effect(s) you identified in Step 2.

4 **State the cause and effect.** A simple cause-and-effect statement might read, "A caused B." A is the cause, and B is the effect. A cause that produced three effects might be stated as, "A caused B, C, and D." A is the cause; its effects are B, C, and D.

A stone tossed into this pond caused the ripples to form. The stone is the cause, and the ripples are the effect.

Practice the Skill

To practice identifying a cause-and-effect relationship, read the paragraph below, using the steps on the previous page.

1 What words signal a possible cause-and-effect situation?

2 Identify the effect by filling in the blank in the following sentence: "Why do _____ happen?" The word you use to fill in the blank is the effect.

3 The effect you identified is triggered by two causes. What are the two causes?

4 State the cause-and-effect relationship in a sentence. Your sentence should give an answer to this question: What causes tsunamis?

A Japanese woodblock print of a tsunami

Tsunamis (soo NAH mees) are powerful waves caused by earthquakes or volcanic eruptions that take place underwater. When an earthquake happens under the ocean floor or when an underwater volcano erupts, both of these actions cause circles of waves like the ones that form when you throw a stone into a pond. The result is a wave that is extremely forceful and fast. In deep water, tsunamis can move as fast as 500 to 600 miles (800 to 960 kilometers) per hour. As a tsunami approaches land, the speed slows down and the wave grows in height, sometimes as high as a ten-story building. The wave pushes inland, carrying boulders, boats, and buildings along until its energy is gone. In 2004, a huge tsunami struck at least 12 countries along the Indian Ocean. Entire villages were destroyed, and at least 225,000 people were killed.

Apply the Skill

Read the passages titled Moving Plates of Rock and Movement and Change Over Time on page 62. Use the steps in the skill to identify one cause that explains why New Zealand and Australia are unique.

The Pacific Islands
Physical Geography

Prepare to Read

Objectives

In this section, you will
1. Examine features of high islands and low islands.
2. Learn about the three main island groups.
3. Find out what kind of climate and vegetation the islands have.
4. Discover how land is used in the Pacific islands.

Taking Notes

As you read this section, look for details about the three major Pacific island groups. Copy the diagram below, and record your findings in it.

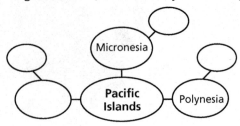

Target Reading Skill

Identify Main Ideas
Sometimes the main idea in a paragraph or reading passage is not stated directly. All the details add up to a main idea, but you must state the main idea yourself. As you read, look for main ideas that are not stated directly.

Key Terms

- **high island** (hy EYE lund) *n.* an island formed from the mountainous top of an ancient volcano
- **low island** (loh EYE lund) *n.* an island formed from coral reefs or atolls
- **atoll** (A tawl) *n.* a small coral island in the shape of a ring
- **coral** (KAWR ul) *n.* a rock-like material made up of the skeletons of tiny sea creatures, most plentiful in warm ocean water

Scuba diving in the Pacific islands

The Pacific Ocean, which covers nearly one third of Earth's surface, is dotted with thousands of islands. Some are barely large enough for a person to stand on. Others cover thousands of square miles. The Pacific islands include the second-largest island in the world. This is New Guinea. Half of this island is actually part of Indonesia. The other half is the independent country of Papua New Guinea (PAP yoo uh noo GIH nee). The Pacific islands also include the world's smallest independent island nation. This is the country of Nauru (NAH oo roo), which has a total land area of just 8 square miles (21 square kilometers).

Geographers divide these thousands of islands into three main groups. Melanesia (mel uh NEE zhuh) means "black islands." Micronesia (my kruh NEE zhuh) means "small islands." Polynesia (pahl uh NEE zhuh) means "many islands." Each of these groups covers a particular area, and any island that falls inside the boundaries of one of these areas belongs to that group.

High Islands and Low Islands

Geographers also divide the Pacific islands into high islands and low islands. **High islands** are mountainous and have been formed by volcanoes. The soil, which consists of volcanic ash, is very fertile. Because of their size and because people can grow crops there, high islands can support more people than low islands.

Low islands are made up of coral reefs or atolls. An **atoll** (A tawl) is a small coral island in the shape of a ring. The ring encloses a shallow pool of ocean water called a lagoon. Often, the lagoon has one or more openings to the sea. An atoll may rise only a few feet above the water. Low islands have this shape and low elevation because they are coral reefs. **Coral** is a rocklike material made up of the skeletons of tiny sea creatures. A reef develops until it nears the surface. Then sand and other debris accumulate on the reef's surface, raising the island above the level of the water.

Far fewer people live on low islands than on high islands. In part, this is because low islands are quite small. Also, low islands have poor, sandy soil and little fresh water, so it is difficult to raise crops. Most low islanders survive by fishing. They may also grow coconuts, yams, and a starchy root called taro.

A traditional house on a high island in Polynesia

✓ **Reading Check** On which type of island do most Pacific island people live?

A Coral Atoll

A South Pacific Atoll
The diagram below shows how a coral atoll is formed. ❶ It begins as a fringe of coral around a volcanic island. ❷ The coral continues to build as the island is worn away. ❸ Eventually, only a ring of coral remains. The aerial view of an atoll at the left shows the ring structure of the coral.

Melanesia, Micronesia, and Polynesia

The island group with the most people is Melanesia, which is north and east of Australia. Most of Melanesia's large islands are high islands. New Guinea, for example, has two ranges of high mountains. The western half of New Guinea is called Irian Jaya (IHR ee ahn JAH yuh). It is part of the country of Indonesia. The eastern half is Papua New Guinea, the largest and most populated Melanesian country. Some smaller Melanesian islands are Fiji, the Solomon Islands, and New Caledonia.

Made up largely of low islands, Micronesia covers an area of the Pacific as large as the continental United States. Most of the islands of Micronesia lie north of the Equator. Some of Micronesia's 2,000 islands are less than 1 square mile (2.6 square kilometers) in area. The largest is Guam, which is 209 square miles (541 square kilometers). Most of Micronesia's islands are divided into groups. The largest are the Caroline, Gilbert, Marshall, and Mariana islands. Guam is part of the Marianas.

Polynesia is the largest island group in the Pacific. It includes the fiftieth state of the United States, Hawaii. Polynesia consists of a great many high islands, such as Tahiti and Samoa. Dense rain forests cover their high volcanic mountains. Along the shores are palm-fringed, sandy beaches. The Tuamotus and Tonga are examples of Polynesia's few low islands and atolls.

✓ **Reading Check** **Which island group contains Hawaii?**

Living in the Pacific Islands
The bottom photo on the opposite page shows a traditional canoe in Fiji. Below left, fishers haul nets in the waters of Fiji. Below right, some people in Papua New Guinea farm for a living. The inset photo on the opposite page shows children playing volleyball in Vanuatu.

Climate and Vegetation of the Pacific Islands

The Pacific islands lie in the tropics. Temperatures are hot year-round. Daytime temperatures can reach as high as the 80s and mid-90s in degrees Fahrenheit (around 30°C). Nighttime temperatures average about 75°F (24°C). The ocean winds keep the temperatures from getting too high.

Some Pacific islands have wet and dry seasons. Most islands, however, receive heavy rainfall all year long. In Hawaii, for example, volcanic peaks such as Mauna Kea (MOW nuh KAY uh) receive 100 inches (250 centimeters) of rain each year. Usually the rain falls in brief, heavy downpours. Some low islands, however, receive only scattered rainfall.

Because of high temperatures, plentiful rainfall, and fertile soil, high islands such as Papua New Guinea and the Hawaiian Islands have rich vegetation. Tropical rain forests cover the hills. Savanna grasses grow in the lowlands. Low islands, on the other hand, have little vegetation. The poor soil supports only palm trees, grasses, and small shrubs.

✓ **Reading Check** **Why do low islands have little vegetation?**

Target Skill **Identify Main Ideas** In one sentence, state what the paragraph at the left is about.

Natural Resources and Land Use

The Pacific island region has few natural resources. The coconut palm is its most important resource. It provides food, clothing, and shelter. Another important resource is fish.

Cash Crops Some Pacific island countries, such as the nation of Fiji, grow cash crops. Fiji is a nation of some 300 islands in Melanesia. The Fiji islands' fertile, volcanic soil and hot, wet climate are good for growing sugar cane. Sugar is a major export for Fiji. Another important cash crop for many Pacific island countries is copra. Copra, or dried coconut, is used in margarine, cooking oils, soaps, and cosmetics. The people in Fiji also work as subsistence farmers, growing their own food crops such as taro, yams, and sweet potatoes.

Tourism The Pacific islands' most valuable resource may be their natural beauty. Tourism provides a key source of income in the region. Many Pacific island nations are working to develop their tourist industries. The greatest number of visitors to the Pacific islands come from Australia. Nearly as many come from the United States.

A worker harvests ripe coconuts in Fiji.

✓ **Reading Check** Give two examples of cash crops grown in the Pacific islands.

Section 3 Assessment

Key Terms
Review the key terms at the beginning of this section. Use each key term in a sentence that explains its meaning.

Target Reading Skill
Read the paragraph titled Tourism, above. Write a sentence that states the main idea.

Comprehension and Critical Thinking
1. (a) Explain Tell the difference between high islands and low islands in the Pacific.

(b) Make Generalizations The people on high islands often have a better standard of living than people on low islands. Explain why this might be so.

2. (a) Recall Name the three Pacific island groups.

(b) Apply Information Why do most of the people in the Pacific islands live in Melanesia?

(c) Draw Conclusions Most Pacific islands have few natural resources. How might this affect trade between these islands and industrial nations around the world?

Writing Activity
Suppose that you have decided to live on one of the Pacific islands. Write a paragraph explaining why you have decided to move. How will you handle the challenges of island life? Will you live on a high island or a low island?

For: An activity on the Pacific islands
Visit: PHSchool.com
Web Code: lcd-6303

◆ Chapter Summary

Section 1: Southeast Asia Physical Geography

- Southeast Asia is divided into mainland and island areas. Mainland Southeast Asia is a peninsula. Island Southeast Asia is part of the Ring of Fire, a region of volcanoes and earthquakes.
- Most of Southeast Asia has a tropical wet climate.
- Farming is a major economic activity in Southeast Asia, although the region's cities and industries have been growing rapidly.
- Southeast Asian rain forests are a source of lumber, medicines, and materials used in industry. The region's remaining rain forests are in danger of destruction from commercial logging and farming.

Section 2: Australia and New Zealand Physical Geography

- Because Australia and New Zealand are far from other landmasses, many of their plants and animals are found nowhere else on Earth.
- Australia is the smallest continent. Most people live along its eastern and southern coasts.
- New Zealand is made up of two mountainous islands.

Cambodia

Section 3: The Pacific Islands Physical Geography

- The Pacific islands are divided into three main groups: Melanesia, Micronesia, and Polynesia.
- Within these groups, there are high islands and low islands.
- Because the Pacific islands lie in the tropics, temperatures are hot all year.
- The Pacific islands have few natural resources, but some island countries are able to grow cash crops such as sugar and copra, or dried coconut. Tourism is growing in importance in the region.

Australia

◆ Key Terms

Use each key term in a sentence that explains its meaning.

1. fiord
2. paddy
3. subsistence farming
4. commercial farming
5. marsupial
6. tectonic plate
7. geyser
8. high island
9. low island
10. coral

Review and Assessment (continued)

◆ Comprehension and Critical Thinking

11. (a) List Which countries make up mainland Southeast Asia?
(b) Explain Why is Malaysia part of both mainland Southeast Asia and island Southeast Asia?

12. (a) Explain Why does Southeast Asia have more than one summer monsoon?
(b) Summarize Describe the effects of summer monsoons in Southeast Asia.

13. (a) Name Which two Southeast Asian countries are among the world's leading rice producers?
(b) Analyze Information Why would a subsistence farmer in Southeast Asia raise rice instead of rubber?

14. (a) Name What is one mountain range in Australia?
(b) Locate Where is this mountain range located relative to Australia's east coast?

15. (a) Recall Describe the major features of New Zealand's geography.
(b) Compare and Contrast How are Australia and New Zealand different from and similar to each other?

16. (a) Identify Where do most people in the Pacific islands live—on high islands or on low islands?
(b) Draw Conclusions You have read about high islands and low islands. What conclusion can you reach about why more people live on one kind than another?

◆ Skills Practice

Identifying Cause and Effect Review the steps you followed to learn this skill. Then reread the first paragraph on page 54. Identify three effects of the eruption of Mount Pinatubo.

◆ Writing Activity: Math

Suppose that it is Monday at 12 noon where you live. Calculate what day and time it is in Bangkok, Thailand; in Jakarta, Indonesia; and in Sydney, Australia. You will need to use a world time zones map, which you can find in an atlas. Do research to learn more about time zones and the International Date Line. Then write a paragraph about the International Date Line.

MAP MASTER™ Skills Activity

Southeast Asia and the Pacific

Place Location For each place listed below, write the letter that shows its location on the map.

1. Malay Peninsula
2. South China Sea
3. Philippine Islands
4. Australia
5. New Guinea
6. Micronesia

Go Online
PHSchool.com Use Web Code lcp-6320 for an interactive map.

Standardized Test Prep

Test-Taking Tips

Some questions on standardized tests ask you to analyze graphic organizers. Study the Venn diagram below. Then follow the tips to answer the sample question.

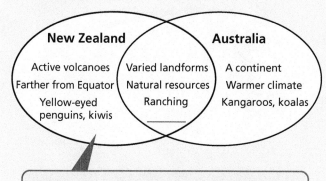

New Zealand

Active volcanoes
Farther from Equator
Yellow-eyed
penguins, kiwis

Varied landforms
Natural resources
Ranching
_____

Australia

A continent
Warmer climate
Kangaroos, koalas

TIP A Venn diagram lists ways that two things are the same and different. This kind of chart is good for writing or note-taking.

Pick the letter that best answers the question.

Which of the following belongs in the blank in the overlapping space?

- **A** compare and contrast
- **B** population mostly in cities
- **C** Great Dividing Range
- **D** geysers

Think It Through The question asks you to choose another example for the overlapping space—in other words, ways that both countries are the same. You can rule out C and D because the Great Dividing Range is in Australia and geysers are only in New Zealand. You can eliminate A, because it describes the chart—not an example in the chart. The correct answer is B, because the population of both countries is mostly in cities.

Practice Questions

Use the tips above and other tips in this book to help you answer the following questions.

1. Thailand, Cambodia, and Vietnam are part of
   - **A** island Southeast Asia.
   - **B** Polynesia.
   - **C** Micronesia.
   - **D** mainland Southeast Asia.

2. Most Australians live along Australia's eastern and southeastern coasts. Based on this information, what conclusion can be drawn about the location of Australia's cities?
   - **A** Most of Australia's cities are located in the interior of the continent.
   - **B** Most of Australia's cities are located along Australia's eastern and southeastern coasts.
   - **C** Most of Australia's cities are located along Australia's northern coast.
   - **D** Most of Australia's cities are located along Australia's western coast.

3. New Zealand's North Island and South Island were formed by
   - **A** volcanoes.
   - **B** coral.
   - **C** earthquakes.
   - **D** geysers.

Use the Venn diagram below to answer Question 4.

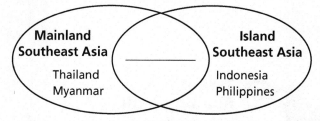

Mainland Southeast Asia

Thailand
Myanmar

Island Southeast Asia

Indonesia
Philippines

4. Which of the following belongs in the blank in the overlapping space?
   - **A** Vietnam
   - **B** Australia
   - **C** Malaysia
   - **D** Cambodia

Go Online
PHSchool.com

Use Web Code **lca-6300** for **Chapter 3 self-test**.

Chapter 4

East Asia: Cultures and History

Chapter Preview

East Asian cultures are among the oldest in the world. In this chapter, you will learn about East Asian cultures and their long histories.

Section 1
Historic Traditions

Section 2
People and Cultures

 **Target Reading Skill**

Context In this chapter, you will focus on using context to help you understand the meanings of unfamiliar words. Context includes the words, phrases, and sentences surrounding a particular word.

► The Great Buddha of Kamakura is the second-largest statue of Buddha in Japan.

MAP MASTER™
Skills Activity

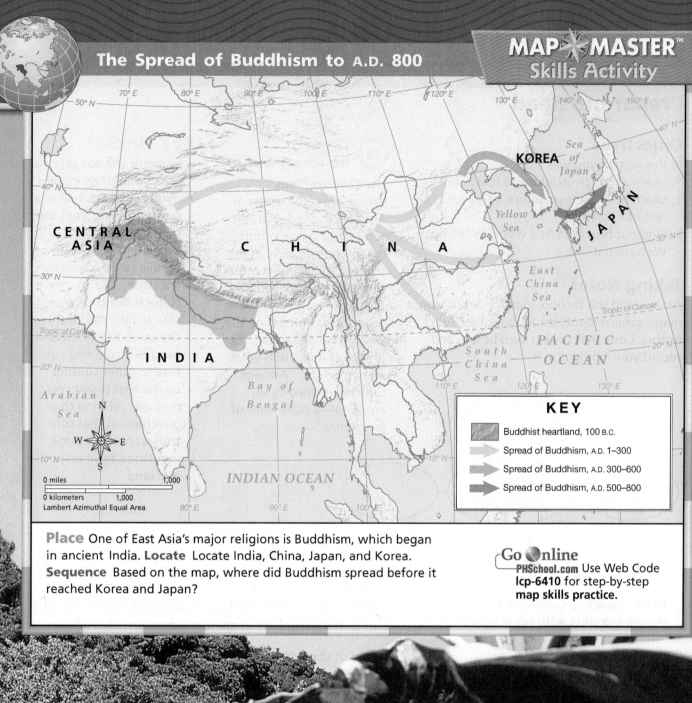

KEY

▨	Buddhist heartland, 100 B.C.
➔	Spread of Buddhism, A.D. 1–300
➔	Spread of Buddhism, A.D. 300–600
➔	Spread of Buddhism, A.D. 500–800

0 miles 1,000
0 kilometers 1,000
Lambert Azimuthal Equal Area

Place One of East Asia's major religions is Buddhism, which began in ancient India. **Locate** Locate India, China, Japan, and Korea. **Sequence** Based on the map, where did Buddhism spread before it reached Korea and Japan?

Go Online
PHSchool.com Use Web Code **lcp-6410** for step-by-step **map skills practice.**

Historic Traditions

Prepare to Read

Objectives

In this section you will
1. Learn about civilizations of East Asia.
2. Learn how Chinese culture influenced the rest of East Asia.
3. Find out how East Asia was affected by Western nations.

Taking Notes

As you read this section, look for details about major achievements throughout East Asia's history. Copy the concept web below, and record your findings in it.

Target Reading Skill

Use Context Clues

When you come across an unfamiliar word, you can sometimes figure out its meaning from clues in the context. The context refers to the surrounding words and sentences. Sometimes the context will define the word. In this example, the phrase in italics tells what an emperor is: "Ancient China was ruled by an emperor—*a male ruler of an empire.*"

Key Terms

- **emperor** (EM pur ur) *n.* a male ruler of an empire
- **dynasty** (DY nus tee) *n.* a series of rulers from the same family
- **clan** (klan) *n.* a group of families with a common ancestor
- **cultural diffusion** (KUL chur ul dih FYOO zhun) *n.* the spreading of ideas or practices from one culture to other cultures
- **communist** (KAHM yoo nist) *adj.* relating to a government that controls a country's large industries, businesses, and land

In this painting, Confucius is shown standing with his students.

More than two thousand years ago, one of the most important thinkers of ancient times gave this advice:

“Let the ruler be a ruler and the subject a subject.

A youth, when at home, should act with respect to his parents, and, abroad, be respectful to his elders. He should be earnest and truthful. He should overflow in love to all, and cultivate the friendship of the good.

When you have faults, do not fear to abandon them.”

These words are from the teachings of Confucius (kun FYOO shus), who lived in China about 500 B.C. He taught that all individuals have duties and responsibilities. If a person acts correctly, the result will be peace and harmony. Confucius's ideas helped to guide Chinese life for hundreds of years.

Civilizations of East Asia

Regions of Asia and Africa produced civilizations earlier than China's. A civilization has cities, a central government, workers who do specialized jobs, and social classes. Of the world's early civilizations, however, only China's has survived. This makes it the oldest continuous civilization in the world. Korea and Japan are not as old, but they, too, have long histories.

China's Middle Kingdom For much of its history, China had little to do with the rest of the world. The Great Wall of China first started in the 600s B.C. as many small unconnected walls between warring states. Over time, it became a symbol of China's desire to keep the world at a distance. In fact, Chinese leaders had such pride that they named their country the Middle Kingdom. To them, it was the center of the universe.

Ancient Achievements The Chinese had reason to believe that their civilization was the greatest in the world. They invented paper, gunpowder, silk weaving, the magnetic compass, the printing press, and clockworks. Chinese engineers were experts at digging canals, building dams and bridges, and setting up irrigation systems. Chinese scientists made major discoveries in mathematics and medicine.

Dynasties in China Starting in ancient times, China was governed by an **emperor**—a male ruler of an empire. An empire is an area of many territories and people that are controlled by one government. A series of emperors from the same family is a **dynasty**. Chinese history is described in terms of dynasties. The chart below lists major dynasties of China.

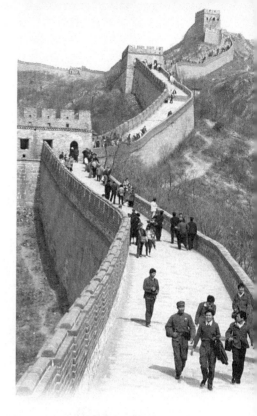

The Great Wall of China

■ **Chart Skills**

The chart below shows major dynasties of China. They ruled China from ancient times to A.D. 1911. **Identify** Which dynasty was the first to develop the Chinese calendar? **Sequence** Which was developed in China first—paper money or iron tools?

Major Dynasties of China

Major Dynasty	Major Achievements
Shang (c. 1766–c. 1122 B.C.)	Well-developed writing, first Chinese calendar, bronze casting.
Zhou (c. 1122–c. 256 B.C.)	Writing laws, iron tools and plows in use.
Qin (221 B.C.–206 B.C.)	First great Chinese Empire. Much of the Great Wall built.
Han (206 B.C.–A.D. 220)	Government based on Confucianism. Buddhism introduced.
Tang (A.D. 618–A.D. 907)	Sculpture and poetry flourish.
Song (A.D. 906–A.D. 1279)	Block printing and paper money developed. Gunpowder first used.
Ming (A.D. 1318–A.D. 1644)	Porcelain, the novel, and drama flourish.
Qing (A.D. 1644–A.D. 1911)	Increased trade with Europe. Last Chinese dynasty.

Use Context Clues
If you do not know what *unified* means, look in the surrounding words for a context clue. Here, the phrase following *unified* explains what the term means.

Korea and China Although Korea's original settlers came from north-central Asia, Korea's history is closely tied to China. Around 1200 B.C., during a time of troubles in China, some Chinese moved to the Korean Peninsula. Later, other Chinese settled in the southern part of the peninsula. In this way, Chinese people brought Chinese knowledge and customs to the Koreans.

As in China, dynasties ruled Korea. While China had many dynasties, Korea had only three. The first was the Shilla. The Shilla dynasty unified Korea as one country in A.D. 668.

Years of Isolation in Japan For much of Japan's history, clans, or groups of families who claim a common ancestor, fought each other for land and power. Around A.D. 500, one clan, the Yamato (yah MAH toh), became powerful. Claiming descent from the sun goddess, Yamato leaders took the title of emperor. Many emperors sat on Japan's throne. For a long time they had little power. Instead, shoguns (SHOH gunz), or "emperor's generals," made the laws. Warrior nobles, the samurai (SAM uh ry), enforced these laws. Together, the shoguns and samurai ruled Japan for more than 700 years.

Japan was isolated from the outside world from about 1640 to 1853. Japanese leaders believed that isolation, or separation, was the best way to keep the country united. Japan finally was forced to trade with the West in the 1800s.

✓ **Reading Check** **Name at least four major achievements of the Chinese civilization.**

■ **Timeline Skills**

Japan has interacted with other countries and regions except for one period in its history. **Note** When did Japan close its borders to the rest of the world? **Analyze Information** Which European country introduced Christianity to Japan?

Events in Japanese History

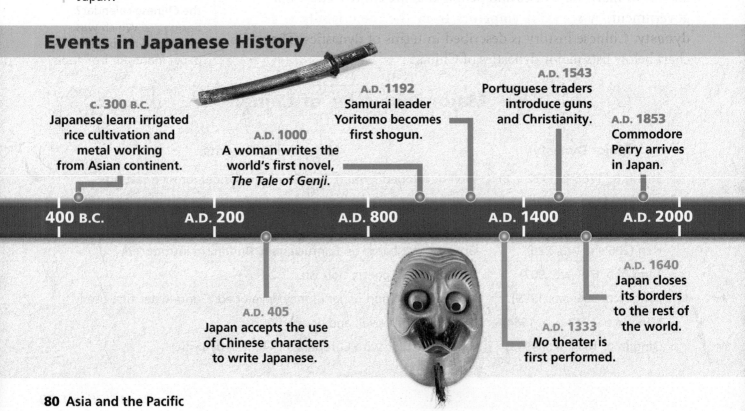

c. 300 B.C.
Japanese learn irrigated rice cultivation and metal working from Asian continent.

A.D. 1000
A woman writes the world's first novel, *The Tale of Genji*.

A.D. 1192
Samurai leader Yoritomo becomes first shogun.

A.D. 1543
Portuguese traders introduce guns and Christianity.

A.D. 1853
Commodore Perry arrives in Japan.

400 B.C.   A.D. 200   A.D. 800   A.D. 1400   A.D. 2000

A.D. 405
Japan accepts the use of Chinese characters to write Japanese.

A.D. 1333
No theater is first performed.

A.D. 1640
Japan closes its borders to the rest of the world.

Paper Making

Civilization developed as people learned first to speak and to draw, and then to write. By the time of the Han dynasty in China, civilization included government, trade, record-keeping, and poetry. Paper was needed for all of these activities. Cai Lun, an official of the Han dynasty, is said to have invented this useful material.

Making paper pulp
People in Xishuangbanna, China, split open bamboo stems to extract pulp.

3 A paper mold—a box with wooden sides and a fine wire screen—is dipped into a vat of pulp and slowly raised.

4 Workers then shake the mold until the water drains off and the wet fibers cover the screen with a thin web of pulp.

2 Workers pound the water-soaked fibers to a pulp.

1 Fibers are gathered from bamboo, mulberry bark, cotton or linen cloth, grass, straw, or wood—and then chopped up, beaten, and soaked in water.

5 While still damp, the sheet of paper is peeled off the mold.

6 The paper sheets are pasted on a wall to dry. A fire might be lit to help the drying process.

Paper dyeing
Women lay out freshly dyed paper to dry in Bhaktapur, Nepal.

ANALYZING IMAGES
Why did it make sense to make paper near a source of water?

The Spread of Cultures in East Asia

In ancient times, China was far ahead of the rest of the world in inventions and discoveries. Thus, it is not surprising that many Chinese discoveries spread to Korea and Japan. This process of **cultural diffusion,** or spreading of ideas from one culture to other cultures, happened early. The teachings of Confucius were among the first ideas to be passed along. The religion of Buddhism (BOOD iz um), which China had adopted from India, later spread to Korea and Japan. East Asian culture owes much to the early exchanges among China, Japan, and Korea. In each case, the countries changed what they borrowed until the element of culture became their own.

✓ **Reading Check** Give an example of cultural diffusion between China and Korea.

Westerners in East Asia

In the 1800s, Europeans and Americans began to produce great amounts of manufactured goods. East Asia seemed to be a good place to sell these products. Western trading ships began to sail to Asian ports.

The Opening of East Asia In 1853, U.S. Commodore Matthew Perry sailed with four warships to Japan. He forced Japan to grant trading rights to the United States. The opening up of China to Europe was different. The British, French, Germans, Portuguese, Russians, and Japanese gained control over parts of China. Other countries then feared losing the opportunity to share in China's riches. In 1899, the United States announced the policy that China should be open for trade with all nations equally. For a while, nations halted their efforts to divide up China.

New Forces in the 1900s Many Chinese blamed the emperor for the foreign powers in their country. In 1911, revolution broke out in China. The rule of emperors ended, and a republic was set up.

Meanwhile, Japan was becoming more powerful. Its leaders sought to control other Asian countries. One of their reasons was to make sure that Japan would have resources to fuel its growing industries. Japanese attacks on other Asian and Pacific lands led to the start of World War II in East Asia in 1941. In 1945, the United States and its allies defeated Japan.

Government in Japan
Japan's legislative branch is called the Diet. The Diet elects a prime minister, who heads the executive branch. Members of the Diet are shown in 2001 applauding the election of Junichiro Koizumi as prime minister. **Analyze Images** *Which man in the photo is Koizumi? Explain your answer.*

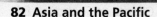

After World War II ended, civil war broke out in China between two groups, the Nationalists and the Communists. The Communists won the war in 1949 and made China a **communist** nation, one in which the government owns large industries, businesses, and most of the country's land.

After World War II, Korea was divided into two parts. Communists ruled North Korea. South Korea turned to Western nations for support. In 1950, North Korea invaded South Korea. The United States sent 480,000 troops to help South Korea. The Korean War lasted for three years, killing about 37,000 U.S. soldiers and more than 2 million Koreans. Neither side won. The battle line at the end of the war, in 1953, remains the border between the two Koreas today.

✓ **Reading Check** How did Japan's actions lead to the start of World War II in East Asia?

American veterans visiting a memorial in South Korea marking the 50th anniversary of the Korean War

Section 1 Assessment

Key Terms
Review the key terms at the beginning of this section. Use each term in a sentence that explains its meaning.

Target Reading Skill
Find the phrase *foreign powers* on page 82. Use context clues to figure out its meaning. What clues helped you figure out its meaning?

Comprehension and Critical Thinking
1. (a) List Name at least four achievements of the Chinese civilization.
(b) Find Main Ideas How was the Chinese civilization ruled from ancient times to 1911?

2. (a) Identify Give one example of cultural diffusion in East Asia.
(b) Make Generalizations Cultural diffusion can take place when people move from one place to another. When they do, they take their culture with them. Based on what you have read in this section, what are some other ways in which cultural diffusion can happen?
3. (a) Recall Why did U.S. Commodore Matthew Perry sail to Japan in 1853?
(b) Compare and Contrast How was the opening up of China to Europe different from the opening up of Japan?

Writing Activity
Suppose that you are a European merchant traveling through China in the 1300s. Use the chart on page 79 to write three short diary entries about the inventions and achievements you find there.

For: An activity on East Asia's history
Visit: PHSchool.com
Web Code: lcd-6401

Skills for Life
Reading Route Maps

Think of three inventions that had an important effect on human progress. What comes to mind: Farming? Books? Cars?

Did you think of *roads?*

The development of road networks has helped human civilization to grow and spread. Roads have been the lifelines of trade, communication, and human migration for thousands of years. Some of the world's oldest roads are in East Asia.

Learn the Skill

A map that shows roads is called a route map. Follow these steps to learn how to read a route map.

1 **Read the title of the map and become familiar with its features.** First, get a general idea of what region the map shows. Use the compass rose to figure out direction on the map.

2 **Study the key to understand its symbols.** Most modern road maps use colored lines to indicate various types of roads, from country roads to interstate highways. Other maps use colors to show land, sea, and air routes. The colors and what they represent are shown in the key. Notice what other symbols in the key represent, including cities.

3 **Trace routes on the map.** Gather information about the route by studying the features on the map. Use the scale of miles to calculate distances. Notice physical features and landmarks along the journey. Make note of any geographic barriers that would affect speed or comfort on the trip.

4 **Interpret the map.** Use information you gather from the map to draw conclusions about the route. On historical maps you can draw conclusions about why travelers and traders took certain routes and traveled at certain times of the year.

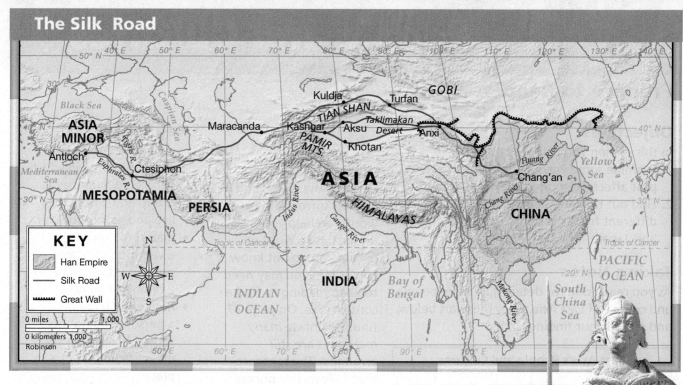

The Silk Road

Practice the Skill

Study the map and follow the steps on the previous page to practice reading a route map.

1 Read the title of the map and study the map to observe its main features. What region does it show? What type of map is it—modern or historical, a standard road map, or some other kind? What is its purpose?

2 Look at the key on this map. What features does it identify?

3 With your finger, start at the city of Chang'an, in China, and trace the general paths of the Silk Road. Using the compass rose, determine the direction of the route. What continents or regions did the Silk Road cross? Where did it end? Did it include travel over mountains?

4 The Silk Road was created over time, as local and regional routes became connected to form one long route. Write a paragraph that describes the route and draws conclusions about how and why it took the particular path shown on the map.

Apply the Skill

Find a street map of your community. Use the steps in the Learn the Skill section to trace the route from your house to your school or to some other location you know, such as a park. Write a paragraph that draws conclusions about the route you found.

Section 2

People and Cultures

Prepare to Read

Objectives

In this section you will
1. Examine some ways in which East Asia's past affects its modern-day culture.
2. Find out how the people of China are different from the people of the Koreas and Japan.

Taking Notes

As you read, look for details about the people and culture of East Asia. Copy the chart below, and record your findings in it.

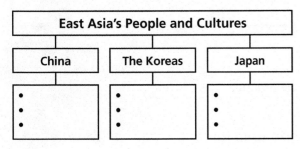

East Asia's People and Cultures		
China	The Koreas	Japan
•	•	•
•	•	•
•	•	•

Target Reading Skill

Use Context Clues
Context, the words and phrases surrounding a word, can help you understand a word or phrase you do not know. Sometimes you may need to keep reading to find a context clue. On page 87, find the phrase *many marriages are still arranged.* The sentence that follows this phrase explains what an arranged marriage is.

Key Terms

- **commune** (KAHM yoon) *n.* a community in which people own land as a group and where they live and work together
- **dialect** (DY uh lekt) *n.* a variation of a language that is unique to a region or an area
- **nomad** (NOH mad) *n.* a person who has no settled home but who moves from place to place
- **homogeneous** (hoh moh JEE nee us) *adj.* identical or similar
- **ethnic group** (ETH nik groop) *n.* a group of people who share such characteristics as language, religion, and ancestry

Two men play a game of Go in a small South Korean village.

The Chinese game weiqi (WAY chee) has ancient cultural roots. One player has 181 black stones standing for night. The other has 180 white stones standing for day. The goal is to surround and capture the opponent's stones. But to the Chinese, weiqi is more than a game. For centuries, Buddhists have used it to discipline the mind. Today, you can see people playing this ancient game throughout East Asia. Another name for this traditional Chinese game is Go.

Tradition and Change

In East Asia, tradition mixes with change in a thousand ways. Businesspeople in Western suits greet each other in the traditional way—with a bow. Ancient palaces stand among skyscrapers. Everywhere in Japan, China, and the Koreas, reminders of the past mingle with activities of the present.

Communism Changes Chinese Farming When the Communists took power in 1949, they began to make major changes. The government ended the old system of land ownership. It created **communes,** communities in which land is held in common and where members live and work together.

Many Chinese farmers were bitter at losing their land. They were accustomed to living in family groups that worked together in small fields. The farmers resisted the communes. Food production fell, and China suffered terrible food shortages. Only when the government allowed some private ownership did food production grow.

Changes in Chinese Life Beginning in the 1970s, the Communists also tried to slow China's population growth by attacking the idea of large families. Chinese couples were supposed to wait until their late twenties to marry. They were not supposed to have more than one child per family. Chinese families with only one child could receive special privileges. For example, couples in urban areas could receive a payment of money. In rural areas, the reward could be more land.

Under communism, the position of women improved. One of the first laws the Communists passed allowed a woman to own property, choose her husband, and get a divorce. Today, however, men still hold most of the power, and many marriages are still arranged. That is, parents or other family members decide who will marry whom.

Shanghai at Night
Shanghai, China, is a bustling city with skyscrapers and superhighways. The small photo shows Nanjing Road, one of the principal streets in Shanghai. **Analyze Images** *Do you think Shanghai is a large or a small city? Explain your answer.*

Japan's Capsule Hotels
In densely populated Japan, people have developed unique ways to use space. Capsule hotels are one such example. They are used mainly by businessmen who have missed the last train home. Each capsule usually has a bed, a television, a radio, and an alarm clock. **Analyze Images** *What are most of the people in the photo doing?*

Use Context Clues Use the last two sentences in this paragraph to help you define *traditional customs*. Check your definition by looking up *traditional* and *custom* in a dictionary.

Old and New in China Old traditions in China are strongest in rural areas. Yet even in the cities, a visitor sees examples of the old China. In cities like Beijing, the capital of China, the streets are filled with three-wheeled cabs pedaled like tricycles. These pedicabs share the roads with buses, cars, and taxis. Tiny shops exist side by side with modern buildings.

Changes in the Koreas In both Koreas, daily life is influenced by long-standing traditions. The family is still important, although the average family is smaller today than before. In rural areas, grandparents, parents, aunts, and uncles may live in one household. In the cities, usually just parents and children live as one household.

As in China, modern ways are much more visible in Korean urban areas. Also, as is true all over the world, the role of women has changed. In the past, Korean women had few opportunities. Today, women can work and vote.

A Blend of Old and New in Japan Japan is the most modern of the East Asian countries. The Japanese use more modern technology than the rest of East Asia. Nearly 80 percent of the population lives in urban areas. Once Japanese workers reach home, however, many still follow traditional customs. For example, they may change into kimonos, or robes. They may sit on mats at a low table to have dinner.

✓ **Reading Check** Which is the most modern country in East Asia?

East Asia's People

East Asia is a mix of cultures both old and new. Within each of the area's countries, however, the people tend to share a single culture.

China: The Han and Other Chinese Ethnic Groups

About 19 of every 20 Chinese people trace their ancestry to the Han ethnic group. As you can see on the map below, the Han live mostly in the eastern half of China. Although they have a common written language, they speak different dialects from region to region. A **dialect** is a variation of a language that is unique to a region or area. The other Chinese come from 55 different minority groups. These groups live mainly in western and southern China. With so many different ethnic groups, China is one of the most ethnically diverse nations in the world.

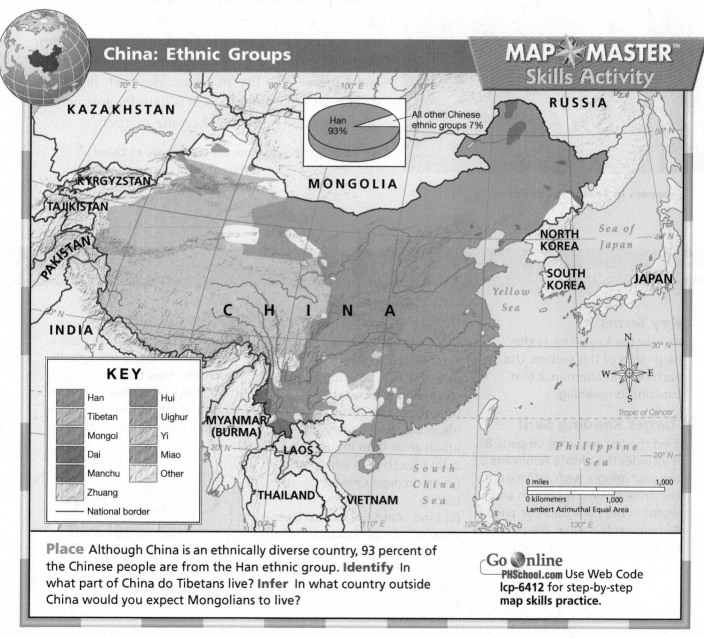

China: Ethnic Groups

MAP★MASTER™
Skills Activity

Han 93%   All other Chinese ethnic groups 7%

KEY

Han | Hui
Tibetan | Uighur
Mongol | Yi
Dai | Miao
Manchu | Other
Zhuang
—— National border

Place Although China is an ethnically diverse country, 93 percent of the Chinese people are from the Han ethnic group. **Identify** In what part of China do Tibetans live? **Infer** In what country outside China would you expect Mongolians to live?

Go Online
PHSchool.com Use Web Code lcp-6412 for step-by-step map skills practice.

Shoppers in Seoul, South Korea

Korea and Japan: Few Minorities Historians believe that the ancient Korean language was brought to Korea by nomads from the north. **Nomads** are people who have no settled home but who move from place to place, usually on a seasonal basis. Over centuries, these groups lost their separate traditions. They formed one **homogeneous** (hoh moh JEE nee us) group, which means identical or similar. Today, even with the division of Korea into two countries, the population is quite homogeneous. There are few minority groups.

Because it is an island nation that isolated itself from the world for a long time, Japan has one of the most homogeneous populations on Earth. Nearly all of the people belong to the same **ethnic group,** a group of people who share such characteristics as language, religion, ancestry, and cultural traditions. Minority groups are few. Small numbers of Koreans and Chinese also live in Japan. However, Japan has strict rules on immigration. It is hard for anyone who is not Japanese by birth to become a citizen.

✓ **Reading Check** **How are the people of China different from the people of the Koreas and Japan?**

Section 2 Assessment

Key Terms

Review the key terms at the beginning of this section. Use each term in a sentence that explains its meaning.

 Target Reading Skill

Find the last sentence on page 86. It includes the phrase *reminders of the past mingle with activities of the present*. Which phrases and words in the paragraph on page 86 help explain what the phrase means?

Comprehension and Critical Thinking

1. (a) Recall In what two major ways did the Communists make changes in the Chinese way of life?
(b) Summarize How is modern life in East Asia more visible in urban areas than in rural areas?
2. (a) Identify To which ethnic group do most Chinese people belong?
(b) Find Main Ideas and Details Why is China said to be an ethnically diverse country?
(c) Summarize Why are the populations of the Koreas and Japan homogeneous?

Writing Activity

Based on what you have read in this section, write a paragraph describing how tradition and change exist together in East Asia. Include at least three supporting details for your topic sentence.

For: An activity on East Asia's culture
Visit: PHSchool.com
Web Code: lcd-6402

Review and Assessment

◆ Chapter Summary

Section 1: Historic Traditions

- China has the oldest continuous civilization in the world. Starting in ancient times, a series of dynasties ruled China.
- Paper, gunpowder, silk weaving, and the magnetic compass are among China's many cultural and technical achievements.
- The Shilla people unified Korea as one country. A series of shoguns ruled Japan for more than 700 years.
- In the 1800s, western nations became interested in East Asia as a market to sell goods.

Japanese *No* mask

Section 2: People and Cultures

- China has been governed under a Communist system since 1949. The Communist party has made major changes in the Chinese way of life.
- Although China is becoming more modern, old traditions are still followed, especially in rural areas of the country.
- As in China, modern ways of life in the Koreas are more visible in urban areas. Japan is the most modern of the East Asian countries but also lives by its historic traditions.
- Most people in China belong to the Han ethnic group. Korea's history resulted in a homogeneous population. As in the Koreas, nearly all Japanese people belong to the same ethnic group.

Shanghai, China

◆ Key Terms

Each of the statements below contains a key term from the chapter. If the statement is true, write *true*. If it is false, rewrite the statement to make it true.

1. An emperor is the male ruler of an empire.

2. A clan is a series of rulers from the same family.

3. A dynasty is a group of families with a common ancestor.

4. Cultural diffusion is the spreading of ideas or practices from one culture to other cultures.

5. People with the same dialect use a variation of a language that is unique to their region or area.

6. A nomad is a community in which people own land as a group and where they live together and work together.

7. A homogeneous group includes people who are identical or similar.

8. An ethnic group shares such characteristics as language, religion, ancestry, and cultural traditions.

◆ Comprehension and Critical Thinking

9. (a) Explain What is a civilization?
(b) Describe What are some achievements of the ancient Chinese civilization?
(c) Make Generalizations Give some examples of how ancient Chinese achievements still affect the world today.

10. (a) Recall To which ethnic group do most of the people in China belong?
(b) Summarize How does China's population differ from the populations of Japan and the Koreas in terms of ethnic diversity?

11. (a) Define What is a dynasty?
(b) Contrast How is China governed today, and how is that government different from China's government in ancient times?

12. (a) Recall About what percentage of people in Japan live in urban areas?
(b) Synthesize Information Give examples of how life in East Asia reflects past traditions and present traditions.
(c) Predict Why might past traditions be followed more in rural areas of East Asia than in urban areas?

13. (a) Recall When did the Communists come into power in China?
(b) Summarize What changes did the Communists make to the Chinese way of life?

◆ Skills Practice

Reading Route Maps In the Skills for Life activity in this chapter, you learned how to read route maps. Review the steps you followed to learn this skill. Then use the map on page 85 to name two rivers in Mesopotamia that the Silk Road crossed. If a traveler was heading west on the Silk Road, which river would he cross first?

◆ Writing Activity: History

As you have read in this chapter, paper was invented in ancient China, as were many other things. Choose one of the inventions named in this chapter, and do research in the library or on the Internet to learn more about it. Find out how it was made and used in ancient China. Also, find out how the invention spread to other parts of the world. Write a paragraph about what you have learned.

MAP✦MASTER™
Skills Activity

Place Location For each place listed below, write the letter from the map that shows its location.

1. Mongolia
2. China
3. Taiwan
4. North Korea
5. South Korea
6. Japan

Go Online
PHSchool.com Use Web Code lcp-6420 for an **interactive map.**

East Asia

Standardized Test Prep

Test-Taking Tips

Some questions on standardized tests ask you to analyze timelines. Study the timeline below. Then follow the tips to answer the sample question.

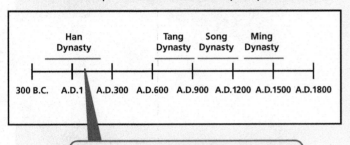

Han Dynasty | **Tang Dynasty** | **Song Dynasty** | **Ming Dynasty**

300 B.C. A.D.1 A.D.300 A.D.600 A.D.900 A.D.1200 A.D.1500 A.D.1800

TIP To read a timeline, first figure out the timespan between dates (in this case it is 300 years). Then line up each event or dynasty with the nearest date or dates and estimate.

Pick the letter that best answers the question.

The world's oldest printed book was found in China. It was made around A.D. 868, during the

A Han dynasty.

B Tang dynasty.

C Song dynasty.

D Ming dynasty.

Think It Through The oldest book was made around A.D. 868. You can eliminate Han and Ming (A and D) because they are not near that date. Now look closely at the timeline: A.D. 868 is between A.D. 600 and A.D. 900. The Song Dynasty started *after* A.D. 900. So the correct answer is B, the Tang Dynasty.

TIP Rewrite the sentence in your own words to make sure you understand what it is asking: *During which dynasty was the oldest book made?*

Practice Questions

Use the tips above and other tips in this book to help you answer the following questions.

1. Based on the timeline above, the Tang dynasty lasted about

   A 100 years.

   B 200 years.

   C 300 years.

   D 400 years.

2. The religion of Buddhism, which China adopted from India, is an example of

   A cultural migration.

   B irrigation.

   C cultural diffusion.

   D Communist rule.

3. Which statement correctly describes Chinese culture?

   A Everyone in China belongs to the same ethnic group.

   B Chinese people speak different dialects from region to region.

   C Old traditions and ways of life are illegal in China.

   D There are two ethnic groups in China.

Go Online
PHSchool.com

Use Web Code **lca-6400** for **Chapter 4 self-test.**

Chapter Preview

In this chapter, you will learn about the cultures and history of three regions in Asia: South Asia, Southwest Asia, and Central Asia.

Target Reading Skill

Word Analysis In this chapter, you will focus on analyzing words. For example, you will learn to break unfamiliar words into parts to understand the words.

▶ Amber Fort is one of the many forts and palaces of South Asia. It is located in India.

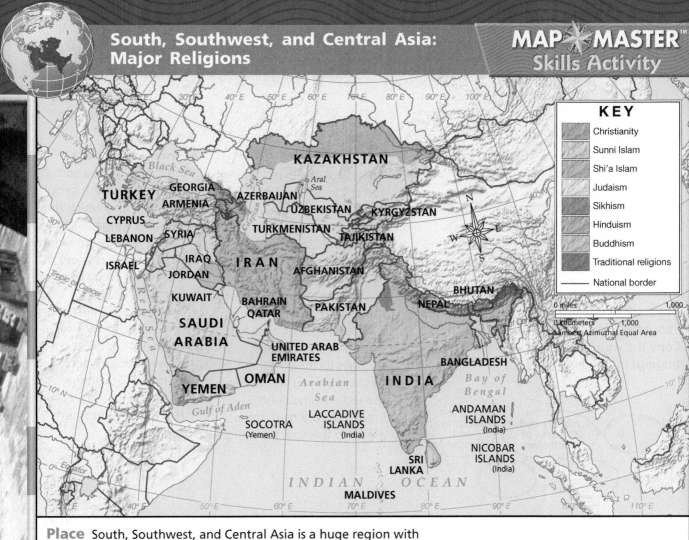

KEY

	Christianity
	Sunni Islam
	Shi'a Islam
	Judaism
	Sikhism
	Hinduism
	Buddhism
	Traditional religions
——	National border

Place South, Southwest, and Central Asia is a huge region with many different religions. They include the two major branches of Islam, Sunni and Shi'a. **Identify** What is the major religion in Saudi Arabia? **Contrast** How is India different from Saudi Arabia in terms of major religions?

Go Online
PHSchool.com Use Web Code lcp-6510 for step-by-step map skills practice.

Prepare to Read

Objectives

In this section, you will

1. Find out which religions became part of South Asian cultures.
2. Understand which empires shaped the history of South Asia.
3. Learn about the present-day religions and languages of South Asian cultures.

Taking Notes

As you read this section, look for main ideas about the history and cultures of South Asia. Copy the web below, and record your findings in it.

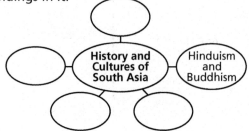

Target Reading Skill

Analyze Word Parts When you come across a word you do not know, break the word into parts to help you recognize it and pronounce it. This may help you find its root and prefix. A root is the part of the word that has meaning by itself. A prefix goes in front of the root and changes its meaning. In this section you will find the word *nonviolent*. Break it into a root and a prefix to learn its meaning.

Key Terms

- **caste** (kast) *n.* in the Hindu religion, a social group into which people are born and which they cannot change; each group with assigned jobs
- **colony** (KAHL uh nee) *n.* a territory ruled by another nation
- **boycott** (BOY kaht) *n.* a refusal to buy or use goods and services to show disapproval or bring about change
- **partition** (pahr TISH un) *n.* a division into parts or portions

In 1921, scientists digging near the Indus River came upon the ruins of an ancient city they called Mohenjo-Daro (moh HEN joh DAH roh). The city was amazingly well planned, with wide, straight streets and large buildings. It had a sewer system and a large walled fortress. Mohenjo-Daro was part of a civilization that developed about 4,500 years ago. The people who lived there were part of the Indus Valley civilization, one of the world's oldest civilizations.

Over the centuries, many other people moved into South Asia. All of them contributed to South Asian culture. South Asian culture, in turn, influenced cultures of other regions. Hinduism (HIN doo iz um) and Buddhism (BOO diz um), two religions that developed in South Asia, are practiced by hundreds of millions of people all over the world.

This ancient statue of a priest-king was unearthed at Mohenjo-Daro.

New Religions

The Indus Valley civilization flourished from about 2500 B.C. to about 1600 B.C. By 1500 B.C., however, the civilization was coming to an end. Scholars are uncertain why this happened.

About the same time that the Indus Valley civilization was weakening, newcomers came to the region, probably from Central Asia. They brought different languages and beliefs to the region. The newcomers merged with the people of the Indus Valley. A new culture combined the ancient languages and beliefs of the region with the language and religion of the newcomers. This mixed culture is known as Aryan culture. The people who practiced this culture are known as Aryans (AYR ee unz).

The Aryans ruled northern India for more than 1,000 years. They divided people into four classes—priests and the educated; rulers and warriors; farmers, artisans, and merchants; and laborers. Europeans later called the division the caste (kast) system. A **caste** is a social group into which people are born and which they cannot change.

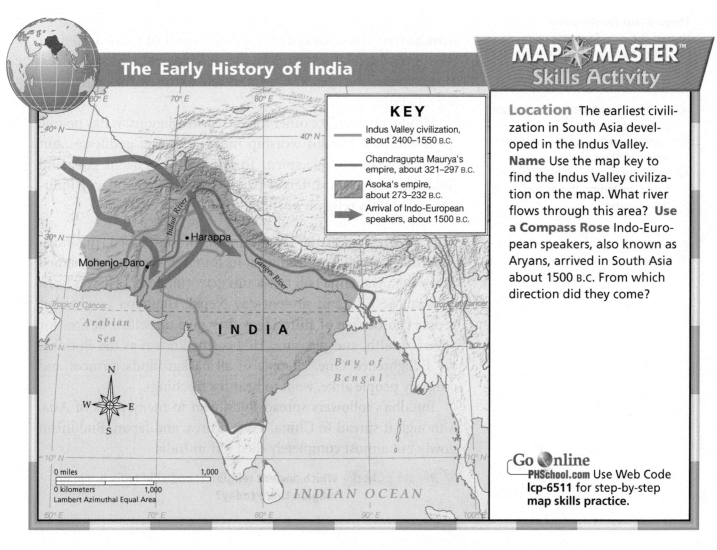

The Early History of India

MAP MASTER™
Skills Activity

KEY

— Indus Valley civilization, about 2400–1550 B.C.

— Chandragupta Maurya's empire, about 321–297 B.C.

▓ Asoka's empire, about 273–232 B.C.

➡ Arrival of Indo-European speakers, about 1500 B.C.

Harappa

Mohenjo-Daro

Indus River

Ganges River

Tropic of Cancer

Arabian Sea

I N D I A

Bay of Bengal

0 miles 1,000
0 kilometers 1,000
Lambert Azimuthal Equal Area

INDIAN OCEAN

Location The earliest civilization in South Asia developed in the Indus Valley. **Name** Use the map key to find the Indus Valley civilization on the map. What river flows through this area? **Use a Compass Rose** Indo-European speakers, also known as Aryans, arrived in South Asia about 1500 B.C. From which direction did they come?

Go Online
PHSchool.com Use Web Code **lcp-6511** for step-by-step map skills practice.

Three Main Hindu Gods
One of the world's oldest religions, Hinduism dates back more than 3,000 years. Shown here are the three main gods in the Hindu trinity

① Brahma is regarded as the creator of the universe.
② Vishnu is worshipped as the pre-server of the universe.
③ Shiva appears in many different forms, including the destroyer of the universe.

Hinduism The caste system was one aspect of a new system of belief that also emerged from Aryan religious ideas and practices. This system of beliefs, Hinduism, is one of the world's oldest living religions.

Hinduism is unlike other major world religions. It has no one single founder. Hindus worship many gods and goddesses, but they believe in a single spirit. To Hindus, the various gods and goddesses represent different parts of this spirit. Today, Hinduism is the main religion of India.

Buddhism Buddhism, like Hinduism, developed in India. According to Buddhist tradition, its founder was a prince named Siddhartha Gautama (sih DAHR tuh GOW tuh muh). He was born in about 560 B.C., in present-day Nepal. Gautama taught that people can be free of suffering if they give up selfish desires for power, wealth, and pleasure. He became known as the Buddha, or "Enlightened One." People of all backgrounds, princes and ordinary people alike, went to hear his teachings.

Buddha's followers spread Buddhism to many parts of Asia. Although it spread to China, Tibet, Korea, and Japan, Buddhism slowly but almost completely died out in India.

✓ Reading Check **Which ancient religion founded in India is a main religion there today?**

From Empires to Nations

Today, South Asia is a region of independent countries. Starting in ancient times, however, a series of empires rose and fell in the region. Before South Asian countries became independent in the 1900s, the region was under European control.

The Maurya Empire Around 321 B.C., a leader named Chandragupta Maurya (chun druh GOOP tuh MOWR yuh) conquered many kingdoms. By the time of his death in 298 B.C., the Maurya Empire covered much of the Indian subcontinent.

Chandragupta's grandson, Asoka (uh SOH kuh), became emperor in 268 B.C. After one bloody battle, Asoka gave up war and violence. He changed his beliefs to Buddhism and vowed to rule peacefully. Asoka had stone pillars set up across India. Carved into the pillars were his laws and beliefs in fair and just government.

The Maurya Empire lost power not long after Asoka's death. By about 185 B.C. the empire collapsed as rival leaders fought for power.

The Gupta Empire About 500 years after the Mauryas, the Gupta Empire again united much of the Indian subcontinent. The Guptas ruled from A.D. 320 to about A.D. 550. Gupta emperors set up a strong central government that was supported by trade and farming.

Under Gupta rule, India enjoyed a period of great cultural achievement. Gupta mathematicians developed the system of writing numerals that we use today. These numerals are called "Arabic" numerals. Arabs carried them from India to Southwest Asia and Europe. People built splendid temples of stone decorated with carvings. Artists created wall paintings of Buddhist stories in temples built inside caves at Ajanta (uh JUN tuh) in western India.

Weak rulers and foreign invaders led to the fall of the Gupta Empire. The empire lasted until about A.D. 550.

The Mughal Empire In the A.D. 700s, people from the north began moving into northern India. They introduced the religion of Islam to the area. According to its followers, Islam is the set of beliefs revealed to the prophet Muhammad. He began teaching these beliefs around A.D. 610 in Southwest Asia. Islam eventually spread westward into North Africa and eastward into Central and South Asia.

This lion sculpture originally stood at the top of one of Asoka's pillars.

Links to Math

Decimal Numbers By about A.D. 600, Indian astronomers were using the decimal system—a numbering system based on tens. Their system also had place values and a zero. This made it easy to add, subtract, multiply, and divide. Europeans were using Roman numerals at this time. They later switched to this decimal, or Hindu-Arabic, system, which is used worldwide today.

The Taj Mahal, India
The Taj Mahal is considered to be one of the world's most beautiful buildings. Emperor Shah Jahan had it built as a tomb for his wife. The small photo shows the actual tomb inside the marble structure. **Analyze Images** *How does the large photo show symmetry in the design of the Taj Mahal?*

Target Skill
Analyze Word Parts
Look for the word *subcontinent* in this paragraph. The prefix *sub-* means "under." Now define the word *subcontinent*.

Among these Muslims, or followers of Islam, who settled in India were the Mughals (MOO gulz). They arrived in the 1500s and established an empire. Akbar (AK bahr), who ruled the Mughal Empire from 1556 to 1605, allowed all people to worship freely, regardless of their religion. He also generously supported the arts and literature.

Akbar's grandson, Shah Jahan (shah juh HAHN), built many grand buildings. Perhaps the greatest is the Taj Mahal (tahzh muh HAHL), which still stands today. He had it built as a magnificent tomb for Mumtaz Mahal (mum TAHZ muh HAHL), his wife. The cost of this and other of Jahan's building projects was enormous. It drained the empire of money and, eventually, helped to cause the empire's collapse in the 1700s.

The British in India By the late 1700s, much of the Indian subcontinent had come under British rule. Until 1858, a trading company known as the British East India Company controlled most of India. The British government ended the rule of the British East India Company in 1858. From that time until 1947, India was controlled by Britain as a colony of Britain's empire. A **colony** is a territory ruled by another nation.

Independence and Division In the early 1900s, a strong independence movement emerged in India. Its leader was Mohandas K. Gandhi (GAHN dee). Gandhi called for people to resist British rule. However, Gandhi stressed that they use nonviolent means. For example, he urged a boycott of British goods. A boycott means a refusal to buy or use goods and services to show disapproval or bring about change. Gandhi played a major part in forcing Britain to grant India its independence in 1947.

As independence approached, Muslims feared that their rights would not be protected in a land where Hindus were the majority. Fighting erupted as demands arose for a state where Muslims would be the majority. In 1947 this led to the partition, or division, of the subcontinent into two nations, Pakistan and India. Muslims would be the majority in Pakistan. Hindus would be the majority in India.

This partition did not stop the fighting. About one million people were killed. Gandhi himself was murdered by a Hindu who was angered at Gandhi's concern for Muslims.

Conflict in South Asia Conflict between India and Pakistan continued throughout the 1900s. In 1971, Indian troops helped East Pakistan break away from Pakistan to form the nation of Bangladesh (BAHNG luh desh). Pakistan and India have fought over the question of which country controls Kashmir (KASH mihr), an area on the border of India and Pakistan. In 1998, both nations tested nuclear weapons. The continuing threat of conflict that might involve nuclear weapons in the region concerns the United States and other countries.

✓ **Reading Check** What are some contributions from the Maurya, Gupta, and Mughal empires?

Indian Independence leader Mohandas Gandhi

Republic Day in India
Every January 26, Indians celebrate Republic Day to mark the adoption of the Indian constitution on January 26, 1950.
Infer Which national flag do you think is shown in the photo?

Selling spices at an open-air market in India

South Asian Cultures Today

South Asia's long history continues to shape its cultures. Two major examples are religion and languages.

Many Religions Hinduism and Islam are the major religions of South Asia today. About 80 percent of the people in India are Hindus. Hinduism is also the major religion in Nepal. Islam is the main religion in Pakistan and Bangladesh. Other religions in South Asia include Christianity, Sikhism (SEEK iz um), and Jainism (JY niz um). Sikhism began as a religion that combined Hindu and Muslim beliefs. Followers of Jainism believe that violence toward or injury of any living thing is wrong.

Many Languages Many different languages are spoken in South Asia. The languages of South Asia generally belong to two families. Dravidian (druh VID ee un) languages are spoken in southern India. Indo-European languages are spoken in northern India and most of the rest of South Asia. The Aryans who came into South Asia in ancient times spoke Indo-European languages. One of the languages in this group is Hindi (HIN dee). About 30 percent of the people in India speak Hindi. Hindi is one of 22 languages recognized by the Indian government. English is also widely used as an official language in India.

✓ **Reading Check** **In which two South Asian countries is Hinduism the major religion?**

Section 1 Assessment

Key Terms
Review the key terms at the beginning of this section. Use each term in a sentence that explains its meaning.

Target Reading Skill
Find the word *uncertain* on page 97 in the first paragraph under the heading New Religions. The prefix *un-* means "not." What is the meaning of *uncertain*?

Comprehension and Critical Thinking
1. (a) Recall Which group of people developed the caste system?
(b) Sequence Which developed first, Hinduism or Buddhism?
2. (a) Name Which empire introduced Islam to South Asia?
(b) Identify Effect What major issues led to the partition of India in 1947?
3. (a) Identify What is the main religion in Pakistan?
(b) Make Generalizations How can the movement of people from one place to another affect language in a region?

Writing Activity
Suppose you are traveling throughout South Asia. Write a letter to your family in which you describe ways in which the history of the region is shown in its present-day culture.

Writing Tip Your letter should begin with a greeting and end with a closing and a signature. The body of the letter contains the information you want to communicate to your reader.

Southwest Asia
Cultures and History

Prepare to Read

Objectives

In this section, you will

1. Find out that one of the world's earliest civilizations grew in Southwest Asia.
2. Understand that three of the world's great religions began in Southwest Asia.
3. Examine the different ethnic groups and religions of Southwest Asia.
4. Learn about the conflict between Arabs and Israelis in Southwest Asia.

Taking Notes

As you read this section, look for details about the three main religions that developed in Southwest Asia. Copy the chart below, and record your findings in it.

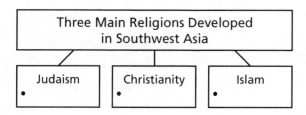

Three Main Religions Developed in Southwest Asia
- Judaism
- Christianity
- Islam

Target Reading Skill

Analyze Word Parts Breaking an unfamiliar word into parts can help you understand the word. Word parts include roots and suffixes. A root is the base of a word that has meaning by itself. A suffix comes at the end of a root word. Suffixes change the meanings of root words. In this section you will read the word *creation*. The suffix *-ion* makes the word a noun. If you know what *create* means, you can figure out the meaning of *creation*.

Key Terms

- **monotheism** (MAHN oh thee iz um) *n.* a belief that there is only one god
- **muezzin** (myoo EZ in) *n.* a person whose job is to call Muslims to pray
- **Holocaust** (HAHL uh kawst) *n.* the systematic killing of more than six million European Jews and others by Nazi Germany before and during World War II

Hammurabi's Code was written about 3,800 years ago in Southwest Asia. People have described its laws as demanding "an eye for an eye." But there was more to the code than that.

> **If the robber is not caught, the man who has been robbed shall formally declare whatever he has lost . . . and the city and the mayor . . . shall replace whatever he has lost for him. . . . If a person is too lazy to make the dike of his field strong and there is a break in the dike and water destroys his own farmland, that person will make good the grain [tax] that is destroyed.**
>
> —*from Hammurabi's Code*

The law punished people severely for wrongdoings. But it also offered justice to people who had been hurt through no fault of their own.

In this ancient carving, Hammurabi receives his code of laws from the sun god.

Mesopotamia

Hammurabi ruled the city of Babylon from about 1800 B.C. to 1750 B.C. He united the region along the Tigris and Euphrates rivers. Located in present-day Iraq, this region was called Mesopotamia, which is derived from Greek words meaning "between the rivers." Mesopotamia was one of the world's earliest civilizations.

The people of Mesopotamia developed a system of writing. They also produced ideas about law that still affect people today. For example, they believed that all citizens must obey the same set of laws.

People had lived in Mesopotamia for thousands of years before Hammurabi united it. By 3500 B.C., the area became a center of farming and trade. The Tigris and Euphrates rivers flooded every year, leaving fertile soil along their banks. People dug irrigation ditches to bring water to fields that lay far from the river. Irrigation helped them to produce crop surpluses, or more than they needed for their own use.

✓ **Reading Check** **In what present-day country did Mesopotamia develop?**

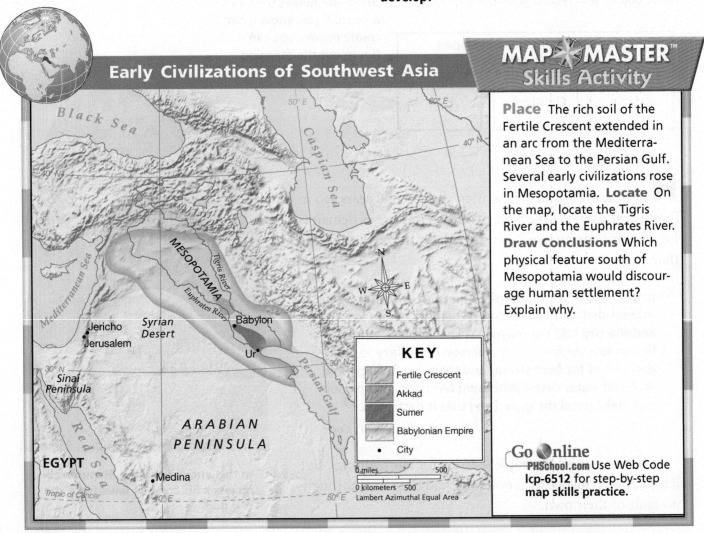

Early Civilizations of Southwest Asia

MAP MASTER™
Skills Activity

Place The rich soil of the Fertile Crescent extended in an arc from the Mediterranean Sea to the Persian Gulf. Several early civilizations rose in Mesopotamia. **Locate** On the map, locate the Tigris River and the Euphrates River. **Draw Conclusions** Which physical feature south of Mesopotamia would discourage human settlement? Explain why.

KEY
Fertile Crescent
Akkad
Sumer
Babylonian Empire
• City

Go Online
PHSchool.com Use Web Code lcp-6512 for step-by-step map skills practice.

0 miles   500
0 kilometers   500
Lambert Azimuthal Equal Area

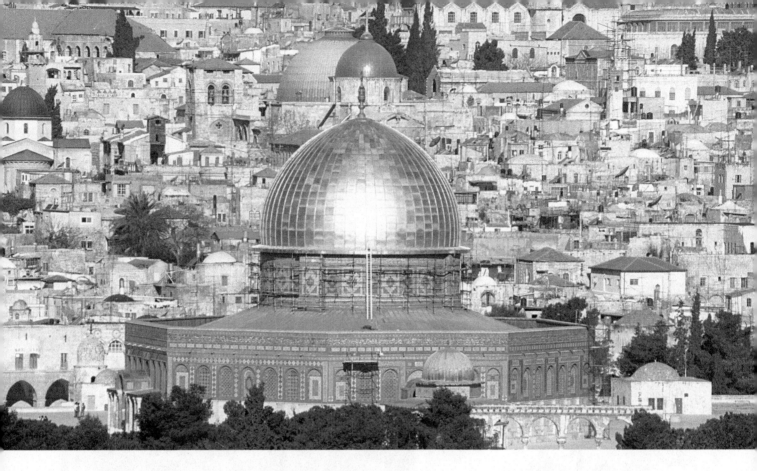

Birthplace of Three Religions

Three of the world's greatest religions—Judaism, Christianity, and Islam—have their roots in Southwest Asia. About 2000 B.C., according to Hebrew religious writings, a man later known as Abraham founded the religion that would become known as Judaism. He lived in present-day Israel. Almost 2,000 years later, Jesus, the founder of Christianity, began preaching in present-day Israel. In about A.D. 600, Islam's founder and prophet, Muhammad, began teaching in present-day Saudi Arabia.

People who practice these three religions share a belief in monotheism. **Monotheism** is a belief in only one god. The followers of these religions also worship the same God—known as Allah in Islam.

Islam Of the three religions, Islam has by far the most followers in Southwest Asia today. They are called Muslims. The sights and sounds of Islam are everywhere in Southwest Asia. One sound is the call of the **muezzin** (myoo EZ in), a person whose job is to call Muslims to pray. Five times a day, Muslims stop what they are doing and pray. In large cities, the call to prayer is broadcast over loudspeakers. Throughout Southwest Asia, as well as other regions in the world, Muslims gather to worship in buildings called mosques. One of the most famous is the Dome of the Rock, shown in the photo on this page.

Jerusalem, A Holy City
Jerusalem is holy to Jews, Christians, and Muslims because events important to their religions took place there. The golden-domed building is the Dome of the Rock. It stands over the rock from which Muslims believe the prophet Muhammad rose into heaven. **Infer** *Why might Muslims from around the world want to visit Jerusalem?*

This woman is praying at the Western Wall, held sacred by Jews as the remains of the Second Temple.

The New Testament of the Christian Bible describes Jesus as a good shepherd who lays down his life for his sheep.

Judaism At the heart of Judaism is the Torah (TOH ruh), five books that make up the Jews' most sacred text. According to the Torah, about 2000 B.C. Abraham, a Mesopotamian man, became convinced that there was one god, not many. He migrated to Canaan, where he became the ancestor of the Jewish people. Canaan was an area of land located along the eastern shore of the Mediterranean Sea. Hundreds of years later, it became known as Palestine. From ancient times, Jews saw Palestine as their homeland. The Torah also contains the Ten Commandments. They established religious duties toward God as well as rules for moral and ethical behavior.

Christianity Christianity first developed around A.D. 30. The religion is based on the teachings of Jesus, a Jew who traveled throughout Palestine. Christians later adopted the Torah as the first five books of the Old Testament of the Christian Bible. The first four books of the New Testament of the Christian Bible are the Gospels. They tell about the life and teachings of Jesus. According to the Gospels, Jesus taught that his followers would have eternal life. Like Islam and Judaism, Christianity began in Southwest Asia and spread throughout the world.

✓ Reading Check Why is Southwest Asia considered the birthplace of Judaism, Christianity, and Islam?

Diverse Cultures in Southwest Asia

More than 3,000 years ago, the land of Southwest Asia was at the center of trading routes that extended across Europe, Africa, and Asia. Time after time, groups from within and outside the region conquered it. The movement of people across Southwest Asia gave the region a unique character. People of many different ethnic groups and religious beliefs settled there.

Arabic-speaking Arabs are the largest ethnic group in the region, and Islam is their main religion. But not all Southwest Asians are Arabs. Many Southwest Asians do not speak Arabic and many people, including Arabic-speaking Arabs, practice religions other than Islam.

A Mix of Ethnic Groups The people in Southwest Asia belong to a mix of ethnic groups. Today, Arabs are the main ethnic group in Saudi Arabia, Jordan, Syria, Iraq, Lebanon, and other countries on the Arabian Peninsula. Arabs also live in territories occupied by Israel. Non-Arab people live mainly in Israel, Turkey, and Iran. In Israel, about 80 percent of the population is Jewish. The remaining 20 percent is mostly Arab. In Turkey, about 80 percent of the population is Turkish. The rest of Turkey's population is Kurdish. Kurdish people also live in communities in Syria, Iraq, and Iran. In Iran, about 50 percent of the people are Persian. The rest belong to a number of different ethnic groups.

A Variety of Religions Except for Israel, the majority of the people in each country in Southwest Asia are Muslim. Even within the Islamic religion, however, there are differences. Muslims are divided into two main groups—Sunnis (SOO neez) and Shi'as (SHEE uz). Today, about 90 percent of Muslims are Sunni. Most of the Muslims in both Iran and Iraq, however, are Shi'as.

In Israel, about 80 percent of the people are Jewish. Muslims make up about 20 percent of the population. A small percentage of people in Israel are Christian. Christians also live in Syria, Turkey, Lebanon, and Iraq.

✓ Reading Check **To which branch of Islam do most Muslims belong?**

About half of Iran's population is Persian.

Scenes of Hope
A Jewish boy and a Palestinian boy walk together in Israel (left). Israeli troops supervise the evacuation of Jewish residents from the Gaza Strip in 2005 (right). **Infer** *Why might friendship and compromise help solve conflict?*

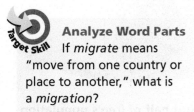

Analyze Word Parts
If *migrate* means "move from one country or place to another," what is a *migration*?

Southwest Asia: Recent History

Differences among various groups of people have led to conflict in Southwest Asia. As you have read, Judaism has ancient roots in Palestine. Over many years, a few Jews continued to live in Palestine. But most had been forced in ancient times to migrate to other parts of the world. In the late 1800s, Jews from around the world began to return to their homeland. This alarmed the Arabs who lived there. For hundreds of years, they had claimed Palestine as their homeland, too.

The Formation of Israel Before and during World War II, Nazi Germany killed more than six million Jews in Europe solely because they were Jewish. This became known as the **Holocaust**. After the war, many of those who had survived decided to migrate to Palestine. On May 14, 1948, Jews declared the formation of their own state, Israel. Their state was recognized by the United Nations.

Arab-Israeli Conflict The day after the state of Israel was declared, the Arab nations of Egypt, Iraq, Jordan, Lebanon, and Syria invaded Israel. These nations supported the Palestinians. Israel drove away the Arab forces. Hundreds of thousands of Palestinians fled from Jewish territory. They lived as refugees in other Arab nations or in territories under Israeli rule. Even larger numbers of Jews were forced to leave Arab countries, and most resettled in Israel. Since 1948, Israel and the Arab nations that border it have fought a number of bloody wars.

Efforts Toward Peace In 1993, Israel and the Palestinian government—known as the Palestine Liberation Organization (PLO)—formally recognized each other. In 2000, fighting broke out between Israel and the Palestinians once again. In 2003, Israeli leaders and the PLO agreed on a new peace plan, which called for the co-existence of Israel and a democratic Palestine. In 2005, Israel withdrew its settlements from the Gaza Strip. Due to renewed fighting in the area, however, future progress is uncertain.

War With Iraq After Iraq's defeat in the 1991 Persian Gulf War, Iraqi leader Saddam Hussein (suh DAHM hoo SAYN) refused to cooperate with United Nations inspectors sent to ensure that Iraq destroyed its most dangerous weapons. In March 2003, U.S. forces attacked Iraq in an invasion supported by Great Britain and several other nations. Three weeks after the start of the war, Saddam fell from power. He was captured by U.S. troops in December 2003. Although Iraq remains unstable, it successfully held democratic national elections and approved a constitution in 2005.

Iraqis line up to vote for new leaders in the city of Suleimaniya in 2005.

✓ **Reading Check** Give one example of conflict in Southwest Asia.

Section 2 Assessment

Key Terms
Review the key terms at the beginning of this section. Use each term in a sentence that explains its meaning.

Target Reading Skill
Define *irrigation*. The root word means "to supply with water by artificial methods." The suffix *–ion* means "act or process."

Comprehension and Critical Thinking
1. (a) Identify Tell where Mesopotamia is located.
(b) Summarize What are two achievements of the civilizations of Mesopotamia?

2. (a) List What three major religions grew in Southwest Asia?
(b) Contrast What do all three religions have in common?
3. (a) Name What is Southwest Asia's main ethnic group today?
(b) Analyze Information Give one example of ethnic or religious diversity in the region of Southwest Asia.
4. (a) Name What area do both Palestinians and Israelis claim as a homeland?
(b) Summarize How has Iraq moved toward establishing a democratic form of government?

Writing Activity
Write a paragraph that begins with this topic sentence: *Southwest Asia is a region with different ethnic groups and religious beliefs.* Include supporting details about at least three countries in the region.

Writing Tip Include at least two sentences about ethnic groups and at least two sentences about religions. Be sure to include supporting details.

Recognizing Bias

A baseball coach chooses his own son over other, better players, to play in a tournament game. The mayor hires her friends to fill important city jobs instead of seeking the most qualified people. The politician who wants to give business to family members says his son-in-law is the best builder to build a new school.

All these situations are examples of bias. Bias is an attitude that favors one way of feeling or acting over any other. Bias prevents someone from making a fair judgment based on facts and reason. Biased speech or writing often contains opinions stated as facts.

Learn the Skill

Knowing how to recognize bias is an important skill you will need in school and in life. To identify bias in what you read, follow the steps below.

1 **Look for opinions.** Opinions are beliefs that cannot be proved. Biased statements often appear to be facts but are actually opinions.

2 **Look for loaded words and phrases and exaggerations.** Loaded words and phrases cannot be proved. They are intended to produce a strong emotional response. To exaggerate means to enlarge a fact or statement beyond what is actual or true.

3 **Look for missing facts.** Biased speech often leaves out facts that do not support the author's bias.

4 **Determine whether the text presents only one point of view.** Writing that is biased presents only one point of view about an issue or a topic. The point of view may be positive or negative.

5 **Determine whether the text contains bias.** Review the text and draw a conclusion about it.

Traveling Through Turkey by Bus

A group of 150 American tourists spent a busy morning at a market in Istanbul, Turkey, arriving at 7 AM just as sellers opened for business.

The Americans were visiting Istanbul on a tour to study the cultures of Turkey. The tourists spent about an hour shopping at the market.

"We usually don't get such a large group so early in the morning," one shop owner commented.

The tourists arrived so early that some shop owners had not yet opened for business. In a narrow section of the market, four tourists bumped into a display and knocked it over. The visitors stopped to help the shop owner fix the display.

The next stop for the Americans' cultural tour will be Turkey's capital, Ankara. The group is traveling through Turkey by bus.

Greedy Tourists Mob Market

A crowd of greedy American tourists invaded a market in the city of Istanbul, Turkey, buying everything in sight.

In a burst of energy rarely seen from Americans who prefer to drive everywhere instead of walk, the bargain-hunters swarmed out of tour buses to examine the products on display. Shop owners were overwhelmed as the impatient Americans roamed through the market.

One group of tourists overturned tables in their quest for bargains.

Americans should use better manners when they shop in other countries instead of barging into stores and being rude.

The next stop for the mob of American tourists is Turkey's capital city, Ankara.

Practice the Skill

Read the two reports above. Then use the steps on the previous page to determine which report shows bias.

1. Opinions often contain words such as *I believe* and *should*. Which report contains an opinion?

2. Look for loaded words or phrases and exaggerations in the reports. How is the phrase "greedy American tourists" an example of a loaded phrase? Which report contains the phrase "buying everything in sight"? Is this a factual statement or an exaggeration?

3. Which report includes facts, such as the number of tourists and the time of day?

4. Which report presents a point of view about American tourists? Is the point of view negative or positive?

5. Based on your review, which report shows bias? State the bias in a complete sentence.

A market in Istanbul, Turkey

Apply the Skill

Find an article about Turkey in the news, either in a newspaper or a magazine. Use the steps shown here to decide whether the article contains bias. Explain your reasoning.

Central Asia
Cultures and History

Prepare to Read

Objectives

In this section, you will

1. Learn that many cultures and peoples influenced Central Asia in ancient times.
2. Discover how Central Asian nations became independent and why they are a focus of world interest.

Taking Notes

As you read this section, look for details about the topics listed in the outline below. Copy and continue the outline and record your details in it.

```
I. Meeting Place of Empires
   A. Early history
      1. _____
      2. _____
   B. The Silk Road
      1. _____
      2. _____
```

 Target Reading Skill

Recognize Word Origins A word's origin is where the word comes from. The word *government* contains the root word *govern*, which comes from the Latin word *gubernare*, meaning "to steer." The suffix *-ment* means "act or process." Knowing a word's origin can better help you understand the word's meaning. How is government related to the process of "steering" a country?

Key Term

- **collective farm** (kuh LEK tiv farhm) *n.* in a Communist country, a large farm formed from many private farms collected into a single unit controlled by the government

American fighter planes prepare for takeoff at an airbase in Central Asia. They are part of a new U.S. military force in the region. American soldiers came to fight a war in Afghanistan in 2001. Now they are based in several Central Asian countries.

American troops are not the only foreign visitors in Central Asia these days. Russian soldiers are also there. Political leaders from various countries are making official visits. Investors and business leaders are arriving too. They are coming from the United States, Russia, China, France, Turkey, and other countries. All these foreign visitors reflect Central Asia's growing international importance. The new countries of Central Asia are becoming the focus of world attention.

A growing film industry is one example of change in Central Asia.

Meeting Place of Empires

Long ago, Central Asia was a meeting place for ancient cultures and peoples. Located between East Asia and Europe, Central Asia was a crossroads for trade caravans and conquering armies. Over time, dozens of ethnic groups settled there. Each group brought new ideas and ways of living.

The Silk Road More than 2,000 years ago, a trade route called the Silk Road linked China and Europe. The Silk Road brought Central Asia into contact with East Asia, Southwest Asia, and Europe. For hundreds of years, caravans brought Chinese silk and Asian spices to the West. They carried items such as glass, wool, gold, and silver to the East. Along with goods, the traders exchanged ideas and inventions. Cities like Samarkand (sam ur KAND), in present-day Uzbekistan (ooz BEK ih stan), grew up at oases along the route and became wealthy centers of trade and learning.

Invasion and Conquest The Silk Road generated wealth, but it also attracted invaders. Waves of conquerors fought to control Central Asia. Although some ruled for hundreds of years, each group was eventually replaced by new invaders.

Each conqueror left a mark on the region. For example, about A.D. 700, a Muslim empire spread across large stretches of Central Asia. The Muslims had the greatest impact on the culture of the region. Many of the people of Central Asia adopted Islam. Today, most people in this region are Muslims.

Links Across The World

Lands for Empires In the 1200s, much of Central Asia was part of the largest land empire the world has ever known. Genghis Khan (GEN gis kahn), a leader of the Mongols, united his nomadic people into a strong fighting force. He conquered much of China and then swept west over Central Asia. At his death in 1227, his empire extended from the Sea of Japan to the Caspian Sea.

Ashgabat's Sunday Market
Ashgabat is the capital and largest city of Turkmenistan. Its Sunday market attracts thousands of people. Here, a family displays the traditional dark red carpets of Turkmenistan. **Compare and Contrast** *How is shopping at an outdoor market similar to and different from the way most Americans shop?*

By the late 1200s, the rise of sea trade led to the decline of the Silk Road. Ships began carrying goods between China and the seaports of Europe. These sea routes were faster and easier than the overland routes across Asia. As a result, trade declined in Central Asia. This, however, did not stop foreign powers from trying to control the region.

Under Russian Rule In the 1800s, both Russia and Britain tried to expand their empires into Central Asia. Russia was more successful. One of the most important cities Russia captured was the city of Tashkent, Uzbekistan, in 1865.

Russia built railroads, factories, and large farms in Central Asia. Some Russians moved into the region, bringing new ways of life. But most people continued to live as they always had. They practiced Islam and lived as nomadic herders.

The Soviet Union In 1922, Russian Communists formed the Soviet Union. The Soviets extended Communist control over a vast area of Central Asia. They divided the region into five separate states, which they called republics. They also forced people to stop living as nomads and give up their traditional way of life. People had to work on **collective farms,** large farms controlled by the government. The Communist government formed collectives by taking over smaller private farms and livestock herds and combining them into larger units. Soviet collectives did not always produce enough food for people to eat. At least one million Central Asians starved to death during the 1930s.

While the Soviets built new industries, schools, and hospitals in Central Asia, they allowed people few freedoms. The Soviets outlawed the practice of religion and tried to stamp out Muslim culture. Many mosques—places of Islamic worship—were torn down in the mid-1900s.

War in Afghanistan In 1979, the Soviets tried to extend their control over Central Asia by invading Afghanistan. Afghan forces fought the Soviets, and the Afghan fighters called themselves mujahedin (moo jah heh DEEN), or Islamic holy warriors. In ten years of warfare, the Soviet army never defeated the Afghan forces. In 1989, the Soviets finally gave up and withdrew their troops.

War continued, however, as the Afghans fought each other for power. Eventually, in the mid 1990s, a group known as the Taliban took control of most of the country. The brutal regime collapsed in 2001 after a U.S.-led military invasion. Hamid Karzai was elected president of Afghanistan in a 2004 democratic election. Members of the National Assembly were elected the following year.

✓ Reading Check **What impact did Soviet rule have on Central Asia?**

A woman in Kyrgyzstan plays a traditional stringed instrument.

After Independence

The Soviet defeat in Afghanistan helped bring an end to Soviet power. In 1991, the Soviet Union broke up. The five Soviet republics of Central Asia became independent nations.

The New States After independence, each of these countries adopted a name that reflected its main ethnic group. The suffix -*stan* is a Persian term that means "place of, or land." So, for example, Kazakhstan means "place of the Kazakhs," or "Kazakh land." Together with Afghanistan, these countries are sometimes referred to as "the Stans."

The new countries are different in many ways. The largest country, Kazakhstan, is mostly flat and has important natural resources, such as oil and natural gas. The smallest country, Tajikistan, is mountainous and very poor. Nevertheless, the countries have many things in common, including Islamic culture. They also face many of the same challenges as they work to develop their economies.

Children at their desks at a school in Kyrgyzstan

Recognize Word Origins

Find the word *governing* in the first sentence of this paragraph. Compare this word to the word *government*. What is the same? What is different?

Challenges and Opportunities Since independence, the new countries of Central Asia have learned to start governing themselves. Most are weighed down by weak economies. Many people do not have jobs. Health care and education are poor and hard to get.

However, all the countries of Central Asia now proudly celebrate their culture and Islam. Mosques that had fallen into ruin are being rebuilt. The people of Central Asia are teaching their children about their religion. Other benefits of independence include the right to use native languages in schools, literature, and the daily news media.

✓ **Reading Check** What does the suffix *-stan* mean in the names of the Central Asian countries?

Section 3 Assessment

Key Terms

Review the key terms at the beginning of this section. Use each term in a sentence that explains its meaning.

 Target Reading Skill

You read about the benefits of independence in Central Asia in this section. The Latin root word *bene* means "good or well." What do you think *benefit* means?

Comprehension and Critical Thinking

1. (a) Recall Where is Central Asia located?

(b) Identify Effects Describe one way that Soviet rule affected Central Asia.

2. (a) Explain How did the Central Asian republics under Soviet control gain their independence?

(b) Identify Central Issues How has Central Asia changed since becoming independent from the former Soviet Union?

(c) Make Generalizations Central Asian countries are now in charge of their own governments. You read that the root word of *governing* means "to steer." How is governing a country related to the idea of steering?

Writing Activity

The countries of Central Asia have many tasks to accomplish as they organize their nations. Using the information in this section, write a list of the challenges facing Central Asian countries. Write a brief explanation of why you think each challenge is an important one to tackle.

For: An activity about Central Asia
Visit: PHSchool.com
Web Code: lcd-6503

Review and Assessment

◆ Chapter Summary

Section 1: South Asia Cultures and History

- Two ancient religions, Hinduism and Buddhism, developed in India. Hinduism is a major religion in South Asia today.
- During its long history, South Asia has been shaped by Indian empires and British rule.
- South Asia's religions and languages have been affected by the region's history.

Ancient Indian sculpture

Section 2: Southwest Asia Cultures and History

- One of the world's earliest civilizations grew in Southwest Asia.
- Three of the world's greatest religions have their roots in Southwest Asia.
- People of many different ethnic groups and religious beliefs settled in Southwest Asia.
- Differences among various people, especially over land claims, have led to conflict and struggle in Southwest Asia.

Section 3: Central Asia Cultures and History

- A crossroads between East Asia and Europe, Central Asia was influenced by many cultures and peoples in ancient times.
- After decades of Soviet rule, independent nations emerged in Central Asia and are working to govern themselves.

Samarkand, Uzbekistan

◆ Key Terms

Each of the statements below contains a key term from the chapter. If the statement is true, write *true*. If the statement is false, rewrite the statement to make it true.

1. According to Hinduism, a caste is a social group into which people are born and which they cannot change.

2. A boycott is a refusal to buy or use goods and services to show disapproval or bring about social or political change.

3. A colony is an independent nation that has its own government.

4. Monotheism is the belief that there is only one god.

5. A muezzin is a person whose job is to call Muslims to prayer.

6. More than six million Jews and others died in the Holocaust.

7. A collective farm is owned and operated by one farmer.

Review and Assessment (continued)

◆ Comprehension and Critical Thinking

8. (a) Identify Identify Mohenjo-Daro.
(b) Sequence When did Aryans first come to South Asia?
(c) Identify Effects What new religion grew out of Aryan beliefs and practices?

9. (a) Recall Who is considered the founder of the religion Buddhism?
(b) Summarize Describe the spread of Buddhism after its founder's death.

10. (a) Identify Who was Asoka?
(b) Identify Effects How did Buddhist beliefs affect Asoka?

11. (a) Name Under which empire did India experience a period of great cultural achievement?
(b) Sequence Which empire followed that one?
(c) Contrast How were these two empires different in terms of religious beliefs?

12. (a) Recall Who played a major part in forcing Britain to grant independence to India?
(b) Analyze Why was India's independence followed by heavy fighting between Hindu and Muslim groups?

13. (a) Recall What are the two main religions in South Asia today?

(b) Apply Information What are other religions in South Asia?

14. (a) Identify Of the three religions founded in Southwest Asia, which has the most followers there today?
(b) Sequence Of the three religions founded in Southwest Asia, which is the oldest?

15. (a) Name What is the largest ethnic group in Southwest Asia today?
(b) Synthesize Information Give an example showing that Southwest Asia is a region of many different ethnic groups and religious beliefs.

◆ Skills Practice

Recognizing Bias Review the steps you followed on page 110 to learn this skill. Then write a sentence that explains what bias is.

◆ Writing Activity: Language Arts

The English language includes contributions from the Arabic language. Use a dictionary to research and learn about the history of these words: *admiral, algebra, cipher, cotton, sherbet,* and *zenith.* Write a paragraph on what you learned about the Arabic and English languages.

MAP★MASTER™
Skills Activity

South, Southwest, and Central Asia

Place Location For each place listed below, write the letter from the map that shows its location.

1. Iraq
2. Israel
3. Kazakhstan
4. Indus River
5. Afghanistan
6. Bangladesh

Go Online
PHSchool.com Use Web Code **lcp-6520** for an interactive map.

Standardized Test Prep

Test-Taking Tips

Some questions on standardized tests ask you to analyze a reading selection. Read the passage below. Then follow the tips to answer the sample question.

> The Silk Road was an important trade route across Central Asia that linked China and Europe more than 2,000 years ago. Caravans carried Chinese silk to the west. They also brought glass, wool, gold, and silver eastward. Merchants traded more than just goods. They also exchanged ideas and inventions. Many ancient cities along the Silk Road, including Samarkand, became wealthy centers of trade and learning.

Pick the letter that best answers the question.

One city that sprang up in Central Asia along the Silk Road was

A China.

B Europe.

C Mohenjo-Daro.

D Samarkand.

TIP Use what you know about geography and history to find the BEST answer choice.

Think It Through Reread the question: The answer must be a city in Central Asia. You can rule out A and B as they are not cities. That leaves C and D. In Section 1, you read that Mohenjo-Daro is an ancient city in South Asia. In Section 2, you read that Samarkand is in Central Asia. The correct answer is D.

Practice Questions

Use the reading selection below to answer Question 1.

> The discovery and production of oil in the Arabian Peninsula brought dramatic changes to Riyadh, Saudi Arabia's capital. Once a small country town, Riyadh is now a modern city with wide highways and skyscrapers of steel and glass. It boasts luxury hotels, large hospitals, and one of the biggest airports in the world. By 2003, Riyadh was one of the world's fastest-growing cities.

1. What conclusion can be made from this reading selection?

   A Riyadh benefited from a worldwide increase in air travel.

   B Riyadh is a fast-growing city because it has luxury hotels.

   C Wealth from Arabian oil production has transformed Riyadh.

   D Riyadh was the smallest town in Saudi Arabia.

Use the tips above and other tips in this book to help you answer the following questions.

2. Which of the following events in South Asia happened last?

   A Asoka ruled the Maurya Empire in India.

   B Aryans came to South Asia probably from Central Asia.

   C India became a colony in the British Empire.

   D During the Gupta Empire, mathematicians developed Arabic numerals.

3. People who practice Judaism, Christianity, and Islam share a belief in

   A the caste system.   B monotheism.

   C many gods.   D Buddha.

Use Web Code **lca-6500** for a **Chapter 5** self-test.

Chapter

6

Southeast Asia and the Pacific Region: Cultures and History

Chapter Preview

In this chapter, you will learn about the cultures and history of Southeast Asia and Australia, New Zealand, and the Pacific islands.

Section 1
Southeast Asia
Cultures and History

Section 2
The Pacific Region
Cultures and History

Target Reading Skill

Sequence In this chapter, you will focus on understanding the order in which a series of events occurs. This is called sequence.

▶ Women sell prepared food and fruits and vegetables at a floating market in Thailand.

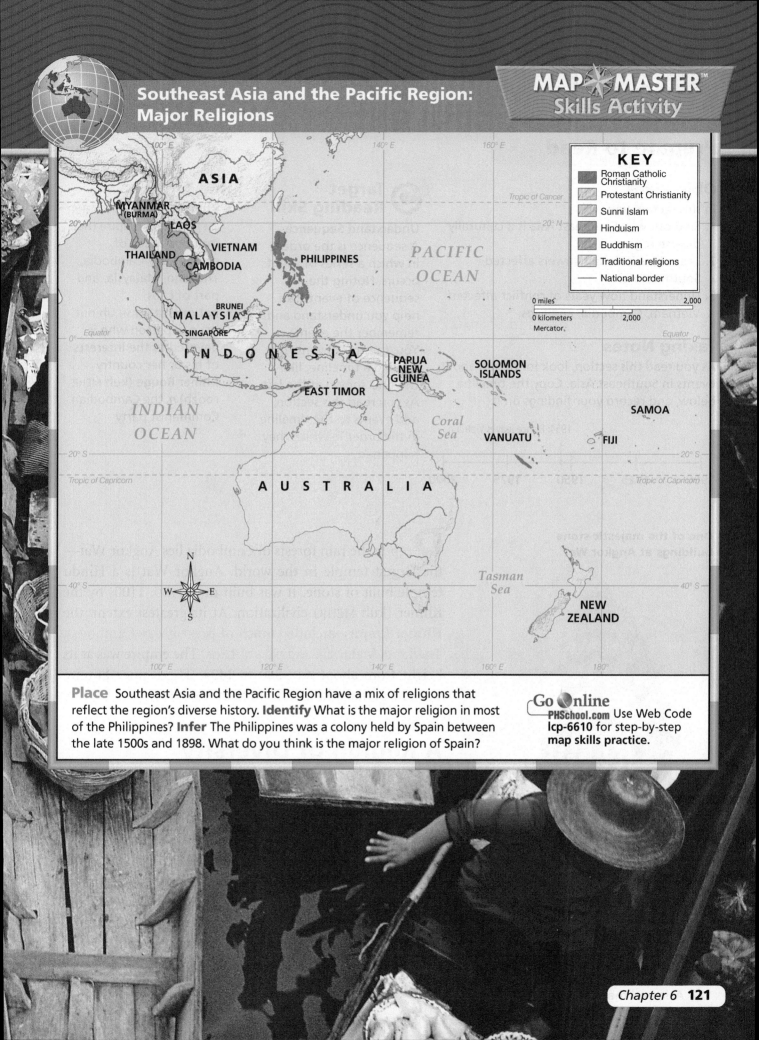

KEY
- Roman Catholic Christianity
- Protestant Christianity
- Sunni Islam
- Hinduism
- Buddhism
- Traditional religions
- National border

0 miles 2,000
0 kilometers 2,000
Mercator.

ASIA

MYANMAR
(BURMA)

LAOS

THAILAND   VIETNAM

CAMBODIA   PHILIPPINES

PACIFIC
OCEAN

Tropic of Cancer

20° N

BRUNEI

MALAYSIA

SINGAPORE

Equator

I N D O N E S I A

PAPUA
NEW
GUINEA

SOLOMON
ISLANDS

Equator

EAST TIMOR

INDIAN
OCEAN

Coral
Sea

SAMOA

VANUATU   FIJI

20° S   20° S

Tropic of Capricorn

A U S T R A L I A

Tropic of Capricorn

N
W   E
S

Tasman
Sea

NEW
ZEALAND

40° S   40° S

Place Southeast Asia and the Pacific Region have a mix of religions that reflect the region's diverse history. **Identify** What is the major religion in most of the Philippines? **Infer** The Philippines was a colony held by Spain between the late 1500s and 1898. What do you think is the major religion of Spain?

Go Online
PHSchool.com Use Web Code
lcp-6610 for step-by-step
map skills practice.

Prepare to Read

Objectives

In this section you will
1. Find out why Southeast Asia is a culturally diverse region.
2. Learn how colonial powers affected Southeast Asia.
3. Understand how years of conflict affected Vietnam, Cambodia, and Laos.

Taking Notes

As you read this section, look for details about events in Southeast Asia. Copy the timeline below, and record your findings on it.

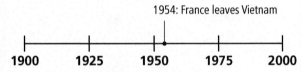

1954: France leaves Vietnam

1900	1925	1950	1975	2000

Target Reading Skill

Understand Sequence
A sequence is the order in which a series of events occurs. Noting the sequence of events can help you understand and remember the events. You can track events by making a timeline, like the one shown at the left. As you read this section, add events to the timeline in the order in which they happened.

Key Terms

- **Khmer Empire** (kuh MEHR EM pyr) *n.* an empire that included much of present-day Cambodia, Thailand, Malaysia, and part of Laos
- **nationalist** (NASH uh nul ist) *n.* a person who is devoted to the interests of his or her country
- **Khmer Rouge** (kuh MEHR roozh) *n.* the Cambodian Communist party

One of the majestic stone buildings at Angkor Wat

Deep in the rain forests of Cambodia lies Angkor Wat—the largest temple in the world. Angkor Wat is a Hindu temple built of stone. It was built in the A.D. 1100s by the Khmer (kuh MEHR) civilization. At its greatest extent, the **Khmer Empire included much of present-day Cambodia, Thailand, Malaysia, and part of Laos.** The empire was at its height from about A.D. 800 to 1434. The Khmer Empire was one of many kingdoms in Southeast Asia.

A Region of Diversity

The peoples of Southeast Asia developed their own cultures before outside influences shaped the region. Southeast Asia's mountains kept groups of people apart from one another. As a result, each group developed its own way of life.

When outside influences came to Southeast Asia, many of them came from India and China. Southeast Asia is located between India and China. Because of this location, the cultures of Southeast Asia were strongly affected by India and China.

The Impact of India and China India affected Southeast Asian cultures mainly through trade. Nearly 2,000 years ago, Indian traders sailed across the Indian Ocean to Southeast Asia. Indians introduced the religion of Hinduism to the region. Later, around A.D. 200, Indians brought Buddhism to Southeast Asia.

Long after Hinduism and Buddhism spread throughout the region, Indians brought Islam to Southeast Asia. Muslim traders from northern India, then under Muslim rule, carried Islam to Indonesia and the Philippines.

China's effect on Southeast Asia was felt primarily in Vietnam. In 111 B.C., the Chinese conquered Vietnam. They ruled the country for more than 1,000 years. During that time, the Vietnamese began using Chinese ways of farming. They also began using the ideas of Confucius, the ancient Chinese philosopher, to run their government.

Major Religions of Southeast Asia Today, there are Hindus in Indonesia and Malaysia. Buddhists and Muslims, however, eventually outnumbered Hindus in the region. Buddhism is the main religion in Myanmar, Thailand, Laos, Vietnam, and Cambodia today. Islam is the religion of the majority of the people in Malaysia and Indonesia. In fact, Indonesia has the largest Muslim population in the world. Singapore has a mix of religions that include Muslims, Buddhists, Hindus, and Christians.

European missionaries brought Christianity to Southeast Asia in the 1500s. Today, most of the people in the Philippines are Christian. There are small groups of Christians in Malaysia and Indonesia, too.

Buddhism in Southeast Asia
According to Buddhist tradition, Buddhism was founded in India in the 500s B.C. by Siddhartha Gautama, known as the Buddha. This gigantic sculpture of the Buddha is in Laos.
Apply Information *Name another Southeast Asian country where Buddhism is the main religion.*

✓ **Reading Check** **What are the major religions of Southeast Asia?**

Colonial Rule in Southeast Asia

Europeans brought more than Christianity to Southeast Asia. Traders from Europe arrived in the region in the 1500s. They hoped to gain control of the rich trade in silks, iron, silver, pearls, and spices. At first, Portugal, the Netherlands, and other European nations built trading posts there. From these small posts, Europeans expanded their power. By the 1800s, European nations had gained control of most of Southeast Asia.

As the map below shows, by 1914 Thailand was the only country in Southeast Asia that was not under colonial rule. Thailand was known as Siam until 1939. Spain ruled the Philippines for about 350 years. In 1898, however, the United States defeated Spain in the Spanish-American War. Control of the Philippines passed to the United States.

Target Skill
Understand Sequence
When did control of the Philippines pass to the United States, before or after the Spanish-American War?

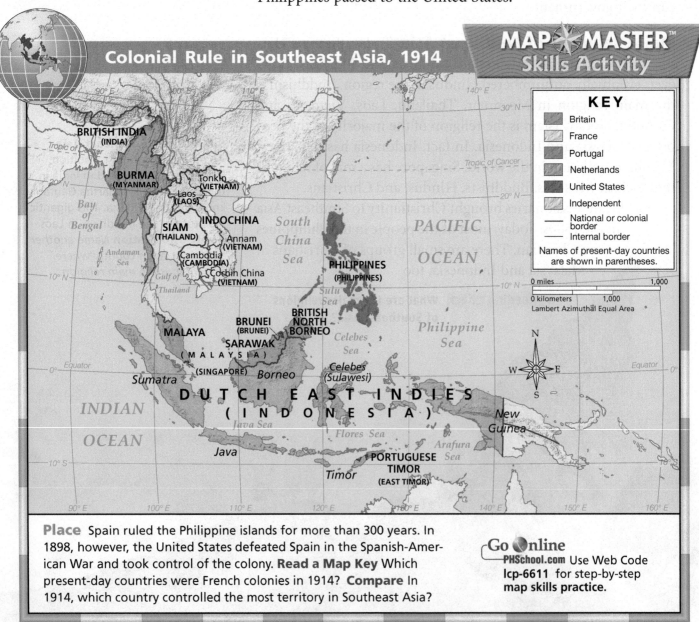

Colonial Rule in Southeast Asia, 1914

MAP MASTER™ Skills Activity

KEY

- Britain
- France
- Portugal
- Netherlands
- United States
- Independent
- —— National or colonial border
- —— Internal border

Names of present-day countries are shown in parentheses.

0 miles 1,000
0 kilometers 1,000
Lambert Azimuthal Equal Area

BRITISH INDIA (INDIA)
Tropic of Cancer
BURMA (MYANMAR)
Tonkin (VIETNAM)
Laos (LAOS)
Bay of Bengal
SIAM (THAILAND)
INDOCHINA
Annam (VIETNAM)
Andaman Sea
Cambodia (CAMBODIA)
Cochin China (VIETNAM)
Gulf of Thailand
South China Sea
PHILIPPINES (PHILIPPINES)
PACIFIC OCEAN
Sulu Sea
MALAYA
BRUNEI (BRUNEI)
BRITISH NORTH BORNEO
SARAWAK (MALAYSIA)
(SINGAPORE)
Celebes Sea
Philippine Sea
Sumatra
Borneo
Celebes (Sulawesi)
INDIAN OCEAN
Equator
DUTCH EAST INDIES (INDONESIA)
Java Sea
Java
Flores Sea
New Guinea
Arafura Sea
Timor
PORTUGUESE TIMOR (EAST TIMOR)

Place Spain ruled the Philippine islands for more than 300 years. In 1898, however, the United States defeated Spain in the Spanish-American War and took control of the colony. **Read a Map Key** Which present-day countries were French colonies in 1914? **Compare** In 1914, which country controlled the most territory in Southeast Asia?

Go Online
PHSchool.com Use Web Code lcp-6611 for step-by-step map skills practice.

Effects of Colonial Rule Colonial rulers built a network of roads, bridges, ports, and railroads in Southeast Asia. Good transportation was essential for the economic success of the colonies. This new network made moving people and goods across the region much easier. The colonial powers also built schools, which helped to produce skilled workers for colonial industries. Education gave some Southeast Asians the skills to become teachers, doctors, government workers, and more.

The Road to Independence By the early 1900s, nationalists were organizing independence movements throughout the countries of Southeast Asia. A **nationalist** is someone who is devoted to the interests of his or her country. But, by the time World War II broke out in 1939, the Japanese had begun to move into Southeast Asia. During the war, the Japanese invaded mainland Southeast Asia and drove out the European colonial powers.

After the Japanese were defeated in World War II, Western nations hoped to regain power in Southeast Asia. But Southeast Asians had other hopes. They wanted independence.

Southeast Asian countries did gain independence. Some, like the Philippines and Burma (now called Myanmar), won their freedom peacefully. Others, including Laos, Cambodia, Vietnam, Malaysia, and Indonesia, had to fight for it.

✔ Reading Check **How did the United States gain control of the Philippines?**

Citizen Heroes

Aung San Suu Kyi

The country of Myanmar has had a military government since 1962. The key leader in Myanmar's fight for democracy was a woman named Aung San Suu Kyi (awn san soo chee). The government tried to stop her efforts. Suu Kyi was placed under house arrest from 1989 to 1995. In 1991, Suu Kyi won the Nobel Peace Prize for her work to bring democracy and human rights to Myanmar through peaceful means. In spite of the government's efforts to stop her, she stayed in Myanmar and continued to work for freedom and democracy.

Vendors display their fruit on bicycles in Hanoi, Vietnam.

Vietnam, Cambodia, and Laos

The road to independence was especially violent in Laos, Cambodia, and Vietnam. These countries were formerly controlled by France. Together, they were known as French Indochina. After World War II ended in 1945, France tried to take back Indochina from Japan. Nationalist forces in Vietnam fought back against the French. In 1954, they forced France to give up power and leave.

The Vietnam War The Vietnamese forces that defeated France declared Vietnam's independence. They wanted Vietnam to be a Communist country. This concerned leaders in the United States. Since the end of World War II, the United States had worked to prevent communism from spreading. Its main rival, the Soviet Union, had worked to expand communism by bringing other countries under its control.

In 1954, Vietnam was divided into two parts. The government of North Vietnam was Communist. The government of South Vietnam was non-Communist. Communist leaders in North Vietnam used force in an effort to unite the country under Communist rule. Helped by the United States, South Vietnam fought back.

At first, the United States sent military advisers and supplies to South Vietnam. Later, it sent hundreds of thousands of American soldiers to Vietnam. After years of fighting, the United States began to withdraw its forces. In 1975, North Vietnam took over South Vietnam and reunited the country under a Communist government.

Cambodia and Laos Cambodia and Laos had gained independence from France in 1953. Pulled into the conflict over Vietnam, both countries went through years of violence as Communists and non-Communists struggled for power. During the war, the United States bombed Cambodia and Laos to destroy Communist North Vietnamese forces there.

In 1975, the Cambodian Communist party called the **Khmer Rouge** (kuh MEHR roozh) took over the government of Cambodia. Opposed to Western ways of life, the Khmer Rouge moved the entire urban population to rural areas and forced them to work in the fields. Over the next four years, the Khmer Rouge killed more than a million Cambodians. Even after the Khmer Rouge leader, Pol Pot, was driven out in 1979, fighting continued. After Pol Pot died in 1998, the Khmer Rouge surrendered, and the country became more stable. A new coalition government formed in 2004. Local elections are scheduled for 2007 and national elections for 2008.

Cambodian children reading in school

✓ **Reading Check** **Which country did the United States support with troops during the Vietnam War?**

Section 1 Assessment

Key Terms
Review the key terms at the beginning of this section. Use each term in a sentence that explains its meaning.

Target Reading Skill
List these events in the order in which they occurred: Vietnam comes under Communist rule; Nationalists organize independence movements throughout Southeast Asia; elections are held in Cambodia.

Comprehension and Critical Thinking
1. (a) Recall Between which two large Asian countries is Southeast Asia located?

(b) Summarize How did this location affect the development of Southeast Asia's cultures?
(c) Apply Information Give one example showing that Southeast Asia has diverse religions.
2. (a) Explain Why did Europeans begin traveling to Southeast Asia in the 1500s?
(b) Identify Effects What were some positive and negative effects of colonial rule in Southeast Asia?
3. (a) Identify What present-day countries made up French Indochina?
(b) Sequence What happened in Vietnam in 1954?
(c) Identify Point of View Why was the United States concerned about Vietnam in 1954?

Writing Activity
Complete this sentence: *Southeast Asian cultures have been shaped by____*. Use your completed sentence as a topic sentence for a paragraph about Southeast Asian cultures. Use the information in this section to write your paragraph.

Writing Tip To complete the topic sentence, review this section. Choose two or three features that have shaped Southeast Asian cultures. Be sure to include supporting details for your topic sentence.

Ena walked into class wearing a bright red silk dress. Her anklet of tiny bells chimed each time she moved. Smiling, she took some objects out of a large box.

Maria watched as Ena put up a beautiful picture of the full moon. Next, Ena placed a small, handmade boat on the table. Then she put a small dish of rice next to it.

Maria looked at the calendar. The date was April 13. Tonight there would be a full moon.

Maria smiled. "Ena is going to tell us about the Cambodian New Year." "How do you know?" Paul asked. Maria laughed. "Yesterday we read about how Cambodians celebrate the New Year," she reminded Paul. "In April when the moon is full, they send boats down the river and make offerings to relatives. Look at what Ena has in her display." Maria had noticed some important details and drew the correct conclusion.

Drawing conclusions means adding clues, or evidence, that you read or see, to what you already know. A conclusion is a judgment.

Learn the Skill

Follow the steps below to learn how to draw a reliable conclusion.

1 **Identify what you know is true.** Use these facts as clues. Maria identified the following facts as clues:

   a. Ena was dressed up and wore an anklet of tiny bells.

   b. Ena displayed a picture of a full moon along with a boat and a bowl of rice.

2 **Add these facts to what you already know.** Maria had heard about the Cambodian New Year. She knew how Cambodians celebrated this special holiday.

3 **Add two or more clues to what you already know to draw a reasoned conclusion.** Maria put together the two clues she saw with what she already knew to reach the conclusion that Ena was going to tell about the Cambodian New Year.

Practice the Skill

Read the passage titled The Vietnam War, on page 126. Then use the steps on the previous page to draw conclusions about why the United States withdrew its troops from Vietnam in 1973.

1 Answer these questions in order to find facts: How did Vietnam become independent after World War II? What country was the main rival of the United States after the end of World War II? Why did the United States send soldiers to Vietnam?

2 Use the facts to build on what you already know. For example, you know that the Vietnamese were successful in driving the French out of their country. If Vietnam had that kind of military success with the French, maybe they could defeat the United States forces, too.

3 Add the clues you have discovered to what you already know. What conclusion can you draw about why the United States withdrew its troops from Vietnam in 1973?

Women dressed in silk clothing attend a New Year's celebration in Hanoi, Vietnam.

Apply the Skill

Turn to page 125 and reread the passage titled Effects of Colonial Rule. Then use the steps in this skill to draw a conclusion about why Southeast Asians fought for independence from their colonial rulers.

Prepare to Read

Objectives
In this section you will
1. Find out how people settled Australia and New Zealand.
2. Learn which groups shaped the cultures of Australia and New Zealand.
3. Understand how Pacific island nations have been affected by other cultures.

Taking Notes
As you read this section, look for details about the cultures and history of Australia, New Zealand, and the Pacific islands. Copy and complete the outline below.

> I. Settlement
>   A. The Maori of New Zealand
>   B. Aborigines in Australia
>   C. The Arrival of the British
> II. The Cultures of Australia and New Zealand

Target Reading Skill

Recognize Signal Words
Signal words point out relationships among ideas or events. To help keep the order of events clear, look for words like *first, before, later, next,* and *recently.* These words help show the order in which events took place. Signal words sometimes, but not always, come at the beginning of a sentence.

Key Terms
- **Maori** (MAH oh ree) *n.* a native of New Zealand whose ancestors first traveled from Asia to Polynesia, and later to New Zealand
- **Aborigine** (ab uh RIJ uh nee) *n.* a member of the earliest people of Australia, who probably came from Asia
- **penal colony** (PEEN ul KAHL uh nee) *n.* a place where people convicted of crimes are sent
- **station** (STAY shun) *n.* in Australia, a large ranch for raising livestock

Stone statues on Easter Island

Hundreds of giant stone statues dot the landscape of Easter Island, a tiny island in the South Pacific. Made of volcanic rock, the statues are from 10 to 40 feet (3 to 12 meters) high. Some weigh more than 50 tons (45 metric tons). A European who saw them in 1722 was amazed:

> **❝ The stone images . . . caused us to be struck with astonishment because we could not comprehend how it was possible that these people, who are devoid of heavy thick timber for making any machines . . . had been able to erect such images. ❞**
>
> —*Dutch explorer Jacob Roggeveen, 1722*

Settlement

Easter Island's statues still impress people. Easter Island is part of the island group of Polynesia. The island belongs to Chile, a country in South America. Scientists have wondered how people first came to this faraway island, as well as to the other parts of the Pacific region.

The Maori of New Zealand The earliest people in New Zealand were the Maori (MAH oh ree). **Maori** are natives of New Zealand. Their ancestors first traveled from Asia to Polynesia. Then, about 1,000 years ago, the Maori traveled across the ocean to New Zealand. According to Maori legend, seven groups set out in long canoes to find a new homeland. A storm tossed their boats ashore on New Zealand. The Maori quickly adapted to their new home. They settled in villages, making a living as hunters and farmers. But the Maori also prized fighting and conquering their enemies. They often fought other groups of Maori over the possession of land. The Maori used storytelling to pass on their beliefs and tales of their adventures.

Recognize Signal Words

In the paragraph at the left, which words signal, or tell you, when and how the Maori came to New Zealand?

Aborigines in Australia Many scientists think that the earliest settlers in Australia, the **Aborigines** (ab uh RIJ uh neez), came from Asia more than 40,000 years ago. For thousands of years, they hunted and gathered food along the coasts and river valleys.

During this time, the Aboriginal population in Australia flourished. People lived in small family groups that moved from place to place in search of food and water. All had strong religious beliefs about nature and the land.

The Arrival of the British In 1788, the British founded the first colony in Australia as a penal colony. **A penal colony** is a remote place where people convicted of crimes are sent. Soon, other colonists settled in Australia. Some worked for the prison facilities. Others went to find new land. Then, in 1851, gold was discovered. The population soared. Not long after, Britain stopped sending convicts to Australia. In 1901, Australia gained its independence.

The British settled New Zealand at about the same time as Australia. In 1840, the British took control of New Zealand. The colony, with its fine harbors and fertile soil, attracted many British settlers. New Zealand gained independence in 1947.

✓ **Reading Check** How did people settle Australia and New Zealand?

Links to **Art**

Maori Canoes The Maori showed their standing in society by the works of art they owned. For instance, a person might own elaborately carved and painted war canoes. Some were as long as 100 feet (30 meters). Human figures were carved along the hull and into the prow, which is the front part of the boat. The figures often had eyes made of mother-of-pearl. Canoes were painted red and decorated with feather streamers. Today these canoes are important artifacts preserved in museums.

The Cultures of Australia and New Zealand

Today, most Australians and New Zealanders are descendants of British settlers. They share British culture, holidays, and customs. Most Australians and New Zealanders enjoy a high standard of living. Employment in farming, mining, manufacturing, and service industries have made the nations prosperous.

Aborigines Since the arrival of Europeans, the Aborigines have suffered great hardships. In the colonial period, settlers forced these native peoples off their lands. Tens of thousands died of European diseases. Others were forced to work on sheep and cattle **stations,** which in Australia are extremely large ranches. The settlers forced Aborigines to adopt European ways. As a result, the Aborigines began to lose their own customs and traditions. More tragically, starting in the 1800s and continuing into the 1960s, Aboriginal children were taken from their families, often by force, to live with non-Aborigines. Today, Aborigines make up less than 1 percent of the country's population.

European and Asian Immigrants People other than the British also settled in Australia. During the gold rush of the 1850s, many people came, including Chinese. Chinese people continue to settle in Australia today. About 2.6 percent of Australia's population is Chinese.

Australians All

About 92 percent of Australians are Caucasian, 7 percent are Asian, and less than 1 percent are Aborigine. Australia's Aborigine heritage was honored at the 2000 Olympic Games when track athlete Kathy Freeman, an Aborigine, lit the Olympic torch. **Summarize** *How were Aborigines affected by the arrival of Europeans?*

Farmers planting vegetables in Tasmania, an island south of Australia

After World War II, many Europeans migrated to Australia. They came from Ireland, Italy, Yugoslavia, Greece, and Germany. In the 1970s, people fleeing the war in Vietnam settled in Australia. Today, people from all over the world continue to arrive.

The Maori Way of Life When New Zealand became a British colony, Britain promised to protect Maori land. Settlers, however, broke that promise. For many years, the settlers and the Maori clashed violently. The settlers defeated the Maori in 1872. After their defeat, the Maori were forced to adopt English ways. Maori culture seemed in danger of being destroyed. Slowly, however, Maori leaders gained more power. Laws now allow the Maori to practice their customs and ceremonies.

Today about 15 percent of New Zealand's population is Maori. Most Maori now live in urban areas. Many speak both Maori and English. Thanks to their artists, writers, and singers, Maori culture is an important part of New Zealand life.

Other Peoples of New Zealand After World War II, many Europeans migrated to New Zealand. People from Polynesia have settled there as well. Today, more Polynesians live in New Zealand's largest city, Auckland, than in any other city in the world. Although most New Zealanders are of European background, the Asian population has grown rapidly.

✔ **Reading Check** **What is the main ethnic group in Australia and New Zealand today?**

The Cultures of the Pacific Islands

Scientists believe that the first people to inhabit the Pacific islands came from Southeast Asia more than 30,000 years ago.

A Variety of Cultures Because of the distances between islands, groups could not easily communicate with one another. Therefore, each group developed its own language, customs, and religious beliefs. However, the island people did have many things in common. Their ocean environment shaped their lives. It fed them and was their main means of transportation and trade. Most built their lives around their small villages.

From Colonies to Independence In the 1800s, Western nations began to take an interest in the Pacific islands. Britain, France, and Germany set up trading posts and naval bases on many islands. By 1900, the United States, Britain, France, and Germany had claimed nearly every island in the region.

After World War II, most Pacific islands gained independence, and life began to improve. By then, traditional island cultures had blended with cultures from Europe, America, and other countries. Most governments were democratic. Most churches were Christian. Many Pacific islanders read and spoke English.

Girls from the Cook Islands, in Polynesia, wearing flower garlands, or *leis*.

✓ Reading Check **What were Pacific island cultures like after World War II?**

Section 2 Assessment

Key Terms
Review the key terms at the beginning of this section. Use each term in a sentence that explains its meaning.

Target Reading Skill
Reread the paragraph on page 131 with the heading The Arrival of the British. Find the words that signal time related to the settlement of Australia.

Comprehension and Critical Thinking

1. (a) **Apply Information** From where do scientists believe the native peoples of Australia came?

(b) **Compare** In what ways are the histories of the Aborigines and the Maori similar?

2. (a) **Recall** From which country are most of the people in Australia and New Zealand descended?

(b) **Identify Effects** How did the settlement of Australia and New Zealand affect native peoples there?

3. (a) **Recall** From where do scientists believe the first people to live in the Pacific islands came?

(b) **Draw Conclusions** Why might people who live on an island be able to preserve their culture for a long period without change?

Writing Activity
Write 10 brief entries for a timeline that shows events in the history and cultures of Australia, New Zealand, and the nearby Pacific islands.

Writing Tip Use complete sentences for your timeline entries. This will help make the sequencing of events easier to follow.

Chapter 6

Review and Assessment

◆ Chapter Summary

Section 1: Southeast Asia Cultures and History

- The people of Southeast Asia developed cultures that later blended with influences from India, China, and Europe.
- By the 1800s, European nations had gained control of most of Southeast Asia.
- After World War II ended in 1945, Southeast Asian countries gained independence.
- After Vietnam became independent, it was divided into Communist North Vietnam and non-Communist South Vietnam. In the Vietnam War, the two sides fought for control of the country for nearly 30 years.
- The United States supported South Vietnam during the Vietnam War. Hundreds of thousands of American soldiers fought in Vietnam. Fighting spread to Cambodia and Laos.
- The Vietnam War ended in 1975 when North Vietnam took over South Vietnam and united the country under a Communist government.

The Cook Islands, Polynesia

Section 2: The Pacific Region Cultures and History

- Aborigines first settled Australia, and the Maori first settled New Zealand.
- In 1788, the British set up their first colony in Australia. Australia was a British colony until it became independent in 1901.
- Britain took control of New Zealand in 1840. New Zealand became independent in 1947.
- Most Australians and New Zealanders are descended from the British and share British culture, holidays, and customs.
- Australia's population now includes Aborigines, Asians, and people with European backgrounds. New Zealand's population includes Maori, Asians, and Polynesians.

Buddha sculpture, Laos

◆ Key Terms

Match the definitions in Column I with the key terms in Column II.

Column I

1. a remote place where people convicted of crimes are sent
2. a member of the earliest people of Australia
3. a person who is devoted to the interests of his or her country
4. in Australia, a large ranch for raising livestock
5. a member of the native people of New Zealand

Column II

A nationalist

B Aborigine

C Maori

D penal colony

E station

◆ Comprehension and Critical Thinking

6. (a) Identify Identify the Khmer Empire.
(b) Identify Cause How did Hinduism and Buddhism come to Southeast Asia?

7. (a) List What are three religions in Southeast Asia today?
(b) Apply Information Name three countries in Southeast Asia in which Buddhism is the main religion today.

8. (a) Identify Identify French Indochina.
(b) Identify Causes Why did the French leave Vietnam in 1954?
(c) Summarize Describe the conflict in Vietnam, including U.S. involvement.

9. (a) Explain How did Aborigines live before the British came to Australia?
(b) Summarize Describe life for the Maori today.

10. (a) Recall What happened in Australia in 1788?
(b) Draw Conclusions How does the history of Australia and New Zealand help explain why their cultures reflect a British heritage?

11. (a) Name On what island group do historians believe the people of the Pacific islands first settled?
(b) Make Generalizations Describe Pacific island cultures after World War II.

◆ Skills Practice

Drawing Conclusions Review the steps you followed on page 128 to learn this skill. Then reread Links to Art on page 131 and draw a conclusion about the level of skill needed to make a Maori canoe.

◆ Writing Activity: Math

Population density is the average number of people living in a square mile or square kilometer. To calculate a country's population density, divide the total population by the total land area. Use an almanac or encyclopedia to find the land areas in square miles and populations for Australia, Thailand, and Vietnam. Be sure to find whole numbers. Calculate the population density of each country to the nearest whole number. Create a table that shows your data. Then write a short paragraph about your findings.

MAP MASTER™ Skills Activity

Southeast Asia and the Pacific Region

Place Location For each place listed below, write the letter from the map that shows its location.

1. Thailand
2. Vietnam
3. Indonesia
4. Australia
5. New Zealand
6. The Philippines

Go Online
PHSchool.com Use Web Code lcp-6620 for an interactive map.

Standardized Test Prep

Test-Taking Tips

Some questions on standardized tests ask you to find cause and effect. Read the passage below. Then follow the tips to answer the sample question at the right.

In the 1100s, the Khmer Empire extended across much territory. It included lands that are now Cambodia and much of Laos, Thailand, and Vietnam. There were many other kingdoms in Southeast Asia at that time. Because of geography, however, the others were small. The mountains of Southeast Asia isolated people, who had little contact with anybody outside their own valley. Each group developed its unique way of life. The region became rich in cultures.

TIP In a cause-and-effect relationship, the effect is what happens and the cause is what makes it happen.

Pick the letter that best answers the question.

Southeast Asia was rich in cultures because—

A the Khmer Empire extended across much territory.

B mountains isolated groups of people in their own valleys.

C there were many other kingdoms in Southeast Asia in the 1100s.

D the Khmer Empire forced different groups to pull together.

TIP Look for words, such as *because, so,* and *as a result* that point to a cause-and-effect relationship.

Think It Through The fourth sentence in the passage says that "because of geography" many Southeast Asian kingdoms were small. You can eliminate A and D because the Khmer Empire did not produce these small kingdoms. C simply restates the idea that the area is rich in cultures. The correct answer is B.

Practice Questions

Use the passage below to answer Question 1.

Beginning in the early 1900s, Australia's population grew steadily. Until the end of World War II in 1945, most of Australia's immigrants came from Great Britain. After the war ended, large numbers of immigrants came from other countries in Europe. In recent years, many immigrants have come from East Asia and Southeast Asia because of Australia's nearby location, and because of Australia's high standard of living.

1. Many immigrants recently have come to Australia from Asian countries because

A they were not welcome in other countries.

B Australia has a high standard of living.

C they could afford to travel to Australia.

D many immigrants from Great Britain were making Asian countries too crowded.

2. During the Vietnam War, fighting spread to

A Malaysia.

B Australia.

C the Philippines.

D Cambodia.

3. The first colony in Australia was set up by

A Great Britain.

B the United States.

C China.

D France.

Go Online
PHSchool.com

Use Web Code lca-6600
for a **Chapter 6 self-test.**

The Clay Marble
By Minfong Ho

Prepare to Read

Background Information

Think of someone you admire. What special gift or quality does that person have? Some people have the ability to show us a new way of looking at things.

In 1980, civil war in Cambodia forced thousands of Cambodians to leave their homes and move to refugee camps near the border of Thailand and Cambodia. Among these refugees were many children. There was very little food, and living conditions were poor. *The Clay Marble* tells the story of twelve-year-old Dara, who lives in one such camp. Dara's friend Jantu, another girl in the camp, makes toys out of little scraps and trinkets she finds at the camp.

Objectives

In this selection, you will
1. Discover how Jantu deals with the challenge of living in a refugee camp.
2. Find out how the author uses point of view to tell a story.

It amazed me, the way she shaped things out of nothing. A knobby branch, in her deft hands, would be whittled into a whirling top. She would weave strips of a banana leaf into plump goldfish or angular frogs. A torn plastic bag and a scrap from some newspaper would be cut and fashioned into a graceful kite with a long tail. A couple of old tin cans and a stick would be transformed into a toy truck.

One of the many refugee camps along the Thai-Cambodian border. The last refugee camp closed in 1999.

Whenever Jantu started making something, she would withdraw into her own private world and ignore everything around her. Leaving me to mind her baby brother, she would hunch over her project, her fierce scowl keeping at bay anybody who might come too close or become too noisy. But if I was quiet and kept my distance, she didn't seem to mind my watching her.

And so I would stand a little to one side, holding the baby on my hip, as Jantu's quick fingers shaped, twisted, smoothed, rolled whatever material she happened to be working with into new toys.

"How do you do it?" I asked her one day, after she had casually woven me a delicate bracelet of wild vines.

"Well, you take five vines of about the same length—elephant creeper vines like this work well—and you start braiding them, see. Like this . . ."

"No, I don't mean just this bracelet," I said. "I mean the goldfish, too, and the kites and toy trucks and . . ."

"But they're all different," Jantu said. "You make them different ways."

"But how do you know what to make? Is there some . . . some kind of magic in your hands, maybe?"

Jantu looked puzzled. "I don't know," she said, turning her hands over and examining them with vague interest. They looked like ordinary hands, the fingernails grimy, the palms slightly calloused. "I don't see anything there," she said. "Nothing that looks like magic." She shrugged and dismissed the subject.

Yet the more I watched her, the more convinced I became that Jantu's hands were gifted with some special powers, some magic. How else could anyone explain how she made that wonderful mobile, of two delicate dolls husking rice?

Even from the start, I knew it was going to be something special. For three days Jantu had kept me busy scrounging up a collection of old cloth and string. Then, as I sat cross-legged watching her, she fashioned two straw dolls in <u>sarongs</u> and straw hats and, with dabs of sticky rice, glued their feet onto a smooth branch. Carefully she tied strings connecting the dolls' wrists and waists, so that when one doll bent down, the other one straightened up. Each doll held a long thin club, with which, in turn, one would pound at a tiny <u>mortar</u> as the other doll lifted up its club in readiness. Jantu held up the mobile and showed me how a mere breath of wind would set the two dolls in motion.

About the Selection

This reading selection is from a chapter in *The Clay Marble*, a novel for young readers written by Minfong Ho and published in 1991.

sarong (suh RAWNG) *n.* a loose garment made of a long strip of cloth wrapped around the body

mortar (MAWRT ur) *n.* a dish in which seed or grain is pounded or ground

✓ **Reading Check**

What materials does Jantu use to make the dolls?

A Cambodian family leaving their refugee camp to return home

recruit (rih KROOT) *v.* to persuade someone to join
resistance army (rih ZIS tuns AHR mee) *n.* an army of people resisting, or opposing, the group holding political power in a country
saunter (SAWN tur) *v.* to walk in an idle or a casual manner

retrieve (rih TREEV) *v.* to get something back again

Pound and lift, up and down, the two dolls took turns crushing the rice with exactly the same jerky rhythm that real village women pounded it to get the brown husks off. There were even some real grains in the miniature mortar set between the two dolls. It was the cleverest thing I had ever seen.

Children crowded around Jantu, pressing in from all sides to watch her work it. "Let me hold it," I begged, standing next to Jantu. "I helped you find the stuff for the dolls."

Jantu nodded. Breathlessly I held it carefully and blew on it. It worked! One of the dolls bent down and pounded the mortar with its club. The other doll straightened up and waited its turn. I was still engrossed with it when someone shouted a warning: "Watch out, Chnay's coming!"

Even in my short stay at the camp, I'd heard of Chnay. He liked to break things, and he was a bully. An orphan, Chnay made his way to the Border alone. Too young to be <u>recruited</u> into the <u>resistance army</u>, Chnay roamed the fields by himself, scrounging for food and sleeping wherever he liked.

Chnay <u>sauntered</u> up and shoved his way through to us. "What've you got there?" he demanded.

"Nothing," I said, trying to hide the toy behind me.

Laughing, Chnay snatched it away from me. One of the dolls was ripped loose and dropped to the ground.

As I bent over to <u>retrieve</u> it, Chnay pushed me aside. "Leave it," he said. "That's for kids. Look what I have." He thrust his arm out. It was crawling with big red ants, the fierce kind that really sting when they bite. "I'm letting them bite me. See?" he bragged. Already small fierce welts were swelling up on his arm, as some ants kept biting him.

"That's dumb!" I exclaimed. Dodging behind him, I tried to snatch the mobile back from him.

Chnay flung the toy to the ground, scattering straw and red ants into the air.

I grabbed on to his hand, but he was taller than I, and much stronger. He shoved me aside and stomped on the dolls until they were nothing but a pile of crushed sticks and rags. Then, kicking aside a boy who stood in his way, Chnay strode off, angrily brushing red ants off his arm.

I squatted down beside the bits of dolls and tried to fit them together, but it was no use. The delicate mobile was beyond repair. I could feel my eyes smarting with angry tears. "I should've held on to it more tightly," I said bitterly. "I shouldn't have let him grab it away from me."

Jantu knelt next to me and took the fragments of the dolls out of my hands. "Never mind," she said quietly, putting them aside. "We can always start something new."

"But it took you so long to make it," I said.

Idly Jantu scooped up a lump of mud from a puddle by her feet and began to knead it in her hands. "Sure, but the fun is in the making," she said.

She looked down at the lump of mud in her hands with sudden interest. "Have you ever noticed how nice the soil around here is?" she asked. "Almost like clay." She smoothed the ball with quick fingers, then rolled it between her palms.

When she opened her palm and held it out to me, there was a small brown ball of mud cupped in it. "For you," she announced.

I looked at it. Compared to the delicate rice-pounding mobile, this was not very interesting at all. "I don't want it," I said. "It's just a mud ball."

"No, it's not. It's a marble," Jantu said. Her eyes sparkling, she blew on it. "There! Now it's a magic marble."

I took it and held it. Round and cool, it had a nice solid feel to it. I glanced at Jantu. She was smiling. Slowly I smiled back at her.

Maybe, I thought, maybe she did put some magic in the marble. After all, why else would I feel better, just holding it?

✓ **Reading Check**

What happens to Jantu's dolls?

About the Author

Minfong Ho (b. 1951) was born in Rangoon, Myanmar (Burma). She grew up in Singapore and Thailand and studied at Cornell University in New York. In 1980, Ho worked as a volunteer in a refugee camp on the Cambodian-Thai border. Her experiences helped her write *The Clay Marble*. She is the author of numerous children's fiction books about life in Southeast Asia.

Review and Assessment

Thinking About the Selection

1. (a) Respond How did you feel about Chnay while reading this selection?
(b) Infer How do you think Jantu felt about what Chnay did to the dolls?
2. (a) Recall How would Jantu act when she started to make something?
(b) Analyze For Jantu, what is important, making toys or the toys themselves? Give evidence for your answer.
3. (a) Recall What does Jantu do with the lump of mud she scoops up?

(b) Contrast How is Dara's opinion of the lump of mud different from Jantu's opinion?
(c) Conclude What symbolic meaning might the clay marble have?

Writing Activity

Write an Essay Choose a person who has been important in your life. Write an essay that tells who the person is and what special qualities he or she has. Tell why these qualities are important to you. Include an introduction and a conclusion in your essay.

Chapter Preview

This chapter focuses on key countries in East Asia: China, Japan, North Korea, and South Korea.

Country Databank

The Country Databank provides data and descriptions of each of the countries of East Asia: China, Japan, North Korea, South Korea, Taiwan, and Mongolia.

Section 1
China
Transforming Itself

Section 2
Japan
Tradition and Change

Section 3
The Koreas
A Divided Land

Target Reading Skill

Comparison and Contrast In this chapter, you will focus on using comparison and contrast to help you analyze information.

▶ Dressed in traditional clothing, a Korean man plays a stringed instrument called a komungo.

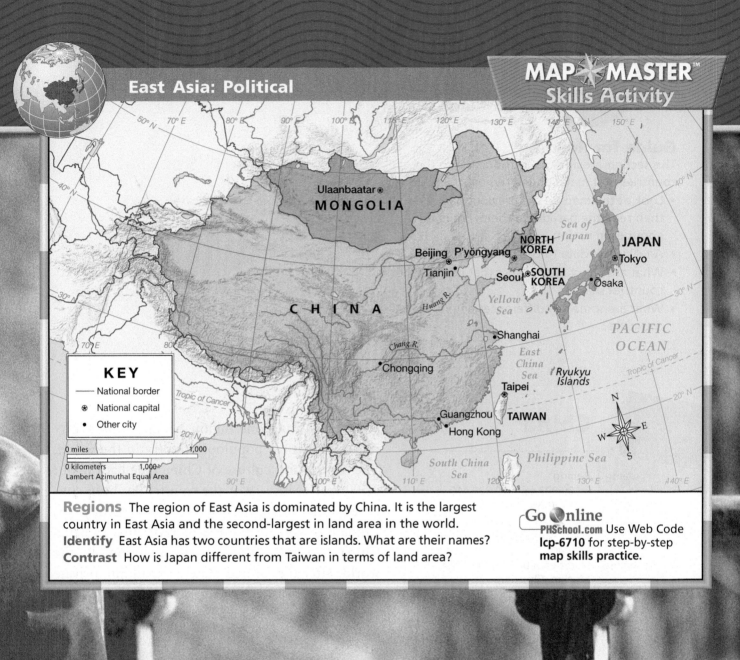

KEY

—— National border
⊛ National capital
• Other city

0 miles 1,000
0 kilometers 1,000
Lambert Azimuthal Equal Area

Regions The region of East Asia is dominated by China. It is the largest country in East Asia and the second-largest in land area in the world.
Identify East Asia has two countries that are islands. What are their names?
Contrast How is Japan different from Taiwan in terms of land area?

Go Online
PHSchool.com Use Web Code **lcp-6710** for step-by-step map skills practice.

Guide for Reading

This section provides an introduction to the countries that make up the region of East Asia.

- Look at the map on the previous page and then read the paragraphs below to learn about each nation.
- Analyze the data to compare the countries.
- What are the characteristics that most of the countries share?
- What are some key differences among the countries?

China

Capital	Beijing
Land Area	3,600,927 sq mi; 9,326,410 sq km
Population	1.31 billion
Ethnic Group(s)	Han, Zhaung, Uygur, Hui, Tibetan, Miao, Manchu, Mongol, Buyi, Korean
Religion(s)	traditional beliefs, Buddhist, Muslim, Christian
Government	Communist state
Currency	yuan
Leading Exports	machinery and equipment, textiles and clothing, footwear, toys and sporting goods, mineral fuels
Language(s)	Mandarin (official), Wu, Cantonese, Hsiang, Min, Hakka, Kan

With more than one billion people, China (CHY nuh) is the most populous country in the world. The history and culture of China date back about 3,500 years. Since 1949, the country has been governed under a Communist system. In recent years, China has worked to build its economy. In 2005, China had the second-largest economy in the world, after the United States. Expanding private businesses and trade with countries around the world have helped China's economy grow rapidly.

Beijing, China

A priest outside a temple in Japan

Japan

Capital	Tokyo
Land Area	144,689 sq mi; 374,744 sq km
Population	127 million
Ethnic Group(s)	Japanese, Korean, Chinese, Brazilian, Southwest Asian
Religion(s)	traditional beliefs, Buddhist, Christian
Government	constitutional monarchy
Currency	yen
Leading Exports	motor vehicles, semiconductors, office machinery, chemicals
Language(s)	Japanese (official), Korean, Chinese

Japan (juh PAN) is an island country located east of North Korea and South Korea. Japan's four main islands and thousands of small islands lie between the Sea of Japan and the Pacific Ocean. Most of Japan's land is rugged and mountainous. Japan succeeded in building a strong economy in the decades after World War II. Although its economy has declined in recent years, Japan still has one of the largest economies in the world. Japan is among the world's leading producers of motor vehicles and electronic equipment.

Mongolia

Capital	Ulaanbaatar
Land Area	600,540 sq mi; 1,555,400 sq km
Population	2.6 million
Ethnic Group(s)	Mongol, Turkic, Tungusic, Chinese, Russian
Religion(s)	Buddhist, Muslim, traditional beliefs, Christian
Government	parliamentary
Currency	tugrik
Leading Exports	copper, livestock, animal products, cashmere, wool, hides, fluorspar, other nonferrous metals
Language(s)	Khalka Mongolian, Kazakh, Chinese, Russian

Mongolia (mahn GOH lee uh) is a landlocked country bordered by Russia to the north and China to the south. Mongolia has very little land suitable for growing crops. Most of the labor force works in raising and herding livestock. Industry in Mongolia takes place chiefly in the capital city of Ulaanbaatar and consists primarily of livestock products, such as dairy products, meats, and woolen textiles. Mongolia is rich in mineral resources as well. The mining of copper, gold, coal, and other minerals contributes to Mongolia's economy.

Introducing East Asia

North Korea

Capital	Pyongyang
Land Area	46,490 sq mi; 120,410 sq km
Population	22.3 million
Ethnic Group(s)	Korean, Chinese, Japanese
Religion(s)	Buddhist, traditional beliefs, Christian
Government	authoritarian socialist
Currency	North Korean won
Leading Exports	minerals, metallurgical products, manufactured goods (including armaments), agricultural and fishery products
Language(s)	Korean (official), Chinese

North Korea (nawrth kuh REE uh) is located on the northern part of the Korean Peninsula. Before World War II ended in 1945, Korea was one country. From 1910 to 1945, Korea was controlled by Japan. When Japan was defeated in World War II, Korea was divided into two parts. The northern part was occupied by the Soviet Union and the southern part was occupied by the United States. In 1948, North Korea and South Korea were established as separate nations. Since then, North Korea has been governed under a communist system. The government supports a huge military and an extensive weapons program, including weapons of mass destruction.

South Korea

Capital	Seoul
Land Area	37,911 sq mi; 98,190 sq km
Population	48.3 million
Ethnic Group(s)	Korean, Chinese
Religion(s)	Christian, Buddhist, traditional beliefs
Government	republic
Currency	South Korean won
Leading Exports	electronic products, machinery and equipment, motor vehicles, steel, ships, textiles, clothing, footwear, fish
Language(s)	Korean (official), Chinese

The nation of South Korea (sowth kuh REE uh) was established in 1948. South Korea is located on the southern half of the Korean Peninsula. South Korea went through many years of political unrest under a number of different rulers. The country's first democratic elections were held in 1987. Since the 1960s, South Korea has achieved remarkable economic growth. Despite an economic slowdown in the late 1990s, South Korea's economy continued to grow in 2002. Its major industries include car production, electronics, shipbuilding, steel, textiles, and footwear. Political relations between South Korea and North Korea have been strained since the Korean War in the 1950s.

Children eating dinner in South Korea

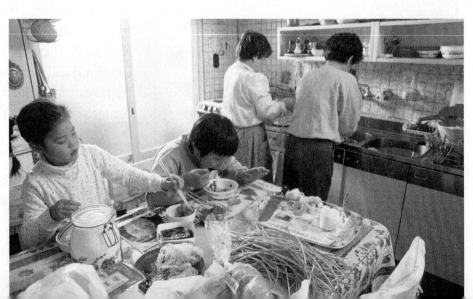

Taiwan

Capital	Taipei
Land Area	12,456 sq mi; 32,260 sq km
Population	22.5 million
Ethnic Group(s)	Taiwanese, Chinese, aborigine
Religion(s)	Buddhist, traditional beliefs, Christian
Government	multiparty democracy
Currency	Taiwan dollar
Leading Exports	machinery and electrical equipment, metals, textiles, plastics, chemicals
Language(s)	Mandarin Chinese (official), Amoy Chinese, Hakka Chinese

SOURCES: DK World Desk Reference Online; CIA World Factbook Online; *World Almanac*, 2003

Taiwan (ty wahn) is an island country located off the southeastern coast of China. The formation of Taiwan as a nation was the result of a power struggle between two political parties in China. One party, the Chinese Communists, gained control of China in 1949. The other party, the Nationalists, fled to Taiwan and set up a government there. During the 1950s and 1960s, Taiwan built a strong economy based on manufacturing industries. Manufacturing is still important in Taiwan today, but growing service industries, such as banking, bring in more money to the nation's economy.

An aerial view of Taipei, Taiwan

Assessment

Comprehension and Critical Thinking

1. Compare Compare the physical size and the population size of China to the other countries in East Asia.

2. Draw Conclusions What are the characteristics that most of the countries share?

3. Contrast What are some key differences among the countries?

4. Categorize What kinds of products are the leading exports of this region?

5. Infer What can you infer about a country if many of its exports are made in factories?

6. Make a Bar Graph Create a bar graph showing the population of the countries in this region.

Keeping Current

Access the **DK World Desk Reference Online** at **PHSchool.com** for up-to-date information about all six countries in this chapter.

Web Code: **lce-6700**

China
Transforming Itself

Prepare to Read

Objectives

In this section, you will

1. Find out how China controlled its economy from 1949 to 1980.
2. Learn about the growth of Taiwan since 1949.
3. Discover how China's government operated after the death of Mao Zedong.
4. Examine aspects of life in China today.

Taking Notes

As you read this section, look for details about how China was governed under the Communist party. Copy the diagram below, and record your findings in it. Write the similarities in the space where the ovals overlap. Write the differences in the space where the ovals do not overlap.

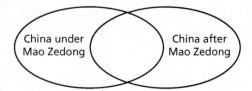

China under
Mao Zedong

China after
Mao Zedong

Target Reading Skill

Compare and Contrast Comparing and contrasting can help you analyze information. When you compare, you look at the similarities between things. When you contrast, you look at the differences. As you read this section, look for similarities and differences in how China was governed under the Communist party. Write the information in your Taking Notes table.

Key Terms

- **radical** (RAD ih kul) *adj.* extreme
- **Red Guards** (red gahrdz) *n.* groups of students who carried out Mao Zedong's policies during the Cultural Revolution
- **free enterprise system** (free ENT ur pryz SIS tum) *n.* an economic system in which people can choose their own jobs, start private businesses, own property, and make a profit
- **gross domestic product** (grohs duh MES tik PRAHD ukt) *n.* the total value of all goods and services produced in an economy

Bicycles remain a major form of transportation in China.

In 1985, the total number of cars, buses, and trucks in all of China was about 320,000. Most people in cities rode bicycles or walked to get around. In 2005, the number of cars, buses, and trucks had grown to about 25 million. During that time, China had experienced tremendous economic growth.

Changes continue as China works to build its economy. In the past, China's Communist government tightly controlled the economy. Today, however, China is in the process of moving toward an economy with fewer government controls.

China's Economy, 1949–1980

In 1949, the Chinese Communist party set up a new government with leader Mao Zedong (mow dzuh doong) in charge. Under Mao, the government took over China's economy. Factories, businesses, and farmland came under the government's control.

The Great Leap Forward In 1958, Mao began a radical, or extreme, program called the "Great Leap Forward." Its goal was to increase output from farms and factories. The program turned out to be a giant step backward. The Communists rushed to increase production by forcing people to work on large communes. But they ignored the need for experience and planning. For example, they ordered a huge increase in steel production. Thousands of untrained workers built backyard furnaces for making steel and other products. Much of the steel they produced was of poor quality and useless.

The focus on industry took farmers away from farming. At the same time, poor weather destroyed crops, resulting in a severe food shortage. Between 1959 and 1961, an estimated 30 million people died from starvation.

The Cultural Revolution In 1966, Mao introduced another radical policy called the Cultural Revolution. His aim was to create a completely new society with no ties to the past. He began by closing schools and urging students to rebel against their teachers and their families. The students formed bands of radicals called Red Guards. These bands destroyed some of China's most beautiful ancient buildings. They beat and imprisoned many Chinese artists, professors, and doctors. Anyone they considered to be against Mao's policies was attacked.

When the Red Guards raged out of control and began to threaten Mao's government, they were imprisoned, too. The Cultural Revolution kept China in turmoil until its conclusion in 1976. Years of chaos left China in disorder, with hundreds of thousands of its citizens dead. The focus on political revolution disrupted China's economic growth.

√ **Reading Check** What was the purpose of China's Great Leap Forward?

China Under Mao
Mao launched the Great Leap Forward in order to improve China's economy. The small photo above shows a poster promoting the program. Mao declared the Cultural Revolution in 1966. In the large photo, Red Guards read a book of Mao's writings. **Summarize** *How did the Great Leap Forward affect China's economy?*

China's Government
China's government is a dictatorship. In a dictatorship, the power to govern is held by one person. By contrast, a democracy is a form of government in which the power to govern rests with the people. A dictatorship has complete power over the people. It may also have control of nearly everything people do. Examples of dictatorships in the past include those in the former Soviet Union and Germany. Shown below is Mao Zedong, leader of China's government from 1949 to 1976.

China launched the world's first magnetic levitation, or maglev, passenger train system. Powerful magnets work to lift and propel the train.

Taiwan Since 1949

After their defeat by the Communists in 1949, the Nationalists fled to Taiwan, an island 100 miles (161 kilometers) off mainland China's southeast coast. They formed a new government and called their country the Republic of China. The Communists on mainland China, however, still claimed the right to rule Taiwan. The Nationalists on Taiwan also claimed the right to rule the rest of China.

In Taiwan, the Nationalists followed the free enterprise system. Under the **free enterprise system,** people can choose their own jobs, start private businesses, own property, and make profits. Taiwan's free enterprise economy quickly became one of Asia's strongest. New programs increased farm output and brought in money to help build new ports and railroads.

Businesses in Taiwan export many goods, such as computer products and electronics, to other countries. These exports, along with new service jobs, have helped the economy grow dramatically. Taiwan has also developed a democratic government. Following the 2000 elections, a new ruling party peacefully took power for the first time in Taiwan's modern history.

✓ **Reading Check** What kind of economic system does Taiwan have?

Changes in China

Meanwhile, many Western countries refused to trade with China. At the same time, some of Mao's policies hurt the country. During the 1970s, the Communists realized that they needed new policies in order to improve China's economy and its relations with the rest of the world.

First, China began repairing relations with the West. In 1971, China was allowed to join the United Nations. In 1972, Richard Nixon became the first American president to visit China. This historic trip opened up trade between the two nations.

China

China has a large and complex economy. Much of China's land is devoted to farming to feed its large population. Most of this land is used for subsistence farming, or growing food mainly for the farm family rather than for sale. Now look at the graphs below. China's exports, or sales to other countries, are greater than its imports, or purchases from other countries. These exports have helped China's economy to grow. Many young workers have moved from rural areas to cities to find higher-paying jobs. However, agriculture remains the main source of jobs in China.

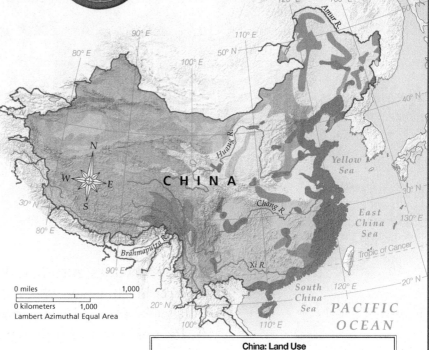

China: Land Use

KEY

- Commercial farming (without rice)
- Commercial farming (with rice)
- Subsistence farming (without rice)
- Subsistence farming (with rice)
- Nomadic herding
- Forestry
- Manufacturing and trade
- Little or no activity
- National border

Foreign Trade

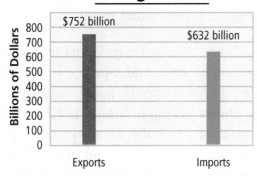

SOURCE: *CIA World Factbook*

Labor Force by Sector

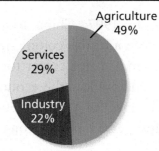

SOURCE: *CIA World Factbook*

Exports by Sector

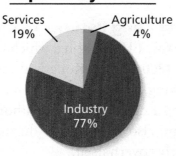

SOURCE: World Trade Organization

Map and Chart Skills

1. **Identify** Which economic sector in China uses the most land and employs the most people?
2. **Contrast** Which economic sector accounts for most of China's exports?
3. **Infer** How might large population movements from rural to urban areas affect farming?

Use Web Code **Ice-6711** for **DK World Desk Reference Online.**

The New China
Sun Dong An Plaza in Beijing, China, includes seven floors of stores, a food court, a multiscreen movie complex, and parking for about 500 cars and about 3,500 bicycles. **Compare and Contrast** *How is Sun Dong An Plaza similar to and different from an American shopping mall?*

New Leaders After Mao died in 1976, moderate leaders gained power in China. By 1981, Deng Xiaoping (dung show ping) was leader of China. Deng carried out a program called the Four Modernizations. This program focused on improvements in farming, industry, science, and defense. During the next 20 years, China gradually allowed some free enterprise. Privately owned Chinese factories began to make electronic equipment, clothes, computer parts, toys, and many other products.

New Economic Plans Under Deng, China set up areas where foreign companies could own and operate businesses. These areas included five "special economic zones" and 14 cities along China's coast. They helped bring in money to China's economy. The Chinese Communist party also allowed some Chinese citizens to run private businesses. By the end of the 1990s, private businesses were producing about 75 percent of China's gross domestic product. **Gross domestic product** is the total value of all goods and services produced in an economy.

Hong Kong Returns to China In 1997, China took back control of Hong Kong, which had been a British colony since the late 1800s. Hong Kong had long been a major center for trade, banking, and shipping. China agreed to allow the economy of Hong Kong to operate without changes for the next 50 years. China also agreed that during this period Hong Kong could largely govern itself.

✓ Reading Check **What happened to Hong Kong in 1997?**

China Today

Today, China is a major economic power. It has formed good relations with many nations. Yet the government has often been criticized for the way it treats its people. China has one political party, which is the Chinese Communist party. Under China's government, its citizens do not have political freedom.

The Chinese government has used violence against people who have called for a democratic government. In 1989, tens of thousands of people gathered in Tiananmen Square in Beijing, China's capital, to demand greater political freedoms. When the people refused to leave, the government sent in tanks and troops. Thousands of people were killed or wounded.

Many nations question how they should relate to a country with such a poor human rights record. Still, most of them continue to remain trade partners with China. China's population makes it a huge market for goods, and China manufactures many items for other countries. In 2003, Hu Jintao became China's president and leader of the Chinese Communist party. Experts on China expected Hu to keep developing an economy with fewer government controls. With the Chinese Communist party firmly in control, however, the country's political system was not expected to change.

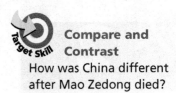

Compare and Contrast
How was China different after Mao Zedong died?

✔ **Reading Check** **How did China's government respond to the democracy movement in 1989?**

Section 1 Assessment

Key Terms
Review the key terms at the beginning of this section. Use each term in a sentence that explains its meaning.

Target Reading Skill
Explain one way China's government was the same and one way it was different after Mao's death?

Comprehension and Critical Thinking

1. (a) Identify Who took control of China in 1949?

(b) Summarize Why did the Chinese government launch the Great Leap Forward?

2. (a) Define What is the Republic of China?

(b) Contrast How is Taiwan different from China?

3. (a) Identify Identify Deng Xiaoping.

(b) Find the Main Idea What economic changes took place under Deng's leadership?

(c) Explain Why has the Chinese government been criticized for the way it treats its people?

Writing Activity
Write a paragraph comparing and contrasting China before and after Mao Zedong's death. Include a description of how China's economy has changed during this time.

> **Writing Tip** Compare and contrast the Great Leap Forward with the Four Modernizations program. How were these programs alike? How were they different?

Section 2

Japan
Tradition and Change

Prepare to Read

Objectives

In this section, you will
1. Learn about the growth of Japan's economy.
2. Find out about successes and challenges in Japan's economy.
3. Examine aspects of life in Japan.

Taking Notes

As you read this section, look for ways in which tradition and change have helped Japan develop its economy. Copy the web diagram below, and record your findings in it.

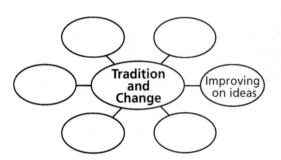

Target Reading Skill

Make Comparisons When you make comparisons, you note how things are alike. As you read this section, compare tradition and change in terms of how they have helped Japan build its economy. Write your information in the Taking Notes web diagram.

Key Terms

- **subsidy** (SUB suh dee) *n.* money given by a government to assist a private company
- **recession** (rih SESH un) *n.* a period during which an economy and the businesses that support it shrink, or make less money
- **birthrate** (BURTH rayt) *n.* the number of live births each year per 1,000 people
- **labor** (LAY bur) *n.* the work people do for which they are paid

A robot demonstration in Japan

In the 1990s, employees of Japanese companies would gather to sing the company song. One song included the words, "Let's put our strength and minds together . . . grow, industry, grow, grow, grow!" A Japanese car company handed out a weekly newsletter that included pep talks to help its employees work more efficiently. Another Japanese car company held an Idea Expo each year. Employees competed in designing unique vehicles. The event reminded workers that each new product is the result of a company-wide team effort.

Harmony and teamwork are important in the Japanese way of life. Tradition and change are also important. Present-day Japan is a modern, urban country where traditional ways blend with the new.

Building a Developed Economy

Once Japan finally opened its ports to other countries in the 1800s, it welcomed new ideas and inventions from the West. For years, the Japanese worked to build major industries. By the 1920s, Japan had become an important manufacturing country.

Japan's Economy After World War II After World War II ended in 1945, however, Japan was in ruins. The United States helped to rebuild Japan's industries. In addition, the Japanese government helped industries by giving them subsidies. A **subsidy** is money given by a government to assist a private company. This allowed companies to build large factories and sell more goods, which boosted the country's economy.

High-Technology Industries Since the 1960s, Japan has produced some of the world's most modern industrial robots. By the 1970s, the Japanese were making more watches and cameras than the Swiss and the Germans. By the 1980s, Japan made and sold a large share of the world's cars, electronic goods, skiing gear, and bicycles. Japan also produced huge amounts of steel, ships, televisions, and CDs.

In addition, Japanese companies improved existing products. For example, the videocassette recorder (VCR) was invented in the United States. But production costs for making VCRs in the United States were thought to be too high. A Japanese company bought the invention. Japan today is a leading maker of VCRs.

Japanese companies also had new ideas of their own. You are probably familiar with portable stereos and small, hand-held electronic games. These products were invented by the Japanese. In 1983, a European company and a Japanese company introduced the first compact disc. Working with European and American companies, Japanese companies also developed the digital video disc (DVD).

✓ **Reading Check** What are some high-technology products made in Japan?

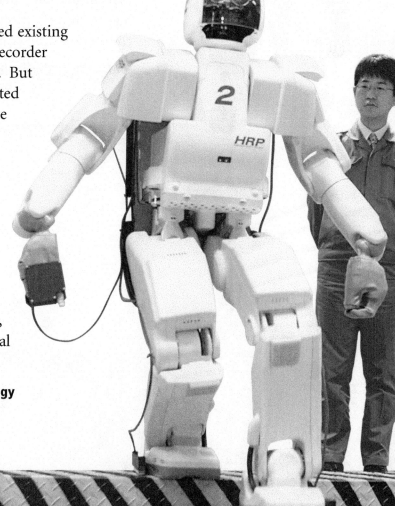

Japan's Robotics Industry
Below, a Japanese robotics designer watches as a humanoid robot steps over a barrier. Increased robot use may be one solution for Japan's labor shortage. **Analyze** *What characteristics does this robot have that would make it suitable as a replacement for a human worker?*

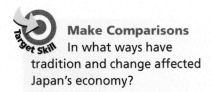

Make Comparisons
In what ways have tradition and change affected Japan's economy?

Successes and Challenges

By the 1980s, Japan had one of the world's largest and strongest economies. Japan's economy depended on exporting its products to the rest of the world. Americans and Europeans eagerly bought Japanese products—particularly cars, television sets, and electronics. Yet Japanese people did not buy many goods from America and Europe.

Other countries grew angry because even though they bought many Japanese products, the Japanese did not buy theirs. This led to poor trade relations between Japan and other countries. On top of that, in the early 1990s, the Japanese economy suffered a severe recession. A **recession** is a period of time when an economy and the businesses that support it shrink, or make less money. To overcome the recession, some companies began laying off their employees. Unemployment in Japan rose.

Since 2004, Japan has experienced improved economic growth, and it still has one of the largest economies in the world. Manufacturing remains an important part of Japan's economy. Today, however, more people work in Japan's service industries than in manufacturing. Service industries include jobs in banking, communications, sales, hotels, and restaurants. More of the country's wealth comes from service industries as well.

✓ **Reading Check** **How was Japan affected by the recession in the 1990s?**

Inspecting a turbine in Yokohama, Japan (large photo); a Japanese-made electronic book reader (small photo)

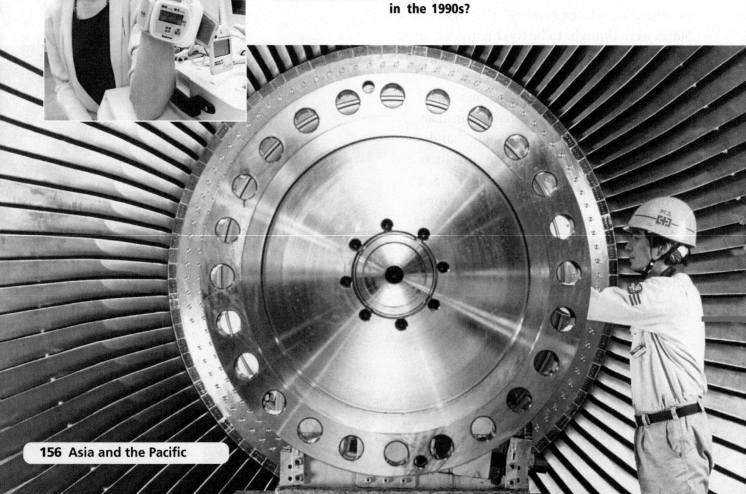

Japan

Japan is one of the world's most densely populated countries. Japan is about the same size as the states of California or Montana. But it has almost half as many people as the entire United States. The bar graph below the map shows that Japan has about the same population density as Massachusetts. Massachusetts is one of the most densely populated U.S. states. Yet, as you can see on the map, forests and farmland cover most of Japan. How is this possible? Japan pre-serves large areas of forest and farm-land because most of its people are crowded into the small part of the country that is urban. Compare the circle graphs below showing land use in Massachusetts and Japan. Even though Japan has nearly the same overall population density as Massa-chusetts, it devotes much less of its space to urban development. This is mainly because its cities are compact, with little of the sprawling suburban development that we know in the United States.

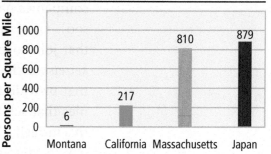

Population Density Comparison

SOURCE: U.S. Census Bureau, Prentice Hall DK World Desk Reference

Land Use

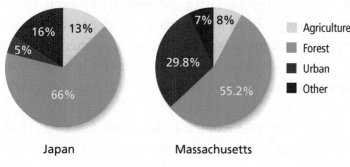

- Agriculture
- Forest
- Urban
- Other

Japan

SOURCE: Statistics Japan, 2003

Massachusetts

SOURCE: U.S. Natural Resources Conservation Service, 1997

Map and Chart Skills

1. **Identify** What percentages of Japan's land are devoted to agriculture and forest?
2. **Compare** Does Japan devote more or less land to agriculture and forest than Massachusetts?
3. **Synthesize** What explains this difference?

Use Web Code **Ice-6712** for **DK World Desk Reference Online.**

Life in Japan

Harmony, ceremony, and order have long been important in Japanese culture. Japanese people have generally followed these traditional values. While the past is honored, however, new ways of living and working have been introduced in Japan. The result is a modern culture with features that are unique to the country.

Working Together Working together as a group has long been a tradition in Japan. One way Japanese manufacturing companies have worked together is by forming *keiretsu* (kay ret soo). This is a Japanese term that describes a group of companies that join together to work toward one another's success. Some *keiretsu* included the companies that make goods, the companies that provide the raw materials for those goods, and the companies that sell the goods. The Japanese car industry has followed this model. Although still part of the country's economy, *keiretsu* have been joined by a growing number of small businesses.

Changing Roles The role of marriage is another example of tradition and change in Japan. Marriage has been the most acceptable social position for a Japanese man or woman. Today, however, more and more Japanese men and women are choosing not to marry or to delay marriage. One result is that Japan's birthrate is low. A country's **birthrate** measures the number of live births each year per 1,000 people.

The role of Japanese women in the work force has changed, too. Before World War II, few women in Japan worked outside the home. Today, there are more Japanese women working full time or part time than women who stay at home full time.

Although about half of Japan's work force is made up of women, men hold most of the management positions. In 2005, women headed about 6 percent of the companies in Japan. This compared with some 40 percent of U.S. companies being headed by women.

Japanese Students
Like American schoolchildren, these Japanese students enjoy clowning for the camera. Most public school students in Japan wear uniforms. **Analyze** *What purpose do you think school uniforms serve?*

Facing the Future As Japan heads into the future, its challenge is to find a way of maintaining its wealth. One of the resources a country needs to produce goods and services is labor. Labor is the work people do for which they are paid. Japan does not have a growing labor force of young workers. In the United States and Europe, a steady supply of immigrants helps keep the labor force growing. In the past, Japan has limited immigration.

Japan's low birthrate affects the labor force. Fewer and fewer workers have to support an aging population no longer working. This makes the cost of producing goods and services higher in Japan than in countries with growing populations.

 Reading Check **Why is the cost of producing goods and services higher in Japan than in other Asian countries?**

Section 2 Assessment

Key Terms
Review the key terms at the beginning of this section. Use each term in a sentence that explains its meaning.

 Target Reading Skill
What are two ways in which tradition and change have helped Japan build its economy?

Comprehension and Critical Thinking
1. (a) Recall Describe what Japan's economy was like by the 1920s.

(b) Summarize Tell how Japan's economy grew from the 1960s to the 1980s.
2. (a) Identify What happened that disturbed Japan's economy in the early 1990s?
(b) Identify Effects How did this affect Japan?
3. (a) Explain What tradition helps explain why Japanese companies formed *keiretsu?*
(b) Identify What is one resource a country needs to produce goods and services?
(c) Draw Conclusions How would a low birthrate affect a country's labor force?

Writing Activity
Japan has an aging population. Based on the information in this section, brainstorm a list of what Japan can do to increase its labor force. Write your list and add a short description of each idea.

For: An activity on Japan
Visit: PHSchool.com
Web Code: lcd-6702

James and his family were going to host a Japanese exchange student for the summer. The student, Hiro, would be arriving in three weeks.

James decided to send information about his town to Hiro. First, he got a map that showed the mountains and lakes in the area. Then, James took photos of his favorite places in town. James added photos of his friends at school and playing soccer. His mother gave him a brochure that told about the area. Finally, James made a video showing his family, his apartment, and even his cat.

Soon, James had a mountain of information. He showed it to his dad.

"You've done a great job," his dad said. "But maybe you should synthesize some of this information. After all, Hiro may not have time to digest all of these things."

When you synthesize information, you combine information from several different sources. You find the main ideas and weave them into a conclusion. Synthesizing information is a very important skill in school and in life.

Learn the Skill

Follow these steps to synthesize information.

1 **Identify the main idea in each piece of information.** Main ideas are big, important ideas that are supported by details. You may want to write the main ideas down. The main idea for James is to tell about his town.

2 **Find details that support your main ideas.** Details will give you more information about your main ideas. One detail that James chose to share was that some children in his town like to play soccer.

3 **Look for connections between the pieces of information.** These connections might be similarities, differences, causes, effects, or examples. Jot down these connections.

4 **Draw conclusions based on the connections you found.** What broad, general statements can you make that tie your main ideas together?

Japan's Modern Economy

Main Ideas	Supporting Details	Connections
1. By the 1980s Japan had one of the world's largest and strongest economies.	• Japan loaned large amounts of money to other countries. • Japan exported its products to the rest of the world.	• Japan imported few goods.
2. In the early 1990s Japan suffered a severe recession.		

Practice the Skill

Use the steps on the previous page to synthesize information about Japan's modern economy. Reread the text on page 156 under the heading Successes and Challenges. Then make a table like the partially completed one above.

1. Study the information about Japan's economy from the 1980s to the present. Add one or two main ideas to the two ideas on the table above.

2. Now find details that support each main idea and add them to the chart. The details already listed add more information about Japan's strong economy in the 1980s.

3. Are the pieces of information connected in some way? Consider cause and effect. The connection already included is a possible cause for the decline in Japan's economy. Add other connections to the chart.

4. Draw some conclusions from the connections you find. See whether you can use these conclusions to answer the question, "Why did Japan's economy decline in the early 1990s?"

The Tokyo Stock Exchange is part of Japan's economy. This stock trader is using a hand signal to show he wants to sell stocks.

Apply the Skill

Use the steps on the previous page to synthesize information about how life has changed in modern Japan. Select information from the text and photos in the section Life in Japan on page 158. Focus on a single aspect of Japanese life, such as family life or work life.

The Koreas
A Divided Land

Prepare to Read

Objectives

In this section, you will

1. Understand why North Korea has been slow to develop.
2. Find out how South Korea became an economic success.

Taking Notes

As you read this section, look for differences between North Korea and South Korea. Copy the table below, and record your findings in it.

North Korea	South Korea
•	• High economic growth

Target Reading Skill

Identify Contrasts When you identify contrasts, you examine differences. North Korea and South Korea are very different. As you read, look for differences between these two countries. Write them down in the Taking Notes table.

Key Terms

- **demilitarized zone** (dee MIL uh tuh ryzd zohn) *n.* an area in which no weapons are allowed
- **truce** (troos) *n.* a cease-fire agreement
- **diversify** (duh VUR suh fy) *v.* to add variety to
- **famine** (FAM in) *n.* a huge food shortage

North Korea and South Korea have a border unlike any other in the world. On a map, the border looks like a simple line. In reality, the border runs through the middle of what former President Bill Clinton called "the scariest place on Earth."

The border runs through the DMZ or **demilitarized zone** (dee MIL uh tuh ryzd zohn), an area in which no weapons are allowed. The DMZ is about 2.5 miles (4 kilometers) wide and about 151 miles (248 kilometers) long. Barbed wire, land mines, watchtowers, and thousands of weapons line both sides.

Children in South Korea

On North Korea's side, an estimated one million troops patrol the border. South Korea has about 600,000 troops. Why does the DMZ exist? In 1953, a **truce,** or cease-fire agreement, ended the Korean War. But no peace treaty was signed. Since then, the world's most heavily armed border has divided the two countries.

More than the DMZ divides the Koreas. The two countries have very different economies and governments as well.

A section of the DMZ that divides North Korea and South Korea

North Korea: Economic Challenges

North Korea (the Democratic People's Republic of Korea) is a communist country under a dictatorship. The government runs the economy. The country has kept itself closed to much of the world. This has kept out new technology and fresh ideas. Yet North Korea is rich in mineral resources. Until the end of World War II, it was the industrial center of the Korean Peninsula.

Today, North Korea manufactures poor-quality goods in government-owned factories. Little has been done to **diversify, or add variety to,** the economy. Although the government briefly opened some private markets in 2004, it still controls the economy. Overall, North Korea's economy is in poor shape.

Farming methods, too, are outdated in North Korea. In 1995, North Koreans faced **famine, or a huge food shortage,** and starvation. North Korean officials estimate that about 220,000 people died from famine between 1995 and 1998. Without farming reforms, food shortages have continued. To help combat starvation, many countries and international organizations provided humanitarian food aid to North Korea. However, in 2005, the government said that it would stop accepting humanitarian aid.

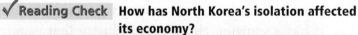

✓ **Reading Check** **How has North Korea's isolation affected its economy?**

A North Korean man saw his South Korean grandmother for the first time in more than 50 years when North Korea allowed separated families to reunite in 2005.

Soccer is a popular sport in South Korea.

Identify Contrasts
How is North Korea's government different from South Korea's government?

South Korea: Economic Growth

In the mid-1950s, South Korea (the Republic of Korea) had agricultural resources but few industries. Fifty years later, South Korea has become a leading economic power.

South Korea is a democracy with an economy based on free enterprise. After World War II, South Korea's factories focused on making cloth and processed foods. Later, South Korea developed heavy industry. Today, South Korea is among the world's leading shipbuilders. It has a growing electronics industry that exports radios, televisions, and computers. South Korea is a leading producer of the silicon chips used in computers. South Korea also has large refineries, or factories that process oil. The oil products are used to make plastics, rubber, and other goods.

The government of South Korea has focused on the growth of industry. But it has also helped farmers. Some programs helped increase crop production. Other programs improved housing, roads, and water supplies and brought electricity to rural areas.

Despite its successes, South Korea faces a number of challenges. Like Japan, it lacks many natural resources. It must import large amounts of raw materials to keep industry running. Major imports are oil, iron, steel, and chemicals.

✓ **Reading Check** **What are some products made in South Korea?**

Years of Tension

Many Koreans hope that one day North Korea and South Korea will once again be one country. But relations between the two Koreas have remained tense since the end of the Korean War. North Korean and South Korean troops have had numerous violent clashes. Better relations seemed possible in 2000. The leaders of the two countries met in Pyongyang, the capital of North Korea, and agreed to work toward peace and cooperation.

COUNTRY PROFILE

Focus on Economics

The Koreas

The Koreas have very different economies. The map at right shows that North Korea is rich in natural resources. However, its communist system has hurt its economy. The graph below shows that South Korea's gross domestic product, or economic output, has soared, while North Korea's has failed to grow.

The Koreas: Natural Resources
KEY
Gold
Silver
Copper
Iron
Lead
Tungsten
Coal
Graphite
Hydroelectric power
Manufacturing
National capital
National border
CHINA
NORTH KOREA
SOUTH KOREA
P'yŏngyang
Seoul
Sea of Japan
Yellow Sea
Korea Strait
Cheju-Do
125° E
130° E
40° N
35° N
N
S
E
W
0 miles 250
0 kilometers 250
Lambert Conformal Conic

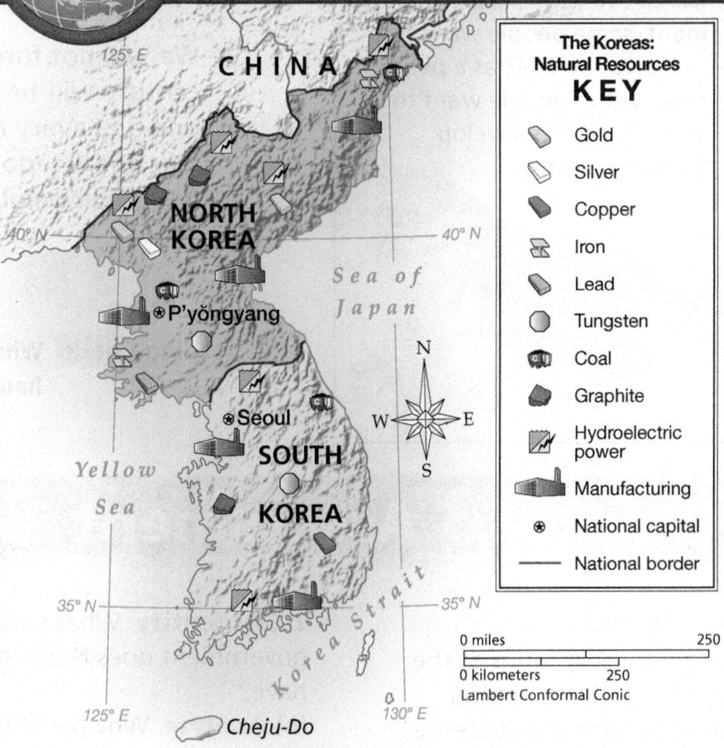

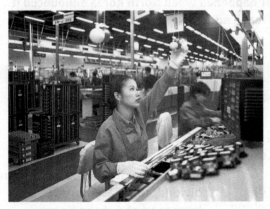

Manufacturing electronics in South Korea

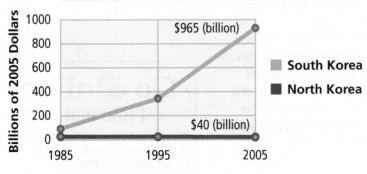

Gross Domestic Product, 1985–2005

Billions of 2005 Dollars
1000
800
600
400
200
0
1985
1995
2005
$965 (billion)
$40 (billion)
South Korea
North Korea

SOURCE: *CIA World Factbook*

Map and Chart Skills

1. **List** Using the map, name at least three natural resources that are found in North Korea but not South Korea.
2. **Contrast** Based on your reading and the graph at the left, discuss the differences between the economies of North and South Korea.

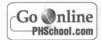

Go Online PHSchool.com Use Web Code **lce-6713** for **DK World Desk Reference Online.**

Nature in the DMZ The land inside the DMZ has been untouched by human settlement for more than 50 years. As a result, the DMZ has become a peaceful haven for wildlife. Living in the DMZ are several rare and endangered species. They include eagles, cranes, and bears. Some people believe there are tigers in the DMZ. If North Korea and South Korea ever sign a peace agreement, some people want to preserve the DMZ as a peace park. Other people want to use the land to develop Korea's economy.

In 2002, North Korea's government made a shocking announcement. Even though it had previously agreed not to, North Korea said it had been developing nuclear weapons. The news damaged hopes for peace between the two countries and caused worldwide concern. In 2005, North Korea announced that it had made nuclear weapons. Later that year, "Six-Party Talks" among North Korea, the United States, Russia, China, Japan, and South Korea led to a new agreement. In exchange for giving up its nuclear weapons, North Korea would receive increased aid and diplomatic relations. However, the agreement has not yet been carried out.

In 2005, U.S. President George W. Bush visited several countries in Asia. On that trip, he said,

> **"We will not forget the people of North Korea. The 21st century will be freedom's century for all Koreans—and one day every citizen of that peninsula will live in dignity and freedom and prosperity at home, and in peace with their neighbors abroad. "**
>
> — *President George W. Bush*

✓ **Reading Check** What happened when North Korea announced it had made nuclear weapons?

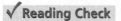

Section 3 Assessment

Key Terms
Review the key terms at the beginning of this section. Use each term in a sentence that explains its meaning.

Target Reading Skill
Using your Taking Notes chart, explain ways in which North Korea and South Korea are different.

Comprehension and Critical Thinking
1. (a) Identify What kind of government and economy does South Korea have?
(b) Identify Causes What are some reasons for South Korea's economic success?

2. (a) Identify What kind of government does North Korea have?
(b) Analyze Why has North Korea's economy lagged behind South Korea's?
3. (a) Explain What event seemed to point to better relations between North Korea and South Korea?
(b) Identify Effects What was the effect of North Korea's development of nuclear weapons?
(c) Draw Inferences What did President Bush mean when he said, "We will not forget the people of North Korea"?

Writing Activity
When North Korea and South Korea were divided, families were divided, too. Based on what you have read about the Koreas, write a paragraph that states your viewpoint on the issue of reunifying the two countries.

For: An activity on the Koreas
Visit: PHSchool.com
Web Code: lcd-6703

Review and Assessment

◆ Chapter Summary

Section 1: China

- China tried two economic programs from 1949 to 1980, including the Great Leap Forward and the Cultural Revolution.
- Under a free enterprise system, Taiwan developed a successful economy.
- After the death of Chinese leader Mao Zedong, China followed a different path that included many changes to develop the economy.
- China today is a major economic power with a government that has fewer controls over the economy, but that does not allow political freedom for its citizens.

Section 2: Japan

- Japan worked hard to build a successful, highly developed economy.
- After an economic decline in the 1990s, Japan continues its recovery with one of the largest economies in the world.
- Japan has a modern culture that combines traditional Japanese values with new ways of working and living.
- One of Japan's challenges for the future is finding a way of maintaining its wealth, despite an aging population and a low birthrate.

China

Section 3: The Koreas

- South Korea has a democratic government with an economy based on free enterprise.
- North Korea has a communist government that controls the economy.

Japan

◆ Key Terms

Match the definitions in Column I with the key terms in Column II.

Column I

1. an economic system in which people can choose their own jobs, start private businesses, own property, and make a profit
2. extreme
3. a huge food shortage
4. to add variety to
5. the number of live births in a nation each year per 1,000 people

Column II

A radical

B free enterprise system

C birthrate

D diversify

E famine

◆ Comprehension and Critical Thinking

6. (a) Identify What was the purpose of the Cultural Revolution?
(b) Compare and Contrast How was the Cultural Revolution similar to and different from the Great Leap Forward?

7. (a) Define Where and what is Taiwan?
(b) Identify Point of View How does the government of Taiwan view China?

8. (a) Explain What was the Four Modernizations program of the 1990s?
(b) Identify Effects Describe one change in China's economy under this program.

9. (a) Note Give examples of some of the high-technology products made in Japan.
(b) Summarize How was the formation of *keiretsu* an example of the Japanese tradition of working together?

10. (a) Define What is labor?
(b) Summarize What is one reason that Japan has a declining labor force?

11. (a) Describe What was North Korea like before the end of World War II?

(b) Contrast How is North Korea's government and economy different from South Korea's?

12. (a) List Name four products that are made in South Korea.
(b) Compare Why is South Korea similar to Japan in terms of what the country must do to keep industry running?

◆ Skills Practice

Synthesizing Information Review the steps you learned in the Skills for Life lesson in this chapter. Then review the text and pictures in Section 1. Synthesize the information and draw a conclusion about how China has changed since 1949.

◆ Writing Activity: Language Arts

Written Chinese is based on characters, rather than on an alphabet. Each Chinese character represents a word or an idea. The complete Chinese writing system has more than 40,000 characters. Use an encyclopedia to look up information about the Chinese language and the Chinese writing system. Write a brief report that describes Chinese writing.

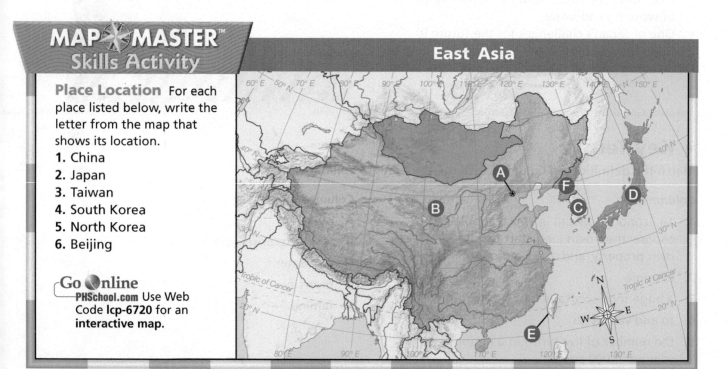

MAP★MASTER™ Skills Activity

East Asia

Place Location For each place listed below, write the letter from the map that shows its location.
1. China
2. Japan
3. Taiwan
4. South Korea
5. North Korea
6. Beijing

Go Online
PHSchool.com Use Web Code lcp-6720 for an interactive map.

Standardized Test Prep

Test-Taking Tips

Some questions on standardized tests ask you to analyze graphic organizers. Study the concept web below. Then follow the tips to answer the sample question at the right.

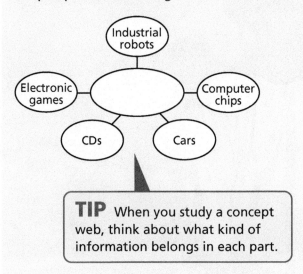

TIP When you study a concept web, think about what kind of information belongs in each part.

Pick the letter that best answers the question.

Which title should go in the center of the web?

A Skiing Gear

B Exports

C Japanese Exports

D Japanese Imports

TIP Read all four answer choices. Then choose the BEST answer from the remaining choices.

Think It Through The question asks you to choose a title for the center of the web—in other words, an idea that covers the information in all of the outer circles. You can rule out A because it is too specific: skiing gear belongs in an outer circle. However, B is too general. Although it is correct, there is probably a better answer. That leaves C or D. Look over the items in the outer circles. Are they goods that Japan sells to the rest of the world (exports) or buys from other countries (imports)? Look for at least one product on the web that you are sure is an export or import. (For instance, do you know any Americans who own a Japanese car?) The correct answer is C.

Practice Questions

Use the tips above and other tips in this book to help you answer the following questions.

1. How are the governments of China and North Korea similar?

   A They are both ruled by kings.

   B They both have communist governments.

   C They both follow the free enterprise system.

   D They both have democratic governments.

2. In Japan, you could expect to find

   A special economic zones.

   B a high birthrate.

   C a growing labor force.

   D an economy based on manufacturing goods for export.

3. In 1997, Hong Kong was returned to

   A Taiwan.

   B China.

   C Japan.

   D South Korea.

Use the concept web below to answer Question 4.

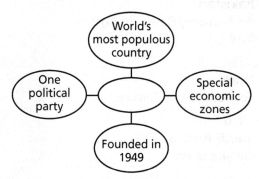

4. Which title should go in the center of the web?

   A Japan

   B North Korea

   C China

   D Taiwan

Use Web Code lca-6700 for **Chapter 7 self-test.**

Chapter

8 South, Southwest, and Central Asia

Chapter Preview

This chapter focuses on four key countries in South Asia and Southwest Asia: India, Pakistan, Israel, and Saudi Arabia. The chapter also focuses on the countries of the Stans, in Central Asia.

Country Databank
The Country Databank provides data and descriptions of each of the countries of South Asia, Southwest Asia, and Central Asia.

 **Target Reading Skill**

Cause and Effect In this chapter, you will practice understanding causes and effects.

▶ **A man docking a small boat in Jordan**

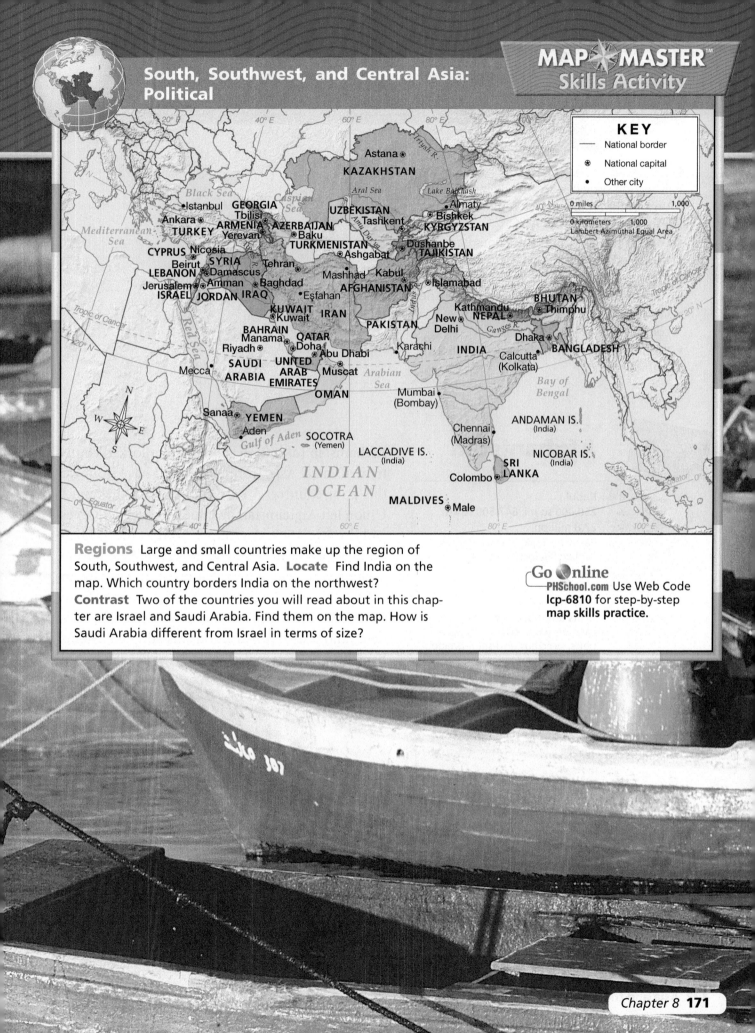

MAP MASTER™
Skills Activity

KEY

— National border

⊛ National capital

• Other city

0 miles   1,000

0 kilometers   1,000
Lambert Azimuthal Equal Area

Regions Large and small countries make up the region of South, Southwest, and Central Asia. **Locate** Find India on the map. Which country borders India on the northwest?

Contrast Two of the countries you will read about in this chapter are Israel and Saudi Arabia. Find them on the map. How is Saudi Arabia different from Israel in terms of size?

Go Online
PHSchool.com Use Web Code
lcp-6810 for step-by-step
map skills practice.

Introducing South, Southwest, and Central Asia

Guide for Reading

This section provides an introduction to the countries that make up the region of South, Southwest, and Central Asia.

- Look at the map on the previous page and then read the paragraphs below to learn about each nation.
- Analyze the data to compare the countries.
- What are the characteristics that most of the countries share?
- What are some key differences among the countries?

Afghanistan

Capital	Kabul
Land Area	250,000 sq mi; 647,500 sq km
Population	27.8 million
Ethnic Group(s)	Pashtun, Tajik, Hazara, Uzbek, Aimaks, Baloch, Turkmen
Religion(s)	Muslim
Government	transitional
Currency	new afghani
Leading Exports	fruits and nuts, handwoven carpets, wool, cotton, hides and pelts, precious and semi-precious gems
Language(s)	Pashtu (official), Dari (official), Tajik, Farsi, Uzbek, Turkmen

Afghanistan (af GAN ih stan) is a landlocked country in Central Asia. Conflict and war have troubled this poor country. A ten-year war with the Soviet Union left Afghanistan in ruins when Soviet forces withdrew in 1989. A group known as the Taliban came to power in 1996 and governed Afghanistan under a very strict interpretation of Islamic law. In 2001, U.S.-led forces drove the Taliban from power. In 2004, Hamid Karzai was elected president, and a new constitution was adopted. Members of the National Assembly were elected in 2005. The new government is working to bring peace to the country.

A girl reading out loud in an Afghanistan classroom

Armenia

Capital	Yerevan
Land Area	10,965 sq mi; 29,400 sq km
Population	3.3 million
Ethnic Group(s)	Armenian, Azeri, Russian, Kurd
Religion(s)	Christian, traditional beliefs
Government	republic
Currency	dram
Leading Exports	diamonds, scrap metal, machinery and equipment, copper ore
Language(s)	Armenian (official), Russian

Located in Southwest Asia east of Turkey, Armenia (ahr MEE nee uh) is a small, landlocked country with an ancient history. Ancient Armenia was the first country in the world to officially adopt Christianity as its religion. The Ottoman Empire conquered Armenia in the 1500s. During World War I, Armenians suffered greatly under Ottoman rule. An estimated 600,000 to 1.5 million Armenians died in what historians called the first genocide in the 1900s. Between 1920 and 1991, Armenia was part of the Soviet Union. Armenia declared its independence from the Soviet Union in 1991.

Azerbaijan

Capital	Baku
Land Area	33,243 sq mi; 86,100 sq km
Population	7.8 million
Ethnic Group(s)	Azeri, Dagestani, Russian, Armenian
Religion(s)	Muslim, Christian
Government	republic
Currency	manat
Leading Exports	oil and gas, machinery, cotton, foodstuffs
Language(s)	Azerbaijani (official), Russian

Azerbaijan (ahz ur by JAHN) is a small country in Southwest Asia located on the west coast of the Caspian Sea. Once part of the Soviet Union, Azerbaijan was the first Soviet republic to declare its independence. Within Azerbaijan is a region called Nagorno-Karabakh (nah GAWR noh kahr ah BAHK). Armenians living in this region wish to become part of Armenia. Between 1988 and 1994, Azerbaijan and Armenia fought a war over which country would control Nagorno-Karabakh. The issue remains a concern today. Azerbaijan has plentiful petroleum and natural gas resources.

Bahrain

Capital	Manama
Land Area	257 sq mi; 665 sq km
Population	656,397
Ethnic Group(s)	Bahraini, Arab, Asian
Religion(s)	Muslim
Government	constitutional hereditary monarchy
Currency	Bahraini dinar
Leading Exports	petroleum and petroleum products, aluminum, textiles
Language(s)	Arabic (official)

Bahrain (bah RAYN) is a tiny island country located in the Persian Gulf east of Saudi Arabia. Bahrain has used its petroleum resources to develop its economy. Aware that it is running out of oil, Bahrain has turned to petroleum processing and refining and has established itself as an international banking center. Unemployment and shrinking oil reserves are major economic problems in Bahrain.

Introducing South, Southwest, and Central Asia

Bangladesh

Capital	Dhaka
Land Area	51,705 sq mi; 133,910 sq km
Population	133.4 million
Ethnic Group(s)	Bengali
Religion(s)	Muslim, Hindu
Government	parliamentary democracy
Currency	taka
Leading Exports	clothing, jute and jute goods, leather, frozen fish and seafood
Language(s)	Bengali (official), Urdu, Chakma, Marma (Magh), Garo, Khasi, Santhali, Tripuri, Mro

Bangladesh (BAHNG luh desh) is located in South Asia. Most of Bangladesh lies on a plain formed by the soil deposited by three powerful rivers that empty into the Bay of Bengal. Most of the country is close to sea level and has a tropical wet climate with heavy rainfall. Low elevation and heavy rainfall contribute to floods that sometimes cause major damage. In 1998, the worst flooding in Bangladesh's history left nearly two thirds of the country underwater. Agriculture is an important part of Bangladesh's economy, and serious flooding can ruin the crops.

Bhutan

Capital	Thimphu
Land Area	18,147 sq mi; 47,000 sq km
Population	2.1 million
Ethnic Group(s)	Bhote, Nepalese, indigenous tribes
Religion(s)	Buddhist, Hindu
Government	monarchy
Currency	ngultrum
Leading Exports	electricity, cardamom, gypsum, timber, handicrafts, cement, fruit, precious stones, spices
Language(s)	Dzongkha (official), Nepali, Assamese

Bhutan (BOO tahn) is a small, landlocked country in South Asia located between India and China. Mountains cover most of Bhutan. These are the Himalayas, the highest mountains in the world. Bhutan's economy is based on agriculture and forestry. Although about 3 percent of Bhutan's land is suitable for growing crops, about 90 percent of the labor force works in farming. Most of the people live in small rural villages. Tourism is an important economic activity in Bhutan. To protect the environment and preserve Bhutan's mostly Buddhist culture, the government limits the number of people who visit Bhutan each year.

Cyprus

Capital	Nicosia
Land Area	3,568 sq mi; 9,240 sq km
Population	767,314
Ethnic Group(s)	Greek, Turkish
Religion(s)	Christian, Muslim
Government	republic
Currency	Cypriot pound and Turkish lira
Leading Exports	citrus, potatoes, grapes, cement, clothing and shoes, textiles
Language(s)	Greek (official), Turkish (official)

Cyprus (SY prus) is an island country located south of Turkey in the Mediterranean Sea. The majority of the people in Cyprus are Greek. About 12 percent of the population is Turkish. In 1974, Turkey invaded Cyprus and won control over a northern region of the island. Today, Greek Cypriots live in the southern two thirds of the island while the Turkish Cypriots occupy the northern third. In 1983, the Turkish region declared independence as a separate nation, which was recognized only by Turkey. The Greek Cypriot region has a prosperous economy.

Georgia

Capital	Tbilisi
Land Area	26,911 sq mi; 69,700 sq km
Population	5 million
Ethnic Group(s)	Georgian, Armenian, Russian, Azeri, Ossetian, Greek, Abkhaz
Religion(s)	Christian, Muslim
Government	republic
Currency	lari
Leading Exports	scrap metal, machinery, tea, chemicals, citrus fruits, other agricultural products
Language(s)	Georgian (official), Abkhazian (official), Russian

Georgia (JAWR juh) emerged as an independent nation in 1991 during the collapse of the Soviet Union. Georgia is located in Southwest Asia between Turkey and Russia. Mountains cover much of the country. Since independence, differences among Georgia's many ethnic groups have led to violence and civil war. Farming is a major economic activity. Georgia is rich in minerals, including copper. An oil pipeline extending from Azerbaijan across Georgia to Turkey is expected to strengthen the economy.

India

Capital	New Delhi
Land Area	1,147,949 sq mi; 2,973,190 sq km
Population	1.05 billion
Ethnic Group(s)	Indo-Aryan, Dravidian, Mongoloid
Religion(s)	Hindu, Muslim, Christian, Buddhist, traditional beliefs
Government	federal republic
Currency	Indian rupee
Leading Exports	textile goods, gems and jewelry, engineering goods, chemicals
Language(s)	Hindi (official), English (official), Urdu, Bengali, Marathi, Telugu, Tamil, Bihari, Gujarati, Kanarese

India (IN dee uh) is the largest country in South Asia and the second-most-populated country in the world. Only China has a larger population than India. India's history dates back to ancient times, with one of the world's earliest civilizations developing in the Indus Valley. A former British colony, India today consists of 28 states governed under a democratic system. A wide range of activities support India's economy. These include farming and modern industries such as textiles, steel, and computer software.

Iran

Capital	Tehran
Land Area	631,660 sq mi; 1,636,000 sq km
Population	66.6 million
Ethnic Group(s)	Persian, Azari, Gilaki and Mazandariani, Kurd, Arab, Lur, Baloch, Turkmen
Religion(s)	Muslim, Jewish, Christian
Government	theocratic republic
Currency	Iranian rial
Leading Exports	petroleum, carpets, fruits and nuts, iron and steel, chemicals
Language(s)	Farsi (official), Azerbaijani, Gilak, Mazanderani, Kurdish, Baluchi, Arabic, Turkmen

Known as Persia until 1935, Iran (ih RAN) became a republic governed under Islamic law in 1979. Islam is the official religion and nearly 100 percent of Iranians are Muslim. Iran's economy depends on the oil industry. Despite recent high oil prices, inflation and unemployment remain high. In 1980, Iraq invaded Iran, beginning an indecisive eight-year war fought over territory claimed by both countries. Iran's commitment to developing nuclear weapons and its support of terrorism have led to tense relations with many countries, including the United States.

Introducing South, Southwest, and Central Asia

Iraq

Capital	Baghdad
Land Area	166,858 sq mi; 432,162 sq km
Population	24.7 million
Ethnic Group(s)	Arab, Kurd, Turkoman, Assyrian
Religion(s)	Muslim, Christian
Government	republic
Currency	Iraqi dinar
Leading Exports	crude oil
Language(s)	Arabic (official), Kurdish, Turkic languages, Armenian, Assyrian

Iraq (ih RAHK) became the focus of world attention when it invaded neighboring Kuwait in 1990. The United States led a group of 32 countries in the Persian Gulf War, defeating Iraq. After the war, the United Nations required Iraq to give up its chemical and nuclear weapons programs. Iraq's refusal to do so led to a second U.S.-led invasion in 2003. Dictator Saddam Hussein and his government were quickly removed, and a new government was elected in 2005. Violence remains a problem.

Israel

Capital	Jerusalem
Land Area	7,849 sq mi; 20,330 sq km
Population	6 million
Ethnic Group(s)	Jewish, Arab
Religion(s)	Jewish, Muslim, Christian
Government	parliamentary democracy
Currency	shekel
Leading Exports	machinery and equipment, cut diamonds, software, agricultural products, chemicals, textiles and clothing
Language(s)	Hebrew (official), Arabic (official), Yiddish, German, Russian, Polish, Romanian, Persian

Israel (IZ ree ul) lies between Egypt and Lebanon and borders the Mediterranean Sea. After World War II, the United Nations allowed Israel to form as a Jewish state, but Arab nations in Southwest Asia opposed its formation. They fought a series of wars in which the Israelis were victorious and gained new territories. However, violence beween Israel and Palestinian residents of these areas continued. Peace talks over the last several decades have been hampered by Palestinian terrorist attacks, aggressive Israeli military counter-terrorism operations, and mistrust on both sides. In 2005, Israel began pulling out of the Gaza Strip and parts of the West Bank.

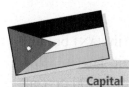

Jordan

Capital	Amman
Land Area	35,510 sq mi; 91,971 sq km
Population	5.3 million
Ethnic Group(s)	Arab, Circassian, Armenian
Religion(s)	Muslim, Christian
Government	constitutional monarchy
Currency	Jordanian dinar
Leading Exports	phosphate, fertilizers, potash, agricultural products, manufactured goods, pharmaceuticals
Language(s)	Arabic (official)

Jordan (JAWRD un) is a Southwest Asian country located northwest of Saudi Arabia. After gaining its independence from the British in 1946, the country was ruled for more than forty years by King Hussein. King Hussein established parliamentary elections and a peace treaty with Israel. After King Hussein's death in 1999, his son, Abdullah, took the throne and worked to bring economic reforms. Recent trade agreements with other countries and increased foreign investment have improved Jordan's economy. The economy is based on tourism, shipping, and the export of phosphate.

Kazakhstan

Capital	Astana
Land Area	1,030,810 sq mi; 2,669,800 sq km
Population	16.7 million
Ethnic Group(s)	Kazakh, Russian, Ukrainian, Uzbek, Uighur
Religion(s)	Muslim, Christian
Government	republic
Currency	tenge
Leading Exports	oil and oil products, ferrous metals, machinery, chemicals, grain, wool, meat, coal
Language(s)	Kazakh (official), Russian, Uighur, Korean, German

Kazakhstan (kah zahk STAHN) is a former Soviet republic, located northwest of China, that struggles to find its national identity. The native people of the area are descendants of Turkic and Mongol tribes who for years did not think of themselves as a nation. Russia conquered these peoples in the 1700s. During the mid-1900s, many Soviet citizens came to cultivate the country's northern pastures as part of a governmental agricultural project. After the country gained independence in 1991, some of these native Russians left. Today, the country is moving quickly to establish a market economy as well as a national identity.

Kuwait

Capital	Kuwait City
Land Area	6,880 sq mi; 17,820 sq km
Population	2.1 million
Ethnic Group(s)	Arab, South Asian
Religion(s)	Muslim, Christian, Hindu, traditional beliefs
Government	nominal constitutional monarchy
Currency	Kuwaiti dinar
Leading Exports	oil and refined products, fertilizers
Language(s)	Arabic (official), English

Kuwait (koo WAYT) is a small country on the Persian Gulf. Its neighbors are Iran, Iraq, and Saudi Arabia. Mainly desert, the country has large oil and gas reserves. Ninety-five percent of its export earnings are from oil. In 1990, Kuwait was invaded by neighboring Iraq. The United States and other countries came to Kuwait's defense in a conflict known as the Persian Gulf War. After the war ended in 1991, Kuwait spent billions on repairs to its oil infrastructure and built a wall on its Iraqi border.

Kuwaitis celebrating the end of the Persian Gulf War

Introducing South, Southwest, and Central Asia

Kyrgyzstan

Capital	Bishkek
Land Area	73,861 sq mi; 191,300 sq km
Population	4.8 million
Ethnic Group(s)	Kyrgyz, Russian, Uzbek, Tatar, Ukrainian
Religion(s)	Muslim, Christian
Government	republic
Currency	som
Leading Exports	cotton, wool, meat, tobacco, gold, mercury, uranium, hydropower, machinery, shoes
Language(s)	Kyrgyz (official), Russian (official)

Kyrgyzstan (kihr gih STAN) is a mountainous Central Asian country located west of China. In the late 1800s, Kyrgyzstan was annexed by Russia. It gained its independence from the Soviet Union more than one hundred years later. Currently, Kyrgyzstan's rural population is growing faster than its urban population. The country is agriculturally self-sufficient, which gives it an economic advantage. Kyrgyzstan is focused on many of the same issues that face other nations in the region. These include improving its economy and making democratic reforms.

Lebanon

Capital	Beirut
Land Area	3,950 sq mi; 10,230 sq km
Population	3.7 million
Ethnic Group(s)	Arab, Armenian
Religion(s)	Muslim, Christian
Government	republic
Currency	Lebanese pound
Leading Exports	foodstuffs, textiles, chemicals, metal products, electrical products, jewelry, paper products
Language(s)	Arabic (official), French, Armenian, Assyrian

Lebanon (LEB uh nahn) is a Southwest Asian nation on the Mediterranean Sea, bordered by Israel and Syria. Although it only became a nation in modern times, it has some of the world's most ancient human settlements. The country has a Muslim majority and a large minority of Christians. Lebanon has suffered from a 16-year civil war, an invasion by Israel in 1981, and fighting between Hezbollah terrorists based in southern Lebanon and Israel in 2006. It faces many challenges as it tries to rebuild. Lebanon has one of the highest literacy rates in the region and is a vibrant economic and cultural center.

Maldives

Capital	Malé
Land Area	116 sq mi; 300 sq km
Population	320,165
Ethnic Group(s)	South Indian, Sinhalese, Arab
Religion(s)	Muslim
Government	republic
Currency	rufiyaa
Leading Exports	fish, clothing
Language(s)	Dhivehi (Maldivian)

Maldives (MAL dyvz) is a group of about 1,300 islands in the Indian Ocean southwest of India. Today, only about 200 of these small coral islands are inhabited. Located at the center of Arab trade routes, the islands were a stopping place for Arab traders who brought Islam with them. For much of their history, the Maldives were ruled by Muslim sultans, but the islands became a British protectorate in 1887. The country gained independence from the British in 1965. A major economic goal for the Maldives is the growth of a tourist trade.

Nepal

Capital	Kathmandu
Land Area	52,818 sq mi; 136,800 sq km
Population	25.9 million
Ethnic Group(s)	Brahman, Chetri, Newar, Gurung, Magar, Tamang, Rai, Limpu, Sherpa, Tharu
Religion(s)	Hindu, Buddhist, Muslim
Government	parliamentary democracy and constitutional monarchy
Currency	Nepalese rupee
Leading Exports	carpets, clothing, leather goods, jute goods, grain
Language(s)	Nepali (official), Maithilli, Bhojpuri

Nepal (nuh PAWL) is a country with a recent history of troubled leadership. Though a kingdom traditionally ruled by a series of royal families, in 1990 Nepal formed a multiparty government with a modern constitution. This began a period of political turmoil, including the killing of most of the royal family, a dissolved parliament, and the postponement of elections. The current king is working to resolve differences and hold elections once again. One of the poorest nations in the world, Nepal's economy depends on agriculture and the tourists who come to see the Himalayas that dominate the country's physical geography.

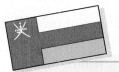

Oman

Capital	Muscat
Land Area	82,030 sq mi; 212,460 sq km
Population	2.7 million
Ethnic Group(s)	Arab, Baluchi, South Asian, African
Religion(s)	Muslim, Hindu
Government	monarchy
Currency	Omani rial
Leading Exports	petroleum, reexports, fish, metals, textiles
Language(s)	Arabic (official), Baluchi

Oman (oh MAHN) shares a western border with Yemen, the United Arab Emirates, and Saudi Arabia. To the east, it is bordered by the Arabian Sea, the Gulf of Oman, and the Persian Gulf. The nation is ruled by a monarch. Although the country is the least developed of the Persian Gulf nations, the current sultan's efforts to modernize have increased Oman's standing in the international community. Oil exports have brought some prosperity to Oman. The country also has a large fishing industry.

Pakistan

Capital	Islamabad
Land Area	300,664 sq mi; 778,720 sq km
Population	147.7 million
Ethnic Group(s)	Punjabi, Sindhi, Pashtun (Pathan), Baloch, Muhajir
Religion(s)	Muslim, Christian, Hindu
Government	federal republic
Currency	Pakistani rupee
Leading Exports	textiles (clothing, cotton cloth, and yarn), rice, other agricultural products
Language(s)	Urdu (official), Punjabi, Sindhi, Pashtu, Baluchi, Brahui

Pakistan (PAK ih stan) is a nation with a history of conflict among its many religious and ethnic groups. Pakistan is located on the shores of the Arabian Sea with India to the east, Iran and Afghanistan to the west, and China to the north. Pakistan was created in 1947, when tensions between Muslims and Hindus caused the British to divide British India into Muslim Pakistan and mostly-Hindu India. In 1971, East Pakistan became the separate country of Bangladesh. Tensions with India have continued since Pakistan was created. At the end of the 1900s, Pakistan began testing nuclear weapons.

Introducing South, Southwest, and Central Asia

Qatar

Capital	Doha
Land Area	4,416 sq mi; 11,437 sq km
Population	793,341
Ethnic Group(s)	Arab, South Asian
Religion(s)	Muslim
Government	traditional monarchy
Currency	Qatari riyal
Leading Exports	petroleum products, fertilizers, steel
Language(s)	Arabic (official)

Qatar (kah TAHR) is an oil-rich monarchy on the northeastern tip of the Arabian Peninsula. The country is a small peninsula in the Persian Gulf. A single family has ruled Qatar since the mid-1800s. With plentiful oil and natural gas resources, Qatar is one of the wealthiest nations in Southwest Asia and provides free health care and education to its citizens. It has a large immigrant population, made up of people from northern Africa, the Indian subcontinent, and Iran, who come to Qatar to work in the oil industry.

Saudi Arabia

Capital	Riyadh and Jiddah
Land Area	756,981 sq mi; 1,960,582 sq km
Population	23.5 million
Ethnic Group(s)	Arab, mixed black and Asian
Religion(s)	Muslim
Government	monarchy
Currency	Saudi riyal
Leading Exports	petroleum and petroleum products
Language(s)	Arabic (official)

Saudi Arabia (SAW dee uh RAY bee uh) is an oil-rich nation bordering the Red Sea and the Persian Gulf north of Yemen. Medina and Mecca, two of Islam's holiest cities, are located in Saudi Arabia. This large country is more than 95 percent desert, but oil discovered there in the 1930s quickly brought it into a position of economic power. In 1990, Saudi Arabia received 400,000 Kuwaiti refugees following Iraq's invasion of Kuwait. It played a key role as a launching point for the United States-led military effort to free Kuwait from Iraqi occupation. Today, the royal family of Saudi Arabia faces the issues of a growing population and a petroleum-dominated economy.

Sri Lanka

Capital	Colombo
Land Area	24,996 sq mi; 64,740 sq km
Population	19.6 million
Ethnic Group(s)	Sinhalese, Tamil, Moor, Burgher, Malay, Vedda
Religion(s)	Buddhist, Hindu, Christian, Muslim
Government	republic
Currency	Sri Lankan rupee
Leading Exports	textiles and clothing, tea, diamonds, coconut products, petroleum products
Language(s)	Sinhala (official), Tamil (official), English (official), Sinhalese-Tamil

Sri Lanka (sree LAHNG kuh) is made up of a large island and several small coral islands in the Indian Ocean off the coast of India. This small nation was controlled by other countries until 1948, when it finally gained its independence. Independence did not, however, bring stability to the country. Civil war between the majority Sinhalese group, made up of Buddhists, and the minority Tamil group, made up mainly of Hindus and Muslims, has raged for more than 20 years. A land of great physical and cultural diversity, Sri Lanka is the world's largest exporter of tea.

A lace shop at an outdoor market in Syria

Syria

Capital	Damascus
Land Area	71,062 sq mi; 184,050 sq km
Population	17.2 million
Ethnic Group(s)	Arab, Kurd, Armenian
Religion(s)	Muslim, Christian
Government	republic under military regime
Currency	Syrian pound
Leading Exports	crude oil, textiles, fruits and vegetables, raw cotton
Language(s)	Arabic (official), French, Kurdish, Armenian, Circassian, Turkic languages, Assyrian, Aramaic

Syria (SIHR ee uh) is a Southwest Asian country on the shores of the Mediterranean Sea, between Lebanon and Turkey. After World War I, the French controlled Syria until its independence in 1946. Since that time, Syria has been governed by a series of military leaders. The country opposes its neighbor, Israel, to whom it lost an area known as the Golan Heights in 1967 during the Arab-Israeli War. Though Syria has large oil supplies, much of its income from oil is spent on military defense.

Tajikistan

Capital	Dushanbe
Land Area	55,096 sq mi; 142,700 sq km
Population	6.7 million
Ethnic Group(s)	Tajik, Uzbek, Russian
Religion(s)	Muslim
Government	republic
Currency	somoni
Leading Exports	aluminum, electricity, cotton, fruits, vegetable oil, textiles
Language(s)	Tajiki (official), Russian

Tajikistan (tah jik ih STAN) is a struggling former Soviet republic located in Central Asia. After gaining independence from the Soviet Union in 1991, the nation went through a five-year civil war and three changes in government. The country has 14 percent of the world's uranium reserves, but has not successfully developed this resource. Tajikistan faces many challenges, including an unstable economy, poor health care, and continuing conflict among ethnic groups.

Introducing South, Southwest, and Central Asia

Turkey

Capital	Ankara
Land Area	297,590 sq mi; 770,760 sq km
Population	67.3 million
Ethnic Group(s)	Turkish, Kurd
Religion(s)	Muslim
Government	republican parliamentary democracy
Currency	Turkish lira
Leading Exports	clothing, foodstuffs, textiles, metal manufactured goods, trasport equipment
Language(s)	Turkish (official), Kurdish, Arabic, Circassian, Armenian, Greek, Georgian, Ladino

Turkey (TUR kee) is a primarily Muslim country that straddles two continents—Asia and Europe. Its location on the Black Sea and Mediterranean Sea has always made it a crossroads of trade and culture. Turkey has a strong economy and has great influence in the region. However, a major fault line leaves many Turkish cities vulnerable to earthquakes. The country's two main ethnic groups, Turks and Kurds, are in conflict. Many Kurds seek to form their own state.

Turkmenistan

Capital	Ashgabat
Land Area	188,455 sq mi; 488,100 sq km
Population	4.7 million
Ethnic Group(s)	Turkmen, Uzbek, Russian, Kazakh
Religion(s)	Muslim, Christian
Government	republic
Currency	manat
Leading Exports	gas, oil, cotton fiber, textiles
Language(s)	Turkmen (official), Uzbek, Russian

Turkmenistan (turk MEN ih stan) is a former Soviet republic which borders the Caspian Sea between Kazakhstan and Iran. Turkmenistan is mostly desert. Only 2 percent of the total land area is suitable for agriculture. The country gained its independence in 1991 and formed a democracy, but the president exercises complete control over the government. Culturally, Turkmenistan is dominated by Sunni Muslims. It has abundant natural gas reserves and is currently working to improve its ability to extract and transport this valuable resource.

United Arab Emirates

Capital	Abu Dhabi
Land Area	32,000 sq mi; 82,880 sq km
Population	2.4 million
Ethnic Group(s)	Arab, South Asian
Religion(s)	Muslim
Government	federation
Currency	UAE dirham
Leading Exports	crude oil, natural gas, reexports, dried fish, dates
Language(s)	Arabic (official), Farsi, Indian and Pakistani languages, English

The United Arab Emirates (yoo NYT id AR ub EM ur uts) was created when seven Southwest Asian states united as a single nation. The United Arab Emirates (UAE) is bordered by the Gulf of Oman and the Persian Gulf between Saudi Arabia and Oman. The UAE is mostly desert. With few water resources, the country relies on an extensive irrigation system. The UAE is rich in oil and natural gas resources. It has a strong economy and good health care and education. It has taken on an important role in the affairs of the region.

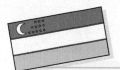

Uzbekistan

Capital	Tashkent
Land Area	164,247 sq mi; 425,400 sq km
Population	25.5 million
Ethnic Group(s)	Uzbek, Russian, Tajik, Kazakh, Karakalpak, Tatar
Religion(s)	Muslim, Christian
Government	republic
Currency	som
Leading Exports	cotton, gold, energy products, mineral fertilizers, ferrous metals, textiles, food products, automobiles
Language(s)	Arabic (official)

Uzbekistan (ooz bek ih STAN) is a former Soviet republic in Central Asia north of Afghanistan. Conquered by Russia in the late 1800s, it came under Communist control in 1924. Heavy growing of cotton and grain by the Soviet Union depleted its water supplies and polluted the land in many areas. Since it gained its independence in 1991, Uzbekistan has looked to develop its extensive mineral and oil resources. However, the country's economy still depends on agriculture. Uzbekistan is one of the largest exporters of cotton in the world.

Yemen

Capital	Sana
Land Area	203,849 sq mi; 527,970 sq km
Population	18.7 million
Ethnic Group(s)	Arab, mixed black and Arab, South Asian
Religion(s)	Muslim
Government	republic
Currency	Yemeni rial
Leading Exports	crude oil, coffee, dried and salted fish
Language(s)	Arabic

Yemen (YEM un) is located at the southern tip of the Arabian Peninsula. Bordered by Saudi Arabia and Oman, it occupies a fertile strip along the Red Sea. Yemen's recent history is one of conflict, including years of civil war that led to the country being divided in half. In 1990, the country was reunited, but still remains politically unstable. Yemen has large oil, gas, and mineral reserves. Agriculture continues to support most of the population.

SOURCES: DK World Desk Reference Online; CIA World Factbook Online; *World Almanac*, 2003

Assessment

Comprehension and Critical Thinking

1. Identify What is the most common ethnic group in the region?

2. Apply Information What is the language in countries that include this ethnic group?

3. Draw Conclusions What are the characteristics that most of the countries share?

4. Contrast What are some key differences among the countries?

5. Summarize In which region is petroleum a leading export, South Asia or Southwest Asia?

6. Make a Bar Graph Create a bar graph showing the population of the four most populous countries in this region.

Keeping Current

Access the **DK World Desk Reference Online** at **PHSchool.com** for up-to-date information about the countries in this chapter.

Go Online
PHSchool.com

Web Code: Ice-6800

Prepare to Read

Objectives

In this section you will
1. Learn about key features of India's population.
2. Examine the state of India's economy.
3. Understand major challenges facing India.

Taking Notes

As you read this section, look for ways in which India's growing population has an effect on its development. Copy the chart below, and record your findings in it.

CAUSE		EFFECTS
• India's population is growing.	⟹	•

Target Reading Skill

Identify Causes and Effects Identifying causes and effects helps you understand how events and situations are related. A cause makes something happen. An effect is what happens as a result. As you read this section, think of India's growing population as a cause. What are the effects of this cause on India's development?

Key Terms

- **textiles** (TEKS tylz) *n.* cloth made by weaving or by knitting
- **malnutrition** (mal noo TRISH un) *n.* poor nutrition caused by a lack of food or an unbalanced diet
- **life expectancy** (lyf ek SPEK tun see) *n.* the average number of years a person is expected to live
- **literacy rate** (LIT ur uh see rayt) *n.* the percentage of a population age 15 and over that can read and write

Students at a private school for boys in Rajasthan, India

In Chapter 7, you read that the gross domestic product (GDP) is the total value of all the goods and services produced in an economy. India's gross domestic product is $3.6 trillion. This makes India's GDP the fourth highest in the world. Yet the standard of living in India is very low compared with many other countries, even though India's GDP is higher. This is because India's $3.6 trillion is shared by more than one billion people. If you divided that $3.6 trillion by India's population, each person would have about $3,300. By comparison, Germany's GDP is about $2.5 trillion. But Germany has a much lower population than India has. If you divided Germany's $2.5 trillion by its population, each person would have about $30,400.

India's large population presents many challenges to the country. At the same time, India's people are an important resource in the drive to develop the country.

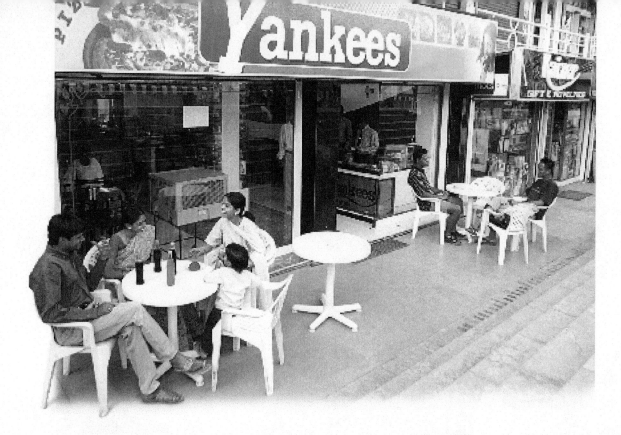

Key Features of India's Population

India is the second-most-populated country in the world. Only China's population is bigger. India's population is changing in ways that affect the country's development.

A Growing Population India has a population of more than one billion people. This large population is growing. India has one of the world's highest population growth rates. By 2050, India is expected to be the world's most populated country.

Growing Urban Areas About 72 percent of India's population lives in rural areas. But with such a large population, that means nearly 300 million people were living in urban areas in 2000. By 2030, the urban population of India is expected to reach more than 600 million. Using 2006 population figures, that equals the combined total populations of the United States, Russia, Mexico, and South Korea.

An Expanding Middle Class About one fourth of India's people lives in poverty. They earn just enough money to buy the food they need to survive. In recent years, however, India's middle class has been growing. People in the middle class are neither very rich nor very poor. They earn enough money to buy goods and services that improve their lives. By some estimates, India's middle class is one of the largest in the world.

India's Middle Class
Although about one fourth of India's population is poor, India has a growing middle class that earns enough money to spend on consumer goods from pizza to cars. The growth of India's middle class is one result of its growing economy. **Analyze Images** *Do you think this photo shows an urban area or a rural area? Explain your answer.*

✓ Reading Check **What are some key features of India's population?**

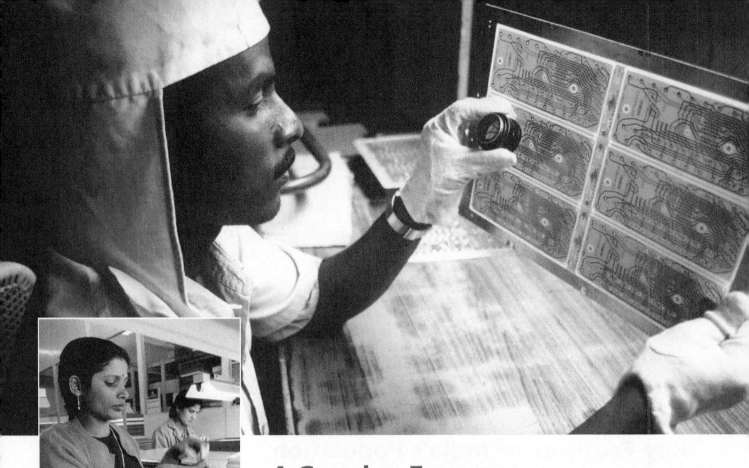

A worker checks electronic circuit boards in Bangalore (large photo); other workers assemble watches (small photo).

A Growing Economy

India has the second-fastest-growing economy in Asia. Only China's economy is growing faster. A democratic government supports India's economy. In the early 1990s, the government made changes to speed economic progress. For example, the government made it easier for foreign companies to do business in India. India's middle class helps the economy, too. The middle class provides a huge market for goods and services produced and sold in India. As the middle class grows, the number of poor people in India is expected to decrease.

Expanding industries in India are also helping the country's economy. One of India's major industries is computer software programming. India has large numbers of highly educated and skilled workers in the computer software industry. India's computer software has become a major export. Products such as electrical appliances are being manufactured in greater numbers. India also has a thriving film industry. More movies are produced in India than in any other country.

India imports more than it exports, but the country can produce all its own food. India exports textiles, or cloth, making cotton and silk clothing that are sold worldwide. Gemstones and jewelry are another major export. The United States buys the largest share of India's exports.

✓ Reading Check **What are some major industries in India?**

India

India has great cultural diversity, or variety. Most Indians are Hindus. As you can see on the map, however, Muslims, followers of Islam, are a majority in one of India's states. But there are Muslims in every other state in India. Millions of Indians practice Christianity, Sikhism, and other religions. Indians also speak hundreds of different languages. Hindi has more speakers than any other language in India. However, many other languages have millions of speakers, and most Indians speak a language other than Hindi.

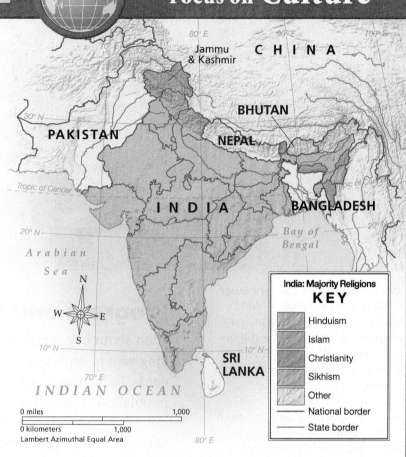

India: Majority Religions
KEY

- Hinduism
- Islam
- Christianity
- Sikhism
- Other
- National border
- State border

0 miles 1,000
0 kilometers 1,000
Lambert Azimuthal Equal Area

Religions

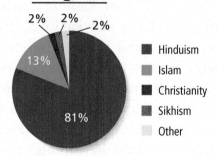

2% 2% 2%
13%
81%

- Hinduism
- Islam
- Christianity
- Sikhism
- Other

SOURCE: *CIA World Factbook*

Where Muslims Live

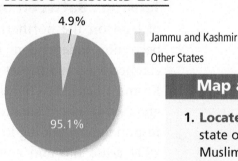

4.9%
95.1%

- Jammu and Kashmir
- Other States

SOURCE: Census of India

Languages

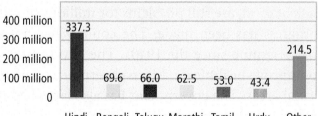

400 million
300 million   337.3
200 million   214.5
100 million   69.6 66.0 62.5 53.0 43.4
0

Hindi Bengali Telugu Marathi Tamil Urdu Other Languages

SOURCE: Census of India, 1991

Map and Chart Skills

1. **Locate** Which is the only state on the map with a Muslim majority?
2. **Note** Based on the graphs, what percentage of India's Muslims live in that state?
3. **Infer** Would you expect states with a Hindu majority to have many people belonging to other religions?

Use Web Code **Ice-6801** for **DK World Desk Reference Online.**

Wind Power and Camel Power
India is a world leader in wind energy production. In many rural villages, however, people still use traditional methods to obtain power. At the right, a camel turns a wheel that pumps water.
Identify Effects *India's monsoons bring strong winds to much of the country. How does this affect the potential to create electricity from wind power?*

Identify Causes and Effects
What effects can a growing population have on the need for jobs, education, and housing?

Progress and Challenges

With about one fourth of its people living in poverty, India has a long way to go before all of its people enjoy higher living standards. India must meet the challenge of taking care of its growing population. The millions of people born each year will need jobs, housing, health care, and education. Food, water, and electricity will also be in higher demand. Another challenge facing India is its relations with its neighbor Pakistan.

Tensions Between India and Pakistan Kashmir is an area of land on the northern borders of India and Pakistan. Since becoming independent in 1947, India and Pakistan have both claimed Kashmir as part of their territory. The disagreement over Kashmir has led to fighting between the two countries. Tensions grew worse after India tested nuclear weapons in 1998. Pakistan responded by holding its own nuclear weapons tests. However, a 2004 cease fire and continuing peace talks have brought new hope to the troubled region.

Health Care Disease and **malnutrition,** or poor nutrition caused by a lack of food, are still problems for millions of Indian people. Yet progress has been made. The country has not suffered from major famine since the 1940s. The government has taken steps to improve health care. More government-paid doctors work in rural areas. The government has also launched programs that protect people from certain diseases.

As a result of these efforts, people in India are living longer. The average life expectancy in India has increased from 53 years in 1981 to 63 years in 2003. **Life expectancy** is the average number of years a person is expected to live. It is an important measure of how well a country is caring for its citizens.

Education Another way that is used to measure how well a country is taking care of its people is the literacy rate. A country's **literacy rate** shows the percentage of the population age 15 and over that can read and write. India's literacy rate is far lower than the literacy rate in the United States, but it is rapidly rising. In 1991, just over 50 percent of India's population were literate. In 2001, the literacy rate had risen to about 65 percent. Thanks to ongoing efforts to improve education, India's literacy rate is continuing to rise.

✓ **Reading Check** How has India improved health care and education for its people?

People in India, like these young students, benefit from being educated.

Section 1 Assessment

Key Terms
Review the key terms at the beginning of this section. Use each term in a sentence that explains its meaning.

Target Reading Skill

Using your Taking Notes chart, identify three effects of India's growing population.

Comprehension and Critical Thinking
1. (a) Recall What is the population of India?
(b) Find Main Ideas Why is India expected to be the world's most populated country by 2050?

(c) Identify Effects One effect of rapid urban growth is increased pollution. What might be some other effects of India's rapid urban growth?
2. (a) Note How does India's middle class help the country's economy?
(b) Identify Causes What are some other factors that are helping India's economy?
3. (a) Explain How have changes in health care increased life expectancy in India?
(b) Predict Give some reasons that a nation would want its citizens to read and write.

Writing Activity
Write an entry in your journal describing some of the challenges India must meet to take care of its growing population. Be sure to consider such factors as food and health care. Which of these challenges do you think is most important? Give one or two reasons for your answer.

For: An activity on India
Visit: PHSchool.com
Web Code: lcd-6801

Pakistan
An Economy Based on Agriculture

Prepare to Read

Objectives

In this section you will
1. Find out that Pakistan's economy is based on agriculture.
2. Learn about Pakistan's industries.

Taking Notes

As you read this section, look for ways in which Pakistan's water supply has affected its economy. Copy the chart below, and record your findings in it.

CAUSE		EFFECTS
• Water is in short supply in Pakistan.	⟹	•

Target Reading Skill

Understand Effects A cause makes something happen. An effect is what happens as the result of a specific cause. Sometimes one cause may produce several effects. As you read this section, note the effects of Pakistan's water supply on its economy. Write the effects in the Taking Notes chart.

Key Terms

- **drought** (drowt) *n.* a long period of dry weather
- **Green Revolution** (green rev uh LOO shun) *n.* a worldwide effort to increase food production in developing countries
- **self-sufficient** (self suh FISH unt) *adj.* able to supply one's own needs without any outside assistance
- **tributary** (TRIB yoo tehr ee) *n.* a river that flows into a larger river

Rainfall is scarce throughout much of Pakistan. What water the country gets is a precious resource. Pakistan's water supply includes three main sources: the Indus River, monsoon rains, and slow-melting glaciers. To make the most of its water supply, Pakistan built the world's largest irrigation system. Without rainfall, however, the gigantic system of dams, canals, ditches, and reservoirs cannot deliver the water needed for Pakistan's farms.

In 2001, Pakistan was in the middle of an extreme **drought**—a long period of dry weather. The government was so concerned over the lack of water that it considered melting part of the glaciers in northern Pakistan. One idea was to spray on charcoal, which would raise the temperature of the ice. Later that year, however, the government decided to give up the plan due to environmental concerns.

Tarbela Dam on the Indus River provides water for irrigation.

An Agricultural Nation

Pakistan's economy is based mostly on agriculture. That is why water is so important there. About half of Pakistan's labor force works in agriculture.

Farming Most of Pakistan's farming takes place in the Indus River basin, where the irrigation system is located. Cotton, wheat, sugar cane, and rice are grown there. Pakistan is among the world's top ten cotton producers. Farmers in Pakistan grow so much rice that the country exports it to other countries.

Wheat is the major food crop in Pakistan. The green revolution has helped Pakistan's farmers grow more wheat. Starting in the 1940s, **the Green Revolution** was a worldwide effort to increase food production in developing countries, including Pakistan and India. The program introduced modern farming methods and special varieties of wheat, rice, and corn that yielded more grain. The year 2000 was the first year in recent history that Pakistan did not have to import wheat. Instead, the country had enough wheat to export its extra to Afghanistan. Becoming self-sufficient in wheat production and having enough to export are major goals in Pakistan. Being **self-sufficient** means Pakistan can supply its own goods without outside assistance.

Wheat Harvest in Pakistan
Although most of Pakistan's wheat is used for food within the country, Pakistan succeeded in exporting wheat for the first time in 2000. **Analyze Images** *How does the lack of modern farm machinery indicate that this wheat was raised by a subsistence farmer?*

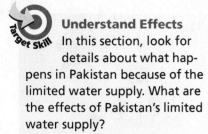

Understand Effects
In this section, look for details about what happens in Pakistan because of the limited water supply. What are the effects of Pakistan's limited water supply?

Managing the Water Supply Pakistan's farmers use thousands of canals and ditches to move water from the Indus River and its tributaries to their fields. A **tributary** is a river that flows into a larger river. In this way, farmers maintain a steady flow of water, even during droughts. As more land is irrigated, more acres are farmed. This increases the amount of crops.

Irrigation solves many farming problems, but it creates others. For example, river water contains small amounts of salts. When water evaporates, the salts are left behind. Over time, salts build up in the soil, causing plant growth to slow. Pakistani scientists are trying to find a way to treat the salt-damaged soil. They are also working to develop a type of wheat that can grow in salty soil.

Pakistanis have another water problem, one that is the opposite of drought. During the monsoon season, damaging floods can occur. One solution is the large dams built by the government. The dams catch and hold monsoon rains. The waters are then released, as needed, into irrigation canals.

✓ **Reading Check** How has irrigation helped Pakistan develop an economy based on agriculture?

Industry in Pakistan

In addition to helping farmers, dams such as the Tarbela—on the Indus River in northern Pakistan—speed industrial growth. Dams capture the energy of rushing water to create hydroelectricity. In Pakistan, hydroelectric power plants produce electricity to run textile mills and other factories. Most industry is located near the sources of hydroelectric power, on the plains of the Indus River.

Links Across The World

Cricket One of the most popular sports in Pakistan is cricket. Played with a bat and a ball, cricket is a team sport widely played in Great Britain and in former colonies of the British Empire. Cricket is also popular in India, Bangladesh, Sri Lanka, Australia, and New Zealand. Like Pakistan, these countries were once British territories. In 1992, Pakistan's international cricket team won the Cricket World Cup.

Making steel at a small factory near Lahore, Pakistan

Pakistan

As the map and graphs show, Pakistan has several different ethnic groups, whose members speak several different languages. However, Islam is very much the dominant religion. Islam is the majority religion for every major ethnic group in Pakistan. Only very small minorities practice religions other than Islam.

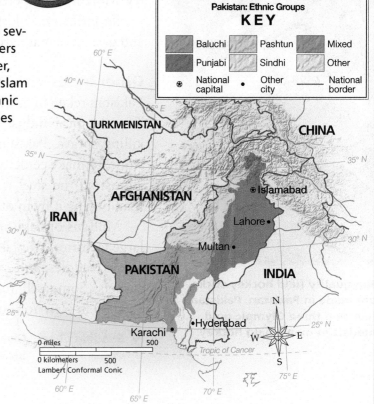

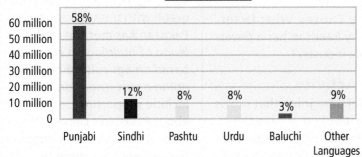

A Pashtun woman in Pakistan

Religions*

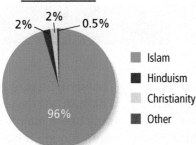

2%   2%   0.5%

96%

- Islam
- Hinduism
- Christianity
- Other

SOURCE: Pakistan Statistics Division
*Numbers may not equal 100% due to rounding.

Languages

58%	12%	8%	8%	3%	9%
Punjabi	Sindhi	Pashtu	Urdu	Baluchi	Other Languages

60 million
50 million
40 million
30 million
20 million
10 million
0

SOURCE: *CIA World Factbook*

Map and Chart Skills

1. **Locate** Based on the map, which two languages are spoken across the largest areas of Pakistan?

2. **Identify** Based on the graph, which of these languages has the most speakers?

3. **Synthesize** What might explain why one language has so many more speakers, even though both are spoken across areas of similar size?

Use Web Code **Ice-6802** for **DK World Desk Reference Online.**

Industry Based on Agriculture Pakistan began its growth in industry by building on what its people knew best: agriculture. Today, Pakistan's economy depends largely on its textile industry. More than 60 percent of the country's exports come from the textile industry. Pakistan's textile products include yarn, cloth, and garments made from cotton grown by the country's farmers.

Other Industries in Pakistan Although most industries in Pakistan relate to farming, the nation has other industries as well. The chemical industry produces paint, soap, dye, and insect-killing sprays. Pakistan uses one of its natural resources, limestone, to make cement. Several steel mills allow Pakistan to make almost all the steel it needs. Producing steel can be less costly than buying it from other countries.

Millions of Pakistanis work in small workshops instead of in large factories. Workshops produce field hockey sticks, furniture, knives, saddles, and carpets. Pakistan is famous for its beautiful carpets. Some sell for as much as $25,000 in Pakistan—and $50,000 in New York or London.

Top-quality field hockey sticks are made in Pakistan. Pakistan has won three Olympic gold medals in men's field hockey.

✓ **Reading Check** Give an example of an industry in Pakistan based on agriculture.

Section 2 Assessment

Key Terms
Review the key terms at the beginning of this section. Use each term in a sentence that explains its meaning.

Target Reading Skill
Describe two or more effects of Pakistan's water supply on the economy. Use the information in your Taking Notes chart.

Comprehension and Critical Thinking
1. (a) Recall Where does most of the farming in Pakistan take place?

(b) Summarize How did the green revolution help Pakistan's farmers grow more wheat?
(c) Identify Effects What is one negative effect of heavy irrigation in Pakistan?
2. (a) Explain How does Pakistan's textile industry help the country's economy?
(b) Identify Causes What factor explains why Pakistan has a developed textile industry?

Writing Activity
Write a brief paragraph that shows your understanding of how the people of Pakistan have responded to conditions in their physical environment. Be sure to include ways Pakistan has developed an economy based mainly on agriculture even though it has a dry climate.

> **Writing Tip** Begin your paragraph with this topic sentence: *Pakistan has met the challenge of building an economy based on agriculture by developing a vast irrigation system.* Include supporting details about Pakistan's climate, the Indus River, Pakistan's irrigation system, and farming.

Prepare to Read

Objectives
In this section you will
1. Discover how Israel's economy has grown and changed over the years.
2. Learn about the different peoples living in Israel.

Taking Notes
As you read this section, look for the major ideas about the economy and cultures of Israel. Copy the diagram below, and record your findings in it.

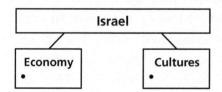

Target Reading Skill
Recognize Multiple Causes Sometimes multiple causes make one effect happen. As you read, look for three causes that have contributed to Israel's success in agriculture.

Key Terms
- **irrigation** (ihr uh GAY shun) *n.* the watering of crops using canals and other artificial waterways
- **kibbutz** (kih BOOTS) *n.* a cooperative settlement
- **West Bank** (west bank) *n.* a disputed region on the western bank of the Jordan River
- **Gaza Strip** (GAHZ uh strip) *n.* a disputed region on the Mediterranean coast

I t is spring in the country of Israel. The khamsin (kam SEEN) has come. The khamsin is a wind—a hot wind—that blows into the country from the south. *Khamsin* means "wind of 50 days."

For many days, the hot khamsin will blow over a harsh landscape. The southern half of Israel is the unforgiving Negev Desert, an arid land of plains and mountains. As the wind continues north, it raises waves on a huge salt-water lake with little life. The lake is called the Dead Sea. The shore of the Dead Sea is the lowest spot on Earth. Rocky highlands lie north of the lake.

Israel is a rugged land, as harsh as the khamsin is hot. Yet the peoples of Israel have turned this dry and rocky place into a country with a modern economy and vibrant cultures.

Harvesting hay on a kibbutz in Galilee, Israel

Israel's Economy

Fresh water and land suitable for farming are in especially short supply in Israel. Historically, people in the region made their living by herding animals across the desert, not by farming.

Agriculture The people of Israel have managed to make farms in their desert. They grow fruits, vegetables, cotton, and other crops. How can they farm in a land with little water?

As in Pakistan, the answer is irrigation. **Irrigation** is the watering of crops using canals and other artificial waterways. Water from the Sea of Galilee, a freshwater lake in northern Israel, is pumped through a vast network of canals and pipelines. Other technological achievements have contributed to Israel's success in agriculture. During the 1950s, the Israelis drained Lake Hula, in northern Israel, and nearby swamps. This created an additional 12,000 acres of farmland.

Another factor in the success of Israeli agriculture has been cooperation among farm workers. Most of them live in small farming villages called *moshavim* (moh shah VEEM). The workers cooperate by combining their money to buy equipment and sharing information about new methods of farming. They also pool their crops to get a better price.

Manufacturing Today, about one in four Israelis work in manufacturing. Major Israeli industries include textiles, processed foods, fertilizers, and plastics. Many companies manufacture goods for the Israeli military. But most Israeli industry is in high technology. Israeli electronic and scientific equipment is respected around the world.

This woman is making electronic cash registers at a factory in Dimona, a town in the Negev Desert.

Kibbutzim Some manufacturing is done on cooperative settlements called kibbutzim. People who live on a **kibbutz** (kih BOOTS) cooperate in all parts of life. They eat together, work together, and share profits equally. Originally, most kibbutzim were farming communities. Today, modern farming machinery has replaced the need for many farm workers. As a result, many kibbutzim have turned to manufacturing.

COUNTRY PROFILE   Focus on **Government**

Israel

Israel controls two types of land. The orange area on the map is Israel within its pre-1967 borders, which the United States and other countries consider part of Israel. Its people are mostly Israeli Jews. Since 1967, Israel has controlled the lands known by the Palestinians as the "occupied territories." The people who live there are mostly non-Israeli Arabs. However, in 2005 Israel withdrew from the Gaza Strip. Including the occupied territories, Israel controls an area slightly larger than New Jersey. Yet the population under Israeli control is larger than New Jersey's. Partly because there is so little land, there are sharp conflicts between Israelis and Arabs over control of this land.

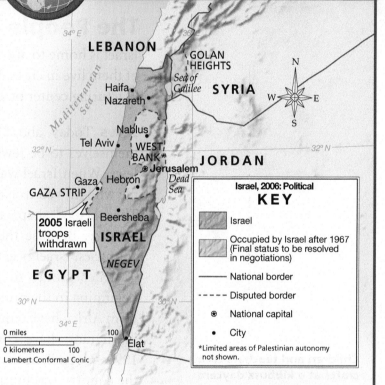

Israel: Population, 2000

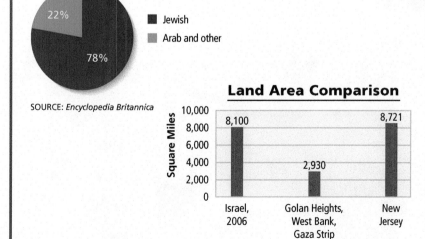

22% — Jewish

78% — Arab and other

SOURCE: *Encyclopedia Britannica*

Land Area Comparison

Square Miles

- Israel, 2006: 8,100
- Golan Heights, West Bank, Gaza Strip: 2,930
- New Jersey: 8,721

SOURCE: *CIA World Factbook*

Map and Chart Skills

1. **Identify** Of the two areas currently under Israeli control, which is larger?
2. **Locate** Which of these areas borders the Sea of Galilee?
3. **Synthesize** What percentage of the population of Israel is not Jewish?

Use Web Code **Ice-6803** for **DK World Desk Reference Online.**

Service Industries Today, service industries are the most important part of the Israeli economy. Service industries are industries that provide services instead of manufactured goods.

One type of service industry is trade. Israel borders the Mediterranean Sea. Its chief port city is Haifa, which has a deep-water harbor, excellent for docking ships. Many Israeli exports leave through Haifa. Many imports arrive there as well. Israel must import much of what it needs, since it has few natural resources. Imports include oil for energy and grain for food.

✓ Reading Check **What industry is the most important part of the Israeli economy?**

The People of Israel

Israel is home to about 6.5 million people. More than 90 percent of them live in cities. Israel's largest cities are Jerusalem, the manufacturing center of Tel Aviv, and the coastal city of Haifa.

Jews Today, about 80 percent of the people of Israel consider themselves to be Jews. Yet there is great diversity among Israeli Jews. When Israel was founded in 1948, most of the Jewish people who moved to Israel came from Europe and North America. They helped shape the culture and government of their new country. Because these people came from modern, developed countries, Israel became a modern, developed country, too.

Later, groups of Jews came from Middle Eastern countries. Beginning in the mid-1970s, tens of thousands of Ethiopian Jews from Africa have emigrated to Israel. More recently, many Jewish immigrants have come from Russia—nearly a million in the 1990s. Overall, nearly 3 million people have settled in Israel since the country was founded.

Children and teachers create crafts at a kibbutz daycare school in Israel.

Religious Diversity Most people in Israel practice Judaism. A small percentage of the country's population is Christian or follows other religions. The single largest religion after Judaism, however, is Islam. About 16 percent of Israel's population is Muslim.

Palestinian Arabs Most Muslims living under Israeli control are Palestinian Arabs. Israel was founded in 1948 on land that was known as Palestine. Both Jews and Palestinian Arabs have long claimed Palestine as their homeland. In a series of wars with its Arab neighbors, Israel won portions of Egypt, Jordan, and Syria. Arabs called these areas the "occupied territories." Today, the occupied territories include the West Bank and the Golan Heights. The **West Bank** is an area on the west bank, or edge, of the Jordan River. Israel gave up control of the Gaza Strip to the Palestinians in 2005. The **Gaza Strip** is a small area of land along the Mediterranean Sea.

For decades, relations between the Palestinians and the Israelis have been marked by violence despite efforts on both sides to achieve peace. Several issues have divided the two groups. For example, many Palestinians fled after the Arab-Israeli wars, and Israelis have opposed the return of large numbers of Palestinians. Many Israelis insisted that a peace agreement protect Israeli settlements in the occupied territories. Palestinians, however, have opposed this idea.

A Palestinian open-air market in Jerusalem, Israel

✓ **Reading Check** What is the single largest religion in Israel after Judaism?

Section 3 Assessment

Key Terms
Review the key terms at the beginning of this section. Use each term in a sentence that explains its meaning.

 ## Target Reading Skill
What are three causes of Israel's success in agriculture?

Comprehension and Critical Thinking
1. (a) Explain How can Israeli farmers grow crops in a desert?

(b) Main Idea What type of industry is most important to the Israeli economy?
(c) Synthesize Information Why do you think high technology has become an important part of the Israeli economy?
2. (a) Recall About what percentage of Israel's population is Muslim?
(b) Identify the Main Idea Give an example of the diversity among Israeli Jews.

Writing Activity
Would you enjoy living on a kibbutz? Write a paragraph that explains why or why not.

Writing Tip Give specific reasons for your explanation. Your first sentence should answer the basic question—whether or not you would like to live on a kibbutz. The following sentences should give specific reasons for your answer.

Saudi Arabia
Oil and Islam

Prepare to Read

Objectives

In this section you will
1. Learn how oil has affected Saudi Arabia's development and economy.
2. Discover how Islam affects everyday life in Saudi Arabia.
3. Understand the main features of Saudi Arabia's government.

Taking Notes

As you read this section, look for ways in which oil and Islam have shaped Saudi Arabia. Copy the table below, and record your findings in it.

Oil	Islam
•	•
•	•

Target Reading Skill

Understand Effects
Sometimes one cause may produce several effects. As you read, note two effects of oil wealth on the development of Saudi Arabia. Write them in your Taking Notes chart.

Key Terms

- **hajj** (haj) *n.* a pilgrimage or journey to Mecca undertaken by Muslims during the month of the hajj
- **Quran** (koo RAHN) *n.* the holy book of Islam
- **monarchy** (MAHN ur kee) *n.* a state or a nation in which power is held by a monarch—a king, a queen, or an emperor

Kingdom Tower in Riyadh

For more than a thousand years, Muslims from all over the world have been making pilgrimages to Mecca, Saudi Arabia. By going to Mecca, they honor the memory of Abraham, who is said to have built the first house of worship there. The pilgrimage to Mecca is called the **hajj** (haj). Muslims must make the hajj at least once in their lifetime. The hajj used to be long, hard, and dangerous. Muslims traveled across mountains and deserts by foot, horse, or camel to reach Mecca. Today, many pilgrims travel there by airplane. Roads link Mecca with other Saudi Arabian cities. Modern hotels line the streets of Mecca. Mecca is the birthplace of Islam's founder, Muhammad, and considered the holiest city in Islam.

Oil Wealth and Saudi Arabia

In 1900, Mecca was a very poor town. Saudi Arabia was one of the poorest countries in the world. Many of its people made a living by herding livestock. Like most of the countries of Southwest Asia, Saudi Arabia is mostly desert.

An Economy Based on Oil But in the 1930s, everything changed. People discovered oil in Southwest Asia. Oil reserves changed the fortunes of Saudi Arabia and several other countries in the region. It made them rich. When night falls in Riyadh (ree YAHD), Saudi Arabia's capital, the skyline begins to glow. The lights of the many apartment and office buildings flicker on. Large buildings line the city streets. When oil prices are high, buildings go up at a rapid pace. Money pours in, allowing communities like Riyadh to modernize. But when oil prices are down, the economy of the entire country is affected. Many large building projects grind to a stop.

Saudi Arabia has the most important oil economy in the world. Under its deserts lie more than 260 billion barrels of oil. Saudi Arabia has about one fourth of the world's oil. No other country on Earth exports more petroleum.

Changes From Oil Wealth Projects paid for with oil money have changed the lives of all Saudi Arabians. Beginning in the late 1960s, the Saudi Arabian government spent billions of dollars from oil sales to modernize the country. The Saudis built modern highways, airports, seaports, and a telephone system. Villages that had always depended on oil lamps were hooked up to electric power grids.

The nation's oil wealth made it possible to build a large school system. Saudi Arabia built thousands of schools. The country has eight major universities. In 1900, many Saudi Arabians could not read or write. But today, Saudi students are becoming doctors, scientists, and teachers.

✓ **Reading Check** **About how much of the world's oil is in Saudi Arabia?**

Understand Effects How does the blue heading signal information on the effects of oil on Saudi Arabia's economy?

Saudi and American men working at the Saudi American Bank in Riyadh

Saudi Arabia

Saudi Arabia has the world's largest known oil reserves. Its economy is heavily dependent on oil. As you can see on the map, much of Saudi Arabia's land area has little or no activity other than oil production. The rest of the land supports a thin population of nomadic herders. One result of Saudi Arabia's heavy dependence on oil is that its gross domestic product per capita, or the average value of goods and services per person, has not increased much over the years. This is because oil prices have been fairly steady in recent years. Although Saudi Arabia has increased oil production, its population has increased, too, so production per person has not changed much.

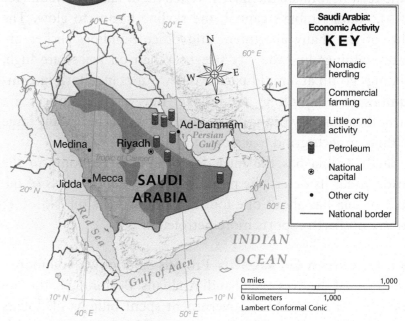

Exports

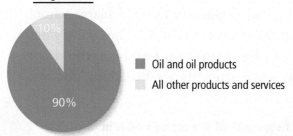

- Oil and oil products
- All other products and services

SOURCE: *CIA World Factbook*

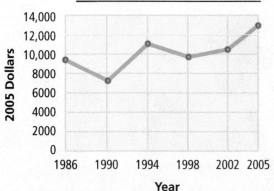

Gross Domestic Product Per Capita, 1986–2005

SOURCE: *CIA World Factbook*

Map and Chart Skills

1. **Identify** What percentage of Saudi Arabia's exports is made up of oil and oil products?
2. **Infer** How does the map help to explain Saudi Arabia's dependence on oil?
3. **Predict** How would Saudi Arabia's economy be affected if oil prices dropped sharply? If oil prices jumped?

Use Web Code **Ice-6804** for **DK World Desk Reference Online.**

Everyday Life in Saudi Arabia

Using their oil wealth, Saudis have imported computers, cellular phones, and televisions. But before a new product is used, the nation's religious leaders study it. They decide whether each import may be used by Muslims. Only imports that they believe do not undermine Muslim values may be used in daily life. In Saudi Arabia, Islam regulates most people's lives.

Islamic Traditions For example, cities like Riyadh have department stores, hotels, and universities. But they have no movie theaters or night clubs. The Wahhabi (wah HAH bee) branch of Islam, which most Saudi Arabians follow, forbids such entertainment.

Alcohol and pork are illegal in Saudi Arabia. All shops close five times a day when Muslims pray. Saudi Arabians use Western inventions to improve their lives, but they make sure these inventions do not interfere with Islamic traditions.

The Role of Women Many laws and traditions in Saudi Arabia deal with the role of women. Women are protected in certain ways, and they are also forbidden to do certain things. For example, when Saudi women go out in public, they must cover themselves with a full-length black cloak. Also, they cannot vote.

However, women in Saudi Arabia today have more opportunities than in the past. Women can work as doctors, as journalists, and in other professions. They can own businesses. Today, more women than men are studying in Saudi Arabian universities.

Despite the changes, women and men usually remain separate. Boys and girls go to different schools. At the university level, women study separately from men. Female students watch male teachers over a video system.

Saudi Arabian Women
According to Islamic law, Saudi Arabian women appearing in public must wear a long, black cloak, a scarf, and a veil covering the face, (bottom photo). The small photo shows a female Saudi doctor examining a male patient.

Drilling for Oil

The modern world depends on oil. Oil affects people every day, in almost every way. It fuels cars, heats homes, and is used to create electricity. Oil is located deep within Earth's surface, on land and under the oceans. The rotary drill, shown here, is often used to extract oil from land. It works like a giant screwdriver. As the drill turns round and round, it forces itself deeper through the ground.

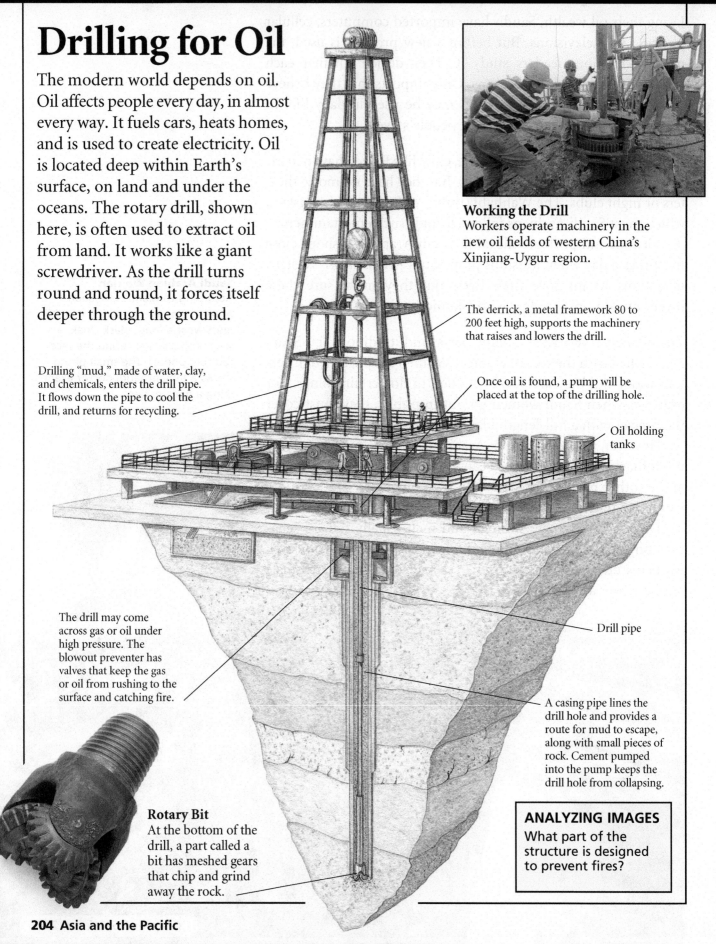

Working the Drill
Workers operate machinery in the new oil fields of western China's Xinjiang-Uygur region.

The derrick, a metal framework 80 to 200 feet high, supports the machinery that raises and lowers the drill.

Drilling "mud," made of water, clay, and chemicals, enters the drill pipe. It flows down the pipe to cool the drill, and returns for recycling.

Once oil is found, a pump will be placed at the top of the drilling hole.

Oil holding tanks

The drill may come across gas or oil under high pressure. The blowout preventer has valves that keep the gas or oil from rushing to the surface and catching fire.

Drill pipe

A casing pipe lines the drill hole and provides a route for mud to escape, along with small pieces of rock. Cement pumped into the pump keeps the drill hole from collapsing.

Rotary Bit
At the bottom of the drill, a part called a bit has meshed gears that chip and grind away the rock.

ANALYZING IMAGES
What part of the structure is designed to prevent fires?

The Influence of the Quran Most of the rules governing daily life in Saudi Arabia come from the Quran, the holy book of Islam. The word *Quran* means "the recitation" or "the reading." It consists of 114 chapters said to have been revealed by God to Muhammad. Muslims view the Quran as a guide for living. It provides guidelines on all aspects of life and religion.

✓ **Reading Check** How is Islam a part of daily life in Saudi Arabia?

The Government of Saudi Arabia

Islam guides more than daily life in Saudi Arabia. Saudi Arabia's government is based on the Quran and Islamic law. The country is an absolute monarchy ruled under Islamic law. A **monarchy** is a state or a nation in which power is held by a monarch. A monarch is a king, a queen, or an emperor.

The king serves as head of the Council of Ministers, which acts as the executive and legislative branches of the government. The king decides who will serve on the Council of Ministers. Traditionally, the Council includes the Crown Prince and members of the royal family. Political parties and elections are not allowed in Saudi Arabia.

✓ **Reading Check** What kind of government does Saudi Arabia have?

Section 4 Assessment

Key Terms
Review the key terms at the beginning of this section. Use each term in a sentence that explains its meaning.

 Target Reading Skill
What are two ways that oil wealth has affected the development of Saudi Arabia?

Comprehension and Critical Thinking
1. (a) Recall On what natural resource is Saudi Arabia's economy based?

(b) Apply Information How did wealth from oil change Saudi Arabia?

(c) Generalize How has the Saudi Arabian government used oil wealth to improve the lives of its citizens?

2. (a) Explain Give two examples of the ways Islam affects daily life in Saudi Arabia.

(b) Identify Point of View How do Muslims view the Quran?

3. (a) Describe Describe Saudi Arabia's system of government.

(b) Evaluate Information Why do you think political parties are not permitted in Saudi Arabia?

Writing Activity
Economists estimate that Saudi Arabia has enough oil to last for about 90 years of production at its present rate. In recent years, the Saudi Arabian government has used oil wealth to develop industries outside of petroleum. These include the iron and steel industries, construction, and chemicals. Write a paragraph that explains why Saudi Arabia might want to diversify its economy.

Writing Tip As you work on your paragraph, keep in mind that petroleum is a nonrenewable resource.

Interpreting Bar Graphs

Look at the picture below. The man is pushing a standard-size oil barrel that holds 42 gallons. The barrel is about the size of a large trash can.

Imagine 20 of these barrels standing together in a corner of your classroom. Would they fill up your classroom? If you stacked them, how many could fit into the room? You could probably squeeze in a few hundred.

If just a few hundred barrels of oil would fill your classroom, imagine how much space 8 million barrels would fill! You probably can't even picture that many barrels. Yet it is important for people to visualize huge numbers like these because they often represent facts we need to understand.

A bar graph is a useful tool for thinking about and comparing large numbers. It is a simple, easy-to-read way of showing a large amount of information.

Learn the Skill

Review the following steps to help you understand how to read bar graphs.

1 **Read the title to see what the bar graph is about.** The title identifies the topic of the bar graph.

2 **Read the labels to find out what each axis represents.** An axis is a line at the side or bottom of a graph. The horizontal axis is called the *x*-axis. Here you will find the categories of your data. The vertical axis is called the *y*-axis. The *y*-axis shows value or quantity.

3 **Look at the data to see if you can find similarities, differences, increases, or decreases.** What information does the horizontal axis show? What information does the vertical axis show?

4 **Make one or more general statements about what the graph shows.** You will have to compare and analyze the data in the bar graph in order to draw a conclusion or make a prediction about the topic of the bar graph.

Practice the Skill

Use the steps you have just learned to read the bar graph on the right.

1 Jot down the subject of the bar graph. What does the bar graph show?

2 Look at the labels. What does the *x*-axis represent? What does the *y*-axis represent?

3 Now compare the data. What information can you read from the *x*-axis and the *y*-axis? Use it to answer the following questions: About how much oil did Saudi Arabia produce in 1998? In 2003? In what year did Saudi Arabia produce 9.5 billion barrels of oil?

4 Analyze the data to make a prediction. From 2002 to 2003, Saudi Arabia increased its crude oil production by about half a billion barrels per year. Based on this rate of increase, how much crude oil would you expect Saudi Arabia to have produced in 2004?

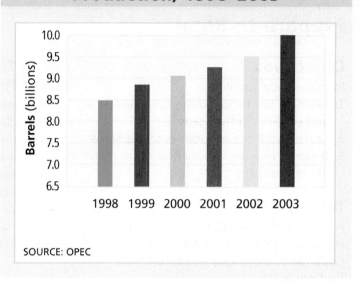

Saudi Arabia Crude Oil Production, 1998–2003

SOURCE: OPEC

Apply the Skill

Follow the steps in this skill lesson to read the bar graph below. What is the bar graph about? What does the *x*-axis represent? The *y*-axis? Which country has the greatest reserves?

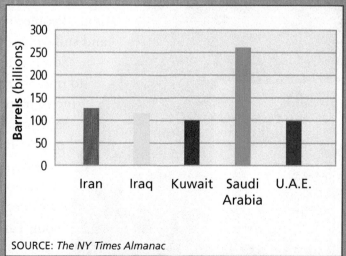

Oil Reserves in Selected Southwest Asian Countries

SOURCE: *The NY Times Almanac*

The Stans
A Diverse Region

Prepare to Read

Objectives

In this section you will

1. Examine the factors that have caused war and conflicts in the Stans.
2. Learn about the economies of the Stans.
3. Discover how environmental issues affect life in the Stans.

Taking Notes

As you read, look for details about the challenges facing Central Asian countries. Copy the chart below, and record your findings in it.

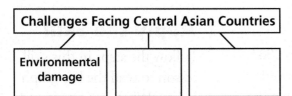

Challenges Facing Central Asian Countries

Environmental damage

Target Reading Skill

Recognize Cause-and-Effect Signal Words
Sometimes certain words, such as *because*, *affect*, or *as a result*, signal a cause or an effect. In this section, look for these words to better understand conditions in Central Asia.

Key Terms

- **refugee** (ref yoo JEE) *n.* a person who flees war or other disasters
- **dictatorship** (DIK tay tur ship) *n.* a form of government in which power is held by a leader who has absolute authority
- **landlocked** (LAND lahkt) *adj.* having no direct access to the sea

Sharbat Gula was a child when she first experienced the hardships of war. The Soviet Union invaded Afghanistan in 1979. Her village was destroyed in the fighting. Her parents were killed. She fled to neighboring Pakistan, where she lived in a camp for **refugees,** people who flee war or other disasters.

In 1985, a photographer named Steve McCurry took a picture of Sharbat at a refugee camp in Pakistan. The picture became famous. People around the world became more aware of the war and suffering in Afghanistan.

Seventeen years later, McCurry went back to the region to find Sharbat. He managed to trace her to a small village in Afghanistan. She was married and had children. She said she hoped that her children would have more opportunities than she had. She hoped they would get an education. Many people in Central Asia share Sharbat's hope for a better life. In addition to Afghanistan, this region includes Kazakhstan, Uzbekistan, Tajikistan, Turkmenistan, and Kyrgyzstan.

Sharbat Gula holds the magazine that made her picture famous.

Warfare and Unrest in Afghanistan

The war that caused Sharbat to flee Afghanistan lasted for ten years, until the Soviet troops withdrew in 1989. But that wasn't the end of the fighting in Afghanistan.

Conflict in Afghanistan A group of militant Islamic people called the Taliban gained power in Afghanistan in 1996. The Taliban established very strict Islamic rule. It limited freedoms and executed or severely punished those who violated their laws. Under the Taliban, girls were not allowed to attend school, and women were barred from working outside the home. Television, music, and the Internet were banned.

The Taliban had the support of radical Muslims from other countries. One of these supporters was Osama bin Laden, a wealthy Saudi Arabian who moved to Afghanistan. In 1996, the Taliban placed bin Laden under its protection.

A Campaign Against Terrorism Bin Laden was the leader of al-Qaeda, a terrorist group. He was the leading suspect in the terrorist attacks of September 11, 2001 that destroyed the World Trade Center in New York City, damaged the Pentagon in Washington, D.C., and killed nearly 3,000 people. Because the Taliban refused to hand bin Laden over to the United States, American troops invaded Afghanistan in October 2001. Aided by Afghan rebels opposed to the Taliban, the United States quickly overthrew the Taliban government. Since 2001, Afghanistan has had a democratic government and, in 2004, Hamid Karzai became the country's first democratically elected president.

✓ **Reading Check** What happened in Afghanistan after the terrorist attacks on September 11, 2001?

An Afghan Classroom
This picture of a girl's school in Kabul was taken when schools reopened after the fall of the Taliban government. The Taliban shut down most schools when it took over in 1996. **Analyze** *Why was the reopening of schools in Afghanistan seen as a return to a stable life?*

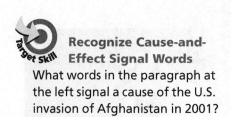

Recognize Cause-and-Effect Signal Words
What words in the paragraph at the left signal a cause of the U.S. invasion of Afghanistan in 2001?

Conflicts in Other Central Asian Countries

Afghanistan was not the only Central Asian country to experience conflict. Tensions among rival leaders, clans, and ethnic groups also affected other countries in the region.

Ethnic Disputes Central Asia is a mixture of various ethnic groups and cultures. For many years, strong Soviet rule kept ethnic and clan tensions under control. As Soviet rule came to an end, however, these tensions increased. In some countries, competing groups came into conflict. In Kazakhstan, for example, disputes arose between Kazakhs and Russians over issues of political and economic power under the new government.

Political Conflicts The situation in Tajikistan was worse. There, conflicts between rival groups erupted in violence. A bloody civil war raged through much of the 1990s and left the country in ruins. In Uzbekistan, conflict broke out in the Ferghana Valley. This fertile region, which borders Tajikistan and Kyrgyzstan, came under attack from radical Muslim groups. They wanted to overthrow the government of Uzbekistan and found an Islamic state.

Uzbekistan's government fought back against its opponents. It jailed critics of the government and outlawed radical groups. Other governments in the region also cracked down on opponents. They curbed political freedoms and violated human rights. Since independence, several countries of Central Asia have turned toward **dictatorship**—a form of government in which authority is held by an all-powerful ruler.

Children in Kyrgyzstan outside a yurt, a portable dwelling used by nomads in Central Asia

Help for Central Asia The United States and other Western countries expressed concern about the rise of dictators in the region. They called on the Stans to create democratic governments. The United States also took steps to help the region. It provided training, equipment, and money—$594 million in 2002—to build democracy and to improve economies. One program, for example, trained judges in Kyrgyzstan and Tajikistan.

✓ **Reading Check** **What conflicts have disrupted life in the Stans?**

COUNTRY PROFILE · Focus on History

The Stans

The Stans' ethnic and religious makeup reflects their history. Over the centuries, waves of invaders have swept across the Stans. People speaking Iranian languages came thousands of years ago. They adopted Islam more than 1,000 years ago. Iranian speakers today include the Tajiks, the Pashtuns, and the Hazaras. About a thousand years ago, invaders brought Turkic languages, such as Uzbek and Kazakh. Finally, during the 1800s, Russians conquered the region. The Russians brought a new religion, Orthodox Christianity. Still, most of the region's people practice Islam.

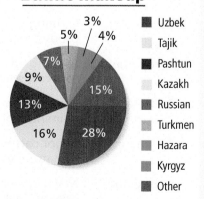

The Stans: Political
KEY
—— National border
⊛ National capital
• Other city

Religions*

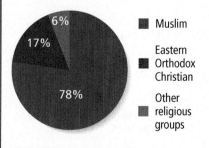

- Muslim
- Eastern Orthodox Christian
- Other religious groups

SOURCE: *CIA World Factbook*
*Numbers may not equal 100% due to rounding.

Ethnic Makeup

3%
5% 4%
7%
9%
13% 15%
16% 28%

- Uzbek
- Tajik
- Pashtun
- Kazakh
- Russian
- Turkmen
- Hazara
- Kyrgyz
- Other

SOURCE: *CIA World Factbook*

Map and Chart Skills

1. **Name** What is the largest ethnic group in the Stans?
2. **Recall** What kind of language does this group speak?
3. **Synthesize** Based on the region's history, which ethnic group probably includes most of the region's Orthodox Christians?

Use Web Code **Ice-6805** for **DK World Desk Reference Online.**

Economic Conditions in Central Asia

The Stans are generally poor countries. Agriculture is the main economic activity, although manufacturing, mining, and energy production are increasingly important. The growth of industry may offer better economic prospects in the future.

Agriculture Farming is the mainstay of Central Asian economies. During the Soviet era, large cotton farms produced huge amounts of cotton for export. Cotton farming is still important in the region—especially around the Ferghana Valley—but other types of farming have also increased. Production of grains, fruits, vegetables, and livestock has grown in recent years.

Some farms in Central Asia are large, like the cotton farms of Uzbekistan, but most are small. For most small farmers, life is a struggle. It is difficult to grow enough food or earn enough money to provide a decent living.

Sharbat Gula's life is typical for people who live in the country. Her village lies in the hills of eastern Afghanistan. Villagers plant small plots of corn, wheat, and rice on terraces built into the hillsides. They may also have a few walnut trees and maybe a sheep or two. To make money, Sharbat's husband works at a bakery in a nearby city. He makes less than one dollar a day. That's barely enough for Sharbat's family to buy the things they need to survive.

■ **Chart Skills**

The Stans are generally poor countries with developing economies.
Compare What is one economic activity all the countries in the Stans have in common?

Economies of Central Asian Countries

Country	Economic Activities
Afghanistan	Farming and livestock raising. Small-scale production of textiles, furniture, cement.
Kazakhstan	Farming, oil and coal mining, steel production, textiles.
Kyrgyzstan	Farming and livestock raising. Cotton, tobacco, wool and meat.
Tajikistan	Mainly farming, mostly cotton. One large aluminum plant.
Turkmenistan	Major cotton-producing country. Production of natural gas, oil, and textiles.
Uzbekistan	Major cotton exporter. Large producer of gold and oil.

Working on a construction site in Turkmenistan

Industry Not all Central Asians live in rural areas, however. Many live in growing cities, like Almaty, Kazakhstan, and Tashkent, Uzbekistan. Many residents live in apartments and work in offices or factories. Many of the industries in the Stans date back to the Soviet era. They are generally old and unproductive. Gradually, however, some factories and mines are being modernized. Much of the focus is on the development of Central Asia's energy and mineral resources.

Several of the Stans are rich in oil, natural gas, and minerals such as coal, gold, iron ore, and uranium. Kazakhstan has major oil reserves, while Turkmenistan is rich in natural gas. Foreign oil and gas companies are exploring ways to develop and export these resources. One problem is that these countries are **landlocked, with no direct access to the sea.** Plans are underway to build pipelines to carry oil and gas out of the region.

✓ **Reading Check** **What are the main features of Central Asian economies?**

Environmental Issues

The new countries of Central Asia face the challenging task of restoring and protecting the environment. In the past, the Soviet Union caused great environmental damage in the region.

One major environmental challenge involves nuclear fallout. For years, the Soviet Union conducted nuclear tests in northern Kazakhstan. Nuclear explosions left the region with severe radiation pollution. Radiation has caused serious health problems, including cancer and birth defects. This pollution will take years, even decades, to clean up.

Links to **Art**

Saving Art Central Asia has a rich artistic tradition. Many works of art have been destroyed, however, as a result of war and other conflicts. In Kabul, Afghanistan, for example, the Taliban destroyed priceless art in the National Museum. They also destroyed two giant Buddha statues at Bamiyan. Efforts are now underway to restore or save the remaining art treasures. Foreign countries and international agencies, such as the United Nations, are working with the Afghan government to preserve the country's artistic heritage. An ancient bronze sculpture from the National Museum in Kabul is shown below.

The natural beauty of the Stans is an important asset for the future. Shown here are the Tian Shan mountains in Kyrgyzstan.

As you read in Chapter 19, another major challenge is the drying of the Aral Sea. For years, the Soviets diverted water from rivers feeding the sea to irrigate cotton fields. As a result, the sea is now drying up.

Still, vast areas of Central Asia remain undeveloped and undamaged. These environmentally healthy lands are a key resource for Central Asia. If the Stans can preserve their environment, it will be an important asset for their future.

✓ **Reading Check** How have environmental problems affected the Stans?

Section 5 Assessment

Key Terms
Review the key terms at the beginning of this section. Use each term in a sentence that explains its meaning.

 ## Target Reading Skill
Review the text about environmental issues. Find the words that signal effects on Central Asia's environment.

Comprehension and Critical Thinking
1. (a) Explain How did the Taliban come to power in Afghanistan?
(b) Summarize Why did the United States invade Afghanistan in 2001?

2. (a) Recall Name a Central Asian country other than Afghanistan that has experienced recent conflicts.
(b) Make Generalizations In general, how has the United States helped Central Asian countries?
3. (a) Identify What is the main economic activity in Central Asian countries?
(b) Apply Information How might mineral resources help Central Asian countries develop their economies?
4. (a) Recall How has nuclear testing affected Kazakhstan?
(b) Identify Causes What caused the Aral Sea to shrink?

Writing Activity
Suppose that you are a news reporter covering Central Asia. Write a brief news report about economic conditions and challenges in Central Asia.

For: An activity on the Stans
Visit: PHSchool.com
Web Code: lcd-6805

Review and Assessment

◆ Chapter Summary

Israel

Section 1: India

- India is the second-most-populated country in the world. India also has a rapidly growing population.
- India has a large middle class that provides a huge market for goods and services.
- Despite India's fast-growing economy, about one fourth of the population lives in poverty.

Section 3: Israel

- Service industries are the most important part of Israel's well-developed economy.
- About 80 percent of the people of Israel are Jewish. About 16 percent are Muslims.
- In 2005, Israel gave control of parts of the occupied territories to the Palestinians.

Section 4: Saudi Arabia

- Oil production is the main economic activity in Saudi Arabia. No other country in the world exports more petroleum.
- Saudi Arabia has used its wealth from oil to make the country more modern.
- Islam guides daily life in Saudi Arabia and is the basis for Saudi Arabia's laws.

India

Section 2: Pakistan

- Pakistan has been working hard to improve its economy.
- Pakistan's economy is based largely on agriculture.
- Pakistan's textile industry is an important part of the economy. Other industries include making chemicals and steel.

Section 5: The Stans

- The countries of Central Asia face many challenges in creating prosperous, stable nations.
- Agriculture is the main economic activity in Central Asia. Manufacturing, mining, and energy production are becoming important.

◆ Key Terms

Each of the statements below contains a key term from the chapter. If the statement is true, write *true*. If it is false, rewrite the statement to make it true.

1. Life expectancy measures the percentage of the population age 15 or over that can read and write.

2. Poor nutrition caused by a lack of food or an unbalanced diet is called malnutrition.

3. Drought, a long period of dry weather, is a major problem in Pakistan.

4. Irrigation is a worldwide effort to increase food production in developing countries.

5. Today, many Muslims make the hajj by airplane.

6. A refugee is a person who flees war or other disasters.

Chapter 8 **215**

Review and Assessment (continued)

◆ Comprehension and Critical Thinking

7. (a) Recall What is the population of India?
(b) Summarize Why is India expected to have the world's largest population by 2050?

8. (a) Explain How does India's middle class help the nation's economy?
(b) Identify Effects What is one effect of India's efforts to improve health care?

9. (a) Explain Why is water shortage a major problem for Pakistan?
(b) Draw Inferences Why might a manufacturing company in Pakistan be located on the plains of the Indus River?
(c) Make Generalizations Why would education be considered important in making a nation more prosperous?

10. (a) Identify Give one example of how technology has helped Israel succeed in agriculture.
(b) Summarize How do the manufacturing and service industries improve Israel's economy?

11. (a) Identify What natural resource has helped Saudi Arabia build its economy and modernize the country?

(b) Identify Effects How has oil wealth affected the lives of Saudi Arabians?

12. (a) Describe What kind of government does Saudi Arabia have?
(b) Analyze What is the connection between Islam and the government of Saudi Arabia?

13. (a) Name Which Central Asian country was controlled by the Taliban?
(b) Summarize What factors have caused wars and conflicts in the Stans?

◆ Skills Practice

Interpreting Bar Graphs Name one Southwest Asian country that is not shown on the graph on the bottom of page 207. How would you find out whether it had any oil reserves?

◆ Writing Activity: Math

Use the Country Databank on pages 172–183 to look up the population of five countries discussed in this chapter. Make a bar graph that shows each country's population. Be sure to label the horizontal axis and the vertical axis of the graph. Include a title for your graph.

MAP MASTER™
Skills Activity

South, Southwest, and Central Asia

Place Location For each place listed below, write the letter from the map that shows its location.

1. Israel
2. India
3. Pakistan
4. Kazakhstan
5. Saudi Arabia
6. Aral Sea

Go Online
PHSchool.com Use Web Code lcp-6820 for an interactive map.

Standardized Test Prep

Test-Taking Tips

Some questions on standardized tests ask you to analyze a reading selection. Read the passage below. Then follow the tips to answer the sample question at the right.

> The Negev Desert takes up two thirds of Israel's land. Only three or four inches of rain fall there each year. Yet Israeli farmers grow fruits and vegetables on the desert. They also plant trees there to prevent erosion. For water, Israeli farmers use an irrigation system that is controlled by computer. Plastic tubes carry underground water straight to the crops. This water is salty, so Israelis developed plants that can soak up the water but not the salt.

TIP Think about the author's purpose as you read. Is the author trying to give information, convince you about something, or explain how something works?

Pick the letter that best answers the question.

This paragraph answers which question?

A What is the Negev Desert in Israel like?

B What are Israeli farms like?

C How has Israel reclaimed the Negev Desert for farmland?

D How can an irrigation system bring water to desert land?

Think It Through Start with the author's purpose: to give you information about Israeli farms in the Negev Desert. What question is the passage answering about Israeli farms on the Negev Desert? You can eliminate D because it is not related specifically to Israeli farms. You can rule out A because it does not address the question of farms at all. That leaves B and C. Both ask questions about Israeli farms, but B does not include the Negev Desert. The correct answer is C.

Practice Questions

Use the tips above and other tips in this book to help you answer the following questions.

Use the passage below to answer Question 1.

> Landlocked Kazakhstan is the largest of the five former Soviet republics in Central Asia. It is about four times the size of Texas. Kazakhstan's most important natural resource is oil. In 2003, the country's oil reserves were estimated to be between 9 and 17.6 million barrels.

1. What information best supports the prediction that Kazakhstan could be a major oil exporter?

   A Kazakhstan is the largest of the former Soviet republics in Central Asia.

   B Kazakhstan is larger than Texas.

   C Kazakhstan's oil reserves are estimated to be as great as 17.6 million barrels.

   D Kazakhstan is landlocked.

2. What is one effect of India's efforts to improve health care?

   A India's literacy rate is increasing.

   B India's life expectancy is increasing.

   C Malnutrition is increasing.

   D India's film industry is growing.

Go Online
PHSchool.com

Use Web Code **lca-6800** for **Chapter 8 self-test.**

Chapter Preview

This chapter focuses on Vietnam, a country in mainland Southeast Asia, and on Australia, the only country that is also a continent.

Country Databank
The Country Databank provides data and descriptions of each of the countries of Southeast Asia and the Pacific Region.

Section 1
Vietnam
A Nation Rebuilds

Section 2
Australia
A Pacific Rim Country

 **Target Reading Skill**

Main Idea In this chapter you will focus on identifying main ideas and supporting details.

▶ Hiking in the mountains of New Zealand

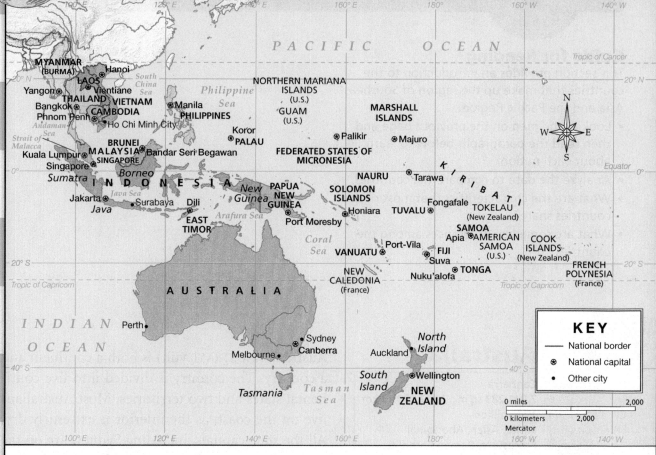

PACIFIC OCEAN

Tropic of Cancer

20° N

MYANMAR
(BURMA) •Hanoi
LAOS
Yangon• •Vientiane
THAILAND **VIETNAM** •Manila
Bangkok• **CAMBODIA** **PHILIPPINES**
Phnom Penh•
*Andaman
Sea* •Ho Chi Minh City

*South
China
Sea*

*Philippine
Sea*

**NORTHERN MARIANA
ISLANDS**
(U.S.)
GUAM
(U.S.)

**MARSHALL
ISLANDS**

•Palikir •Majuro

*Strait of
Malacca*
Kuala Lumpur• **BRUNEI**
MALAYSIA• •Bandar Seri Begawan
SINGAPORE
Singapore•
Borneo
0°
Sumatra **I N D O N E S I A**
Jakarta• •Surabaya Dili•
Java Sea
Java **EAST
TIMOR**

PALAU
Koror⊛

**FEDERATED STATES OF
MICRONESIA**

*New
Guinea* **PAPUA
NEW
GUINEA** **SOLOMON
ISLANDS**
•Honiara
Arafura Sea •Port Moresby
NAURU
•Tarawa
TUVALU⊛

K I R I B A T I

Equator 0°

Fongafale• **TOKELAU**
(New Zealand)

N
W E
S

*Coral
Sea* **VANUATU** •Port-Vila
FIJI •
•Suva
**NEW
CALEDONIA**
(France) Nuku'alofa• ⊛**TONGA**

SAMOA
Apia•⊛**AMERICAN
SAMOA**
(U.S.)

**COOK
ISLANDS**
(New Zealand)
**FRENCH
POLYNESIA**
(France)

20° S

Tropic of Capricorn *Tropic of Capricorn*

**I N D I A N
O C E A N**
Perth•

A U S T R A L I A

•Sydney
Melbourne• ⊛Canberra

*North
Island*
Auckland•
•Wellington
**NEW
ZEALAND**

*South
Island*

40° S 40° S

Tasmania *Tasman
Sea*

KEY
―― National border
⊛ National capital
• Other city

0 miles   2,000
0 kilometers   2,000
Mercator

Regions Much of Southeast Asia and the Pacific Region is located between the Tropic of Cancer and the Tropic of Capricorn.
Identify Which countries have land south of the Tropic of Capricorn?
Contrast What climate would you expect most of these countries to have? Explain your answer.

Go Online
PHSchool.com Use Web Code
lcp-6910 for step-by-step
map skills practice.

Introducing Southeast Asia and the Pacific Region

Guide for Reading

This section provides an introduction to the countries that make up the region of Southeast Asia and the Pacific Region.

- Look at the map on the previous page and then read the paragraphs below to learn about each nation.
- Analyze the data to compare the countries.
- What are the characteristics that most of the countries share?
- What are some key differences among the countries?

Australia

Capital	Canberra
Land Area	2,941,283 sq mi; 7,617,930 sq km
Population	19.6 million
Ethnic Group(s)	white, Asian, Aboriginal
Religion(s)	Protestant, Roman Catholic, traditional beliefs
Government	democratic, federal-state system recognizing the British monarch as sovereign
Currency	Australian dollar
Leading Exports	coal, gold, meat, wool, aluminum, iron ore, wheat, machinery and transport equipment
Language(s)	English (official), Italian, Cantonese, Greek, Arabic, Vietnamese, Aboriginal languages

Australia (aw STRAYL yuh) is both a continent and a country. The country is divided into five continental states and two territories. Most Australians live on the coast, as the interior is extremely dry. All the state capitals, including Sydney, are on the coast. The national capital, Canberra, is located inland. Australia is a country of great physical diversity, from deserts to snow-capped mountains. It also has the Great Barrier Reef, the largest coral reef in the world. Tourism is Australia's main industry, although it also has important farming and mining industries.

Wool is a leading Australian export.

Brunei

Capital	Bandar Seri Begawan
Land Area	2,035 sq mi; 5,270 sq km
Population	366,000
Ethnic Group(s)	Malay, Chinese, indigenous tribes
Religion(s)	Muslim, Buddhist, Christian, traditional beliefs
Government	constitutional sultanate
Currency	Brunei dollar
Leading Exports	crude oil, natural gas, refined products
Language(s)	Malay (official), English, Chinese

Brunei (broo NY) is a largely Muslim country in Southeast Asia. The same family, the Sultanate of Brunei, has been in power for more than six hundred years. At one point between the 1400s and 1600s, the nation controlled parts of Borneo and the Philippines. Later, the country experienced problems related to royal succession, colonization, and piracy. In the late 1800s, Brunei came under British rule for almost one hundred years, until it gained its independence in 1984. The nation is rich in oil and natural gas and has a relatively strong economy.

Cambodia

Capital	Phnom Penh
Land Area	68,154 sq mi; 176,520 sq km
Population	14.5 million
Ethnic Group(s)	Khmer, Vietnamese
Religion(s)	Buddhist
Government	multiparty democracy under a constitutional monarchy
Currency	riel
Leading Exports	clothing, timber, rubber, rice, fish
Language(s)	Khmer (official), French, English

Cambodia (kam BOH dee uh) is located on the Gulf of Thailand in Southeast Asia. It is bordered by Thailand, Vietnam, and Laos. Communist Khmer Rouge forces took over Cambodia in 1975. More than a million people died or were executed when the Khmer Rouge ordered the evacuation of all cities and towns. After decades of violent political conflict, the surrender of the Khmer Rouge in 1998 brought renewed political stability to Cambodia. Today, with massive international donations, Cambodia struggles to maintain a stable government and establish a working economy.

East Timor

Capital	Dili
Land Area	5,794 sq mi; 15,007 sq km
Population	820,000
Ethnic Group(s)	Austronesian (Malayo-Polynesian), Papuan, Chinese
Religion(s)	Roman Catholic, Muslim, Protestant, Hindu, Buddhist, traditional beliefs
Government	republic
Currency	U.S. dollar
Leading Exports	coffee, sandalwood, marble
Language(s)	Tetum (Portuguese-Austronesian) (official), Portuguese (official), Indonesian, English

East Timor (eest TEE mawr) is located in Southeast Asia, northwest of Australia. East Timor includes the eastern half and the Oecussi region of the island of Timor as well as two smaller islands. Once a Portuguese colony, East Timor declared its independence in 1975. Nine days after declaring independence, however, it was invaded and occupied by Indonesia. In 1999, the United Nations supervised an election in which the people of East Timor voted for independence from Indonesia. Though Indonesian militias protested with violence, East Timor was internationally recognized as an independent democratic nation in May 2002.

Introducing Southeast Asia and the Pacific Region

Federated States of Micronesia

Capital	Palikir
Land Area	271 sq mi; 702 sq km
Population	135,869
Ethnic Group(s)	Micronesian, Polynesian
Religion(s)	Roman Catholic, Protestant
Government	constitutional government
Currency	U.S. dollar
Leading Exports	fish, clothing, bananas, black pepper
Language(s)	English (official), Trukese, Pohnpeian, Mortlockese, Losrean

The Federated States of Micronesia (FED ur ayt id stayts uv my kruh NEE zhuh) is an island group in the North Pacific Ocean. It consists of all the Caroline Islands except Palau. Once under United States control, the Federated States of Micronesia (FSM) became independent in 1986. The United States still provides the country with financial aid and military protection. The FSM is working to overcome long-term concerns such as high unemployment, overfishing, and dependence on United States aid. Most Micronesians live without running water or electricity.

Fiji

Capital	Suva
Land Area	7,054 sq mi; 18,270 sq km
Population	856,346
Ethnic Group(s)	Fijian, South Asian, white, other Pacific Islander, East Asian
Religion(s)	Hindu, Protestant, Roman Catholic, Muslim
Government	republic
Currency	Fiji dollar
Leading Exports	sugar, clothing, gold, timber, fish, molasses, coconut oil
Language(s)	English (official), Fijian, Hindi, Urdu, Tamil, Telugu

Fiji (FEE jee) is an island group in the South Pacific Ocean. Fiji consists of two main islands and hundreds of smaller islands. After nearly one hundred years as a British colony, Fiji became an independent democracy in 1970. Fiji has a history of ethnic conflict between native Fijians and those of Indian ancestry. This conflict has caused great political instability over the past few decades and has weakened Fiji's economy.

Indonesia

Capital	Jakarta
Land Area	705,188 sq mi; 1,826,440 sq km
Population	231.3 million
Ethnic Group(s)	Javanese, Sundanese, Madurese, coastal Malay
Religion(s)	Muslim, Protestant, Roman Catholic, Hindu, Buddhist
Government	republic
Currency	rupiah
Leading Exports	oil and gas, electrical appliances
Language(s)	Bahasa Indonesia (official), Javanese, Sundanese, Madurese, Dutch

Indonesia (in duh NEE zhuh) is an island nation located between the Indian and Pacific Oceans. It is Southeast Asia's largest and most populous country, and the world's largest archipelago. It is also the world's most populous Muslim nation. Once known as the Dutch East Indies, Indonesia achieved independence from the Netherlands in 1949. When a giant tsunami struck in 2004, parts of Indonesia faced destruction, and about 129,000 people were killed. Although poverty and terrorism remain problems, the nation's government and economy have grown more stable.

Kiribati

Capital	Bairiki (Tarawa Atoll)
Land Area	313 sq mi; 811 sq km
Population	96,335
Ethnic Group(s)	Micronesian, Polynesian
Religion(s)	Roman Catholic, Protestant, Muslim, traditional beliefs
Government	republic
Currency	Australian dollar
Leading Exports	copra, coconuts, seaweed, fish
Language(s)	English (official), Micronesian dialect

Kiribati (kihr uh BAS) is a group of 33 coral atolls in the Pacific Ocean. It lies on the Equator about halfway between Hawaii and Australia. Once called the Gilbert Islands, part of a British colony, Kiribati became independent in 1979. Great Britain had mined the islands for their phosphate deposits for decades. Although the phosphate ran out in 1980, Kiribati succeeded in winning some payment from Britain for what it had taken. With very few natural resources, Kiribati has a limited economy. However, it grows enough food to support its citizens without imports.

Laos

Capital	Vientiane
Land Area	89,112 sq mi; 230,800 sq km
Population	5.8 million
Ethnic Group(s)	Lao Loum, Lao Theung, Lao Soung, Vietnamese, East Asian
Religion(s)	Buddhist, traditional beliefs
Government	communist state
Currency	new kip
Leading Exports	wood products, clothing, electricity, coffee, tin
Language(s)	Lao (official), Mon-Khmer, Yao, Vietnamese, Chinese, French

Laos (LAH ohs) is a landlocked Communist country in Southeast Asia bordered by Vietnam, Cambodia, Thailand, Myanmar, and China. After six hundred years as a monarchy, Laos became a communist nation in 1975. The country has many mineral resources and produces large amounts of coffee and timber. Still, it is one of the world's least developed countries and depends on foreign aid. Laotians are mostly Buddhists. The majority of the population lives in rural areas and works in farming.

Malaysia

Capital	Kuala Lumpur and Putrajaya
Land Area	126,853 sq mi; 328,550 sq km
Population	22.7 million
Ethnic Group(s)	Malay, East Asian, indigenous tribes, South Asian
Religion(s)	Muslim, Buddhist, traditional beliefs, Hindu, Christian
Government	constitutional monarchy
Currency	ringgit
Leading Exports	electronic equipment, petroleum and liquefied natural gas, wood
Language(s)	Bahasa Malaysia (official), Malay, Chinese, Tamil, English

Malaysia (muh LAY zhuh) consists of a peninsula and the northern third of the island of Borneo in the South China Sea. It shares borders with Thailand, Indonesia, Singapore, and Brunei. The country, made up of parts of former British colonies, was formed in 1963. Although Malaysia is considered a developing country, its economy was one of the fastest growing in the world from 1987 to 1997. The Asian financial crash of 1997 slowed but did not stop this growth. Malaysia exports large amounts of oil, natural gas, and palm oil.

Introducing Southeast Asia and the Pacific Region

Marshall Islands

Capital	Majuro
Land Area	70 sq mi; 181.3 sq km
Population	73,360
Ethnic Group(s)	Micronesian
Religion(s)	Christian
Government	constitutional government in free association with the United States
Currency	U.S. dollar
Leading Exports	copra (dried coconut), coconut oil, handicrafts
Language(s)	English (official), Marshallese (official), Japanese, German

The Marshall Islands (MAHR shul EYE lundz) is a group of 34 islands in the North Pacific Ocean. Once under United States control, the Marshall Islands became independent in 1986. The island nation maintains ties to the United States and heavily depends on it for economic support. The money the United States provides the islands makes up almost two thirds of its total income. The Marshall Islands faces ongoing problems of few natural resources, high unemployment, and poverty.

Myanmar

Capital	Rangoon
Land Area	253,953 sq mi; 657,740 sq km
Population	42.2 million
Ethnic Group(s)	Burman, Shan, Karen, Rakhine, East Asian, South Asian, Mon
Religion(s)	Buddhist, Christian, Muslim, traditional beliefs
Government	military regime
Currency	kyat
Leading Exports	clothing, food, wood products, precious stones
Language(s)	Burmese (Myanmar) (official), Karen, Shan, Chin, Kachin, Mon, Palaung, Wa

Myanmar (MYUN mahr), also known as Burma, is a Southeast Asian nation bordered by Thailand, China, India, the Andaman Sea, and the Bay of Bengal. There are mountains in the north, but the fertile Irrawaddy basin dominates the rest of the country. Myanmar is rich in natural resources, and its economy is mainly agricultural. Once a British colony, Myanmar gained its independence in 1948. Since that time, it has had a history of ethnic conflict and political instability. Today, its government is run by the military.

Nauru

Capital	Yaren District
Land Area	8 sq mi; 21 sq km
Population	12,329
Ethnic Group(s)	Nauruan, Pacific Islanders, East Asian, white
Religion(s)	Protestant, Roman Catholic
Government	republic
Currency	Australian dollar
Leading Exports	phosphate
Language(s)	Nauruan (official), Kiribati, Chinese, Tuvaluan, English

Nauru (nah OO roo) is an island in the South Pacific Ocean. The world's smallest independent republic, Nauru was once a German, and then a British colony. It gained its independence in 1968. For decades, the United Kingdom, New Zealand, and Australia mined Nauru for its phosphate. The income from phosphate, Nauru's only export, has made its people very wealthy. However, mining activities caused great environmental damage. With phosphate mining expected to run out, Nauru faces the great challenge of keeping its economy from collapsing.

Sea kayaks in Milford Sound in Fiordland National Park, New Zealand

New Zealand

Capital	Wellington
Land Area	103,737 sq mi; 268,680 sq km
Population	3.8 million
Ethnic Group(s)	white, Maori, Pacific Islander, Asian
Religion(s)	Protestant, Roman Catholic
Government	parliamentary democracy
Currency	New Zealand dollar
Leading Exports	dairy products, meat, wood and wood products, fish, machinery
Language(s)	English (official), Maori (official)

New Zealand (noo ZEE lund) is made up of two large islands and a number of smaller islands in the South Pacific Ocean. It lies about 1,000 miles southeast of Australia. Settled by the Polynesian Maori in about A.D. 800, New Zealand became a British colony during the 1800s and an independent nation in 1907. New Zealand's economy is based on agricultural exports—particularly butter and wool—as well as manufacturing. New Zealand has some of the world's most varied scenery, and tourism is an important industry.

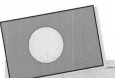

Palau

Capital	Koror
Land Area	177 sq mi; 458 sq km
Population	19,409
Ethnic Group(s)	Palauan, Asian, white
Religion(s)	Christian, traditional beliefs
Government	constitutional government in free association with the United States
Currency	U.S. dollar
Leading Exports	shellfish, tuna, copra, clothing
Language(s)	Palauan (official), English (official), Japanese, Angaur, Tobi, Sonsorolese

Palau (pah LOW) is an archipelago made up of several hundred islands in the North Pacific Ocean southeast of the Philippines. Palau, once governed by the United States and the United Nations, became independent in 1994. It is now a constitutional democracy, but maintains close ties to the United States and relies on it for financial aid. Its economy is developing and is primarily agricultural, with a growing tourism industry.

Introducing Southeast Asia and the Pacific Region

Papua New Guinea

Capital	Port Moresby
Land Area	174,849 sq mi; 452,860 sq km
Population	5.2 million
Ethnic Group(s)	Melanesian, Papuan, Negrito, Micronesian, Polynesian
Religion(s)	Protestant, Roman Catholic, traditional beliefs
Government	constitutional monarchy with parliamentary democracy
Currency	kina
Leading Exports	oil, gold, copper ore, logs, palm oil, coffee, cocoa, crayfish, prawns
Language(s)	English (official), Pidgin English, Papuan, Motu, around 750 native languages

Papua New Guinea (pap YOO uh noo GIH nee) is a group of islands—including the eastern half of the island of New Guinea—located between the Coral Sea and the South Pacific Ocean. Papua New Guinea became independent from Australia in 1975. Since then, its political situation has been somewhat unstable due to conflicts between many political parties. Papua New Guinea's people are extraordinarily diverse, with around 750 different languages spoken there. Its economy is mainly agricultural, though it has significant mineral and oil resources as well. A gas pipeline between Papua New Guinea and Australia is expected to bring in almost $220 million per year.

Philippines

Capital	Manila
Land Area	115,123 sq mi; 298,170 sq km
Population	84.5 million
Ethnic Group(s)	Malay, East Asian
Religion(s)	Roman Catholic, Protestant, Muslim, Buddhist
Government	republic
Currency	Philippine peso
Leading Exports	electronic equipment, machinery and transport equipment
Language(s)	English (official), Filipino (official), Tagalog, Cebuano, Hiligaynon, Samaran, Ilocano, Bikol

The Philippines (FIL uh peenz) is an island nation in the western Pacific Ocean, between the Philippine Sea and the South China Sea. It consists of more than 7,000 islands, about 1,000 of which are inhabited. The Philippines became independent from the United States in 1946. Since that time, it has suffered a troubled political history, including dictatorships. The Philippines has more than 100 ethnic groups and is the only Christian nation in Southeast Asia. It has large mineral deposits that have not been fully developed.

Samoa

Capital	Apia
Land Area	1,133 sq mi; 2,934 sq km
Population	178,631
Ethnic Group(s)	Samoan, mixed white and Polynesian, white
Religion(s)	Protestant, Roman Catholic
Government	constitutional monarchy
Currency	tala
Leading Exports	fish, coconut oil and cream, copra
Language(s)	Samoan (official), English (official)

Samoa (suh MOH uh) is a group of nine volcanic islands located in the South Pacific Ocean. Only four of the nine islands are inhabited, and more than 70 percent of the population lives on one island. Samoa became independent from New Zealand in 1962, when it established a democratic government. Samoa is one of the world's least developed countries and is dependent on foreign aid. However, its expanding manufacturing and tourism industries and increasing agricultural exports are helping its economy to grow.

Singapore

Capital	Singapore
Land Area	264 sq mi; 683 sq km
Population	4.5 million
Ethnic Group(s)	East Asian, Malay, South Asian
Religion(s)	Buddhist, Muslim, Christian, Hindu, traditional beliefs
Government	parliamentary republic
Currency	Singapore dollar
Leading Exports	machinery and equipment (including electronics), consumer goods, chemicals, mineral fuels
Language(s)	Malay (official), English (official), Mandarin (official), Tamil (official)

Singapore (SING uh pawr) is a group of islands located in Southeast Asia between Malaysia and Indonesia. Singapore was established as a British trading colony in 1819. It became independent in 1965. Singapore is currently one of the most important trading ports in Asia and one of the world's most prosperous countries. Ethnic Chinese make up about 80 percent of its population.

Solomon Islands

Capital	Honiara
Land Area	10,633 sq mi; 27,540 sq km
Population	494,786
Ethnic Group(s)	Melanesian, Polynesian, Micronesian, white, East Asian
Religion(s)	Protestant, Roman Catholic, traditional beliefs
Government	parliamentary democracy
Currency	Solomon Islands dollar
Leading Exports	timber, fish, copra, palm oil, cocoa
Language(s)	English (official), Pidgin English, Melanesian Pidgin

The Solomon Islands (SAHL uh mun EYE lundz) is a group of islands in the South Pacific Ocean east of Papua New Guinea. The Solomons are an archipelago of several hundred islands spread over 250,000 square miles. Most are coral reefs, and the majority of the population lives on the six largest islands. The Solomon Islands have been settled for thousands of years. In 1978, the island nation achieved independence from the United Kingdom. However, ethnic conflict and a high crime rate have caused instability and weakened the economy in recent years.

Thailand

Capital	Bangkok
Land Area	197,594 sq mi; 511,770 sq km
Population	62.5 million
Ethnic Group(s)	Thai, East Asian
Religion(s)	Buddhist, Muslim, Christian, Hindu
Government	constitutional monarchy
Currency	baht
Leading Exports	computers, transistors, seafood, clothing, rice
Language(s)	Thai (official), Chinese, Malay, Khmer, Karen, Miao

Thailand (TY land) is located in Southeast Asia, between the Andaman Sea and the Gulf of Thailand. It is bordered by Laos, Cambodia, Myanmar, and Malaysia. Thailand's central plain is fertile and densely populated. The country has enjoyed rapid economic growth in recent decades. However, this growth has used up many of its natural resources and strained its water supplies. Thailand, once called Siam, is the only Southeast Asian country that has never been taken over by a European power. It is now a constitutional monarchy.

Introducing Southeast Asia and the Pacific Region

Tonga

Capital	Nuku'alofa
Land Area	277 sq mi; 718 sq km
Population	106,137
Ethnic Group(s)	Polynesian, white
Religion(s)	Christian
Government	hereditary constitutional monarchy
Currency	pa'anga (Tongan dollar)
Leading Exports	squash, fish, vanilla beans, root crops
Language(s)	Tongan (official), English (official)

Tonga (TAHNG guh) is an archipelago of 170 islands located in the South Pacific Ocean northeast of New Zealand. Tonga's economy is based on agriculture and tourism but depends heavily on foreign aid. The country also imports much of its food. Tonga remains the only monarchy in the Pacific region and its king controls the nation's politics, despite calls in recent years for greater democracy.

Tuvalu

Capital	Fongafale
Land Area	10 sq mi; 26 sq km
Population	10,800
Ethnic Group(s)	Polynesian, Micronesian
Religion(s)	Protestant, traditional beliefs
Government	constitutional monarchy with a parliamentary democracy
Currency	Australian dollar and Tuvaluan dollar
Leading Exports	copra, fish
Language(s)	English (official), Tuvaluan, Kiribati

Tuvalu (too vuh LOO) is a tiny island group located in the South Pacific Ocean. It lies about halfway between Hawaii and Australia, or about 650 miles north of Fiji. Tuvalu has a total land area of about 10 square miles (26 square kilometers). Tuvalu was part of a British colony until its independence in 1978. Tuvalu's economy is based mainly on subsistence farming and fishing. However, the tiny nation also gets about $50 million per year from leasing out its Internet domain name ".tv."

Vanuatu

Capital	Port-Vila
Land Area	4,710 sq mi; 12,200 sq km
Population	196,178
Ethnic Group(s)	Melanesian, white, Southeast Asian, East Asian, Pacific Islander
Religion(s)	Protestant, Roman Catholic, traditional beliefs
Government	parliamentary republic
Currency	vatu
Leading Exports	copra, kava, beef, cocoa, timber, coffee
Language(s)	Bislama (official), English (official), French (official)

Vanuatu (van wah TOO) is a small island nation located in the South Pacific Ocean. It lies about three quarters of the way from Hawaii to Australia, or about 500 miles west of Fiji. Vanuatu is an archipelago of 80 volcanic islands spread over about 4 50 miles. However, only about 12 of the islands are of any size. Vanuatu was once called the New Hebrides. The islands were settled in the 1800s and ruled jointly by Great Britain and France from 1906. In 1980, Vanuatu became an independent republic. The economy is based primarily on agriculture and fishing.

Vietnam

Capital	Hanoi
Land Area	125,621 sq mi; 325,360 sq km
Population	81.1 million
Ethnic Group(s)	Vietnamese, East Asian, Hmong, Thai, Khmer, Cham
Religion(s)	Buddhist, Christian, traditional beliefs, Muslim
Government	communist state
Currency	dông
Leading Exports	crude oil, marine products, rice, coffee, rubber, tea, clothing, shoes
Language(s)	Vietnamese (official), Chinese, Thai, Khmer, Muong, Nung, Miao, Yao, Jarai

SOURCES: DK World Desk Reference Online; CIA World Factbook Online; *World Almanac,* 2003

Vietnam (vee et NAHM) is located along the eastern coast of the Indochinese peninsula in the South China Sea. France occupied Vietnam during the late 1800s. France continued to rule until 1954, when Communist forces under leader Ho Chi Minh defeated the French and took over the northern part of the country. The United States then helped South Vietnam resist Communist rule by fighting the North Vietnamese in the Vietnam War. The United States withdrew its military forces in 1973, and all of Vietnam was united under Communist rule. Still recovering from years of war, the government has allowed some private enterprise to strengthen its weak economy.

A woman weaves in a village in Vietnam. Most people in Vietnam live in rural areas.

Assessment

Comprehension and Critical Thinking

1. Name Name two Southeast Asian countries that are island nations.

2. Draw Conclusions What are the characteristics that most of the countries share?

3. Contrast What are some key differences among the countries?

4. Categorize Which countries in the region have monarchies?

5. Contrast How are the governments of Laos and Vietnam different from those of the other countries in the region?

6. Make a Bar Graph Create a bar graph showing the land area of the five most populous countries in this region.

Keeping Current

Access the **DK World Desk Reference Online** at **PHSchool.com** for up-to-date information about all the countries in this chapter.

Go Online
PHSchool.com

Web Code: lce-6900

Vietnam
A Nation Rebuilds

Prepare to Read

Objectives

In this section you will
1. Find out how Vietnam was divided by conflicts and war.
2. Learn how Vietnam has rebuilt its economy.

Taking Notes

As you read this section, look for details about how Vietnam has developed since the Vietnam War. Copy the diagram below and record your findings in it.

Target Reading Skill

Identify Main Idea The main idea of a paragraph tells what the whole paragraph is about. On page 234, the main idea of the paragraph with the heading Rebirth in Ho Chi Minh City is "Vietnam's greatest successes have been in rebuilding its cities." As you read this section, identify the main idea of each paragraph that follows a blue heading.

Key Terms

• **civil war** (SIV ul wawr) *n.* a war between political parties or regions within the same country
• **domino theory** (DAHM uh noh THEE uh ree) *n.* a belief that if one country fell to communism, neighboring nations would also fall, like a row of dominoes

New industries in Vietnam

It is summer in Vietnam, more than 25 years after the end of the Vietnam War. In countryside villages, people seed, harvest, and plow rice fields just as their parents and grandparents did. Unlike their parents and grandparents, however, many of these villagers are making money. In the cities, people are working in such growing industries as manufacturing and telecommunications. Private ownership of companies in Vietnam has been growing since the mid-1990s. Like China, communist Vietnam is taking steps toward an economy that allows some free enterprise.

Decades of Conflict and War

The people of Vietnam have survived a long period of conflict. First, an alliance of Communists and Nationalists in Vietnam fought against France from 1946 to 1954. Second, a civil war followed. A **civil war** is a war between political parties or regions within the same country. During the Vietnam War, North Vietnam fought South Vietnam and its ally, the United States.

Vietnam Divided After the French defeat in 1954, a treaty divided Vietnam into northern and southern parts. Communists controlled the northern half. A non-communist government supported by the United States ruled South Vietnam. The treaty said that, eventually, an election would be held to reunite the country under one government.

These elections were never held, largely because the United States and Ngo Dinh Diem (en GOH din dee EM), the leader of South Vietnam, feared that the Communists might win. At that time, U.S. leaders believed in the **domino theory.** They thought that a Communist victory would cause other countries in Southeast Asia to fall to communism, like a row of dominoes.

Meanwhile, the Communists were trying to take over the south by force. In 1959, they launched a war to achieve this goal. They were led by Communist leader Ho Chi Minh (hoh chee min). Ho Chi Minh's forces were called the Viet Cong.

Presidential Palace in Hanoi
The Presidential Palace is used as offices for Vietnam's government. The palace was built by the French and used as headquarters for the French government until 1954. Note the flag of Vietnam is displayed. **Analyze Images** *How are change and continuity shown in this photo?*

U.S. troops taking part in a mission in South Vietnam in 1967

Water Puppets In Vietnam, a type of puppet theater uses a pond for a stage. Water puppet shows started centuries ago. In these shows, a puppeteer guides wooden figures so that they appear to wade through the water. The puppets are attached to rods and strings hidden underwater. Audiences sit at the water's edge. Stage settings of trees and clouds are also placed on the pond.

American Involvement in the Vietnam War Communist leader Ho Chi Minh wanted to unite Vietnam under northern rule. Operating from the north, he aided Communist forces in the south. As the Communists threatened South Vietnam, the United States took an active role. At first, the United States sent thousands of military advisors to help the South Vietnamese. Later, hundreds of thousands of American troops arrived. Through the 1960s, the United States sent more troops to Vietnam. By 1968, there were more than 500,000 U.S. troops in Vietnam.

By the early 1970s, Vietnam had been at war for more than 30 years. The fighting spread to neighboring Laos and Cambodia as well. North Vietnam sent supplies along the Ho Chi Minh Trail through Laos and Cambodia to its troops in South Vietnam. In 1970, the United States bombed the Ho Chi Minh Trail and then invaded Cambodia. In 1971, South Vietnamese troops attacked North Vietnamese bases in Laos.

As the fighting continued, American casualties increased. Millions of people in the United States were calling for an end to the war. In 1973, the United States finally ended its part in the war when the last American combat soldiers left South Vietnam. More than 3 million Americans had served in the Vietnam War. More than 58,000 American troops died in the war, and another 150,000 were seriously wounded.

✓ **Reading Check** Why did North Vietnam launch a war against South Vietnam?

Vietnam

Most people in Vietnam are ethnic Vietnamese, but Vietnam has more than 90 ethnic minorities. Ethnic Vietnamese live mainly in the lowlands of the north, the south, and a thin coastal strip. Fertile soils in the lowlands support a dense population, as you can see on the map. The largest minority, the ethnic Chinese, live mainly in lowland cities. Other minorities inhabit the rugged highlands, where farming is difficult and population densities are low.

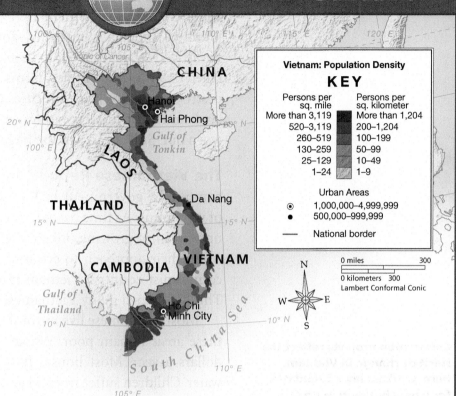

Vietnam: Population Density

KEY

Persons per sq. mile	Persons per sq. kilometer
More than 3,119	More than 1,204
520–3,119	200–1,204
260–519	100–199
130–259	50–99
25–129	10–49
1–24	1–9

Urban Areas
◉ 1,000,000–4,999,999
• 500,000–999,999
— National border

0 miles 300
0 kilometers 300
Lambert Conformal Conic

Ethnic Groups

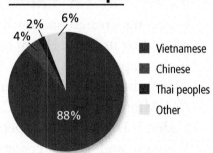

- Vietnamese
- Chinese
- Thai peoples
- Other

2% 4% 6% 88%

SOURCE: DK World Desk Reference

Peoples of Vietnam

Ethnic Group	Where They Live
Vietnamese	Coastal strip, lowlands, major cities
Chinese	Major cities, northern lowlands
Tai peoples	Northern highlands
Hmong peoples	Northern highlands
Other minorities	Northern and central highlands, border regions

SOURCE: Ethnologue

Map and Chart Skills

1. **Identify** What percentage of Vietnam's people are ethnically Vietnamese or Chinese?

2. **Describe** These groups live in the fertile lowlands, with more than 259 persons per square mile. Do these lowlands cover more than 50 percent of Vietnam's area?

3. **Analyze** How can you explain the difference between these percentages?

Use Web Code **Ice-6901** for **DK World Desk Reference Online.**

After the Vietnam War

After the United States pulled out its troops, North Vietnam conquered South Vietnam in 1975. In 1976, the country was reunited under a communist government. Vietnam had been devastated by the war. More than a million Vietnamese had been killed or wounded. Homes, farms, factories, and forests had been destroyed. Bombs had torn cities apart. Fields were covered with land mines, or hidden explosives. The Vietnamese people were worn out. Still ahead was the huge effort of rebuilding.

The Vietnamese Rebuild In the years after the war, the communist government in Vietnam strictly controlled the lives of its citizens. As time passed, however, it was clear that the economy was not growing. Like the Chinese, the Vietnamese had to adapt their approach to economic growth. Although it is still a communist country, Vietnam now allows some free enterprise. This has helped many Vietnamese improve their lives.

Most Vietnamese live in rural areas. In spite of some progress, these areas remain poor. Whole families live on a few hundred dollars a year. Most houses have no indoor toilets or running water. Children suffer from a lack of healthy food. Vietnam is still among the poorest nations in Asia.

Contruction projects reflect the spirit of change in Vietnam. Here, workers lay a foundation for a new building in Ho Chi Minh City.

Rebirth in Ho Chi Minh City Vietnam's greatest success has been in rebuilding its cities. Hanoi in the north is the capital. The city of Saigon (sy GAHN), in the south, was renamed Ho Chi Minh City after the Communist leader. It is the most prosperous city in Vietnam and is the center of trade. Americans who visit Ho Chi Minh City today find some of the same things they would find at home, such as American-style ice cream and cable news networks on television.

Some Vietnamese who live in the city enjoy greater prosperity. They buy designer clothing and watches, stereo systems, video recorders, and jewelry. Many of these people run restaurants or hotels, buy and sell land or buildings, or own factories, all of which help stimulate Vietnam's economy.

A girl from the Hmong ethnic group (left) and a city shopper (inset) show rural and urban life in Vietnam.

Economic Recovery In 1986, Vietnam's government began an economic recovery program aimed chiefly at attracting foreign investors. As a result, Vietnam became one of the fastest-growing economies in the world. From 1990 to 1997, the economy grew each year by an average of about 8 percent. Agricultural output doubled, turning Vietnam from a country once dependent on food imports to the world's second-largest exporter of rice. Government-led reforms have helped modernize the economy and promote economic growth in the 2000s. After committing to trade agreements with other countries, including the United States, Vietnam's exports have greatly increased.

Identify Main Ideas Which sentence states the main idea in the paragraph on this page?

 **Reading Check** Which city in Vietnam is the most prosperous and the nation's center of trade?

Section 1 Assessment

Key Terms
Review the key terms at the beginning of this section. Use each term in a sentence that explains its meaning.

Target Reading Skill
Write the main idea of each paragraph that follows a blue heading in this section.

Comprehension and Critical Thinking
1. (a) Recall When did the United States withdraw from the Vietnam War?

(b) Summarize What conflicts have divided Vietnam since the end of World War II?
2. (a) Describe Describe conditions in Vietnam when the Vietnam War ended.
(b) Make Generalizations What successes has Vietnam had in rebuilding its economy?
(c) Identify Point of View Why do you think Saigon was renamed Ho Chi Minh City after the Vietnam War?

Writing Activity
Write a summary that describes Vietnam since the Vietnam War. Use this title for your summary: Vietnam: A Country, Not a War. Focus on the country's economic development.

Writing Tip Be sure to look closely at the pictures and the Country Profile in this section to help you as you write your description.

Rice is one of the most important crops in Vietnam. It is grown on almost 75 percent of all cultivated land. Most Vietnamese farmers live in the lowland and delta area. This area's wetlands and heavy rains make it perfect for growing rice.

Most Southeast Asian farmers grow rice the same way that their ancestors did thousands of years ago. They build shallow fields called paddies. They flood the paddies with water. They plant rice in seedling beds. Farmers transplant the rice seedlings in the paddies by hand. They also harvest the rice by hand.

You've just read a description of how rice is grown. But sometimes it is easier to figure out how something works by following the steps in a flowchart.

Traditional Rice Farming

> Farmers build a rice paddy.

> The paddy is flooded with water.

> Farmers use water buffalo to plow and smooth out the paddy.

> Farmers prepare seedling beds alongside the paddy and plant rice seed in seedling beds.

> After seedlings are 4 to 6 inches tall, farmers transplant them into the paddy.

> Farmers weed, fertilize, and add water regularly to the paddy.

> When the rice turns from green to gold, it is harvested.

A flowchart shows the sequence of steps used to complete an activity. It shows the steps in the order they happen. Sometimes the steps are illustrated. A flowchart usually uses arrows to show how steps follow one another.

Learn the Skill

Here are the steps you will need to follow when you read a flowchart.

1. **Read the title.** Read the title first to find out what the flowchart is about. The title of the flowchart at the left is Traditional Rice Farming.

2. **Find the arrows.** The arrows will tell you the order in which you should read the chart. Find the beginning and start there.

3. **Read the flowchart carefully.** If there are illustrations, study them, but be sure to read the text next to them. Think about how one step leads to the next step. What are the connections? If there are no illustrations, try imagining each step to help you understand the sequence.

Practice the Skill

Use the steps and the flowchart on the previous page to practice reading a flowchart.

1 Read the title of the flowchart first. Explain what the flowchart will tell you.

2 Find the beginning of the chart. Identify the first step of the chart. Start there and follow the arrows through each step.

3 Now read the flowchart carefully. Your reading of the flowchart should help you understand the steps in traditional rice farming. Now answer these questions: What is the first step in traditional rice farming? What happens after the paddy is flooded with water? Where do the farmers prepare seedling beds? How tall are the rice seedlings when the farmers transplant them into the paddy? How do the farmers know when it is time to harvest the rice?

Traditional Rice Processing

Thresh, or beat, the rice plants to separate the rice husks from the plant.

Dry the rice husks.

Thresh the rice husks to remove the rice grains from the husks.

Thresh the rice again to separate the husks from rice grains.

Store the rice in a dry place.

Apply the Skill

Use the steps in this skill to read the flowchart above. What is the chart about? How are the rice husks separated from the plant? Why is the rice threshed three times?

Australia
A Pacific Rim Country

Prepare to Read

Objectives

In this section you will
1. Learn about the major economic activities in Australia.
2. Find out how Aboriginal people in Australia are working to improve their lives.

Taking Notes

Copy the diagram. As you read, record details about Australia's economy.

Trade

Australia

Target Reading Skill

Identify Supporting Details On page 240, look at the paragraph with the heading Ranching. The first sentence is the main idea. The rest of the sentences support the main idea. What details in this paragraph explain the part ranching plays in Australia's economy?

Key Terms

- **outback** (OWT bak) *n.* the dry land consisting of plains and plateaus that makes up much of central and western Australia
- **artesian well** (ahr TEE zhun wel) *n.* a well from which water flows under natural pressure without pumping

Michael Chang owns a successful trading company in Sydney, Australia's largest city. From his office in a modern glass skyscraper, he sometimes watches Sydney's busy harbor. What interests him most are the large cargo ships.

John Koeyers and his family own a huge cattle ranch in northwest Australia. He uses helicopters and trucks to round up the herds on his ranch. The Koeyers sell most of their cattle to companies in Asian nations.

Charlie Walkabout is director of Anangu Tours. Anangu Tours is owned and run by Aboriginal people. The company has won awards for its tours of Uluru, also known as Ayers Rock.

Sydney, Australia, has a beautiful and busy harbor.

Economic Activities

Michael Chang, the Koeyers, and Charlie Walkabout are all Australians. The meaning of *Australian* has changed since Australia achieved independence. It is no longer "British." It now reflects the diversity of Australia's people. Today, Australia has close ties with other nations of the Pacific Rim. These nations border the Pacific Ocean. They include Japan, South Korea, China, and Taiwan. The United States is another major Pacific Rim nation. It is one of Australia's key trading partners. Australia's economy depends on trade with Pacific Rim countries.

Trade Michael Chang's trading company is just one of hundreds of companies that do business with Pacific Rim countries. He sends various products to many countries in Asia. Rancher John Koeyers is involved in trade, too. Large cargo ships transport his cattle to South Korea and Taiwan. Other cargo ships carry products such as Australian wool and meat to foreign markets. Cargo ships also carry Australia's minerals to Japan.

Farming It seems strange that farm products are an important export for Australia, because only about 7 percent of Australia's land is good for farming. Most of this land is in southeastern Australia and along the east coast. The country's few rivers are in those areas. Farmers use the river water to irrigate their crops. Australian farmers raise barley, oats, and sugar cane. However, their most valuable crop is wheat. Australia is one of the world's leading wheat growers and exporters.

Target Skill **Identify Supporting Details**
What details in this paragraph explain the meaning of the "Pacific Rim"?

Ranching Ranching is another major part of Australia's economy. Australian sheep and cattle provide lamb, mutton, and beef for export. Australia is the world's leading wool producer. Most cattle and sheep are raised on large ranches called stations. Some of the largest stations are in the outback. The **outback** is the name Australians use for the dry land that makes up much of the central and western part of the country. Few people live on its plains and plateaus.

COUNTRY PROFILE
Focus on Geography

Australia

Australia is a large but thinly populated country. It covers about the same area as the United States, not including Alaska and Hawaii. But it has only about 20 million people, a smaller population than Texas. As the graph shows, most of its people live in urban areas. Australia's largest urban areas lie along its southeast coast. On the map, they are the areas labeled "manufacturing and trade." They cover only a very small part of the country. Much of the country consists of huge ranches and farms—labeled "livestock raising" and "commercial farming" on the map—and large deserts—labeled "limited economic activity." There are also forests in the southeast and aboriginal land, used for hunting and gathering, mainly in the north.

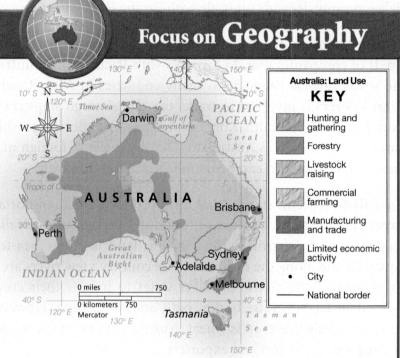

Australia: Land Use
KEY
- Hunting and gathering
- Forestry
- Livestock raising
- Commercial farming
- Manufacturing and trade
- Limited economic activity
- • City
- — National border

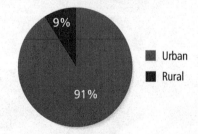

Urban and Rural Population

- Urban 91%
- Rural 9%

SOURCE: DK World Desk Reference

Map and Chart Skills

1. **Recall** Where do most Australians live?
2. **Infer** About how many people live in Australia's rural areas?
3. **Compare** How does Australia's population density compare with that of the United States?

Use Web Code **Ice-6902** for **DK World Desk Reference Online.**

For example, the Koeyers' ranch is in a hot, dry area in northwest Australia. It covers 1 million acres (404,686 hectares) and has about 7,000 head of cattle. Another outback station, near Alice Springs in the center of Australia, is even larger. It covers nearly 12,000 square miles (31,080 square kilometers)—larger than the state of Maryland. Even with this much land, sometimes the cattle can barely find enough grass for grazing. Fresh water also is scarce. Rain falls rarely, and the region has only a few small streams. To supply water for their cattle, ranchers use underground **artesian wells.** These are wells from which water flows under natural pressure without pumping.

✓ **Reading Check** **How does ranching help Australia's economy?**

British Heritage in Australia
The majority of Australians have a British ancestry. Australia's British heritage is shown in Australia's national flag, which includes the flag of the United Kingdom. Australia's flag also includes the Southern Cross, a constellation visible in the Southern Hemisphere. **Conclude** *Why is the Southern Cross an appropriate symbol for Australia?*

Aborigines: Improving Lives

The people of Anangu Tours are proud of the awards they have won for their tours of Uluru. Aboriginal guides conduct the tours in their own language and an interpreter translates the words into English. Aboriginal people in Australia are working hard to preserve their culture. They are having a growing role in the economic life of the country.

Aboriginal leaders have worked to improve the lives of their people. Their schools now teach Aboriginal languages. Aborigines again celebrate important events with ancestral songs and dances. Artists have strengthened Aboriginal culture by creating traditional rock paintings and tree bark paintings.

Aboriginal leaders have helped their people in another important way, too. They have influenced the government of Australia. The government has begun to return Aboriginal land to them. The government has also built schools and hospitals on their land. It has begun to protect some of their sacred places as well.

Aborigines have gained more rights. But their main goal is to regain their ancestral lands. Though Australia's courts have helped, many ranchers and farmers now live on those lands. These people strongly oppose giving the land back. This issue may take many years to resolve.

✓ **Reading Check** **What is a main goal for Aboriginal people in Australia?**

Australian Aboriginal cave paintings date back thousands of years and are among the world's earliest art.

Section 2 Assessment

Key Terms
Review the key terms at the beginning of this section. Use each term in a sentence that explains its meaning.

Target Reading Skill
Find the text on ranching on page 806. What details support the information about ranching in Australia?

Comprehension and Critical Thinking
1. (a) Explain What is the Pacific Rim?

(b) Apply Information Based on what you know about Australia's location, explain why Australia's economy depends on trade with Pacific Rim countries.

2. (a) Recall Give two examples showing how Aboriginal people are working to improve their lives.

(b) Compare As the United States grew, Native Americans were forced from their homelands and moved to reservations. For years, Native Americans have been fighting to regain their original homelands. How does this compare with the history and struggle of the Aborigines?

Writing Activity
Use the information in this section and in the Country Profile on page 786 to write an article about Australia for a news magazine. The article should describe the main types of work people do in Australia.

For: An activity about Australia
Visit: PHSchool.com
Web Code: lcd-6902

Review and Assessment

◆ Chapter Summary

Section 1: Vietnam
- After decades of conflict and war, Vietnam is now a communist country that allows some free enterprise.
- In recent years, Vietnam has made great strides toward modernizing and strengthening its economy.
- Vietnam has become a leading exporter of rice.

Section 2: Australia
- Australia is a Pacific Rim country with an economy based on trade.
- Farming and ranching are key parts of Australia's economy.
- Aboriginal people in Australia are working to preserve their culture and have a role in the economic life of the country.

Vietnamese water puppets

Sydney, Australia

◆ Key Terms

Match the definitions in Column I with the key terms in Column II.

Column I

1. a well from which water flows under natural pressure without pumping

2. a war between political parties or regions within the same country

3. a belief that if one country fell to communism, neighboring nations would also fall, like a row of dominoes

4. the dry land that makes up much of central and western Australia

Column II

A civil war

B outback

C artesian well

D domino theory

Review and Assessment (continued)

◆ Comprehension and Critical Thinking

5. **(a) Recall** Who was Vietnam in conflict with from 1946 to 1954?
(b) Explain What were the Viet Cong?
(c) Summarize Describe the involvement of the United States in the Vietnam War.

6. **(a) Recall** Why did the United States end its involvement in the Vietnam War?
(b) Identify Effects What was one result of the Vietnam War?

7. **(a) Note** Where do most people in Vietnam live?
(b) Contrast How are rural areas in Vietnam different from Ho Chi Minh City?

8. **(a) Name** What is the capital of Vietnam?
(b) Locate In what part of Vietnam is Hanoi located?
(c) Apply Information Why was Saigon renamed Ho Chi Minh City?

9. **(a) Recall** On what kinds of products does Australia depend for a prosperous foreign trade?
(b) Infer Why do few people make their home in Australia's outback?

10. **(a) Note** What are important goals for Australia's Aboriginal people?
(b) Conclude How is Anangu Tours helping to preserve Aboriginal culture?

◆ Skills Practice

Using a Flowchart In the Skills for Life activity in this chapter, you learned how to read a flowchart. Review the steps you learned to use this skill. Then use the flowchart on page 236 to tell what happens after farmers transplant rice seedlings into the rice paddy.

◆ Writing Activity: Language Arts

Storytelling is an important part of Aboriginal culture. Do library research to find and read an Aboriginal folk tale from Australia. Write a report that summarizes the folk tale.

MAP★MASTER™
Skills Activity

Southeast Asia and the Pacific Region

Place Location For each place listed below, write the letter from the map that shows its location.

1. Pacific Ocean
2. Australia
3. Vietnam
4. Philippines
5. Sydney
6. New Zealand

Go Online
PHSchool.com Use Web Code **lcp-6920** for an **interactive map.**

Standardized Test Prep

Test-Taking Tips

Some questions on standardized tests ask you to analyze point of view. Read the passage below. Then, follow the tips to answer the sample question.

> In 1973, the United States ended its part in the Vietnam War. American military advisers and troops were sent home. As American helicopters flew off from the capital, someone watching them said, "I had better hurry to the American embassy. Maybe one of my American friends there can help me escape from Vietnam and go to America."

Pick the letter that best answers the question.

Which onlooker might have made that statement?

TIP Be sure you understand the question. Who said the words that begin, "I had better hurry to the American embassy . . ."?

A a North Vietnamese soldier who had been fighting for years

B an American soldier who got separated from his company

C a South Vietnamese woman who had worked for the Americans

D a protestor who had been supporting North Vietnam during the war

Think It Through You can eliminate A and D because neither person would have friends at the American embassy. You can eliminate B because an American soldier would not have a reason to escape from Vietnam. The correct answer is C.

Practice Questions

Use the tips above and other tips in this book to help you answer the following questions.

1. What did the United States fear would happen if it did NOT help South Vietnam fight against North Vietnam?
   A The French would take control.
   B North Vietnam would invade China.
   C Communists would take over South Vietnam.
   D The United States would lose control of North Vietnam.

2. The Vietnam War finally ended in 1975 when
   A North Vietnam surrendered.
   B U.S. forces invaded Cambodia.
   C North Vietnam gained control over all of South Vietnam.
   D the United States signed a peace treaty with North Vietnam.

3. Some of Australia's trading partners in the Pacific Rim include the United States, China, Taiwan, and
   A India.
   B Italy.
   C Egypt.
   D Japan.

Use Web Code **Ica-6900** for **Chapter 9 self-test.**

Projects

Create your own projects to learn more about Asia and the Pacific. At the beginning of this book, you were introduced to the **Guiding Questions** for studying the chapters and special features. But you can also find answers to these questions by doing projects on your own or with a group. Use the questions to find topics you want to explore further. Then try the projects described on this page or create your own.

1. **Geography** What are the main physical features of Asia and the Pacific?

2. **History** How have ancient civilizations of Asia and the Pacific influenced the world today?

3. **Culture** What are the main characteristics of the cultures of Asia and the Pacific?

4. **Government** What types of government exist in Asia and the Pacific today?

5. **Economics** How do the people of this region make a living?

Project
RESEARCH EXPORTS AND TRADE

Asia and the Pacific Trade Fair

With your class, plan a trade fair for the countries of Asia and the Pacific. As you read this book, choose a country to research. Find out about its major products, factories, and trading partners. Set up a booth to show and tell visitors about trade in your country. Bring books about the country and make posters, pamphlets, and charts for your booth.

Project
CREATE A MAP AND POSTER DISPLAY

Agriculture in Asia and the Pacific

Draw a large map of Asia and the Pacific and hang it in your classroom. As you read about different kinds of farm products, mark them on the appropriate location on your map. Choose ten farm products and design a small poster for each one. On each poster, write the farm product and a country in Asia and the Pacific where this product comes from. Find or draw a picture for each poster.

Table of Contents

The World: Political

CENTRAL AMERICA
AND THE CARIBBEAN
For detail, see map
North and South
America: Political

0 miles   2,000

0 kilometers   2,000
Robinson

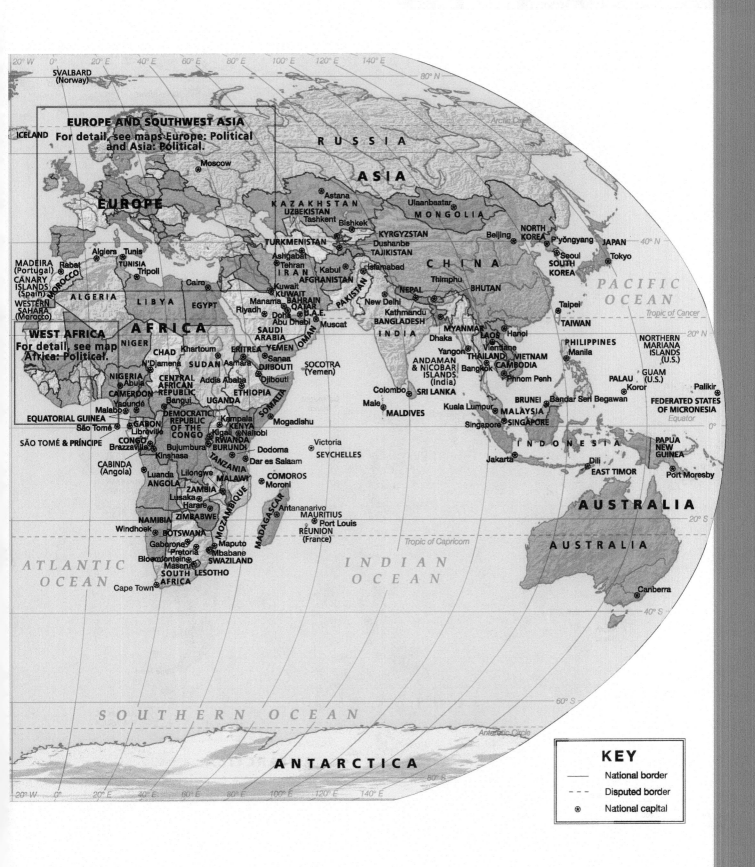

SVALBARD
(Norway)

20° W   0°   20° E   40° E   60° E   80° E   100° E   120° E   140° E   80° N

ICELAND

Arctic Circle

EUROPE AND SOUTHWEST ASIA
For detail, see maps Europe: Political
and Asia: Political.

RUSSIA

ASIA

Moscow ⊗

EUROPE

⊗ Astana   Ulaanbaatar ⊗
KAZAKHSTAN   MONGOLIA
UZBEKISTAN
Tashkent ⊗ Bishkek ⊗
KYRGYZSTAN   Beijing ⊗   NORTH
TURKMENISTAN   Dushanbe ⊗   KOREA ⊗ P'yŏngyang ⊗   JAPAN   40° N
Ashgabat ⊗   TAJIKISTAN   CHINA   Seoul ⊗ Tokyo ⊗
Tehran ⊗   Thimphu ⊗   SOUTH
Algiers ⊗ Tunis ⊗   IRAN Kabul ⊗   KOREA
MADEIRA   Rabat ⊗ TUNISIA   ⊗ Islamabad   PACIFIC
(Portugal)   Tripoli   Kuwait ⊗ AFGHANISTAN NEPAL BHUTAN   OCEAN
CANARY   MOROCCO   Manama ⊗ BAHRAIN PAKISTAN New Delhi ⊗ Taipei ⊗   Tropic of Cancer
ISLANDS   Cairo ⊗ Riyadh ⊗ QATAR Kathmandu ⊗   TAIWAN
(Spain)   ALGERIA   LIBYA   EGYPT Doha ⊗ U.A.E. BANGLADESH   20° N
WESTERN   Abu Dhabi ⊗ Muscat ⊗ MYANMAR LAOS NORTHERN
SAHARA   SAUDI   INDIA Dhaka ⊗ Hanoi ⊗   PHILIPPINES MARIANA
(Morocco)   WEST AFRICA   AFRICA ARABIA YEMEN   VIETNAM Manila ⊗ ISLANDS
For detail, see map   NIGER Khartoum ⊗ ERITREA ⊗ Sanaa SOCOTRA Yangon ⊗ THAILAND   (U.S.)
Africa: Political.   CHAD   Asmara ⊗ DJIBOUTI (Yemen) Bangkok ⊗ CAMBODIA GUAM
N'Djamena ⊗ SUDAN   Djibouti ⊗   Phnom Penh ⊗ PALAU (U.S.)   Palikir ⊗
NIGERIA   CENTRAL Addis Ababa ⊗   Colombo ⊗ SRI LANKA   Koror ⊗   FEDERATED STATES
⊗ Abuja   AFRICAN   ETHIOPIA   Male ⊗   BRUNEI ⊗ Bandar Seri Begawan OF MICRONESIA
CAMEROON   REPUBLIC UGANDA   MALDIVES Kuala Lumpur ⊗   Equator
Yadundé ⊗ Bangui ⊗   Kampala ⊗ KENYA Mogadishu ⊗   Singapore ⊗ MALAYSIA   0°
Malabo ⊗ DEMOCRATIC Kigali ⊗ Nairobi ⊗   SINGAPORE ⊗
EQUATORIAL GUINEA   REPUBLIC RWANDA   INDONESIA   PAPUA
São Tomé ⊗ GABON OF THE Bujumbura ⊗ BURUNDI   NEW
SÃO TOMÉ & PRÍNCIPE Libreville ⊗ CONGO   Dodoma ⊗ Victoria ⊗   GUINEA
CONGO Kinshasa ⊗ TANZANIA Dar es Salaam ⊗ SEYCHELLES   Jakarta ⊗ Dili ⊗
Brazzaville ⊗   EAST TIMOR Port Moresby ⊗
CABINDA   Luanda ⊗ Lilongwe ⊗   COMOROS
(Angola)   ANGOLA   MALAWI ⊗ Moroni ⊗   AUSTRALIA
Lusaka ⊗ ZAMBIA MOZAMBIQUE Antananarivo ⊗ MAURITIUS   AUSTRALIA   20° S
NAMIBIA   Harare ⊗ ZIMBABWE MADAGASCAR Port Louis ⊗
Windhoek ⊗   BOTSWANA   RÉUNION
Gaborone ⊗ Maputo ⊗   (France)   Tropic of Capricorn
Bloemfontein ⊗ Pretoria ⊗ Mbabane ⊗
Maseru ⊗ SWAZILAND   INDIAN   40° S
SOUTH LESOTHO
Cape Town ⊗ AFRICA   OCEAN
ATLANTIC
OCEAN

Canberra ⊗

60° S

SOUTHERN OCEAN

Antarctic Circle

ANTARCTICA

20° W   0°   20° E   40° E   60° E   80° E   100° E   120° E   140° E   80° S

KEY
—— National border
- - - Disputed border
⊗ National capital

The World: Physical

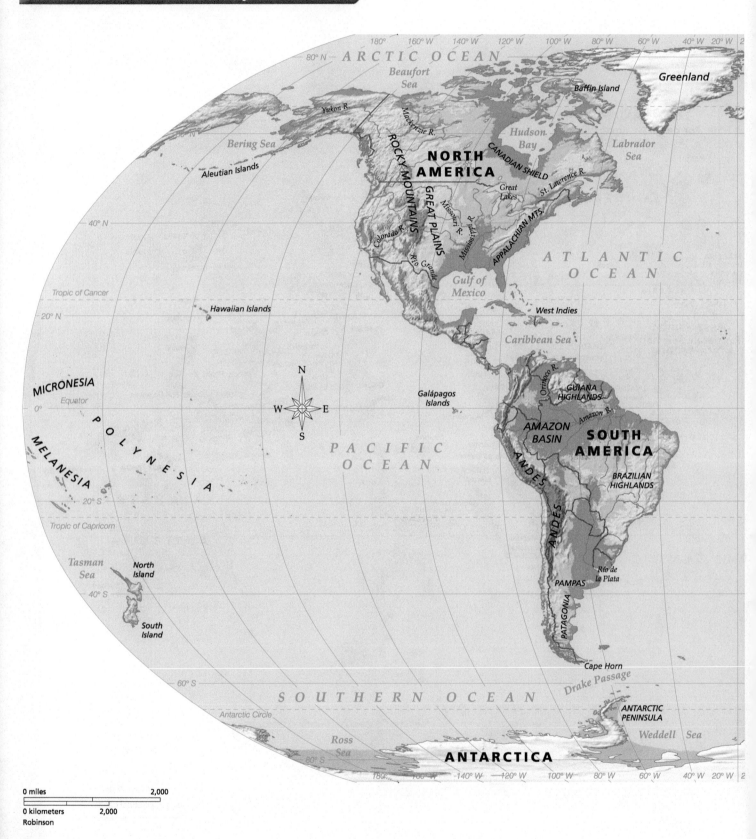

0 miles 2,000

0 kilometers 2,000

Robinson

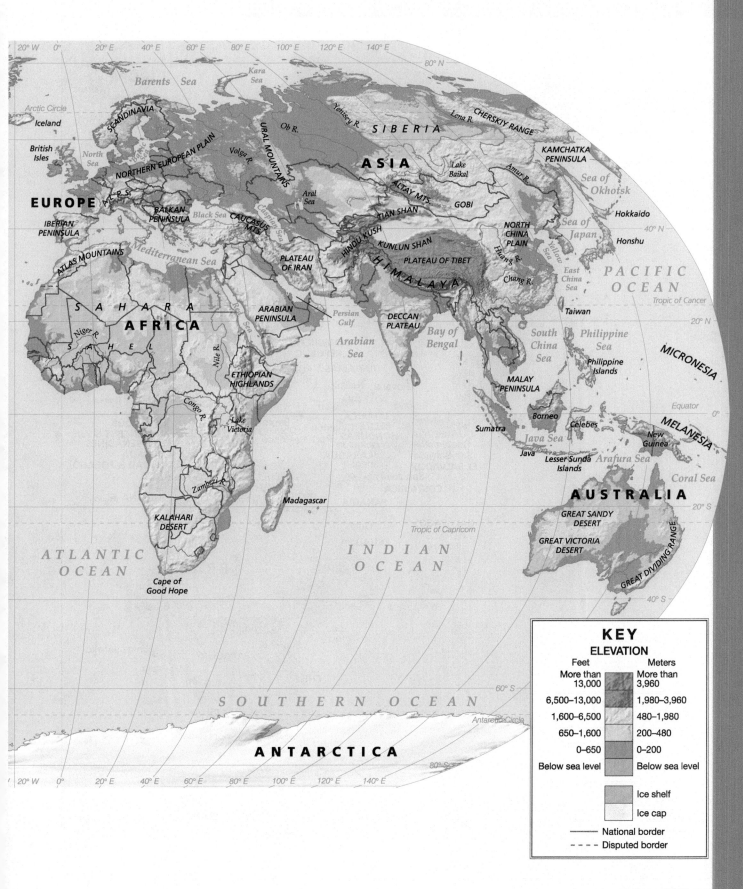

KEY

ELEVATION

Feet		Meters
More than 13,000		More than 3,960
6,500–13,000		1,980–3,960
1,600–6,500		480–1,980
650–1,600		200–480
0–650		0–200
Below sea level		Below sea level

Ice shelf

Ice cap

—————— National border

- - - - - Disputed border

North and South America: Political

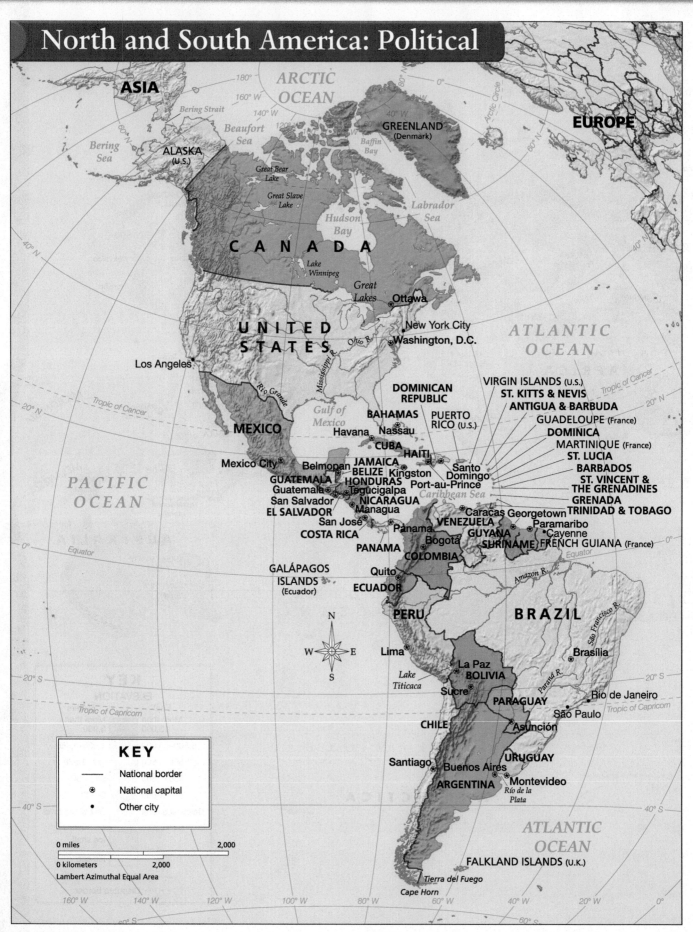

ASIA

ARCTIC OCEAN

180°
160° W
140° W
120° W
Bering Strait
Beaufort Sea
Bering Sea

EUROPE

GREENLAND
(Denmark)

ALASKA
(U.S.)

Baffin Bay

Great Bear Lake

Great Slave Lake

Hudson Bay

Labrador Sea

C A N A D A

Lake Winnipeg

Great Lakes

Ottawa

New York City
Washington, D.C.

ATLANTIC OCEAN

U N I T E D
S T A T E S

Ohio R.

Los Angeles

Mississippi R.

Rio Grande

Tropic of Cancer

Gulf of Mexico

MEXICO

Havana

Mexico City

CUBA

Belmopan
GUATEMALA
Guatemala
San Salvador
EL SALVADOR

BELIZE
HONDURAS
Tegucigalpa
NICARAGUA
Managua

JAMAICA
Kingston

Nassau

BAHAMAS

DOMINICAN REPUBLIC

PUERTO RICO (U.S.)

HAITI

Port-au-Prince

Santo Domingo

VIRGIN ISLANDS (U.S.)
ST. KITTS & NEVIS
ANTIGUA & BARBUDA
GUADELOUPE (France)
DOMINICA
MARTINIQUE (France)
ST. LUCIA
BARBADOS
ST. VINCENT &
THE GRENADINES
GRENADA
TRINIDAD & TOBAGO

Caribbean Sea

Tropic of Cancer

20° N

PACIFIC OCEAN

San José
COSTA RICA

PANAMA

Panama

VENEZUELA

Caracas

Bogotá

Georgetown
GUYANA
SURINAME
Paramaribo
Cayenne
FRENCH GUIANA (France)

COLOMBIA

GALÁPAGOS ISLANDS
(Ecuador)

Quito

ECUADOR

Equator

Amazon R.

Equator

PERU

Lima

Lake Titicaca

N
W   E
S

La Paz
BOLIVIA
Sucre

BRAZIL

São Francisco R.

Brasília

Rio de Janeiro

São Paulo

Tropic of Capricorn

PARAGUAY
Asunción

CHILE

Paraná R.

20° S

URUGUAY

Santiago
Buenos Aires
ARGENTINA
Montevideo
Río de la Plata

KEY

—— National border
⊛ National capital
• Other city

40° S

ATLANTIC OCEAN

0 miles   2,000
0 kilometers   2,000
Lambert Azimuthal Equal Area

FALKLAND ISLANDS (U.K.)

Tierra del Fuego

Cape Horn

160° W   140° W   120° W   100° W   80° W   60° W   40° W   20° W

North and South America: Physical

ASIA

ARCTIC OCEAN

EUROPE

Bering Strait

Beaufort Sea

Mt. McKinley 20,320 ft (6,194 m)

Greenland

Alaska Range

Bering Sea

Baffin Bay

Davis Strait

Aleutian Islands

Gulf of Alaska

Great Bear Lake

Baffin Island

Labrador Sea

Mackenzie R.

Great Slave Lake

Hudson Bay

Newfoundland

ROCKY MOUNTAINS

CANADIAN SHIELD

GREAT PLAINS

Lake Winnipeg

Great Lakes

Missouri R.

Appalachian Mts.

Colorado R.

Ohio R.

ATLANTIC OCEAN

Tropic of Cancer

Mississippi R.

Baja California

Rio Grande

Gulf of Mexico

Sierra Madre Occidental

Sierra Madre Oriental

Gulf of California

Yucatán Peninsula

Cuba

Hispaniola

Lesser Antilles

Greater Antilles

Caribbean Sea

PACIFIC OCEAN

Isthmus of Panama

Orinoco R.

Guiana Highlands

Galápagos Islands

Equator

AMAZON BASIN

Amazon R.

ANDES

São Francisco R.

Brazilian Highlands

Lake Titicaca

Parná R.

Tropic of Capricorn

ANDES

Gran Chaco

Paraguay R.

Paraná R.

Aconcagua 22,834 ft (6,960 m)

Pampas

Río de la Plata

Patagonia

ATLANTIC OCEAN

Falkland Islands

Tierra del Fuego

Cape Horn

KEY

ELEVATION

Feet	Meters
More than 13,000	More than 3,960
6,500–13,000	1,980–3,960
1,600–6,500	480–1,980
650–1,600	200–480
0–650	0–200

Ice cap

National border

0 miles 2,000

0 kilometers 2,000

Lambert Azimuthal Equal Area

N W E S

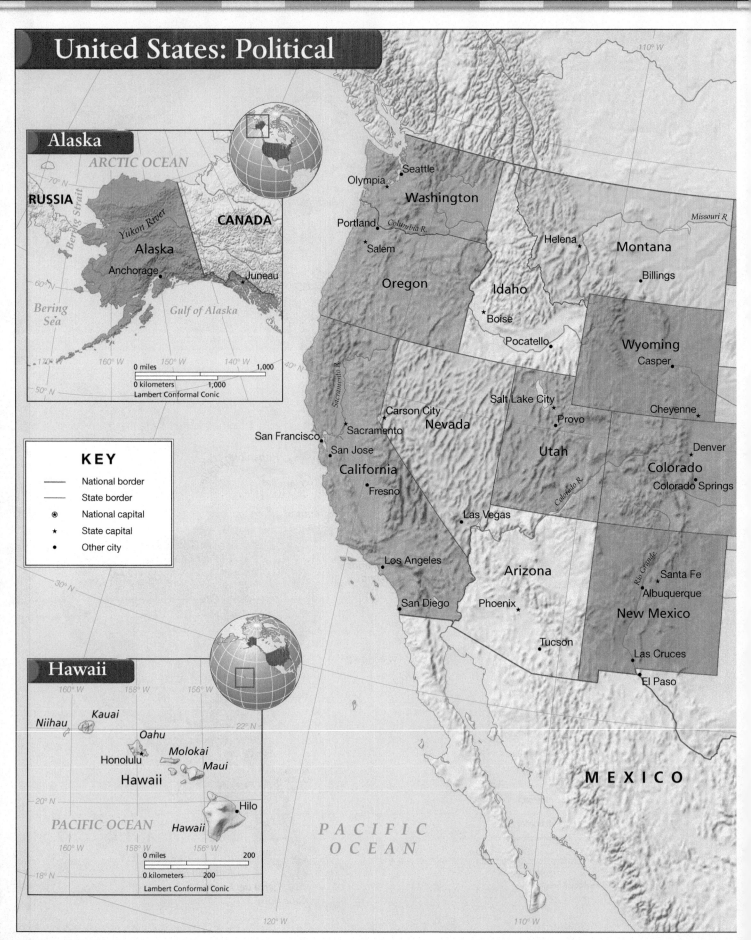

United States: Political

Alaska

ARCTIC OCEAN

70° N

RUSSIA

Arctic Circle

CANADA

Bering Strait

Yukon River

Alaska

60° N

Anchorage

Juneau

Bering Sea

Gulf of Alaska

170° W   160° W   150° W   140° W   1,000

50° N

0 miles   1,000
0 kilometers   1,000
Lambert Conformal Conic

KEY

———	National border
———	State border
⊛	National capital
★	State capital
•	Other city

30° N

Hawaii

160° W   158° W   156° W

Niihau

Kauai

22° N

Oahu

Molokai

Honolulu

Maui

Hawaii

20° N

PACIFIC OCEAN

Hawaii

18° N

Hilo

160° W   158° W   156° W   200

0 miles   200
0 kilometers   200
Lambert Conformal Conic

110° W

Seattle

Olympia

Washington

Missouri R.

Portland   Columbia R.

Salem

Helena

Montana

Oregon

Idaho

Billings

Boise

Pocatello

Wyoming

Casper

Sacramento R.

Carson City

Salt Lake City

Cheyenne

Sacramento

Nevada

Provo

San Francisco

Utah

Denver

San Jose

Colorado

California

Colorado Springs

Fresno

Colorado R.

Las Vegas

Arizona

Santa Fe

Los Angeles

Rio Grande

Albuquerque

Phoenix

New Mexico

San Diego

Tucson

Las Cruces

El Paso

120° W

PACIFIC OCEAN

MEXICO

110° W

CANADA

North Dakota
Bismarck
Fargo

Minnesota

South Dakota
Pierre
Sioux Falls

Minneapolis
St. Paul
Mississippi R.

Lake Superior

Wisconsin
Milwaukee
Madison

Michigan
Grand Rapids
Lansing

Lake Huron

Lake Ontario

Maine
Augusta
Portland

Vermont
Montpelier
New Hampshire
Concord

Albany
Boston
Massachusetts

Nebraska
Omaha
Lincoln

Iowa
Des Moines

Lake Michigan

Chicago
Cedar Rapids

Fort Wayne
Indiana

Detroit
Lake Erie

New York
Buffalo

Providence
Hartford
Rhode Island
Connecticut

New York City

Illinois
Springfield

Indianapolis

Ohio
Columbus

Cleveland
Pittsburgh

Harrisburg

Pennsylvania

New Jersey
Trenton
Philadelphia
Delaware
Dover

Missouri R.

Kansas City
Topeka
Jefferson City

Kansas
Wichita

Arkansas R.

Louisville

St. Louis

Cincinnati
Ohio R.

West
Virginia

Charleston

Frankfort

Baltimore
Washington, D.C.
Annapolis
Maryland

District of Columbia
Richmond

Virginia
Norfolk

Missouri

Kentucky

Oklahoma
Tulsa
Oklahoma City

Arkansas
Fort Smith
Little Rock

Nashville
Memphis

Tennessee
Tennessee R.

Knoxville

Raleigh

North Carolina
Charlotte

South Carolina
Columbia

ATLANTIC
OCEAN

Red R.

Texas

Mississippi R.

Mississippi
Jackson

Alabama
Birmingham
Montgomery

Atlanta

Georgia
Columbus

Charleston

Savannah

Dallas
Fort Worth

Shreveport
Louisiana
Baton Rouge

Gulfport
New Orleans

Mobile

Jacksonville

Tallahassee

Austin
Houston
San Antonio

Florida
Orlando
Tampa

Miami

Gulf of Mexico

N
W E
S

0 miles   250
0 kilometers   250
Lambert Azimuthal Equal Area

100° W
90° W
80° W
70° W
50° N
40° N
30° N

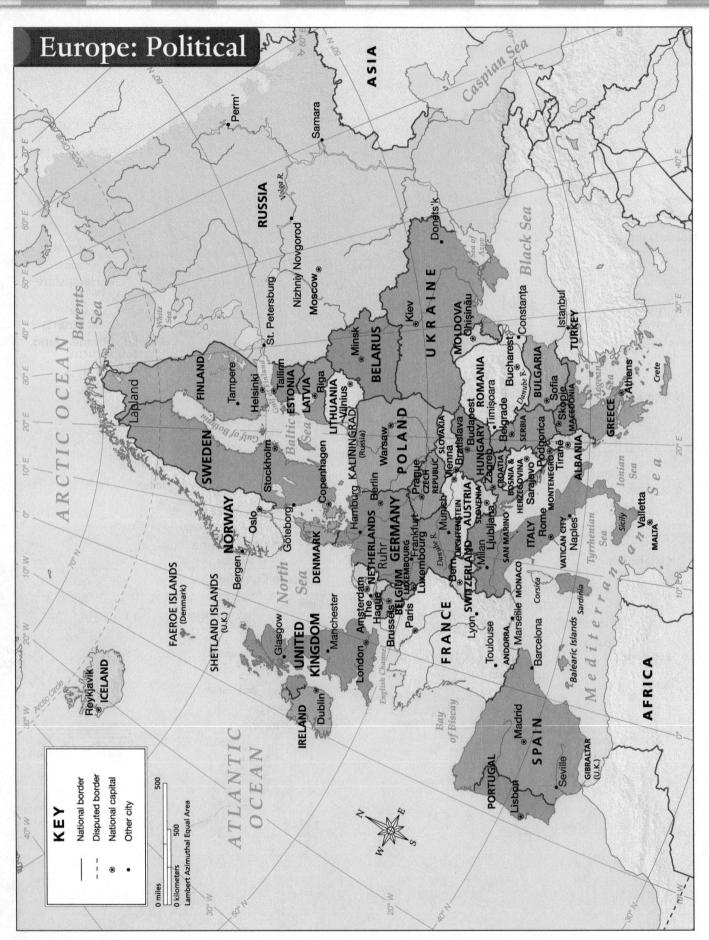

Europe: Political

ASIA

RUSSIA

Caspian Sea

Perm'

Samara

Volga R.

Nizhniy Novgorod

Moscow ⊛

St. Petersburg

Barents Sea

White Sea

ARCTIC OCEAN

Lapland

FINLAND

Tampere

Helsinki ⊛

SWEDEN

Gulf of Bothnia

Stockholm ⊛

Göteborg

NORWAY

Oslo ⊛

Bergen

Minsk ⊛

BELARUS

Kiev ⊛

UKRAINE

Donets'k ⊛

Sea of Azov

Black Sea

MOLDOVA

Chişinău ⊛

ROMANIA

Timişoara

Bucharest ⊛

Constanţa

Danube R.

BULGARIA

Sofia ⊛

Istanbul

TURKEY

Tallinn ⊛

ESTONIA

Riga ⊛

LATVIA

LITHUANIA

Vilnius ⊛

KALININGRAD
(Russia)

POLAND

Warsaw ⊛

Gulf of Finland

Baltic Sea

Copenhagen ⊛

DENMARK

Hamburg

GERMANY

Berlin ⊛

Ruhr

Frankfurt

Prague ⊛

CZECH
REPUBLIC

SLOVAKIA

Bratislava ⊛

Vienna ⊛

AUSTRIA

HUNGARY

Budapest ⊛

Zagreb ⊛

CROATIA

SLOVENIA

Ljubljana ⊛

Belgrade ⊛

SERBIA

BOSNIA &
HERZEGOVINA

Sarajevo ⊛

MONTENEGRO

Podgorica ⊛

Tiranë ⊛

ALBANIA

MACEDONIA

Skopje ⊛

GREECE

Athens ⊛

Aegean Sea

Crete

Ionian Sea

NETHERLANDS

Amsterdam

The Hague

BELGIUM

Brussels ⊛

LUXEMBOURG

Luxembourg ⊛

Paris ⊛

FRANCE

Danube R.

Bern ⊛

LIECHTENSTEIN

SWITZERLAND

Munich

Milan

SAN MARINO

MONACO

ITALY

Rome ⊛

VATICAN CITY

Naples

Corsica

Sardinia

Tyrrhenian Sea

Sicily

Valletta ⊛

MALTA

Mediterranean Sea

Lyon

Marseille

Toulouse

ANDORRA

Barcelona

Balearic Islands

Madrid ⊛

SPAIN

Seville

GIBRALTAR
(U.K.)

PORTUGAL

Lisbon ⊛

Bay of Biscay

English Channel

London ⊛

UNITED
KINGDOM

Glasgow

Manchester

IRELAND

Dublin ⊛

North Sea

SHETLAND
ISLANDS (U.K.)

FAEROE ISLANDS
(Denmark)

ICELAND

Reykjavik ⊛

Arctic Circle

ATLANTIC
OCEAN

AFRICA

KEY

——	National border
– – –	Disputed border
⊛	National capital
•	Other city

0 miles 500
0 kilometers 500

Lambert Azimuthal Equal Area

N E S W

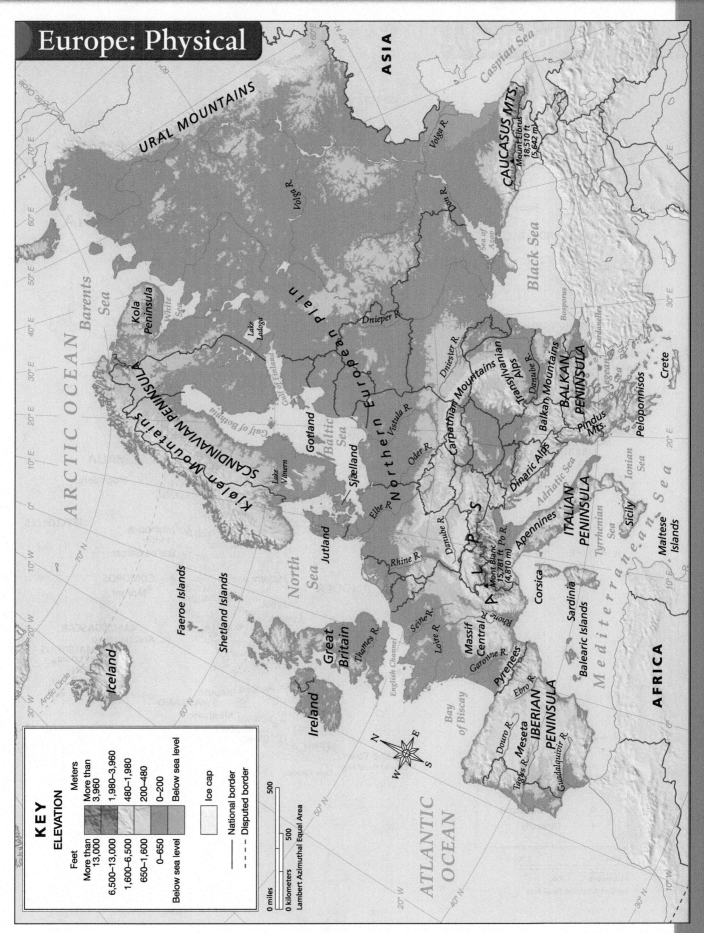

Europe: Physical

ASIA

URAL MOUNTAINS

Caspian Sea

CAUCASUS MTS.
Mount Elbrus
18,510 ft
(5,642 m)

Volga R.

Volga R.

Don R.

Sea of Azov

Dnieper R.

Black Sea

Bosporus

ARCTIC OCEAN

Barents Sea

Kola Peninsula

White Sea

Lake Ladoga

Northern European Plain

Dniester R.

Carpathian Mountains

Transylvanian Alps

Danube R.

Balkan Mountains

BALKAN PENINSULA

Dardanelles

Aegean Sea

Crete

Gulf of Finland

Vistula R.

Pindus Mts.

Peloponnisos

SCANDINAVIAN PENINSULA

Kjølen Mountains

Gulf of Bothnia

Oder R.

Dinaric Alps

Baltic Sea

Gotland

Sjælland

Elbe R.

Adriatic Sea

Ionian Sea

Lake Vänern

Apennines

ITALIAN PENINSULA

Tyrrhenian Sea

Sicily

Maltese Islands

Mediterranean Sea

North Sea

Jutland

Danube R.

ALPS

Mont Blanc
15,781 ft
(4,810 m)

Corsica

Sardinia

Balearic Islands

Rhine R.

Great Britain

Thames R.

Seine R.

Loire R.

Massif Central

Rhône R.

English Channel

Faeroe Islands

Shetland Islands

Ireland

Iceland

Garonne R.

Pyrenees

Ebro R.

IBERIAN PENINSULA

Meseta

Douro R.

Tagus R.

Guadalquivir R.

Bay of Biscay

ATLANTIC OCEAN

AFRICA

Arctic Circle

N
E
S
W

KEY
ELEVATION

Feet	Meters
More than 13,000	More than 3,960
6,500–13,000	1,980–3,960
1,600–6,500	480–1,980
650–1,600	200–480
0–650	0–200
Below sea level	Below sea level

Ice cap

—— National border

– – – Disputed border

0 miles 500

0 kilometers 500

Lambert Azimuthal Equal Area

Africa: Political

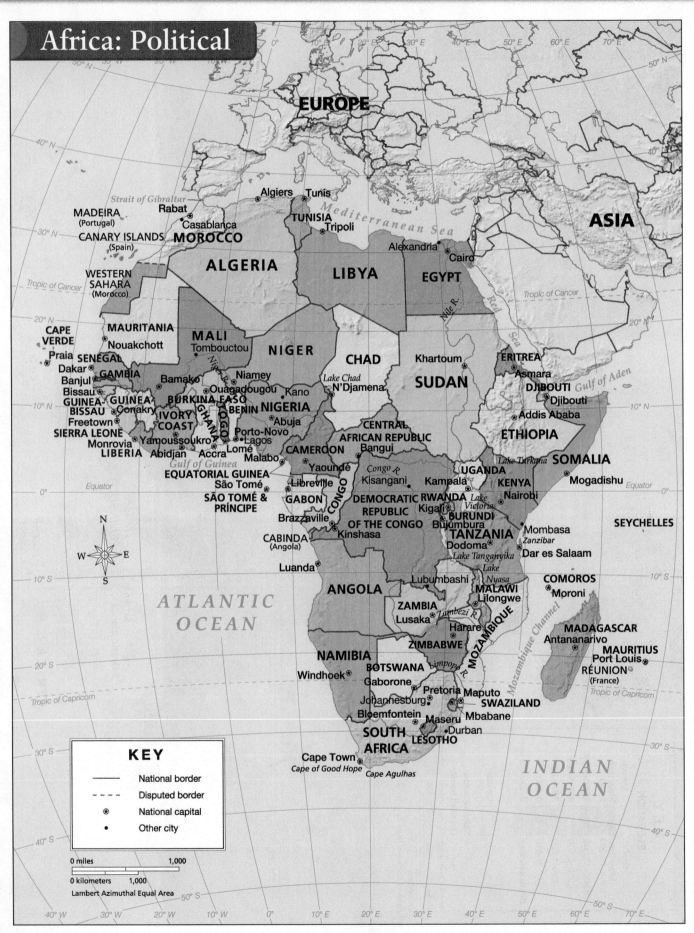

EUROPE

ASIA

Strait of Gibraltar
MADEIRA (Portugal)
Rabat
Casablanca
CANARY ISLANDS (Spain)
MOROCCO
WESTERN SAHARA (Morocco)
Tropic of Cancer

Algiers Tunis
TUNISIA
Tripoli
Mediterranean Sea
Alexandria
Cairo
LIBYA
EGYPT
ALGERIA

CAPE VERDE
Praia
MAURITANIA
Nouakchott
SENEGAL
Dakar
GAMBIA
Banjul
Bissau
GUINEA-BISSAU
GUINEA
Conakry
Freetown
SIERRA LEONE
Monrovia
LIBERIA
Abidjan

MALI
Tombouctou
Bamako
Niamey
Ouagadougou
BURKINA FASO
IVORY COAST
Yamoussoukro
Accra
Lomé
GHANA
Niger R.
NIGER
Kano
BENIN
NIGERIA
Abuja
Porto-Novo
Lagos
Malabo

CHAD
Lake Chad
N'Djamena
Khartoum
SUDAN
Nile R.
Red Sea
Tropic of Cancer

ERITREA
Asmara
DJIBOUTI
Djibouti
Gulf of Aden
Addis Ababa
ETHIOPIA

CENTRAL AFRICAN REPUBLIC
Bangui
CAMEROON
Yaoundé
EQUATORIAL GUINEA
São Tomé
SÃO TOMÉ & PRÍNCIPE
GABON
Libreville
CONGO
Brazzaville
CABINDA (Angola)
Kinshasa
DEMOCRATIC REPUBLIC OF THE CONGO
Kisangani
Congo R.

SOMALIA
Mogadishu
Lake Turkana
UGANDA
Kampala
RWANDA
Kigali
BURUNDI
Bujumbura
KENYA
Nairobi
Lake Victoria
TANZANIA
Dodoma
Mombasa
Zanzibar
Dar es Salaam
Lake Tanganyika

Gulf of Guinea
Equator

SEYCHELLES

N
W E
S

ATLANTIC OCEAN

Luanda
ANGOLA
Lubumbashi
ZAMBIA
Lusaka
Zambezi R.
Harare
ZIMBABWE
Limpopo R.
NAMIBIA
Windhoek
BOTSWANA
Gaborone
Johannesburg
Pretoria
Maputo
SWAZILAND
Mbabane
Bloemfontein
Maseru
LESOTHO
Durban
SOUTH AFRICA
Cape Town
Cape of Good Hope
Cape Agulhas

Lake Nyasa
MALAWI
Lilongwe
MOZAMBIQUE
Mozambique Channel
COMOROS
Moroni
MADAGASCAR
Antananarivo
MAURITIUS
Port Louis
RÉUNION (France)
Tropic of Capricorn

INDIAN OCEAN

KEY

— National border
--- Disputed border
⊛ National capital
• Other city

0 miles   1,000
0 kilometers   1,000
Lambert Azimuthal Equal Area

258 Reference

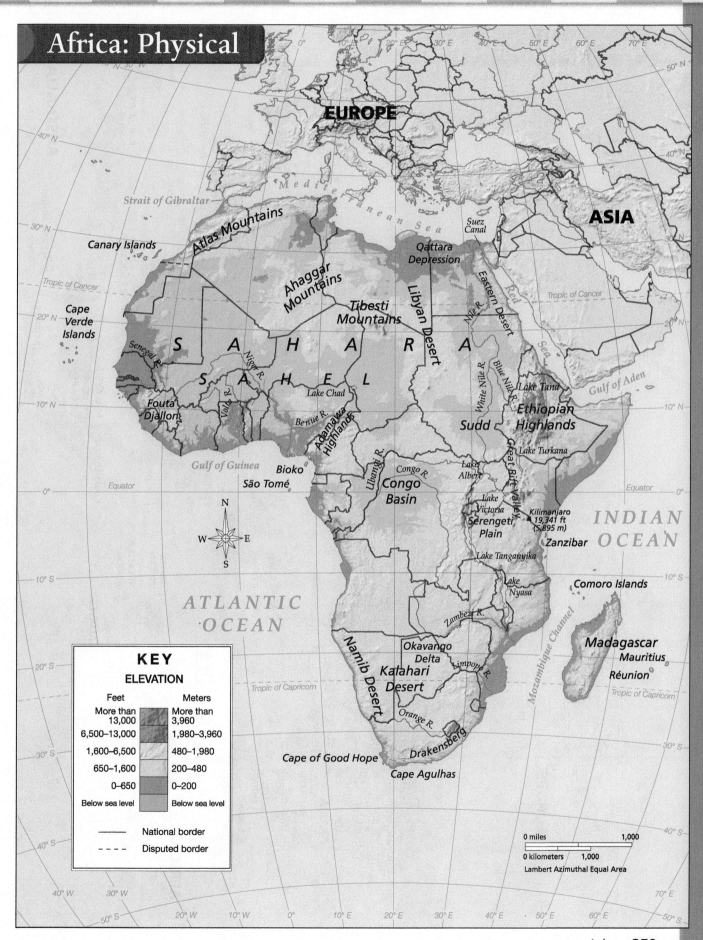

Africa: Physical

EUROPE

ASIA

Mediterranean Sea

Strait of Gibraltar

Canary Islands

Suez Canal

Qattara Depression

Atlas Mountains

Ahaggar Mountains

Tibesti Mountains

Libyan Desert

Tropic of Cancer

Cape Verde Islands

S A H A R A

Nile R.

Eastern Desert

Red Sea

Tropic of Cancer

Senegal R.

S A H E L

Niger R.

Lake Chad

White Nile R.

Blue Nile R.

Lake Tana

Gulf of Aden

Fouta Djallon

Volta R.

Benue R.

Adamawa Highlands

Sudd

Ethiopian Highlands

Lake Turkana

Gulf of Guinea

Bioko

São Tomé

Ubangi R.

Congo R.

Congo Basin

Lake Albert

Great Rift Valley

Equator

Lake Victoria

Serengeti Plain

Kilimanjaro
19,341 ft
(5,895 m)

INDIAN OCEAN

Zanzibar

Lake Tanganyika

ATLANTIC OCEAN

Lake Nyasa

Comoro Islands

Zambezi R.

Mozambique Channel

Madagascar

Mauritius

Réunion

Namib Desert

Okavango Delta

Kalahari Desert

Limpopo R.

Tropic of Capricorn

Tropic of Capricorn

Orange R.

Drakensberg

Cape of Good Hope

Cape Agulhas

KEY
ELEVATION

Feet		Meters
More than 13,000		More than 3,960
6,500–13,000		1,980–3,960
1,600–6,500		480–1,980
650–1,600		200–480
0–650		0–200
Below sea level		Below sea level

——— National border

- - - Disputed border

N
W E
S

0 miles 1,000
0 kilometers 1,000
Lambert Azimuthal Equal Area

Asia: Political

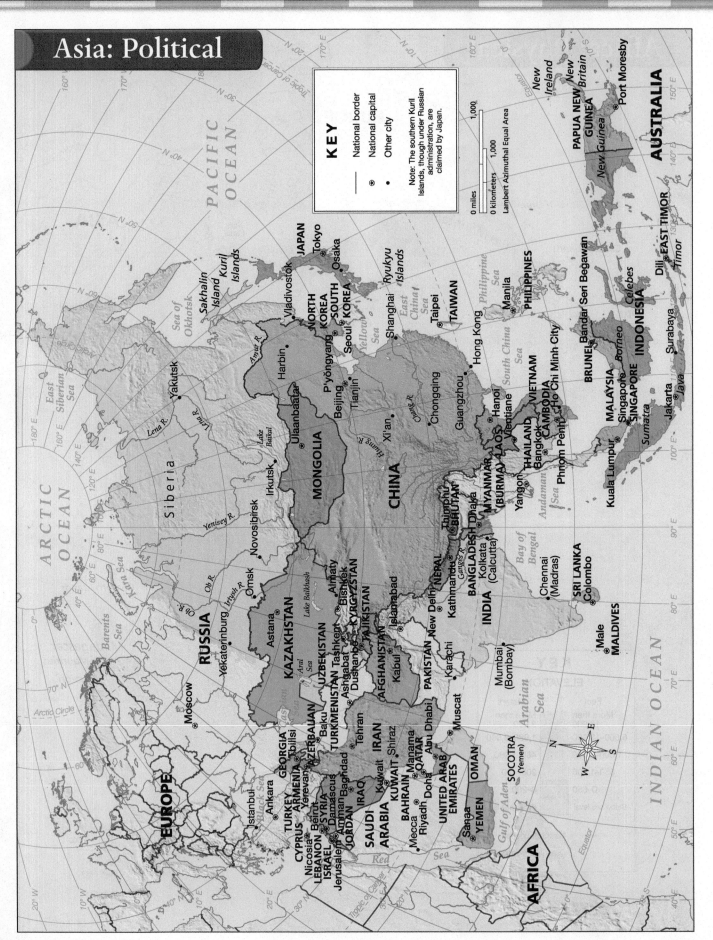

KEY

National border
⊛ National capital
• Other city

Note: The southern Kuril Islands, though under Russian administration, are claimed by Japan.

0 miles 1,000
0 kilometers 1,000
Lambert Azimuthal Equal Area

PACIFIC OCEAN

ARCTIC OCEAN

Arctic Circle

Tropic of Cancer

East Siberian Sea

Sea of Okhotsk

Sakhalin Island

Kuril Islands

JAPAN
Tokyo
Vladivostok
Osaka
NORTH KOREA
P'yŏngyang
SOUTH KOREA
Seoul
Harbin

Ryukyu Islands

East China Sea

Shanghai

Yellow Sea

TAIWAN
Taipei

Philippine Sea

PHILIPPINES
Manila

New Ireland
New Britain
PAPUA NEW GUINEA
New Guinea
Port Moresby

AUSTRALIA

Barents Sea

Kara Sea

ARCTIC OCEAN

Yakutsk

Lena R.

Lena R.

Siberia

Lake Baikal

Irkutsk

Amur R.

Beijing
Tianjin

MONGOLIA
Ulaanbaatar

CHINA
Xi'an
Chongqing
Guangzhou
Hong Kong

Huang R.

Guang R.

South China Sea

Hanoi
VIETNAM
Vientiane
LAOS
Bangkok
THAILAND
CAMBODIA
Phnom Penh
Ho Chi Minh City

MALAYSIA
Kuala Lumpur
BRUNEI Bandar Seri Begawan
Borneo
SINGAPORE
Singapore
INDONESIA

Celebes

Sumatra
Java
Jakarta
Surabaya

Dili EAST TIMOR
Timor

MOSCOW

EUROPE

Black Sea

Istanbul
Ankara
TURKEY
CYPRUS
Nicosia
LEBANON Beirut
SYRIA
ISRAEL
Jerusalem
Damascus
JORDAN
Amman
Baghdad
IRAQ
Mecca
Riyadh

SAUDI ARABIA

Red Sea

AFRICA

Yenisey R.

RUSSIA

Yekaterinburg

Omsk
Novosibirsk

Ob R.
Irtysh R.

Astana
KAZAKHSTAN

Aral Sea

Lake Balkhash

Almaty
Bishkek
KYRGYZSTAN
Tashkent
UZBEKISTAN
TAJIKISTAN
Dushanbe
TURKMENISTAN
Ashgabat

AFGHANISTAN
Kabul
Islamabad

PAKISTAN

Karachi

GEORGIA
Tbilisi
ARMENIA
Yerevan
AZERBAIJAN
Baku
Tehran
IRAN
Shiraz

KUWAIT
Kuwait
BAHRAIN Manama
QATAR
Doha
Abu Dhabi
UNITED ARAB EMIRATES

OMAN
Muscat

Caspian Sea

Kura Sea

NEPAL
Kathmandu
New Delhi
Thimphu
BHUTAN
BANGLADESH
Dhaka
Kolkata (Calcutta)

INDIA

Ganges R.

Bay of Bengal

Chennai (Madras)

SRI LANKA
Colombo

Mumbai (Bombay)

Male
MALDIVES

Arabian Sea

YANGON
MYANMAR (BURMA)

Andaman Sea

INDIAN OCEAN

SOCOTRA (Yemen)

Gulf of Aden

Sanaa
YEMEN

N
W E
S

Equator

Tropic of Cancer

Asia: Physical

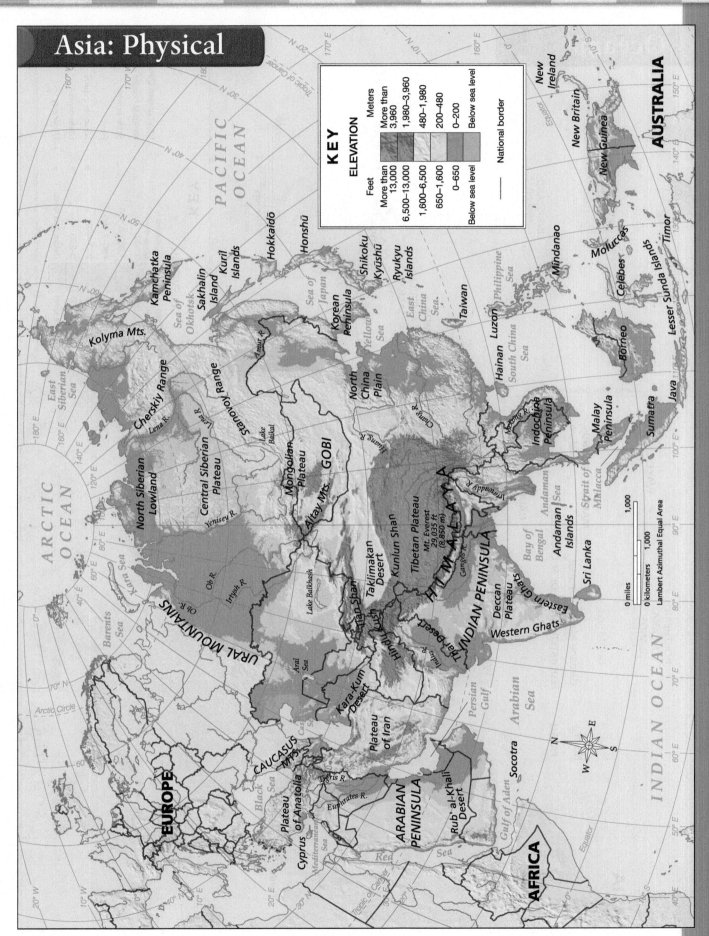

KEY

ELEVATION

Feet	Meters
More than 13,000	More than 3,960
6,500–13,000	1,980–3,960
1,600–6,500	480–1,980
650–1,600	200–480
0–650	0–200
Below sea level	Below sea level

National border

PACIFIC OCEAN

ARCTIC OCEAN

INDIAN OCEAN

AUSTRALIA

EUROPE

AFRICA

New Ireland

New Britain

New Guinea

Mindanao

Moluccas

Celebes

Borneo

Lesser Sunda Islands

Timor

Java

Sumatra

Philippine Sea

Luzon

Hainan

South China Sea

Taiwan

Malay Peninsula

Strait of Malacca

Andaman Sea

Andaman Islands

Indochina Peninsula

Mekong R.

Irrawaddy R.

Bay of Bengal

Sri Lanka

Eastern Ghats

Western Ghats

Deccan Plateau

INDIAN PENINSULA

Ganges R.

Thar Desert

Indus R.

HIMALAYA

Mt. Everest 29,035 ft (8,850 m)

Tibetan Plateau

Kunlun Shan

Taklimakan Desert

Tian Shan

Hindu Kush

Kara-Kum Desert

Aral Sea

Lake Balkhash

GOBI

Altay Mts.

Mongolian Plateau

Lake Baikal

Huang R.

Chang R.

North China Plain

Yellow Sea

East China Sea

Korean Peninsula

Sea of Japan

Honshū

Shikoku

Kyūshū

Ryukyu Islands

Hokkaidō

Kuril Islands

Sakhalin Island

Sea of Okhotsk

Kamchatka Peninsula

Kolyma Mts.

Cherskiy Range

Stanovoy Range

Lena R.

Amur R.

Central Siberian Plateau

North Siberian Lowland

Yenisey R.

Ob R.

Irtysh R.

East Siberian Sea

Kara Sea

Barents Sea

URAL MOUNTAINS

Ob R.

CAUCASUS MTS.

Black Sea

Caspian Sea

Plateau of Anatolia

Cyprus

Mediterranean Sea

Tigris R.

Euphrates R.

Plateau of Iran

Persian Gulf

Arabian Sea

ARABIAN PENINSULA

Rub' al-Khali Desert

Socotra

Gulf of Aden

Red Sea

Tropic of Cancer

Arctic Circle

Equator

0 miles 1,000

0 kilometers 1,000

Lambert Azimuthal Equal Area

Oceania

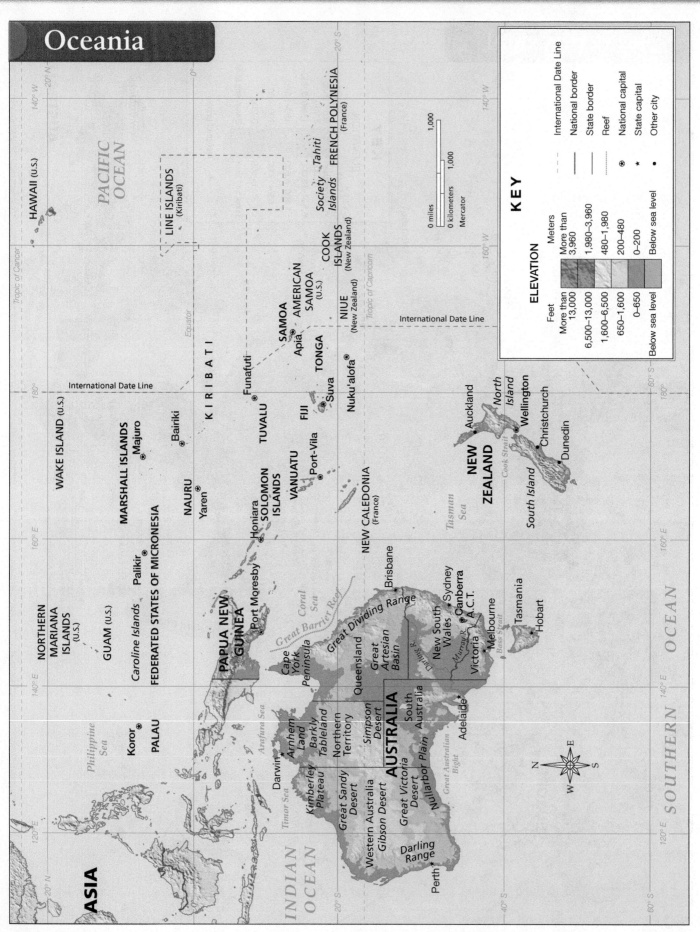

KEY

ELEVATION

Feet	Meters
More than 13,000	More than 3,960
6,500–13,000	1,980–3,960
1,600–6,500	480–1,980
650–1,600	200–480
0–650	0–200
Below sea level	Below sea level

International Date Line
National border
State border
Reef
⊛ National capital
★ State capital
• Other city

0 miles 1,000
0 kilometers 1,000
Mercator

PACIFIC OCEAN

HAWAII (U.S.)

LINE ISLANDS (Kiribati)

FRENCH POLYNESIA (France)

Society Islands
Tahiti

COOK ISLANDS (New Zealand)

AMERICAN SAMOA (U.S.)

NIUE (New Zealand)

SAMOA
Apia

TONGA
Nuku'alofa ⊛

Tropic of Cancer

Equator

Tropic of Capricorn

International Date Line

KIRIBATI

Funafuti ⊛
TUVALU

FIJI
Suva

WAKE ISLAND (U.S.)

MARSHALL ISLANDS
Majuro ⊛

Bairiki ⊛

NAURU ⊛
Yaren

SOLOMON ISLANDS
Honiara ⊛

VANUATU
Port-Vila ⊛

NEW CALEDONIA (France)

NORTHERN MARIANA ISLANDS (U.S.)

GUAM (U.S.)

Caroline Islands
Palikir ⊛
FEDERATED STATES OF MICRONESIA

PAPUA NEW GUINEA
Port Moresby ⊛

Philippine Sea

Koror ⊛ PALAU

ASIA

Cape York Peninsula

Great Barrier Reef

Coral Sea

Arafura Sea

Timor Sea

Darwin ★
Arnhem Land

Kimberley Plateau

Barkly Tableland

Northern Territory

Simpson Desert

Queensland

Great Artesian Basin

Great Dividing Range

Brisbane ★

New South Wales
Sydney
Canberra ⊛
A.C.T.

Murray R.
Darling R.

Victoria
Melbourne ★

Tasmania
Hobart ★

Bass Strait

AUSTRALIA

South Australia
Adelaide ★

Great Sandy Desert

Western Australia
Gibson Desert

Great Victoria Desert

Nullarbor Plain

Great Australian Bight

Darling Range

Perth ★

INDIAN OCEAN

NEW ZEALAND

Auckland
North Island
Wellington ⊛
Christchurch
Dunedin

South Island

Cook Strait

Tasman Sea

SOUTHERN OCEAN

N
E
S
W

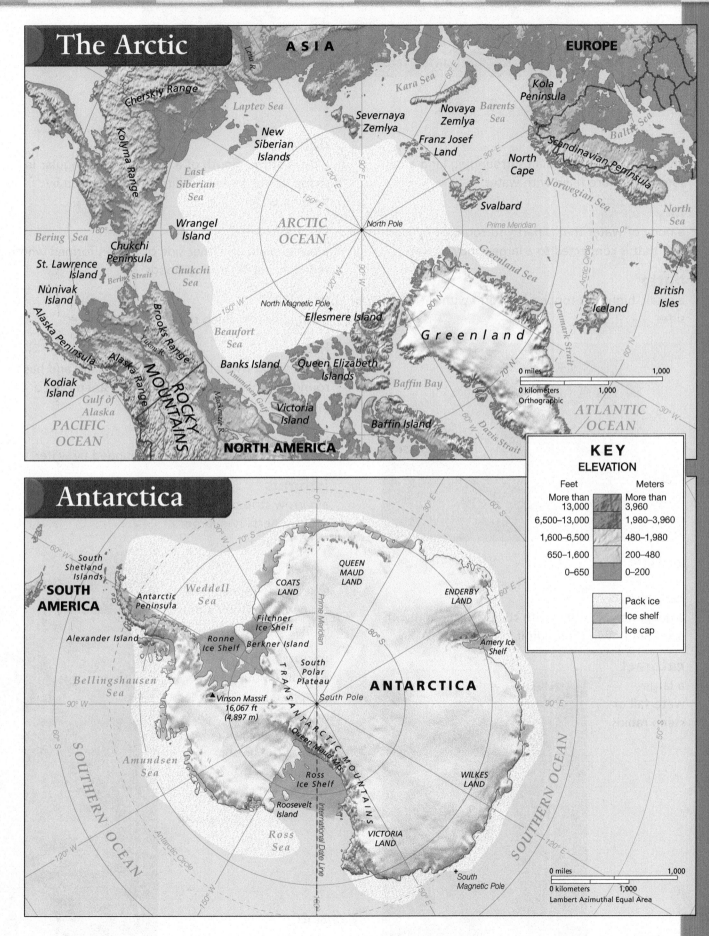

The Arctic

ASIA

EUROPE

Cherskiy Range

Kolyma Range

Laptev Sea

New Siberian Islands

Severnaya Zemlya

Kara Sea

Novaya Zemlya

Barents Sea

Franz Josef Land

Kola Peninsula

North Cape

Scandinavian Peninsula

Baltic Sea

East Siberian Sea

ARCTIC OCEAN

North Pole

Prime Meridian

Svalbard

Norwegian Sea

Greenland Sea

North Sea

Bering Sea

Wrangel Island

Chukchi Peninsula

Chukchi Sea

Arctic Circle

British Isles

St. Lawrence Island

Bering Strait

North Magnetic Pole

Beaufort Sea

Ellesmere Island

Iceland

Denmark Strait

Nunivak Island

Brooks Range

Yukon R.

Banks Island

Queen Elizabeth Islands

Greenland

Alaska Peninsula

Alaska Range

ROCKY MOUNTAINS

Amundsen Gulf

Victoria Island

Baffin Bay

0 miles 1,000

0 kilometers 1,000
Orthographic

Kodiak Island

Gulf of Alaska

Mackenzie R.

Baffin Island

Davis Strait

ATLANTIC OCEAN

PACIFIC OCEAN

NORTH AMERICA

Antarctica

South Shetland Islands

SOUTH AMERICA

Antarctic Peninsula

Weddell Sea

COATS LAND

QUEEN MAUD LAND

ENDERBY LAND

Alexander Island

Filchner Ice Shelf

Ronne Ice Shelf

Berkner Island

Prime Meridian

Amery Ice Shelf

Bellingshausen Sea

South Polar Plateau

ANTARCTICA

Amundsen Sea

Vinson Massif 16,067 ft (4,897 m)

South Pole

TRANSANTARCTIC MOUNTAINS

Queen Maud Mts.

WILKES LAND

Ross Ice Shelf

Roosevelt Island

International Date Line

VICTORIA LAND

SOUTHERN OCEAN

Ross Sea

Antarctic Circle

South Magnetic Pole

0 miles 1,000

0 kilometers 1,000
Lambert Azimuthal Equal Area

KEY
ELEVATION

Feet	Meters
More than 13,000	More than 3,960
6,500–13,000	1,980–3,960
1,600–6,500	480–1,980
650–1,600	200–480
0–650	0–200

Pack ice

Ice shelf

Ice cap

Glossary of Geographic Terms

basin
an area that is lower than surrounding land areas; some basins are filled with water

bay
a body of water that is partly surrounded by land and that is connected to a larger body of water

butte
a small, high, flat-topped landform with cliff-like sides

▲ **butte**

canyon
a deep, narrow valley with steep sides; often with a stream flowing through it

cataract
a large waterfall or steep rapids

◀ **cataract**

delta
a plain at the mouth of a river, often triangular in shape, formed where sediment is deposited by flowing water

flood plain
a broad plain on either side of a river, formed where sediment settles during floods

glacier
a huge, slow-moving mass of snow and ice

hill
an area that rises above surrounding land and has a rounded top; lower and usually less steep than a mountain

island
an area of land completely surrounded by water

isthmus
a narrow strip of land that connects two larger areas of land

mesa
a high, flat-topped landform with cliff-like sides; larger than a butte

mountain
a landform that rises steeply at least 2,000 feet (610 meters) above surrounding land; usually wide at the bottom and rising to a narrow peak or ridge

▶ **glacier**

◀ delta

mountain pass
a gap between mountains

peninsula
an area of land almost completely surrounded by water but connected to the mainland

plain
a large area of flat or gently rolling land

plateau
a large, flat area that rises above the surrounding land; at least one side has a steep slope

river mouth
the point where a river enters a lake or sea

strait
a narrow stretch of water that connects two larger bodies of water

tributary
a river or stream that flows into a larger river

valley
a low stretch of land between mountains or hills; land that is drained by a river

volcano
an opening in Earth's surface through which molten rock, ashes, and gases escape from the interior

▶ volcano

Gazetteer

A

Alice Springs (23°42' S, 133°53' E) a town in Northern Territory, Australia, p. 241

Almaty (43°15' N, 76°57' E) the largest city of Kazakhstan, a country in Central Asia, p. 213

Angkor Wat (13°26' N, 103°52' E) an archaeological site in present-day Angkor, in northwest Cambodia; the world's largest religious temple complex, p. 122

Aral Sea (45° N, 60° E), an inland saltwater sea in Kazakhstan and Uzbekistan, p. 46

Auckland (36°52' S, 174°46' E) the largest city in New Zealand, located on North Island, p. 64

B

Bangladesh (24° N, 90° E) a coastal country in South Asia, officially the People's Republic of Bangladesh, p. 174

C

Canterbury Plain (44° S, 172° E) the lowland area of east-central South Island, New Zealand, p. 65

Central Asia a region in Asia including Kazakhstan, Kyrgystan, Tajikistan, Turkmenistan, Uzbekistan, and others, p. 44

Chang (32° N, 121° E) the longest river in Asia, flowing through China to the East China Sea, p. 11

E

East Asia a region of Asia including China, Japan, Mongolia, North Korea, South Korea, and Taiwan, p. 9

Eastern Ghats (14° N, 79° E) a mountain range forming the eastern edge of the Deccan Plateau in India, p. 32

Euphrates River (31° N, 46° E) a river that flows south from Turkey through Syria and Iraq; the ancient civilizations of Babylon and Ur were situated near its banks, p. 37

G

Ganges River (23° N, 90° E) a river in India and Bangladesh flowing from the Himalaya Mountains to the Bay of Bengal; considered by Hindus to be the most holy river in India, p. 32

Great Dividing Range (25° S, 147° E) a series of plateaus and mountain ranges in eastern Australia, p. 63

Great Wall of China (41° N, 117° E) a fortification wall which, with all its extensions, stretched 4,000 miles (6,400 km) through China; under construction from about 600 B.C. to A.D. 1600, p. 79

H

Himalayas (28° N, 84° E) the Central Asian mountain range extending along the India-Tibet border, through Pakistan, Nepal, and Bhutan, and containing the world's highest peaks, p. 11

Hindu Kush (36° N, 72° E) a mountain range in Central Asia, p. 45

Ho Chi Minh City (10°45' N, 106°40' E) the largest city in Vietnam, named for a former President of North Vietnam; formerly Saigon, p. 234

Huang (38° N, 118° E) the second-longest river in China; it flows across northern China to the Yellow Sea; also known as the Yellow River, p. 11

I

Indus River (24° N, 68° E) a river rising in Tibet and flowing through India and Pakistan into the Arabian Sea, p. 32

Iraq (33° N, 44° E) a country in Southwest Asia, officially the Republic of Iraq, p. 36

J

Java (7° S, 110° E) the fourth-largest island in the Republic of Indonesia, an archipelago in the Indian and Pacific oceans, p. 55

K

Kashmir (34° N, 76° E) a disputed territory in northwest India, parts of which have been claimed by India, Pakistan, and China since 1947, p. 101

Kazakhstan (48° N, 68° E) the largest country in Central Asia, officially the Republic of Kazakhstan, p. 44

Kuwait (29° N, 48° E) a country in Southwest Asia, officially the Republic of Kuwait, p. 177

M

Mecca (21°27' N, 39°49' E) a city in western Saudi Arabia; birthplace of the prophet Muhammad and most holy city for Islamic people, p. 200

Mediterranean Sea (35° N, 20° E) the large sea that separates Europe and Africa, p. 37

Melanesia (13° S, 164° E) the most populous of the three groups of Pacific islands; includes Fiji, Papua New Guinea, and others, p. 68

Mesopotamia a historic region in western Asia between the Tigris and Euphrates rivers; one of the cradles of civilization, p. 37

Micronesia (11° N, 159° E) one of the three groups of Pacific islands; includes Guam, the Marshall Islands, and others, p. 68

Middle Kingdom the name given to China by its Chinese leaders, p. 79

Mount Everest (27°59' N, 86°56' E) the world's highest mountain peak, located in the Himalaya range in South Central Asia, p. 11

Mount Fuji (35°22' N, 138°44' E) the highest mountain in Japan; a dormant volcano and sacred symbol of Japan, p. 10

N

Negev Desert (30° N, 35° E) a triangular, arid region in southwest Israel, touching the Gulf of Aqaba, p. 195

North China Plain a large, fertile plain in northeastern China, p. 11

North Island (39° S, 176° E) the smaller and more northern of the two islands composing New Zealand, p. 64

P

Palestine (32° N, 35° E) a historical region at the east end of the Mediterranean Sea, now divided between Israel and Jordan, p. 106

Pamir (38° N, 73° E) a mountain range in Central Asia, p. 45

Papua New Guinea (6° S, 150° E) an island country in the southwest Pacific; the eastern half of New Guinea, officially the Independent State of Papua New Guinea, p. 68

Philippines (13° N, 122° E) an island country in Southeast Asia, officially the Republic of the Philippines, p. 54

Polynesia (4° S, 156° W) largest of the three groups of Pacific islands, includes New Zealand, Hawaii, Easter, and Tahiti islands, p. 68

These girls live in Polynesia.

R

Riyadh (24°38' N, 46°43' E) the capital of Saudi Arabia, p. 201

Rub' al-Khali (20° N, 51° E) the largest all-sand desert in the world, located on the Arabian peninsula; the "Empty Quarter," p. 35

S

Samarkand (39°40' N, 67°15' E) a city in Uzbekistan, p. 113

Seoul (37°33' N, 125°58' E) the capital of South Korea, p. 13

Silk Road a 4,000-mile-long ancient trade route linking China to the Mediterranean area in the west, p. 85

South Asia a region of Asia that includes Afghanistan, Bangladesh, Bhutan, India, Maldives, Nepal, Pakistan, and Sri Lanka, p. 31

Southeast Asia a region of Asia including Brunei, Cambodia, Indonesia, Laos, Malaysia, Myanmar (Burma), Philippines, Singapore, Thailand, Timor, and Vietnam, p. 55

South Island (43° S, 171° E) the larger and more southern of the two islands composing New Zealand, p. 65

Southwest Asia a region of Asia including Iran, Iraq, Israel, Jordan, Kuwait, Lebanon, Saudi Arabia, Syria, Turkey, and others, p. 36

Sydney (33°52' S, 151°13' E) the capital of New South Wales, on the southeastern coast of Australia, and the largest city in Australia, p. 238

T

Taiwan (23° N, 121° E) a large island country off the southeast coast of mainland China, formerly Formosa; since 1949, the Nationalist Republic of China, p. 147

Thailand (15° N, 100° E) a country in Southeast Asia, officially the Kingdom of Thailand, p. 227

Tigris River (31° N, 47° E) a river that flows through Turkey, Iraq, and Iran to the Persian Gulf; the ancient civilizations of Nineveh and Ur were situated near its banks, p. 37

V

Vietnam (16° N, 108° E) a country in Southeast Asia, officially the Socialist Republic of Vietnam, p. 229

W

Western Ghats (14° N, 75° E) a mountain range forming the western edge of the Deccan Plateau in India, p. 32

A desert in Southwest Asia

Glossary

A

Aborigine (ab uh RIJ uh nee) *n.* a member of the earliest people of Australia, who probably came from Asia, p. 131

alluvial (uh LOO vee ul) *adj.* made of soil deposited by rivers, p. 32

archipelago (ahr kuh PEL uh goh) *n.* a group of islands, p. 12

artesian well (ahr TEE zhun wel) *n.* a well from which water flows under natural pressure without pumping, p. 241

atoll (A tawl) *n.* a small coral island in the shape of a ring, p. 69

B

birthrate (BURTH rayt) *n.* the number of live births each year per 1,000 people, p. 158

boycott (BOY kaht) *n.* a refusal to buy or use goods and services to show disapproval or bring about change, p. 101

C

cash crop (kash krahp) *n.* a crop that is raised or gathered to be sold for money on the local or world market, p. 34

caste (kast) *n.* in the Hindu religion, a social group into which people are born and which they cannot change; each group has assigned jobs, p. 97

civil war (SIV ul wawr) *n.* a war between political parties or regions within the same country, p. 231

clan (klan) *n.* a group of families with a common ancestor, p. 80

collective farm (kuh LEK tiv fahrm) *n.* in a Communist country, a large farm formed from many private farms collected into a single unit controlled by the government, p. 114

colony (KAHL uh nee) *n.* a territory ruled by another nation, p. 100

commercial farming (kuh MUR shul FAHR ming) *n.* the raising of crops and livestock for sale on the local or world market, p. 58

commune (KAHM yoon) *n.* a community in which people own land as a group and where they live and work together, p. 87

communist (KAHM yoo nist) *adj.* relating to a government that controls a country's large industries, businesses, and land, p. 83

coral (KAWR ul) *n.* a rocklike material made up of the skeletons of tiny sea creatures, most plentiful in warm ocean water, p. 69

cultural diffusion (KUL chur ul dih FYOO zhun) *n.* the spreading of ideas or practices from one culture to other cultures, p. 82

D

deciduous (dee SIJ oo us) *adj.* falling off or shedding, as in leaves, seasonally or at a certain stage of development, p. 17

demilitarized zone (dee MIL uh tuh ryzd zohn) *n.* an area in which no weapons are allowed, p. 162

developed country (dih VEL upt KUN tree) *n.* a country with many industries and a well-developed economy, p. 21

developing country (dih VEL up ing KUN tree) *n.* a country that has low industrial production and little modern technology, p. 21

dialect (DY uh lekt) *n.* a variation of a language that is unique to a region or area, p. 89

dictatorship (DIK tay tur ship) *n.* a form of government in which power is held by a leader who has absolute authority, p. 210

diversify (duh VUR suh fy) *v.* to add variety to, p. 163

domino theory (DAHM uh noh THEE uh ree) *n.* a belief that if one country fell to communism, neighboring nations would also fall, like a row of dominoes, p. 231

double-cropping (DUB ul KRAHP ing) *v.* to grow two or more crops on the same land in the same season or at the same time, p. 24

drought (drowt) *n.* a long period of dry weather, p. 190

dynasty (DY nus tee) *n.* a series of rulers from the same family, p. 79

E

emperor (EM pur ur) *n.* a male ruler of an empire, p. 79

ethnic group (ETH nik groop) *n.* a group of people that share such characteristics as language, religion, ancestry, and cultural traditions, p. 90

F

famine (FAM in) *n.* a huge food shortage, p. 163

fertile (FUR tul) *adj.* able to support plant growth, p. 11

fiord (fyawrd) *n.* a long, narrow inlet or arm of the sea bordered by steep cliffs created by glaciers, p. 65

free enterprise system (free ENT ur pryz SIS tum) *n.* an economic system in which people can choose their own jobs, start private businesses, own property, and make a profit, p. 150

G

Gaza Strip (GAHZ uh strip) *n.* a disputed region on the Mediterranean coast, p. 199

geyser (GY zur) *n.* a hot spring that shoots a jet of water and steam into the air, p. 64

Green Revolution (green rev uh LOO shun) *n.* a worldwide effort to increase food production in developing countries, p. 191

gross domestic product (grohs duh MES tik PRAHD ukt) *n.* the total value of all goods and services produced in an economy, p. 152

H

hajj (haj) *n.* a pilgrimage or journey to Mecca undertaken by Muslims during the month of the hajj, p. 200

high island (hy EYE lund) *n.* an island formed from the mountainous tops of ancient volcanoes, p. 69

Holocaust (HAHL uh kawst) *n.* the systematic killing of more than six million European Jews and others by Nazi Germany before and during World War II, p.108

homogeneous (hoh moh JEE nee us) *adj.* to be the same or similar, p. 90

I

irrigation (irh uh GAY shun) *n.* the artificial watering of crops using canals and other artificial waterways, p. 196

K

Khmer (kuh MEHR) *n.* an empire that included much of present-day Cambodia, Thailand, Malaysia, and part of Laos, p. 122

A kibbutz in Israel

Khmer Rouge (kuh MEHR roozh) *n.* a Communist party that took over the government of Cambodia in 1975, p. 127

kibbutz (kih BOOTS) *n.* a cooperative settlement, p. 197

L

labor (LAY bur) *n.* the work people do for which they are paid, p. 159

landlocked (LAND lahkt) *adj.* having no direct access to the sea, p. 213

life expectancy (lyf ek SPEK tun see) *n.* the average number of years a person is expected to live, p. 189

literacy rate (LIT ur uh see rayt) *n.* the percentage of a population age 15 and over that can read and write, p. 189

low island (loh EYE lund) *n.* an island formed from coral reefs or atolls, p. 69

M

malnutrition (mal noo TRISH un) *n.* poor nutrition caused by a lack of food or an unbalanced diet, p. 188

Maori (MAH oh ree) *n.* a native of New Zealand whose ancestors first traveled from Asia to Polynesia, and later to New Zealand, p. 131

marsupial (mahr SOO pea ul) *n.* an animal that carries its young in a body pouch, such as a kangaroo, p. 62

monarchy (MAHN ur kee) *n.* a state or a nation in which power is held by a monarch—a king, queen, or emperor, p. 205

monotheism (MAHN oh thee iz um) *n.* a belief that there is only one god, p. 105

monsoon (mahn SOON) *n.* a wind that changes direction with the change of season, occurring especially in southern Asia and Africa, p. 15

muezzin (myoo EZ in) *n.* a person whose job is to call Muslims to pray, p. 105

N

nationalist (NASH uh nul ist) *n.* person who is devoted to the interests of his or her country, p. 125

nomad (NOH mad) *n.* a person who has no settled home but moves from place to place, p. 90

nonrenewable resource (nahn rih NOO uh bul REE sawrs) *n.* a natural resource that cannot be replaced once it is used, p. 39

O

oasis (oh AY sis) *n.* an area in a desert region where fresh water is usually available from an underground spring or well, p. 36

outback (OWT bak) *n.* the dry land consisting of plains and plateaus that makes up much of central and western Australia, p. 240

P

paddy (PAD ee) *n.* a level field that is flooded to grow rice, especially in Asia, p. 58

partition (pahr TISH un) *n.* a division into parts or portions, p. 101

penal colony (PEEN ul KAHL uh nee) *n.* a place where people convicted of crimes are sent, p. 131

petroleum (puh TROH lee um) *n.* an oily liquid formed from the remains of ancient plants and animals; used as a fuel, p. 39

plateau (pla TOH) *n.* a raised area of level land bordered on one or more sides by steep slopes or cliffs, p. 10

population density (pahp yuh LAY shun DEN suh tee) *n.* the average number of people living in a square mile or square kilometer, p. 13

Q

Quran (koo RAHN) *n.* the holy book of Islam, p. 205

R

radical (RAD ih kul) *adj.* extreme, p. 149

recession (rih SESH un) *n.* a period during which an economy and the businesses that support it shrink, or make less money, p. 156

Red Guards (red gahrdz) *n.* groups of students who carried out Mao Zedong's policies during the Cultural Revolution, p. 149

refugee (ref yoo JEE) *n.* a person who flees war or other disasters, p. 208

S

self-sufficient (self suh FISH unt) *n.* able to supply one's own needs without outside assistance, p. 191

standard of living (STAN durd uv LIV ing) *n.* a measurement of a person's or a group's education, housing, health, and nutrition, p. 39

station (STAY shun) *n.* in Australia, a large ranch for raising livestock, p. 132

steppe (step) *n.* vast, mostly level treeless plains that are covered in grass, p. 45

subcontinent (SUB kahn tih nunt) *n.* a large land-mass that is a major part of a continent, p. 30

subsidy (SUB suh dee) *n.* money given by a government to assist a private company, p. 155

subsistence farming (sub SIS tuns FAHR ming) *n.* farming that provides only enough food for a family or a village, p. 58

T

tectonic plate (tek TAHN ik playt) *n.* a huge slab of rock that moves very slowly over a softer layer beneath the surface of Earth, p. 62

terrace (TEHR us) *n.* a horizontal ridge made in a hillside to create farmland, save water, or lessen erosion, p. 24

textiles (TEKS tylz) *n.* cloth made by weaving or knitting, p. 186

tributary (TRIB yoo tehr ee) *n.* a river that flows into a larger river, p. 192

truce (troos) *n.* a cease-fire agreement, p. 163

typhoon (ty FOON) *n.* a tropical storm in which winds reach speeds greater than 74 miles per hour and that occurs over the Pacific Ocean, p. 16

W

West Bank (west bank) *n.* a disputed region on the western bank of the Jordan River, p. 199

Handcrafted textiles in Syria

Index

Acknowledgments

Cover Design

Pronk&Associates

Staff Credits

The people who made up **World Studies** team—representing design services, editorial, editorial services, educational technology, marketing, market research, photo research and art development, production services, project office, publishing processes, and rights & permissions—are listed below. Bold type denotes core team members.

Greg Abrom, Ernie Albanese, Rob Aleman, Susan Andariese, **Rachel Avenia-Prol,** Leann Davis Alspaugh, Penny Baker, Barbara Bertell, **Peter Brooks,** Rui Camarinha, **John Carle,** Lisa Del Gatto, Paul Delsignore, Kathy Dempsey, Anne Drowns, Deborah Dukeshire, Marlies Dwyer, **Frederick Fellows,** Paula C. Foye, Lara Fox, Julia Gecha, Mary Hanisco, Salena Hastings, Lance Hatch, Kerri Hoar, Beth Hyslip, Katharine Ingram, Nancy Jones, John Kingston, Deborah Levheim, Constance J. McCarthy, **Kathleen Mercandetti,** Art Mkrtchyan, Ken Myett, **Mark O'Malley,** Jen Paley, Ray Parenteau, **Gabriela Pérez Fiato,** Linda Punskovsky, Kirsten Richert, **Lynn Robbins,** Nancy Rogier, Bruce Rolff, Robin Samper, Mildred Schulte, **Malti Sharma,** Lisa Smith-Ruvalcaba, Roberta Warshaw, Sarah Yezzi

Additional Credits

Jonathan Ambar, Tom Benfatti, Lisa D. Ferrari, Paul Foster, Florrie Gadson, Ella Hanna, Philip Gagler, Jeffrey LaFountain, Karen Mancinelli, Michael McLaughlin, Lesley Pierson, Pronk&Associates, Debi Taffet

The DK Designs team who contributed to **World Studies** were as follows: Hilary Bird, Samantha Borland, Marian Broderick, Richard Czapnik, Nigel Duffield, Heather Dunleavy, Cynthia Frazer, James A. Hall, Lucy Heaver, Rose Horridge, Paul Jackson, Heather Jones, Ian Midson, Marie Ortu, Marie Osborn, Leyla Ostovar, Ralph Pitchford, Ilana Sallick, Pamela Shiels, Andrew Szu. Tokeley.

DK Maps

Maps and globes were created by DK Cartography. The team consisted of: Tony Chambers, Damien Demaj, Julia Lunn, Ed Merritt, David Roberts, Ann Stephenson, Gail Townsley, Iorwerth Watkins

DK Illustrations

Richard Bonson/DK Images: **81**, Chris Orr/DK Images: **203**, Jun Park: **69**

Photos

Cover Photos: tl, Ted Meed/Getty Images, Inc.; **tm,** British Museum London, UK/Bridgeman Art Library; **tr,** Anthony Cassidy/Getty Images, Inc.; **b,** Vince Streano/Getty Images, Inc.

Title Page: Vince Streano/Getty Images, Inc.

Table of Contents: iv b, Boden-Ledingham/Masterfile; **v, tr,** H.Spichtinger/zefa; **v, br,** Artbase Inc.; **vi b,** Janet Wishnetsky/CORBIS; **vii tr,** Tim Flach/Getty Images; **1 mr,** AFP/CORBIS;

Learning With Technology: xiii, Discovery School Channel

Reading and Writing Handbook: RW, Michael Newman/PhotoEdit; **RW1,** Walter Hodges/Getty Images, Inc.; **RW2,** Digital Vision/Getty Images, Inc.; **RW3,** Will Hart/PhotoEdit; **RW5,** Jose Luis Pelaez, Inc./Corbis

MapMaster: M, James Hall/Dorling Kindersley; **M1,** Mertin Harvey/Gallo Images/Corbis; **M2–3 m,** NASA; **M2–3,** (globes) Planetary Visions; **M6 tr,** Mike Dunning/Dorling Kindersley; **M5 br,** Barnabas Kindersley/Dorling Kindersley; **M10 b,** Bernard and Catherine Desjeux/Corbis; **M11,** Hutchison Library; **M12 b,** Pa Photos; **M13 r,** Panos Pictures; **M14 l,** Macduff Everton/Corbis; **M14 t,** MSCF/NASA; **M15 b,** Ariadne Van Zandbergen/Lonely Planet Images; **M16 l,** Bill Stormont/Corbis; **M16 b,** Pablo Corral/Corbis; **M17 t,** Les Stone/Sygma/Corbis; **M17 b,** W. Perry Conway/Corbis

Regional Overview: 2 l, David Ball/Corbis; **3 bl,** Massimo Listri/Corbis; **4 t,** José Fuste Raga/Corbis; **4 bl,** Paul A. Souders/Corbis; **5 t,** James A. Sugar/Corbis; **5 b,** David Samuel Robbins/Corbis; **6 l,** Richard T. Nowitz/Corbis; **6 br,** Jeremy Horner/Corbis; **7 tr,** Damien Simonis/Lonely Planet Images; **7 bl,** Bohemian Nomad Picturemakers/Corbis

Chapter One: 8f l, Royalty-Free/Corbis; **8f r,** PhotoDisc/Getty Images, Inc.; **8–9,** Boden-Ledingham/Masterfile; **10 bl,** Dallas&John Heaton/CORBIS; **11 tr,** Karen Su/Getty Images; **12 bl,** Michael S. Yamashita/CORBIS; **13 tr,** Catherine Karnow/CORBIS; **14 b,** Scott Markewitz/Getty Images; **16 ml,** Private Collection/Ancient Art and Architecture Collection Ltd/ Bridgeman Art Library; **17 tr,** Heatons/Firstlight.ca; **19 tr,** Mug Shots/CORBIS; **19 tr(inset),** Kevin Schafer/CORBIS; **20 bl,** AFP/CORBIS; **22-23 b,** Liu Liqun/CORBIS; **23 tr,** Keren Su/CORBIS; **23 br,** Keren Su/CORBIS; **24 tl,** B.S.P.I/CORBIS; **25 ml,** Karen Su/Getty Images; **25 mr,** Scott Markewitz/Getty Images

Chapter Two: 28f l, Royalty-Free/Corbis; **28f r,** PhotoDisc/Getty Images, Inc.; **28–29,** Galen Rowell/CORBIS; **30 b,** Alan Kearney/Getty Images; **33 b,** Will Curtis/Getty Images; **33 lr,** Eisenhut&Mayer/Foodpix; **33 mr,** Artbase Inc.; **34 tl,** R. Ian Lloyd/Masterfile; **35 b,** George Steinmetz; **37 b,** George Gerster/Photo Researchers Inc.; **37 mr,** H. Spichtinger/zefa; **39 r,** George Steinmetz; **40 tl,** Israel Talby; **41 tr,** Hugh Sitton/Getty Images; **42 bl,** Myrleen Ferguson/Photoedit Inc.; **43 tr,** Business Essentials/Artbase Inc.; **43 br,** Donovan Resse/Getty Images; **43 tr(inset),** George Steinmetz; **44 bl,** TASS/Sovfoto/Sergei Kazak; **45 tr,** James Strachan/Getty Images; **47 tr,** Reuters/CORBIS; **48 tl,** TASS-S-54679/ Sovfoto/Eastfoto; **49 ml,** James Strachan/Getty Images; **49 tr,** Israel Talby

Chapter Three: 52f l, Royalty-Free/Corbis; **52f r,** PhotoDisc/Getty Images, Inc.; **52–53,** Paul A. Souders/CORBIS; **54 bl,** Photodisc/ArtBase Inc.; **55 br,** Dorling Kindersley/DK Images; **56-57 bg,** ACE; **57 in,** AFP/CORBIS; **58 ml,** Martin Puddy/Getty Images; **58 b,** R.Ian Lloyd/Masterfile; **60 tl,** Frank Siteman/Maxximages.com; **61 br,** Tui De Roy/Auscape; **61 mr,** Artbase Inc.; **62 ml,** Jeremy Woodhouse/Masterfile; **62 t,** Tim Flach/Getty Images; **64 t,** Mike Langford/Auscape; **65 tr,** John Lamb/Getty Images; **66 b,** William Gottlieb/CORBIS; **67 bg,** The Bridgeman Art Library/Getty Images; **68 bl,** G.Bell/Zefa/ Masterfile; **69 bm,** Yann Arthurs-Bertrand/CORBIS; **69 tr,** Trip/Ask Images; **70 br,** Photography.com.au; **70 bl,** Photography.com.au; **70-71 bg,** Macduff Everton/Getty Images; **71 mr,** James Strachan/Getty Images; **72 tl,** Trip/M.Jelliffe; **73 tr,** AFP/CORBIS; **73 bm,** Jeremy Woodhouse/Masterfile; **73 bm,** Tim Flach/Getty Images

Chapter Four: 76e l, Royalty-Free/Corbis; **76e r,** PhotoDisc/Getty Images, Inc.; **76f l,** GeoStock/Getty Images, Inc.; **76f ml,** Comstock; **76f mr,** PhotoDisc/Getty Images, Inc.; **76f r,** SW Productions/Getty Images, Inc.; **76–77,** John Dakers:Eye Ubiquitous/CORBIS; **78 bl,** Bridgeman Art Library; **79 tr,** Carl & Ann Purcell/CORBIS; **80 b,** © Lee Boltin/Boltin Picture Library; **81 t,** DK Images; Wolfgang Kaehler/Corbis; **81 b,** Macduff Everton/Corbis; **82 bl,** Haruyoshi Yamaguchi/CORBIS/Sygma; **83 tr,** AFP/Getty Images; **84 l,** Michael S.Yamashita/CORBIS; **85 mr,** Werner Forman/Art Resource, NY; **86 bl,** SETBOUN/CORBIS; **87 t,** Daryl Benson/Masterfile; **87 mr,** Dale Wilson/Masterfile; **88 t,** Paul Chesley/Getty Images; **90 tl,** James A.Sugar/CORBIS; © Lee Boltin/Boltin Picture Library; **91 mr,** Dale Wilson/Masterfile

Chapter Five: 94f l, Royalty-Free/Corbis; **94f r,** PhotoDisc/Getty Images, Inc.; **94–95,** Bob Krist/CORBIS; **96 bl,** Archivo Iconografico S.A./CORBIS; **98 tl,** Michael Freeman/CORBIS; **98 tm,** Burstein collection/CORBIS; **98 tr,** Burstein collection/CORBIS; **99 tr,** Camermann International; **100 t,** Miles Ertman/Masterfile; **100 inset,** Archivo Iconografico S.A./CORBIS; **101 tl,** Hulton Deutsch Collection/CORBIS; **101 b,** Kapoor Baldev/CORBIS; **102 tl,** Frans Lemmens/ZEFA/Masterfile; **103 br,** Gianni Dagli Orti/CORBIS; **105 t,** Shai Ginott/CORBIS; **106 tr,** Paul Chesley/Getty Images; **106 l,** Scala/Art Resource; **107 r,** Peter Turnley/Corbis; **108 tl,** Ricki Rosen/CORBIS; **108 tr,** Eddie Gerald/Alamy Images; **109 tr,** Pool/Reuters/CORBIS; **110 l,** Ed Brock/CORBIS; **111 r,** David W.Hamilton/Getty Images; **112 bl,** Dean Conger/CORBIS; **113 t,** DanielSheehan/The Image Works; **113 br,** The Bridgeman Art Library/Getty Images; **114 t,** David Samuel Robbins/CORBIS; **115 br,** David Samuel Robbins/CORBIS; **116 tr,** Nevada Weir/CORBIS; **117 tl,** Camermann International; **117 mr,** Daniel Sheehan/The Image Works

Chapter Six: 120e l, Royalty-Free/Corbis; **120e r,** PhotoDisc/Getty Images, Inc.; **120f l,** GeoStock/Getty Images, Inc.; **120f ml,** Conmstock; **120f mr,** PhotoDisc/Getty Images, Inc.; **120f r,** SW Productions/Getty Images, Inc.; **120–121,** David Noton/Masterfile; **122 bl,** DK Images; **123 b,** Manfred Gottschalk/agefotostock/firstlight.ca; **125 tl,** Miles Ertman/Masterfile; **126 t,** Paul Chesley/Getty Images; **127 tr,** Howard Davies/CORBIS; **128 bl,** Chad Elhers/Getty Images; **128 inset,** Foodphotography/MaxXimages.com; **129 b,** Leonard de Selva/CORBIS; **130 bl,** Kevin Schafer/Getty Images; **131 b,** Graeme Matthews/PhotoNewZealand.com; **132 br,** Reuters/CORBIS; **132 bl,** Rob Walls; **133 t,** R. Ian Lloyd/Masterfile; **134 tl,** Nicolas DaVore/Getty Images; **135 bl,** Manfred Gottschalk/agefotostock/firstlight.ca; **135 tr,** Nicolas DaVore/Getty Images; **138 b,** Time-Life Pictures/Getty Images; **140 tl,** Jason Bleibtreu/CORBIS/Sygma

Chapter Seven: 142f l, Royalty-Free/Corbis; **142f r,** PhotoDisc/Getty Images, Inc.; **142–143,** John Elk/Getty Images; **144 b,** Grant Faint/Getty Images; **145 t,** Don Stevenson/ MaxXImages.com; **146 b,** Nathan Benn/CORBIS; **147 m,** Bill Lai/IndexStock/MaxX Images; **148 bl,** Chris Shinn/Getty Images; **149 t,** Bettmann/CORBIS; **149 mr,** Collection:Stefan Landsberger; **150 ml,** Bettmann/CORBIS; **150 br,** Reuters/CORBIS; **152 t,** Walter Bibikow/Getty Images; **152 inset,** Walter Bibikow/Getty Images; **154 bl,** APWideWorld; **155 br,** Reuters/Corbis; **156 ml,** AFP/CORBIS; **156 b,** Alan Levinson/Getty Images; **158-159 t,** Ettagale Blauer/Laure Communications; **160 ml,** Bob Daemmrich/StockBoston; **161 mr,** The Cover Story/CORBIS; **162 b,** Janet Wishnetsky/CORBIS; **163 b,** AP Wide World Photos; **164 t,** APWideWorld; **165 ml,** DigitalVision/Artbase Inc.; **166 ml,** CORBIS/Artbase Inc.; **167 tr,** Chris Shinn/Getty Images; **167 mr,** Reuters/Corbis

Chapter Eight: 170f l, Royalty-Free/Corbis; **170f r,** PhotoDisc/Getty Images, Inc.; **170–171,** Annie Griffiths Belt/CORBIS; **172 r,** AFP/CORBIS; **177 b,** Peter Turnley/CORBIS; **181 t,** Alison Wright/CORBIS; **184 bl,** Anna Clopet/CORBIS; **185 t,** Kapoor Baldev/CORBIS; **186 t,** Derimais Lionel/CORBIS/Sygma; **186 in,** David H. Wells/CORBIS; **188 tl,** Michael S. Yamashita/CORBIS; **188 tr,** Sheldon Collins/CORBIS; **189 tr,** David Katzenstein/CORBIS; **190 bl,** Christine Osborne/CORBIS; **191 t,** Johnathan Blair/CORBIS; **191 in,** Johnathan Blair/CORBIS; **192 br,** AFP/CORBIS; **193 ml,** AntoineSerra/CORBIS; **194 tl,** AFP/CORBIS; **195 br,** RichardT. Nowitz/CORBIS; **196 b,** Ricki Rosen/Saba/CORBIS; **198 b,** Zev Radovan/PhotoEdit Inc.; **199 tr,** Izzet Keribar/Coral Planet; **200 bl,** James Sparshatt/CORBIS; **201 b,** John Moore/The Image Works; **203 in,** Jacques Langeuin/ CORBIS/Sygma; **203 b,** David Turnley/CORBIS; **204 t,** DK Images; Still Pictures; **204 bl,** DK Images; **206 l,** Caroline Penn/CORBIS; **207 b,** R. Ian Llloyd; **208 bl,** Steve McCurry/Magnum Photos Inc.; **209 t,** AFP/CORBIS; **210 b,** Janet Wishnetsky/CORBIS; **212 bl,** Zylberman Lauren/CORBIS/Sygma; **213 br,** Volker Thewalt; **213 tl,** Zylberman Lauren/CORBIS/Sygma; **214 tr,** James Strachan/Getty Images

Chapter Nine: 218e l, Royalty-Free/Corbis; **218e r,** PhotoDisc/Getty Images, Inc.; **218f l,** GeoStock/Getty Images, Inc.; **218f ml,** Comstock; **218f mr,** PhotoDisc/Getty Images, Inc.; **218f r.** SW Productions/Getty Images, Inc.; **218–219,** Philip&Karen Smith/Getty Images; **220 b,** J.Raga/Zefa/Masterfile; **225 t,** Paul A.Souders/CORBIS; **229 m,** Alyx Kellington/MaxXimages.com; **230 ml,** Owen Franken/CORBIS; **230 b,** Steve Raymer/CORBIS; **231 t,** R. Ian Lloyd/Masterfile; **232 bl,** Dallas&John Heaton/CORBIS; **232 tr,** Bettman/CORBIS; **234 bl,** Tim Page/CORBIS; **235 tl,** Charles Coates/Impact Photos; **235 tr,** AP WideWorld; **237 b,** BohemianNomadPicturemakers/CORBIS; **238–239 b,** Ray Juno/CORBIS; **241 t,** CORBIS/Artbase Inc.; **242 mr,** John Van Hasselt/CORBIS; **243 mc,** Ray Juno/CORBIS; **243 tr,** Dallas&John Heaton/CORBIS

Projects: 246 b, Robert Essel NYC/Corbis; **246 mr,** AFP/Corbis

Reference: 247, China Tourism Press/Getty Images

Gazetteer: 267 br, Nicolas DaVore/Getty Images; **268 b,** George Steinmetz

Glossary: 270 br, Zev Radovan/PhotoEdit Inc.; **272 b,** Alison Wright/CORBIS

Text

138, Excerpt from *The Clay Marble* by Minfong Ho. Copyright © 1991 by Minfong Ho.

Note: Every effort has been made to locate the copyright owner of material used in this textbook. Omissions brought to our attention will be corrected in subsequent editions.